To
LOUISE POUND

WITHDRAWN

FOLKLORE IN THE ENGLISH
& SCOTTISH BALLADS

THE UNIVERSITY OF CHICAGO PRESS
CHICAGO, ILLINOIS

—

THE BAKER & TAYLOR COMPANY
NEW YORK

THE MACMILLAN COMPANY OF CANADA, LIMITED
TORONTO

THE CAMBRIDGE UNIVERSITY PRESS
LONDON

THE MARUZEN-KABUSHIKI-KAISHA
TOKYO, OSAKA, KYOTO, FUKUOKA, SENDAI

THE COMMERCIAL PRESS, LIMITED
SHANGHAI

FOLKLORE
IN THE
ENGLISH & SCOTTISH
BALLADS

BY

LOWRY CHARLES WIMBERLY

Associate Professor of English in the University of Nebraska

THE UNIVERSITY OF CHICAGO PRESS
CHICAGO · ILLINOIS

PREFACE

❦

THIS volume presents an exhaustive survey of those customs and beliefs that in the English and Scottish popular ballads center about religion and magic. The chief problems encountered were those of identification and classification, but I feel confident that the various heads under which I have assembled my materials are such as to avoid any exclusion of matters that should find a place in this book. The principal regret entailed by such a survey is that the investigator must often give but a glance at folklore items meriting prolonged study. A work of this kind, however, should suggest to others many opportunities for further research. An inquiry might well be made, for instance, into the displacement in balladry of pagan by Christian elements; or a study of Celtic elements in the English ballads might be undertaken; and there is opportunity to throw light upon the original character of our ballads by an examination of those vestigial supernatural features that appear in songs like *Lady Isabel and the Elf-Knight, Child Waters,* and *The Lass of Roch Royal.* Within the limits of this work I have been unable to treat these problems in detail, although I have not passed them by altogether unnoticed.

In addition to making a survey or analysis of ballad folklore I have thought it well to give a survey of critical opinion wherever such opinion would serve to substantiate my own interpretation of the ballad evidence and wherever it would furnish the reader with something of a consensus of scholarly opinion respecting the significance of folksong from the standpoint of folklore. That such a survey of opinion has been included will not, I hope, cause the reader to overlook the chief object of this work; namely, that of gleaning directly from the ballads a rich harvest of early beliefs and customs that have to do with ideas of the soul, the nature of the Otherworld, Otherworld denizens, and various other matters, such as modes of enchantment and disenchantment. In this study I have devoted a chapter to the ballad revenant, considering this Otherworld being along with the fairy and the witch. Important materials having to do with death and burial and closely related to ghostlore I have presented in my doctoral dissertation under the title *Death and Burial Lore in the English and Scottish Popular Ballads*. This work has been published recently in the "University of Nebraska Studies in Language, Literature, and Criticism," No. 8.

I owe my initial interest in the British ballads to Professor Louise Pound, of the University of Nebraska, whose contributions on the subject of ballad origins are well known. The present survey was made at the suggestion of Professor Hutton Webster, who was my teacher in social anthropology. Both Miss Pound and Mr. Webster have been unstinted in their encouragement, and have shown their interest by reading the work in manuscript and proof. That any student of the ballads is indebted beyond measure to Professor Child goes without saying, and I trust that this survey of ballad-lore may be taken as a recognition of those opportunities for investigation made possible by this great scholar in the domain of folksong.

LOWRY C. WIMBERLY

UNIVERSITY OF NEBRASKA

FOREWORD

❦

FOLKLORE, as the late Joseph Jacobs once remarked, "has somewhat the versatility of the elephant's trunk, in that it can deal with the most trivial of children's rhymes, while at times laying hands upon the very secrets of man's being and inmost thoughts." It is a branch of social anthropology which deals with primitive culture and also with the vestiges of such culture. The early folklorists did little more than gather miscellaneous "popular antiquities," these being then duly tabulated, like the exhibits in some provincial museum, with little or no regard for questions of origin and interpretation. Aubrey, Brand, and their successors in the British Isles and on the Continent accomplished useful work as collectors, and there is still much to be done by those who follow in their footsteps. Today, however, folklore presumes to be a science. It asks Why? and Whence? and Whither? It seeks to extract some meaning from the enormous mass of materials now at its disposal.

The folklorist ordinarily confines his attention to traditional stories, songs, proverbs, riddles, games, ceremonies, and superstitious beliefs and observances found among the more backward classes in all European lands. The folk, whose lore he gathers and dissects, are country dwellers for the most part, illiterate peasants, untraveled, *adscripti glebae*, and, until recently, little affected by the swirling currents of modern "progress." How truly primitive they remain, despite fifteen hundred years of Christianity and Christian civilization, is an impressive and somewhat disconcerting discovery. We begin to realize the extent of our intellectual heritage from prehistoric and heathen ancestors when we come upon so many "relics of

[ix]

savage ignorance" at our very doors. Happily, to such relics the folklorist gives his most studious hours.

There are other sources of folklore whose value is still inadequately appreciated. The great literary productions of the Middle Ages in Europe preserve much evidence as to bygone beliefs and customs. *Beowulf* and other remains of Old English poetry and prose, the *Nibelungenlied*, the *Eddas* and the sagas, the *chansons de geste*, including the *Song of Roland*, the Arthurian romances, the Finnish *Kalevala*, *Reynard the Fox*, and the *Gesta romanorum*—to name but a few outstanding examples—contain abundant data awaiting elucidation by investigators who combine the requisite linguistic and literary equipment with competence in folklore studies. This literature is mostly anonymous, as are the Gothic cathedrals. Like the latter, too, it reflects the spirit of an entire age, of an entire social group, of an entire cultural *stratum*. Much of it is essentially folk-literature, even though its present form may be due to the labors of forgotten monks and minstrels.

Dr. Wimberly's work, the first part of which now lies before the reader, presents the folklore in the ballads, specifically English and Scottish ballads, with only incidental reference to those of continental countries. It is the author's intention to assemble all the evidence of this sort yielded by British balladry. The present investigation relates to religion and magic, that is, to what from our sophisticated point of view is labeled "superstition." The second part of the work, now in active preparation, will deal with old-time rites and ceremonies imbedded in balladry.

No similar investigation of such wide scope and exhaustive character has been made. Previous workers in this field, either because they shrank from the laborious delving required, or, more probably, because of unfamiliarity with the methods and results of folklore study, have usually limited themselves to considerations of ballad form. Ballad content has been quite neglected, or treated incidentally, or discussed with specific reference to some theory as to the relation between folksong and art song. The ballads as repositories of folklore have shared the neglect accorded to the epics and romances of the Middle Ages. Dr. Wimberly's researches thus fill a gap in our knowledge of the ballads and likewise suggest profitable methods of approach to other varieties of folk-literature.

Our author pronounces no judgment upon the vexed question of ballad origins. The nature of his work does not require him to do so. For him it matters little whether the English and Scottish ballads represent the immediate and spontaneous productions of the communal mind, or whether they imply individual authorship. In either case the stuff of the ballads preserves what was believed and felt and done in former days. It is the business of the folklorist, here, as elsewhere, to go straight to the facts and let the facts speak for themselves. How well Dr. Wimberly has done this must be apparent even to the reader who runs as he reads.

HUTTON WEBSTER

CONTENTS

CONTENTS

INTRODUCTION

❖

THE best traditional ballads, as the poet Gray said of *Child Maurice*, begin "in the fifth act of the play." The climax is upon one at the outset and the action falls precipitously to the close, often a tragic close—the death by violence of the hero or the heroine or of both. The ballad expends a tremendous force in its brief dramatic portrayal. Such a ballad is *The Bonny Hind*, that terrible Scotch song of brother-sister love. The tragic horror of this piece is matched by that in another ballad, *Sheath and Knife*, or by that in the story of Kullervo found in the Finnish epic *Kalevala*. There is little or no exposition in these ballads, much less any detailed description. There is no emphasis on the setting in the literary or critical sense of that term. But in a larger sense the little drama of folksong is enacted in a setting with which the ordinary reader, perhaps even a reader like the scholarly Gray, is wholly unacquainted. This setting or cultural milieu, so essential to an appreciation of the ballad story, it is the good fortune of the folklorist to be able in some measure to supply.

An American Indian sun-dance or an Australian *corroboree* is an exciting spectacle for the uninitiated, but for one who understands something of the culture whence it springs it is a hundred fold more heart-moving. And is not Gray's fifth act infinitely more touching when read in the light of that bygone culture or way of life in which the ballad plot was conceived or to which it owes its inspiration? *Earl Brand* or *The Douglas Tragedy*, a song better preserved in Norse than in English tradition, sings of defeated love. A witness of the fight between her lover and her relatives—father and brethren—the stolen bride lets slip

[1]

the name of her lover and so names him dead. Let us give two lines from Prior's translation of the Danish ballad:

> *The moment Guldborg named his name,*
> *A fatal blow, the deathblow came.*

Does not the tale gain immeasurably in power when we appreciate the tragic awfulness of this slip of the tongue, when we know that in olden times, as among savages today—Australian aborigines, for instance—a man's life was thought to be bound up with his name and that one must therefore keep his name secret from his enemies?

The beautiful ballad of *The Twa Sisters* likewise finds true expression only when we are aware of that ancient philosophy which held that the soul might at death pass into any one of a number of forms, that of a tree, a bird, or a serpent, or that it might, as in this song of a murdered maiden, reside in the bones or in the hair—bodily relics which, when fashioned into a harp or viol, sing out an accusation of the murderess. The terror of Greek tragedy lives in these little songs, as does the grim fatalism of Northern poetry, in such a song, again, as *The Cruel Brother*, the catastrophe in which springs from the old incident of slighted fraternal authority. But it is not the purpose of this study to dwell upon the ballad theme, however arresting that theme may be. Indeed, we shall in the following pages often lose sight of the ballad story, for the work of the folklorist is minutely analytical. Still we may in our undertaking do service to the theme of folksong by piecing together that rich mosaic of thought which is the ballad's, a philosophy of life which, viewed as a whole, is seen to reflect in no fragmentary manner the culture of an earlier day.

In this book, then, I have approached the English and Scottish traditional ballads from the point of view of folklore and anthropology. So far as British popular poetry is concerned, I have tried to make an exhaustive survey of those beliefs and customs that have to do with religious conceptions, or, speaking somewhat less broadly, that have to do with ideas both of religion and magic. The early or primitive mind best reveals itself on its religico-magical side. Hence I have felt that once we gain an insight into religion and magic as reflected in balladry we shall have gone far toward discovering what our folksong holds of primitive thought.

The term "folklore" is employed here in its widest sense, in that sense which Sir James G. Frazer gives it in his *Folk-Lore in the Old Testament*, or—covering in this study a narrower range of subjects—as virtually equivalent to the term "tradition" as defined by E. S. Hartland in *The Science of Fairy Tales*. Frazer remarks in the former work:

Such survivals are included under the head of folk-lore, which, in the broadest sense of the word, may be said to embrace the whole body of a people's traditionary beliefs and customs, so far as these appear to be due to the collective action of the multitude and cannot be traced to the individual influence of great men.[1]

Hartland says:

By Tradition I mean the entire circle of thought and practice, custom as well as belief, ceremonies, tales, music, songs, dances and other amusements, the philosophy and the superstitions and the institutions, delivered by word of mouth and by example from generation to generation through unremembered ages: in a word, the sum total of the psychological phenomena of uncivilized man.[2]

It should be stated at the outset that the following investigation has to do with the matter rather than with the manner of the ballads, and is not concerned with problems of form and structure. Nor is this work concerned with questions of provenience. The affiliation, through their ideas, of the ballads with romances, for example, or with *Märchen*, I shall, where possible, take into account, but not with a view to reopening questions of derivation and origin. I shall duly observe, however, as the occasion arises, that so far as their materials go, the ballads need not yield in point of priority to the romances, and that many of them "stand," to use the words of Andrew Lang, "on much

[1] I, vii. [2] P. 34.

[3]

the same footing as the *Märchen* or popular tales of the world."[1] In fact, it is largely the object of this study to show that in general the superstitions and usages reflected in folk-poetry[2] have their basis in those traditions upon which romances and popular tales have frequently drawn —traditions which carry one back ultimately to the people themselves.

Before defining further the scope of this investigation, I wish, by way of introduction, (1) to assemble as rapidly as possible the views of certain students of folk-belief and custom respecting the amount and significance of the material in the ballads; (2) to give the opinions of scholars as to the value of such material, its value, that is, for purposes of arriving at a knowledge of beliefs and observances current at one time or another in actual life; (3) to point out the essentially pagan character of folk-poetry; and (4) to make a brief comparison, from the standpoint of folklore, between the matter of romance and that of balladry.

However widely scholars may differ as to the origin and composition of the ballads, there is, in general, substantial unanimity as regards the wealth and significance of the customs, beliefs, and superstitions embodied in traditional poetry. "In many ways," remarks T. F. Henderson, "they [the ballads] bring us into immediate contact with the antique, pagan, savage, superstitious, elemental character-istics of our race."[3] That Mr. Henderson is disposed to regard these characteristics of the ballads as carried on from "old forgotten romances" does not, so far as the pres-ent investigation is concerned, detract from the value of his testimony. For even though it be granted that English and Scottish folksong is, in the words of Gregory Smith, "part of the literary débris of the Middle Ages,"[4] yet one

---

[1] "The Ballads," Chambers' *Cyclopaedia of English Literature*, I (1901), 521.

[2] With respect to the phrase "folk-poetry," I shall throughout this study bear in mind the words of Professor G. L. Kittredge: "Poetry of the folk is, perhaps, a dangerous phrase; but it is too convenient to be lightly rejected, and, if we proceed with caution, we may employ it without disaster" (Sargent-Kittredge, *English and Scottish Popular Ballads*, p. xii).

[3] *Scottish Vernacular Literature*, p. 370.   [4] *The Transition Period*, p. 186.

must arrive finally, although it be through other forms of literature, at a point in the history of the ballad where one comes in touch with that "taste and sentiment" which, according to Courthope, characterize the ballads and which "the people contributed to" their "making."[1] Granted, for the moment, that the ballads do derive chiefly from old romances, "they have to some extent embalmed," to return to the observations of Henderson, ". . . . the essence of what the old romances embalmed—the sentiments, passions, beliefs, forms of thought, and imaginative wonder and dread of our pagan ancestors." But we need not rest the case with Mr. Henderson. "It can hardly be questioned, by any one who takes the trouble to think about the matter," writes Professor W. P. Ker, "that there is this strange excellence in the ballads, this power, not merely of repeating old motives, but of turning the substance of daily life into poetry."[2] "The ballads preserve many archaic literary traits along with the emotions and culture of a vanished age," remarks Miss Louise Pound in her *Poetic Origins and the Ballad*.[3] "The ballad-maker," says Andrew Lang, "works on the original data of world-wide popular tradition."[4] And Francis B. Gummere observes "that curious old ideas prevail about behavior on occasions such as childbirth and funeral. Minor superstitions abound which are derived from a lapsed mythology and a superseded habit of dealing with the other world."[5]

Prefatory to the observations of certain scholars who have evaluated the materials of popular literature in their relation to actual customs and superstitions, we should meet the criticism that the presence of a set of ideas in a given ballad or tale is not necessarily proof that these ideas are or ever were the property of those people among whom the ballad or tale is found. It is not my intention to attempt a reconstruction of the philosophy and life of the English and the Scotch on the strength of the data furnished

---

[1] *History of English Poetry*, I, 445.

[2] "On the Danish Ballads," *Scottish Historical Review*, V (1908), 401.

[3] P. 109. [4] *Op. cit.*, I, 522. [5] *The Popular Ballad*, p. 298.

by the songs which they sing or have sung. The matter of the ballads is all the more significant in that these traditional songs are, in general—especially as regards the lore which they embody—not confined to England and Scotland. Indeed, our best ballads are almost as little characterized by insularity as are popular tales. It is one of the traits of folk-poetry that, generally speaking, it belongs to no particular time or place.[1] Hence, one does not hesitate to agree with W. R. Halliday that to "use the incidents of folk-tales as evidence for the aboriginal habits or institutions of the people who now tell them, is hazardous in the extreme."[2] My position is that although certain incidents and ideas found in the ballads may not reflect the "aboriginal habits or institutions" of the people who sing the ballads, they do, at least, mirror the life and thought of the people from whom the substance of traditional poetry originally sprang. As a matter of fact, however, it will be obvious time and again in the following study that the folk-poetry under consideration does transcribe ideas and practices which were, and often still are, current among the people of the British Isles. That these same beliefs and customs may be duplicated in the traditions of Scandinavia or Greece, in ancient Hebrew or Egyptian culture, or in the thought and usages of the Melanesians or the Amerindian races is no reason for saying that they do not belong also to the traditions of the English and the Scotch. This universality of the customs and superstitions portrayed in British balladry justifies us all the more in regarding traditional songs as invaluable documents for the folklorist and the anthropologist.

But we must further inquire as to whether the thought and life depicted in the ballads is to be taken as genuine evidence of the culture of any people whatsoever. Or is the matter of folksong pure fiction, at best a fantastic idealization of life spun from the dreams of some medieval

[1] On the localization of the ballads see "Localizing of Ballad-Stories," Child's *English and Scottish Popular Ballads*, V, 487.

[2] "Notes on Indo-European Folk-Lore," *Folk-Lore*, XXXIV, 126.

bard? We may without hesitation answer this question in the negative. As repositories of superstitions and usages which are, or have been, actually held and practiced, the ballads are on a par with folktales and myths. Recognizing the importance of popular stories as representative of the life of the people, Sir G. L. Gomme[1] quotes the words of J. F. Campbell:

Thus, writing, in 1860, of his grand collection of "Highland Tales,"[2] Mr. Campbell very truly says: "The tales represent the actual every-day life of those who tell them, with great fidelity. They have done the same, in all likelihood, time out of mind, and that which is not true of the present is, in all probability, true of the past; and therefore something may be learned of forgotten ways of life."

"We have already learned," says W. Crooke, "to look to the folk-tales for the most trustworthy indications of popular belief."[3] As commentaries on the foregoing statements by Campbell and Crooke, we could ask for nothing better than J. A. MacCulloch's *Childhood of Fiction* and E. S. Hartland's *Science of Fairy Tales*. Mr. MacCulloch, in the former work, observes:

Many of our European folk-tales are thus hoary with age—transcripts of the ideas, beliefs, and customs of a forgotten world, which tell their story as plainly as do the weapons of stone and bronze, the monumental remains, or the rock-shelters, hut circles, or lake dwellings, found all over the world.[4]

The first section of W. Y. Wentz's *Fairy-Faith in Celtic Countries* "deals with the living Fairy-Faith among the Celts themselves; the second, with the recorded and ancient Fairy-Faith as we find it in Celtic literature and mythology."[5] And that Mr. Wentz finds the recorded fairy faith to square generally with the living faith is evidenced by such of his conclusions as the following: "All this matter is definitely enough in line with the living

[1] *Folklore as an Historical Science*, p. 48.
[2] *Popular Tales of the West Highlands*, I, lxix.
[3] *The Popular Religion and Folk-Lore of Northern India*, II, 263.
[4] P. 13; cf. *ibid.*, pp. vii, 20.   [5] P. xviii.

Fairy-Faith";[1] or "The recorded or manuscript Fairy-Faith of the Gaels corresponds in all essentials with the living Gaelic Fairy-Faith."[2]

Professor Franz Boas, in attempting to reconstruct the life of the Tsimshian tribes, bases his "data solely on the recorded mythology." "It is obvious," says this scholar, "that in the tales of a people those incidents of the every-day life that are of importance to them will appear either incidentally[3] or as the basis of a plot. Most of the references to the mode of life of the people will be an accurate reflection of their habits." And he goes on to say that "material of this kind does not represent a systematic description of the ethnology of the people, but it has the merit of bringing out those points which are of interest to the people themselves. They present in a way an auto-biography of the tribe."[4] "The worst stories," observes Gummere, "come directly from life, and ballad or tale simply follows fact,—a hint for the too eager discoverer of a literary origin for every narrative in verse."[5] To gain a complete and fair view of the old Teutonic faith we must, according to York Powell, go to early Norse documents: "It is in the accurate prose of Ari and the old verse in these volumes that all of direct evidence that can be recovered is practically contained."[6] Need we go beyond statements like the foregoing in order to show that the tale, the myth, or the ballad is a legitimate hunting ground for the folk-lorist or anthropologist? One would hate to see works on old ideas and customs, such works as Brand's *Popular Antiquities* or Aubrey's *Remaines,* deprived of the evidence

[1] P. 289.

[2] P. 307.

[3] It is often true that in balladry a belief or custom finds depiction only incidentally, in a mere phrase, a line, or a stanza at the most, but this incidental depiction is the best sort of guaranty that we have a bona fide representation of an actual superstition or usage.

[4] *Bureau of American Ethnology,* Thirty-first Report (1909–10), p. 393; see also *Anthropology in North America* (1915), p. 333.

[5] *Op. cit.,* p. 172.

[6] Vigfusson-Powell, *Corpus poeticum boreale,* I, 426.

yielded by literature, whether that literature be of the "popular" or of the "artistic" sort.

It should be obvious to anyone, however, who is at all familiar with traditional tales and songs that care must be taken not to regard as details on a single canvas observances and habits of thought which in reality may be widely remote from one another. English and Scottish balladry —to regard Professor Child's collection as definitive— embraces some three hundred pieces, most of them with a number of different versions, each of which has had a more or less unique history—some of them rescued at one time, some at another, some in one locality, some in another locality, from the stream of oral transmission, with the natural result that the investigator is confronted with a medley of ideas which, even in the case of a single ballad, may typify various levels of culture. The ballads again in this respect resemble *Märchen*, and what MacCulloch says for folk-stories is exactly applicable to folk-poetry:

> The ideas of later ages have entered into and coloured these primitive stories; comparatively modern social customs and names jostle those of a remote antiquity without any feeling of incongruity; the tales have a firm root in a past paganism, but they are full of later Christian conceptions. Tales which bristle with the marvellous, and introduce us to ogres and witches and enchanted heroes and heroines, to animals and things which talk and act like men, to the weirdest and most irrational customs and ideas, speak also of gunpowder and tobacco, of cannons and muskets, of cities, palaces, hotels, coaches, and other things of later civilization; or make the most evidently pagan ogres, monsters, or personages of mythical antiquity indulge in church-going and other Christian practices; or refer to the Sultan or Boney in the most matter-of-fact way. But all this is only the veneer of a later age; the material of the stories is old, so old as to be prehistoric.[1]

We may now turn our attention for a moment to the pagan character of the ballads. The remains of heathendom in folksong are especially marked, and as regards this "veneer of a later age," which characterizes *Märchen*, one need not hesitate to affirm, even upon a cursory reading of traditional poetry, that the ideas and practices imbedded

[1] *Op. cit.*, p. 3.

in British balladry may be referred almost wholly to a pagan culture. This is not to say that the ballads had always to go back to a remote antiquity for their materials. That much of ballad-lore does descend from such antiquity there is no question, but it should be pointed out here— without, again, however, any intention of discussing ballad origins—that until comparatively recent times many parts of the British Islands have been characterized by a state of uncivilization. Dalyell, a Scottish author, writing in 1835, says that "Scotland, until the most modern date, was an utter stranger to civilisation,"[1] a condition of society comparable to that of Spenser's Ireland,[2] and which, as Gomme points out, "obtained in the northern counties of England, and in other parts."[3] An abundance of superstitions and primitive ideas, as well as customs, were, then, ready at hand for the maker of the ballads. In any event, whether or not the English ballads drew chiefly for their incidents and beliefs upon the traditions of the British Isles, it is true that these songs reflect a way of life with which the balladist could not have been altogether unacquainted.

But it is not the purpose of this study to show how the remains of paganism came to be recorded in balladry but to show simply that such remains are there recorded. Nor do I intend to discriminate, to the point of exclusion, against ideas not heathen, for I shall include not only the "remaines of gentilisme" but all remains whatsoever. The body of evidence to be presented in the following pages will, however, if allowed to speak for itself, bear out beyond question what York Powell, for example, has to say about the religion of folksong. This scholar remarks:

The religion of the Scottish ballads, save for the few poems that deal with the popular Catholic mythology, is absolutely as heathen as that of the Helgi Lays; the sacredness of revenge, remorse, and love, the horror of treason, cruelty, lust, and fraud are well given, but of Christianised feelings there are no traces. The very scheme, on which the ballads and lays are alike built, the hapless innocent death of a

[1] *Darker Superstitions of Scotland*, pp. 197 f.
[2] *View of the State of Ireland* (1596).   [3] *Op. cit.*, p. 183.

hero or heroine, is as heathen as the plot of any Athenian tragedy can be.[1]

Again, what Professor Johannes Steenstrup, expressing the views of Svend Grundtvig, says for the traditional poetry of Denmark, may, with equal propriety, be said for the ballads of England and Scotland. Regarding the clerical or religious ballads[2] as farther removed from the true spirit of the folk than are those pieces which do not derive from sacred tradition, but not going so far as Vilmar and Böhme, who "show no inclination to recognize a clerical or religious popular ballad," Steenstrup observes:

Concerning all others the rule holds good that however many remarkable and marvelous things happen, miracles never find a place. It is not by prayers and petitions to God and to the saints that metamorphosed knights and maidens get their own shape back again, nor is it by making the sign of the cross nor by reading the Scriptures that evil is bested. The intervention of the Virgin Mary or of holy men is unnecessary; that which heals or reshapes, that which draws the frigid lover to longing is mysterious remedies, the various instruments of superstition, the token and the mystic word. Runes have a wonderful alluring power, a man's life is bound up in his name as if in a mathematical power, and with or against this one can work precisely as though it were the man himself. In a kiss lies witchcraft, which releases that which is bewitched, and drinking a man's warm blood and tasting of his flesh leads to metamorphosis.[3]

On the whole, Steenstrup might have been writing of the British ballads. Again, speaking of incidents of transformation and deliverance in folksong, he observes: "For the remarkable circumstance connected with these, and one which indicates great age, is that the trace of Christianity which appears in them never touches their essential nature."[4]

From the standpoint of the matter of traditional poetry

[1] Vigfusson-Powell, *op. cit.*, I, 507.

[2] On the English ballads and the Church see Louise Pound, *op. cit.*, pp. 162–91.

[3] *The Medieval Popular Ballad* (trans. E. G. Cox), pp. 179 f.

[4] *Ibid.*, p. 181. This is well illustrated for British balladry in a Shropshire version of *The Wife of Usher's Well*, where the return of the dead is brought about by a miracle; see *infra*, pp. 401 f.

we may draw some general comparisons between the ballads and the romances. However he might have summed up his views had he lived to write his introduction to the whole subject of balladry, there is no doubt that Professor Child would have taken into account the matter of balladry as well as the form. With respect to Svend Grundtvig's *Danmarks gamle Folkeviser* and Child's companion work, *The English and Scottish Popular Ballads*, Axel Olrik well observes: "The most characteristic feature in both works is the certainty with which true folk-tradition is distinguished from literary emendation. Both authorities had a lively sense of what folk-poetry will say."[1] Professor Olrik's is indeed a profound observation. The student of traditions must be ever grateful when he recalls how closely Child scrutinizes the matter of the ballads, how readily he detects the counterfeit and modern whether in form or substance, how offended he is, for example, by the fulsomeness of Buchan's blind beggar, who was guilty among other crimes of rationalizing his talking birds into parrots.[2]

That Professor Child guarded jealously the right of the ballad to sing of old ideas without echoing the voice of romance is clear from what he says, in his Introduction to *Earl Brand*, concerning the familiar ballad commonplace of plants which spring from the graves of lovers:

> The idea of the love-animated plants has been thought to be derived from the romance of Tristan, where it also occurs; agreeably to a general principle, somewhat hastily assumed, that when romances and popular ballads have anything in common, priority belongs to the romances. The question as to precedence in this instance is an open one, for the fundamental conception is not less a favorite with ancient Greek than with mediaeval imagination.

The views of Child with respect to priority of tale, chronicle, romance, or ballad are again forcibly put in his Introduction to *Sir Aldingar*, the chief incident in which, trial

---

[1] Review of the Kittredge-Sargent edition of the Child collection, *Folk-Lore*, XVIII, 470; trans. A. F. Major from *Danske Studier* (1907).

[2] On the general authenticity of Buchan's ballad texts see, however, Alexander Keith in his introductory essay to his edition of Gavin Greig, *Last Leaves of Traditional Ballads and Ballad Airs*, pp. xix ff.

by combat, is widely paralleled in romance, chronicles, and
continental balladry. Child observes:

> There is little or nothing in all these tales that can be historically
> authenticated, and much that is in plain contradiction with history.
> Putting history out of the question, there is no footing firmer than air
> for him who would essay to trace the order of the development. Even
> if we exaggerate the poverty of human invention so far as to assume
> that there must have been a single source for stories so numerous and
> so diversified in the details, a simple exposition of the subject-matter,
> with subordinate connections, seems all that it is safe, at present, to
> attempt.[1]

And he adds in a footnote: "Grundtvig, admitting that
the time has not come for anything more, sketches an hypothesis of the evolution and transmission of the story,
'as a mere experiment.' "[2]

"Ballads," says Gummere, "have, as a rule, better
claims to priority than the romances can offer."[3] Moreover, Gummere goes so far as to distinguish, in a general
way, at least, between the matter of the ballads and that
of the romances:

> Theirs [the ballads] is the romance of tradition, a kind of obsolete
> reality, as different from literary romance of the past as it is from mod-
> ern realism. They have not much of the fantastic element so plentiful
> in popular tales, and speak more willingly of old custom than of old
> myth.[4]

Mr. Courthope, as we have already pointed out, regards
the ballads as deriving from literary romances, but Andrew
Lang observes:

> We have already remarked on a few samples of that class of ballads
> which may be regarded as *précis* of literary romances or *chansons de
> geste*. But the *matter* even of these is "the legacy of oral tradition," as
> Professor Child shows, contrary to the opinion of Mr. Courthope, whose
> chapter on ballads does not display any special acquaintance with the
> comparative study of the world's ancient, traditional, and popular
> narratives in verse and prose.[5]

[1] *Op. cit.*, II, 43 f.   [2] *Ibid.*, p. 44 n.   [3] *Op. cit.*, p. 68.

[4] "The Mother-in-Law," *Kittredge Anniversary Papers*, p. 16. See also the
same author, *The Popular Ballad*, pp. 38 ff.; *Old English Ballads*, pp. xxvii ff.

[5] "The Ballads," Chambers' *Cyclopaedia of English Literature*, I, 522.

In the same connection Lang remarks further: "In perhaps more numerous cases the popular ballad does *not* 'reproduce, in a mould peculiar to itself, the subject-matter of the older gests, romances, or lays.' The ballad-maker works on the original data of world-wide popular tradition."[1] C. S. Baldwin does not hesitate to say that the ballads are nearer than the romances to the actual superstitions of the people: "In being oral the ballads were adapted to the common people; and they were popular in other ways. The romances took folklore, indeed, but transformed it; the ballads kept more of the original telling of the folk, at once strong and eerie."[2]

Certainly one would not argue that the matter as well as the manner of balladry is unique. The ballad is a literary genre—popular or otherwise—chiefly by virtue of its form, and Gummere is right, in the main, when he says that "the differencing quality of the ballad of tradition lies not in its subject, which may be anything, not in its setting, which may be anywhere, but in its actual structure."[3] But it can be little questioned that the naïve ballad manner, the impersonal note of folksong, and the tendency of traditional poetry to employ, as W. M. Hart so well points out, "no special art for the treatment of the supernatural,"[4] do keep the matter of the ballads in immediate touch with the "original telling of the folk." Böhme recognizes the nearness of the ballads to the people when he says that spiritual songs are wanting in the genuine folktone which is characteristic of the true ballads.[5] Professor Ker insists upon the form of the ballads, but he is careful to observe that this form determined at times what the ballads might or might not say.

The ballads are not merely a limb of the great mediaeval body of romance; they are a separate form. They are not mere versified folklore, because their form—the *Idea* of a Ballad—makes them reject some of the most delightful fairy tales as unfit for their poetical scope. They

---

[1] *Ibid.* [2] *English Medieval Literature*, p. 236.
[3] *Popular Ballad*, p. 71.
[4] *Ballad and Epic*, p. 21. [5] *Altdeutsches Liederbuch*, pp. xlvi, 676.

are not degradations of longer stories, for even when they have the same plot, they make a different thing of it. Griselda has Boccaccio, Petrarch, and Chaucer as her advocates, but they leave the ballad of *Fair Annie* unimpeached, and no one of their versions can take the place of it. The story is much the same as theirs if you reduce it to an abstract summary, but that is not the ballad.[1]

Professor Ker in his essay on the Danish ballads compares the ballads with the poems of the *Elder Edda*, and brings out the relative "unliterariness" of folksong: "There are no extant Anglo-Saxon ballads; and though the heroic poems of the 'Elder Edda' are like ballads in many things, they are much more ambitious and self-conscious, much more literary, than the *Folkeviser*."[2] In the same essay he says of the ballads that "though they are often childish and illiterate, and touched with the common weaknesses, they are not simply degraded versions of old noble legends, and they cannot be understood by means of any such theory."[3]

It would seem, then, if we are to take the testimony of scholarship, that there is reason for thinking that the ballad, largely by virtue of its peculiar form, stands nearer to the people than do the romances or other literary types, and mirrors more faithfully than they the beliefs and customs of the folk. In any event, however, questions of manner and priority aside, or whether the ballads derive from the romances or the other way about, we may, so far as the lore of traditional song is concerned, take the position outlined by Lang in his *Collection of Ballads:*

Some writers have decided, among them Mr. Courthope, that our traditional ballads are degraded popular survivals of literary poetry. The plots and situations of some ballads are, indeed, the same as those of some literary mediaeval romances. But these plots and situations, in Epic and Romance, are themselves the final literary form of *Märchen*, myths and inventions originally *popular*, and still, in certain cases, extant in popular form among races which have not yet evolved, or borrowed, the ampler and more polished and complex *genres* of literature. Thus, when a literary romance and a ballad have the same theme,

---

[1] "On the History of the Ballads: 1100–1500," *Proceedings of the British Academy*, IV, 25.

[2] "On the Danish Ballads," *Scottish Historical Review*, V, 385.

[3] *Ibid.*, p. 387.

the ballad may be a popular degradation of the romance; or, it may be the original popular shape of it, still surviving in tradition. A well-known case in prose is that of the French fairy tales.[1]

In this connection we should also give Lang's profound observations on the importance of the anthropological study of literary origins. He remarks:

> Literary origins can only be studied, like all other origins, in the light of a wide knowledge of the popular literature of the world, peasant, barbaric, and savage. The fallacy of supposing that a rite, or myth, or custom, or belief, or romantic incident is necessarily derived from its civilised or literary counterpart, and that popular examples of the same ideas are necessarily later, borrowed, and degenerate, has long been abandoned by anthropologists, and ought not to be accepted by literary students.[2]

It would, as Lang implies, be a mole-eyed type of scholarship which would be content to treat the incident, say, of the swan-maiden as a purely literary incident and overlook the occurrence of this story in savage traditions. Again, it may be important to know that the Oversea Otherworld idea is present in both romance and balladry, but it is much more important to know that it is present in savage beliefs current in Polynesia, for example, or among the American Indians. To trace a given motif from one literary document to another and to rest the case there must strike the folklorist or anthropologist as scholastic gymnastics and nothing more, if the same motif, that of the bridge of the dead, for instance, is found the world over in primitive traditions.

We may at this point raise the question as to the literariness of certain incidents in the ballads—literariness in the sense of being merely figurative or metaphorical. Is the singing-bone incident in *The Twa Sisters*, for instance, to be regarded as nothing more than a pretty fancy or conceit, or does it reflect actual thought? We are safe in saying that this incident does find its counterpart or its source in living ideas and, moreover, that the employment of such an incident in an obviously metaphorical sense would be

---

[1] Pp. xiii f.   [2] Chambers, *op. cit.*, I, 524.

good evidence that the original stuff of folksong had been
tampered with. This lack in the ballads of the metaphorical goes far to prove what we have already pointed out,
that the ballads give a bona fide record of the stuff of actual tradition. As regards the absence from balladry of the
figurative and the symbolical, we may say that the philosophy imbedded in folksong is often at one with savage
thought, for the primitive man has few or no symbols in
our sense of the term.[1] The passing of the soul into the
form of a bird or of a tree is actual fact for the primitive
mind; it is likewise actual fact for the ballads. Says
Gomme:

> Between the butterfly and the moth there is, perhaps, not much
> to distinguish from the point of view of poetical fancy. In the parish
> of Ballymoyer in Ireland butterflies "are said to be the souls of your
> grandfather." But poetical fancy dies away as we find out that the
> same conception is found in different places attached to birds and
> animals.[2]

Our ballad of *The Twa Sisters* is not striving for poetic
effect when it relates that the harp made from the drowned
sister's bones sings out an accusation of the murderess.
And that a man's personality or soul is somehow bound up
with his name is no idle fancy, but, as in the ballad of *Earl
Brand*, is a hard fact to reckon with when one is exchanging
death strokes with an enemy.

In balladry animals talk and act like human beings,
maidens have Otherworld lovers, flowers and herbs have
magic potency, and even inanimate objects, such as a
sword, have the power of speech. To embrace a fairy or
kiss a ghost places the earthly man under the jurisdiction
of the Otherworld, and music has power to bring the dead
from the grave or lure mortals to the elfin hill. But all
this is, in folksong, pure matter of fact, not in the least to
be questioned. Speaking of the ballad's naïve acceptance of
the supernatural, W. M. Hart says: "Thus there is, in
Clerk Colvill, no mystery, no vagueness in the suggestions.

[1] Cf. Wundt, *Elements of Folk Psychology* (trans. E. L. Schaub), p. 201.
[2] *Ethnology in Folklore*, p. 159.

To meet a mermaid washing her silken sark by the stream was evidently common experience; no special artifice was necessary to get such a story believed."[1] Again, Mr. Hart observes: "Janet's confession that her lover is an elfin grey occasions no surprise; in fact there is no reply to her confession, and thereafter we see her in no company but Tam Lin's."[2] Rationalization of this or that ancient trait occurs now and then in folksong, but it is easily detected, as when one sees in Buchan's parrots an attempt to make plausible for the modern mind the primitive talking bird. With respect to the superstition of the bird-soul, Dr. Frazer says that what is "metaphor to a modern European poet was sober earnest to his savage ancestor, and is still so to many people."[3] For a generation far removed, however happily or unhappily, from the primitive man's outlook, a generation which has experienced the enlightenment wrought by scientific truth, there may be found in the ancient ballads merely a residue of quaint beauty—not even that, perhaps, but, as Tylor so well remarks, this is because the old animistic philosophy has gone from us, "dissipating from such fancies their meaning, and with their meaning their loveliness. Still, if we look for living men to whom trees are, as they were to our distant forefathers, the habitations and embodiments of spirits, we shall not look in vain."[4] In the ballads this old philosophy —animistic or even pre-animistic—prevails, and was regarded by the ballad-maker or, at least, by those in whom, at whatever remote period, ballad ideas originated, as none other than a true philosophy. On the whole, it may safely be said—to revert to a comparison of the ballad with more "literary" genres—that the lore yielded by folksong is likely to have greater value than that yielded by more diffuse and more artistic forms. The ballads, since they are impersonal, brief, and swiftly dramatic, gave the author little opportunity for the exercise of poetic fancy and confined him to a more immediate and closely literal tran-

---

[1] *Ballad and Epic,* p. 28. [3] *The Golden Bough,* III, 34.
[2] *Ibid.,* p. 27. [4] *Primitive Culture,* II, 220 f.

script of actuality. In romances, on the other hand, greater
latitude was allowed the fancy or imagination of the author.
It is noteworthy, in this connection, that the most fanciful
creatures of balladry, such as fire-breathing fiends, five-
headed giants, and so on, are found in those ballads—*King
Arthur and King Cornwall* (30),[1] for instance—which are
more or less related to romance.

But, to dwell for a while longer on the unmetaphorical
character of the ballad, let us grant, for the moment, that
a given incident, like that of the love-animated plants in
Earl Brand (7), was regarded by the balladist as nothing
other than a beautiful fancy, nay, more, was simply caught
up by him as an altogether meaningless formula; even then
we should be justified in looking upon the ballad as a repos-
itory of genuine folk-belief current at one time or another
—this despite the fact that the formula in which the belief
has been handed down may have had no significance for
the balladist or his audience, just as it may have no meaning for the lay reader of the twentieth century. In this
vestigial sense, then, if in no other, ancient belief and custom have survived in the ballad in the same way that early
thought survives among us today in certain—to us—
meaningless customs, such as our saying "God bless you"
when a person sneezes, or raising our hats merely as a mark
of courtesy, whereas this act once signified homage. So,
again, it is possible that the ballad-maker had no conception of the primitive or early rationale which underlies the
episode in *Lamkin* (93) of catching the blood of the murdered lady. We are inclined to give the balladist the bene-
fit of the doubt, but he may or may not have regarded this
act as being motivated in the belief that the blood is sacred
and is a vehicle for the soul. In this work, then, we would
not always insist that the beliefs and customs recognized
by a sound folkloristic interpretation as residing in a given
incident were so recognized by those who made the ballads.

I may now say whatever else is needed to define the

[1] The ballad numbers used throughout this work are those of Child, *English
and Scottish Popular Ballads.*

scope of my study of religion and magic in balladry. I have already indicated that this investigation makes no pretense to side either with those who hold to the "communal" view of ballad origins or with those who hold to the theory of "individual authorship."[1] We should here, however, give a moment's consideration to the question as to whether the ballads have emerged from the upper or the lower levels of society—a matter which has arisen in connection with controversies about the origin of "folksong." In the main, it is immaterial, from the standpoint of the lore of balladry, whether for traditional poetry we "assume composition in aristocratic circles" or whether we refer the ballads to "the lower classes of the people" and grant that "the same habit of thought, the same standard of action, ruled alike the noble and his meanest retainer."[2] Irrespective of their origin among one class or the other, it is altogether probable that the ballads mirror ideas which were entertained by people in both high and low stations in life. As regards the epoch—the late sixteenth century—represented by the chronicle ballad *Northumberland Betrayed by Douglas*, Child says: "Witchcraft was rife at the epoch of this ballad, nor was the imputation of it confined to hags of humble life. The Lady Buccleuch, the Countess of Athole, and the Lady Foullis were all accused of practising the black art."[3] It is well known, of course, as Gomme points out, that "lawyers, magistrates, judges, nobles, and monarchs" have, in the United Kingdom, figured in the history of witchcraft.[4] Even Francis Bacon and Thomas Browne were not uninfluenced by the vulgar conceptions of sorcery. The ballads themselves, if one is to impute to

---

[1] For expositions of these opposing views, see respectively (and especially) F. B. Gummere, *The Popular Ballad*, and Louise Pound, *Poetic Origins and the Ballad*; "The Term: 'Communal,'" *Publications of the Modern Language Association*, XXXIX, 440-54.

[2] See Louise Pound, *Poetic Origins and the Ballad*, pp. 95 ff.; Gummere, *Old English Ballads*, p. xxvii; "Ballads," *A Library of the World's Best Literature*, III, 1307.

[3] *Op. cit.*, III, 410 f.

[4] *Folklore as an Historical Science*, pp. 202 ff.

them a professional origin by virtue of the upper strata of society therein represented, furnish the best kind of evidence that witchlore, fairy-lore, and ghostlore were by no means peculiar to the peasants but were much in evidence among lords and ladies as well.

But, again, questions of origin aside, I find ample justification for my study in showing through the following material that balladry contains a world of early and primitive thought—this though the ballads represent different cultural strata and derive their elements from various sources, from medieval literature, from chronicles, from classic sources, and from tradition, sacred or otherwise.[1] As I have already indicated, it has been necessary to give the term "folklore" a wide meaning in order to include under it the many customs and beliefs that center about conceptions of the Otherworld as it is portrayed in folksong. Problems of division have not always been easy of solution. I have experienced certain difficulties in arrangement of the material, chiefly because of the confusion of faiths represented in the ballads. The striking, and, indeed, significant, similarity between ghost and fairy in English folksong I have taken as sufficient justification in a great many cases for treating ghost beliefs and fairy-lore together, as in the chapters on the Otherworld spell. It has been impossible to avoid repetition of incidents and items, but in view of the scope of the investigation I feel that repetition is not altogether a fault.

I have based my investigation upon Professor Child's great ballad collection, *The English and Scottish Popular Ballads*.[2] Needless to say, without Child's work, which is virtually definitive for the traditional poetry of England and Scotland, it would be exceedingly difficult to do justice

[1] Professor Gummere's words in his essay "The Mother-in-Law" (*Kittredge Anniversary Papers*, p. 16) not inadequately describe the purpose of my study: "What sort of evidence can the ballads, which rest upon tradition of five or six centuries at the utmost, give for a state of affairs which belongs by the hypothesis to a far older date?"

[2] *Op. cit.* (1882–98), ten parts, two to a volume, the tenth part, with the apparatus of investigation, edited by G. L. Kittredge.

[21]

to a study of the sort undertaken in the present volume. "It is unnecessary to indicate," says Andrew Lang, "more than one authority on the subject of ballads. Professor Child, of Harvard, ... has collected all known ballads, with all accessible variants, and has illustrated them with an extraordinary wealth of knowledge of many literatures."[1] Of Professor Child's materials I have of course taken advantage. Indispensable to the student are Child's extensive notes on the folksong of other peoples, his careful analyses of the lore of such songs, and his comparison of the matter of balladry with that of folktales current in Europe and in other parts of the world. This great scholar was painstaking, too, in his recognition of the matter of romance as reflecting, paralleling, or in some few obvious instances, as actually furnishing the materials of the ballads—all this, to be sure, along with repeated insistence upon the integrity of the ballad, a full appreciation of both the form and the substance of traditional song. Moreover, Professor Child was ever awake to living traditions, those beliefs and practices existent among the people, and recorded many of these traditions in connection with the materials of the ballads. In short, Child went a long way toward fixing the lore of the ballads in its proper place in the context of universal tradition. And, indeed, it has been my task not only to make easily accessible for scholars a great body of ballad traditions but also to assemble Child's observations on these traditions.

In addition to Child I have, of course, drawn upon the works of other great folklorists and students of the English ballads, chief among them Andrew Lang, Francis B. Gummere, George L. Kittredge, T. F. Henderson, W. P. Ker, F. York Powell, Walter M. Hart, Louise Pound, Frank Sidgwick, Lucy Broadwood, and Charlotte S. Burne. Many of the general and special works on folklore and anthropology which I have consulted are given in the Bibliography at the end of this study. Especially helpful have been the volumes of the *Folk-Lore Record*,

[1] "The Ballads," Chambers, *op. cit.*, I, 524.

the *Folk-Lore Journal*, *Folk-Lore*, and many other publications of the Folk-Lore Society. A number of rather slight dissertations on the folklore elements in British balladry appeared shortly after the publication of Child's work, but these studies have not afforded me any considerable help in the preparation of this volume. I may mention here Georg Rüdiger's *Zauber und Aberglaube in den englisch-schottischen Volksballaden* and Konrad Ehrke's *Das Geistermotiv in den schottisch-englischen Volksballaden.*

As for variants of the English and Scottish ballads not included in Professor Child's collection and recovered since the completion of his work, I have made a careful analysis of many texts, but on the whole these variants—recovered in the British Islands and in America—have not, from the standpoint of the lore they embody, yielded a great deal over and above what is to be found in the Child versions. In fact, what Professor Kittredge says about the definitiveness of Child's work might be said as regards the balladlore therein represented: "Professor Child's great collection . . . . comprises the whole extant mass of this material."[1] Or, again, "little or nothing of value remains to be recovered in this way."[2] This is not to disparage the results obtained by the untiring efforts of ballad collectors since Child and since the foregoing observations made by Professor Kittredge some twenty years ago. Many excellent texts have been recovered from oral tradition and are still being recovered, but these variants, even though occasionally not inferior to the Child versions, seldom, as already indicated, throw additional light upon the lore of the ballads. Nevertheless, in order to make my study as representative as possible, I have not infrequently cited such texts, confining myself chiefly to those printed in the *Journal of the Folk-Song Society*, the *Journal of American Folk-Lore*, the excellent anthologies of which Cecil Sharp was sole or joint editor, particularly his *English Folk Songs*

[1] *English and Scottish Popular Ballads*, the Sargent-Kittredge edition of the Child collection (1904), p. xiii.

[2] Introductory to Child, *English and Scottish Popular Ballads*, I, xxviii.

from the Southern Appalachians, the late Gavin Greig's *Folk-Song of the North-East* and his *Last Leaves of Traditional Ballads and Ballad Airs*, Alfred Williams' *Folk Songs of the Upper Thames*, Josephine McGill's *Folk Songs of the Kentucky Mountains*, Louise Pound's *American Ballads and Songs*, Loraine Wyman and Howard Brockway's *Lonesome Tunes*, John Harrington Cox's *Folk-Songs of the South*, and texts in other works which, with the foregoing, are listed in my Bibliography.

In bringing to a close this general Introduction I should like to make it clear that the investigation in hand is not meant to be comparative in the sense that it attempts a correlation of the lore found in all ballads whatsoever. Continental popular poetry contains traditions paralleling those in British balladry, as well as significant matters not present in English song, but an inclusion of such matters, however desirable, is not possible within the limits of this study. My work can be described as comparative only in the sense that it recognizes the universality of the traditions embodied in British balladry, and, more narrowly, in the sense that it consults foreign analogues of the English ballads when such reference aids in restoring certain items of folklore that have obviously been lost from the English pieces. The superstition of dead-naming may, for example, be claimed for the ballad *Earl Brand* and the related *Erlinton* by reference to Scandinavian analogues of the former piece. So, too, the character of the dead man in *Sweet William's Ghost* is more clearly understood when we compare him with the revenant in the Norse ballad *Aage og Else*.

I have not, then, attempted a comparative study but have selected for examination a definite *corpus* of folk-poetry, just as one might make an investigation of the lore contained in certain romances or *Märchen* or in Chaucer's poetry, or just as one might—as did Charlotte Burne, Walter Gregor, and William Henderson—make a survey of the beliefs and customs current in particular regions of England and Scotland. As a result of my classification of the ballad-lore surveyed in this study I feel that I have got together and given due emphasis to a body of beliefs and practices that should, in an organized form, be brought to the attention of scholarship. This proper emphasis upon and evaluation of ballad traditions cannot be given even in such a work as Professor Child's collection where observations upon this or that tradition as preserved in this or that ballad are necessarily scattered here and there. But that which balladry has to say, for instance, about the dead man or the fairy, is seen at once to be significant when the matters relating to one or the other of these supernatural beings are grouped together under appropriate heads.

PART I
THE PAGAN OTHERWORLD

INTRODUCTORY

✤

ENGLISH and Scottish balladry embodies no definite system of beliefs, no official religion. There is, on the contrary, a constant merging and overlapping of beliefs. Hence, in a study of the Otherworld one soon realizes how many and varied are the elements that make up the mosaic of ballad ideas. At first thought one is likely to look upon this collocation of cults, this fusion or confusion of faiths, as arising from differences in ballad lineage, as being a compound of elements deriving in part, at least, from medieval literature, from classic sources, and from tradition, sacred or otherwise. This survival side by side of dissimilar or even contradictory notions of the Otherworld is not, however, the consequence altogether of the origin and history of traditional poetry. Such a commingling of faiths results chiefly from the fact that the ballads, whether they be classified as minstrel, historical, or purely traditional songs, were in close *rapport* with the folk-consciousness. Hence, they simply mirrored the strange heterogeneity of ideas that existed in the popular mind. Like admixtures of various religious ideas are, of course, found in traditions the world over—in the beliefs of primitive peoples[1] or in those of peoples more advanced, the Teutons, say.[2]

Attention will be directed in the following pages to the presence side by side in balladry of several general views of the after-life—the continuation of the soul in the shape of a bird, an animal, a tree, or in other forms; immortality in the tomb; and the existence of the departed in some more or less remote and general dwelling place. The realm of

[1] See "State of the Dead," *Encyclopaedia of Religion and Ethics*, XI, 826 f.

[2] See Vigfusson-Powell, *Corpus poeticum boreale*, I, 420.

spirits is not, of course, to be taken in the following chapters as always signifying the land of the dead. It will be necessary, in order to give full depiction to the ballad Otherworld, especially in its pagan aspects, to include a great deal of material on fairies and fairyland. There is, however, sufficient justification for treating the ghost world along with the fairy realm in the fact that at bottom ghost and fairy traditions have much in common. Hartland's observation on popular tales is applicable to the ballads: "The line which separates fairies and ogres from the souls of men has gradually grown up through ages of Christian teaching; and, broad as it may seem to us, it is occasionally hardly visible in these stories."[1]

To the extent of devoting separate chapters to Christian ideas of the after-life I have attempted to set forth pagan Otherworld beliefs apart from those that have derived from Christianity. But to return to the vagueness and confusion that often characterize ballad allusions to the Otherworld—one is confronted everywhere in folk-poetry with a palimpsest of ideas—it is not impossible, despite this merging of faiths, to piece together from fragmentary evidence scattered here and there, a presentable description of the Otherworld of traditional poetry.

Before passing to a survey of the various conceptions of spiritland or of the fairy world we may quote, as evidential of the ballad faith in another life, those affecting lines from *Lord Thomas and Fair Annet*. Fair Annet, mortally wounded by the brown bride, is besought by her lover to await him in her passing:

> *"Now stay for me, dear Annet," he sed,*
> *"Now stay, my dear," he cry'd;*
> *Then strake the dagger untill his heart,*
> *And fell deid by her side.* [73 A 28]

One may give, too, those beautiful lines of *Sweet William's Ghost* which, as Professor Ker observes, express the

[1] *Science of Fairy Tales*, pp. 42 f.

"ghostly regret for the living world." "Midd-larf" means "middle-earth":

> "*O cocks are crowing a merry midd-larf,*
> *A wat the wilde foule boded day;*
> *The salms of Heaven will be sung,*
> *And ere now I'le be misst away*" [77 B 8].

Chapter I

TRANSMIGRATION BELIEFS AND IDEAS
OF THE SOUL

❧

BRITISH folksong embodies early and widespread conceptions of the soul, and in these ideas, if anywhere, we find the remains of paganism. The soul at death may take on various forms. It may be transformed into a plant, an animal, a bird, a fish, or into an inanimate object, such as a stone; or it may reside in, or be of the nature of, certain parts of the body—the blood, the bones, or the hair. Again, the soul may be associated with some personal belonging, such as the name or an ancestral sword. Prefatory to a survey of soul beliefs in balladry it should be said that posthumous metamorphosis of man into a plant or animal or other forms does not, as a rule, carry with it the idea of retribution. In other words, it is not, according to the ballads, necessarily the wicked man who undergoes transformation at death. With the exception of the notable instances of transmigration immediately to be considered, metamorphosis seems not to be punitive, for it is generally the good man or woman, the hero or heroine, who is changed into a flower, a bird, or an animal.

TRANSMIGRATION

The reticence of the ballad, along with the occasional disposition of the popular muse to render old ideas haphazardly or not at all, or, worse yet, to rationalize them, throws the student back at times upon little more than inference. But we could hardly ask for a clearer illustration of metensomatosis or transmigration than that offered by two of our best ballads, *The Cruel Mother* and *The Maid*

[33]

and the Palmer. In both these pieces transformation is associated with retribution. According to the former ballad, the ghosts of two murdered babes announce certain seven-year penances which the mother must undergo; namely, as in the Harris text, transmigration into a bird, a fish, and an eel:

> *"Ye sall be seven years bird on the tree,*
> *Ye sall be seven years fish i the sea.*

> *"Ye sall be seven years eel i the pule,*
> *An ye sall be seven years doon into hell"* [20 J].

It is noteworthy that the transmigrations are in gradation downward to hell, as also in texts I and K. Hell is likewise the final stage for the murderess in *The Maid and the Palmer* (21 A, B). The infanticide in *The Cruel Mother* (20) welcomes them all but cries (I), "heavens keep me out of hell"; (J), "for gudesake, keep me frae hell." Bird transformation occurs in other versions of this piece (K, I): "a bird in the tree"; "fowl in the woods." The Findlay text also gives the bird and fish transformations.[1] W. R. Mackenzie's "New World" text reads: "seven more like an owl in the woods."[2] Other examples of the bird-soul will be discussed presently.

For the fish metamorphosis in *The Cruel Mother*, version I has "a fish in the floods"; Mackenzie, "like a whale in the sea."[3] The eel is an obnoxious creature in *Lord Randal* (12) and is one of the shapes through which Tam Lin (39 C 9, I 44) passes in the process of his disenchantment. In *The Twa Magicians* (44), a transformation-conflict ballad, the lady is changed into an eel, among other shapes. Still other ballads offer instances of transformation into a fish. The sister in *The Laily Worm* (36) is changed by her witch stepmother into "the machrel of the sea." Kempion

---

[1] Child, *English and Scottish Popular Ballads*, V, 212.

[2] *The Quest of the Ballad*, p. 105. Cf. text, Greig, *Last Leaves of Traditional Ballads and Ballad Airs* (ed. Alexander Keith), p. 22: "fish in the flood," "bird in the wood," "seven year a warnin bell," "seven year in deeps o hell."

[3] *Loc. cit.*

(34 B 15) asks a maiden, enchanted as a "fiery beast," if it was a "fish intill the sea" that had "misshapit" her. *The Great Silkie of Sule Skerry* (113) tells a story of a seal-lover. The mermaid in *Clerk Colvill* (42 A, B) is at will a lady on the land or a "fish intill the sea."

The ballad of *The Maid and the Palmer*, like that of *The Cruel Mother*, reflects the belief in retribution through transmigration. The penances in the latter piece belong properly, however, to the former ballad.[1] An unchaste woman who has slain six of her nine babes is sentenced by an old palmer to a series of seven-year penances (21 A):

> *"Penance I can giue thee none,*
> *But 7 yeere to be a stepping-stone.*
>
> *"Other seaven a clapper in a bell,*
> *Other 7 to lead an ape in hell."*

Sharpe's text (B) gives simply "stone" and "porter of hell;" a fragment from Scott's recollection reads: "Seven years ye shall be a stone."[2] These instances of metempsychosis are clearly evidential of animistic thought. With reference to the Norse versions, Child observes: ". . . . The penance in the English ballads is completely different in kind, consisting not in exaggerated austerities, but partly, at least, in transmigration or metensomatosis."[3] The stone metamorphosis in *The Maid and the Palmer* doubtless reflects the widespread belief in the retributive character of petrifaction or transformation into a stone, a belief exemplified in the notion that certain stones or rocks were once human beings, thus transformed by way of punishment.[4] In connection with the stepping-stone in version A of the English ballad it is interesting to note that in a Norwegian tale, *Vesle Aase Gaasepige*, there is a stepping-

[1] See Child, *op. cit.*, I, 218.

[2] *Ibid.*, p. 233.

[3] *Ibid.*, p. 230. For the penances in foreign analogues see *ibid.*, pp. 228 ff.

[4] See Hartland, *The Legend of Perseus*, III, 95–147; MacCulloch, *Childhood of Fiction*, p. 156 n.

stone which, if stepped on, reveals unchastity.[1] Other references in British balladry reflect the widespread belief in the magic character of stones.[2] In Norse balladry we find an occasional instance of a supernatural creature who is punished or made harmless by being turned into stone. Thus St. Olave in the Danish song *Saint Olave's Voyage* turns his elfin and witch enemies to stone:

> They sail'd across the hills of Scone,
> And froze the swarthy Elves to stone.

> There stood a hag with spinning wheel;
> "And why should we thine anger feel?"

> "Saint Olave, thou, with ruddy beard,
> Thy ship has through my cellar steer'd."

> The Saint look'd back, "Thou hag of Scone,
> Stand there and turn to granite stone."[3]

In Scandinavian tradition, and in traditions generally, the creatures of darkness are sometimes changed into stone by the sun or the light of day.[4] In a Moravian ballad of the same tenor as *The Maid and the Palmer* a maiden is turned into a pillar of salt.[5]

The transformation into "a clapper in a bell" (21 A) is matched by that into a "church bell" in *The Cruel Mother*

[1] G. W. Dasent, *Popular Tales from the Norse* (2d ed.), p. 478.

[2] A stone figures in a chastity test in *Willie o Winsbury* (100 A 4 f.). There is a "marriage-stane" in Greig's copy of *Young Beichan* (53) (*Folk-Song of the North-East*, Vol. I, art. 78, text A). A purse of gold is told on a stone in *The Knight and the Shepherd's Daughter* (110 F 32). Magic may be at work in the following instances: In *The Twa Sisters* (10 B, C, E, M, O, Q) one or both of the sisters, just before the drowning of the younger, stand on a stone. So in a Danish version: "As on a stone the younger trod, she thrust her into the rushing flood" (R. C. Prior, *Ancient Danish Ballads*, I, 382). Just before meeting her murderer, the lady in *Lamkin* (93 A, D, H, I, J, M, N, Q) "steppit on a stane"; cf. text, *Rymour miscellanea*, II, 137. About to be hanged, the sons in *The Clerk's Twa Sons o Owsenford* (72 C 39) are required to lay their black hats "down on a stone."

[3] R. C. Prior, *op. cit.*, I, 360; cf. the ballad *Rosmer*, *ibid.*, III, 56, 60.

[4] Cf. Bugge, *The Home of the Eddic Poems* (trans. W. H. Schofield), pp. 239 f., 259.

[5] See Child, I, 231.

(20 I 17) or "Seven years to ring a bell" (K 7, L 9), or, again, "Seven yeare a tinglin bell."[1] Church bells have an extensive lore. They were, in all likelihood, doubly efficacious against the powers of darkness by virtue of their association with the Church and by reason of the metal in them.[2] The line (21 A 14) "Other 7 to lead an ape in hell" is a humorous play on the hell-portership in 21 B and 20 I, K.[3]

The foregoing songs, *The Cruel Mother* and *The Maid and the Palmer*, furnish the sole examples in British balladry of what is, unquestionably, a belief in transmigration or metamorphosis of a retributive character. But there are many other instances in our traditional poetry of the belief—transmigration to be inferred or not—that the soul may at death be transformed into a plant, a bird, or an animal, or that a human being, through magic and without dying, may undergo like metamorphoses. A number of our ballads have to do with purely magical transformations. Among these are the excellent songs of *Kemp Owyne* (34), *Allison Gross* (35), *The Laily Worm* (36), and *King Henry* (32). *Tam Lin* (39) is the best of our shape-shifting ballads. *The Twa Magicians* (44), "a base-born cousin of a pretty ballad known over all Southern Europe, and elsewhere,"[4] illustrates the transformation-combat motif. *The Earl of Mar's Daughter* (270)—a poor piece, with, however, Scandinavian analogues of some merit—tells the ancient story of the lover in bird shape.[5] The types of metamorphoses exemplified in our songs of magic will be alluded to from time to time in the following pages.

THE PLANT SOUL

The universal and primitive idea of tree or flower metamorphosis is illustrated by the familiar ballad common-

[1] *Ibid.*, V, 212.
[2] See John Aubrey, *Remaines of Gentilisme and Judaisme*, pp. 19, 96, 131; Charlotte Burne, *Shropshire Folk-Lore*, pp. 600 ff.; W. Henderson, *Folk-Lore of the Northern Counties*, p. 62.
[3] On leading apes in hell see *infra*, pp. 426 f.
[4] Child, I, 399.   [5] See *ibid.*, V., 38 ff.

place of love-animated plants that spring from the graves of lovers. Numerous students of folklore have recognized the significance of the ballad incident as reflecting the belief that the soul may at death pass into a tree.[1] That this incident occurs with amazing persistency in the myths, legends, folktales, and ballads of all European countries, and, indeed, in traditions throughout the world from China to Australia or North America, goes far to show that the lore of folksong is a faithful transcript of early and primitive thought. Child describes the incident as it occurs in folksong:

> The beautiful fancy of plants springing from the graves of star-crossed lovers,[2] and signifying by the intertwining of stems or leaves, or in other analogous ways, that an earthly passion has not been extinguished by death, presents itself, as is well known, very frequently in popular poetry. Though the graves be made far apart, even on opposite sides of the church, or one to the north and one to the south outside of the church, or one without kirk wall and one in the choir, however separated, the vines or trees seek one another out, and mingle their branches or their foliage.[3]

In the traditions of peoples among whom our ballads are, or are not, found, there are numberless parallels to the foregoing incident.[4]

This commonplace of sympathetic plants occurs in a number of ballads. It is especially well preserved in the Motherwell text of *Earl Brand* (7 C). Here the lovers are expressly said to grow up as plants, a reading that is nearer the original idea than are somewhat more fanciful readings in other versions:

[1] See E. S. Hartland, *Primitive Paternity*, I, 158; MacCulloch, *op. cit.*, pp. 115 f. n.; W. Crooke, "On Homeric Folk-Lore," *Folk-Lore*, XIX, 65 f.; Burne, *op. cit.*, p. 546 n.; George Henderson, *Survivals in Belief among the Celts*, p. 182.

[2] In this incident there is, of course, more than mere poetic fancy. It was in all likelihood not regarded as only so much imagery even by the ballad-maker himself.

[3] *Op. cit.*, I, 96.

[4] See Child's many examples, *ibid.*, pp. 93, 94, 96–98, 200, 489, 506; II, 205–6, 498; III, 498, 510; IV, 443, 450; V, 31, 285 f.

The one was buried in Mary's kirk,
    The other in Mary's quire;
The one sprung up a bonnie bush,
    And the other a bonny brier.

These twa grew, and these twa threw,
    Till they came to the top,
And when they could na farther gae,
    They coost the lovers' knot.

One could not ask for better evidence of the primitive character of ballad tradition.[1] The idea that the soul may
become a tree is obvious enough in a Russian ballad: "A
Cossack blossoms into a thorn, a maid into an elder; his
mother goes to pull up the thorn, hers to pluck up the
elder. 'Lo, this is no thorn! it is my son!' 'Lo, this is no
elder! it is my daughter!' "[2] In view of the primitive belief
that the soul may at death issue from the mouth, there is
an interesting reading of our ballad commonplace in a version of *Fair Margaret and Sweet William*, a text recorded
in the *Journal of the Folk-Song Society:*

And out from her mouth there sprung a rose,
    And out of his a briar.[3]

"The Teutons and the Celts, and other peoples, seem,
with regard to the tree-soul, to think alike," says George
Henderson in his *Survivals in Belief among the Celts*.[4] In

---

[1] The nearness of ballad-lore to primitive thought is well borne out by what
MacCulloch (*Childhood of Fiction*, p. 115) says about folk-stories, which in many
ways are at one with balladry: "When a tree or plant springs from the grave of
the victim, or from any part of him, the identity of tree and victim is evident.
. . . . Actual instances of the belief that sacred trees are the dead transformed,
or are the habitation of the ghost, are found in Australia, the Philippine Islands,
among the Damaras, and the Santals, who hold that the good are transformed
into trees at death."

[2] See Child, *op. cit.*, II, 498.

[3] III, 64 f. In Child's No. 91 A 29 the dying heroine has a "scope" (gag)
"into her cheek and into her chin, all to keep her life till her dear mother came."
Is there a possible allusion here to the belief that the life (soul) may leave by
the mouth?

[4] P. 181.

comparison with the Barra version of the story of Deirdre he gives the ballad incident of the loving plants as found in Percy's *Fair Margaret and Sweet William* (74). He then goes on to observe that there "originally underlay this the idea of the instantaneous passage of the soul into a flower, a bush, a tree, just as Daphne and Syrinx, when they cannot elude the pursuit of Apollo or Pan, change themselves into a laurel or a reed."[1] In connection with our ballad commonplace Child likewise takes note of the Deirdre story[2] and the incident therein of how the bad king persecutes the lovers by cutting down the trees that spring from their graves. But neither Child nor Henderson observes that this act of vengeance is not altogether absent from the British songs. It is present in Scott's version of *Earl Brand*. Here the Black Douglas, the maiden's father, pulls up the brier which grows from the lover's grave and throws it "in St. Mary's Loch":

> *But bye and rade the Black Douglas,*
> *And wow but he was rough!*
> *For he pulld up the bonny brier,*
> *And flang't in St. Mary's Loch* [7 B 20].[3]

In the Scotch-Gaelic version of the Deirdre story cited by Child the lovers are buried on opposite sides of a loch, over which the trees unite. May not the loch here account for the loch in Scott's ballad? There is also something of this cruelty to the dead lovers in *Lady Alice* (85). In version A the priest of the parish severs the intertwining roses; in B— and here one sees how "poetic invention" may obscure the original lore of traditional song—it is a "cold north-easterly wind" that "cut this lilly in twain."

The foregoing citations from the ballads, though sufficing to illustrate the belief in the tree-soul, are no indication of the frequent occurrence of the loving-plant incident

---

[1] P. 182.   [2] *Op. cit.*, III, 498.

[3] Cf. text, Greig, *Traditional Ballads and Ballad Airs*, p. 250b: "He pulled oot the bonnie brier bush, threw it in St. Mary's Loch." Cf. also text of No. 64 (Child, IV, 466): An "ill French lord" "pu'd up the bonnie brier."

even in British folksong. It is an incident which can be used to conclude any tragic love ballad.[1] In all but two of the Child pieces the plants that spring from the graves are either a brier and a rose or a brier and a birk.[2] *The Lass of Roch Royal* (76 C) has a thorn and a brier; *Lady Alice* (85 B), a lily. Sophie Jewett observes that "most commonly, especially in the German, it is the lily that blossoms on the grave of knight or maiden."[3] In continental ballads the plants—given here, wherever possible, as they are paired in folksong—are, among others, the following: linden, pinks, lilies, clump of reeds and cypress, thorn and elder, pines, pomegranate and almond tree, rose tree and grapevine, vine and pine, rosemary and a white flower, yew trees, plane and linden, oak and birch, rose and sage, poplar and pine, reeds and lemon tree, thorn and orange tree, golden willow and cypress, maple and birch, silver willow and golden willow.[4] "It will be noticed," says Miss

[1] This commonplace occurs in the following British ballads: 7 B, C, I, 64 A, E, also *ibid.*, E (Child, II, 111), and a further text (Child, IV, 465); 73 A; B, E, F, G, Dh (Child II, 198), and G (Child, V, 224); 74 A, B, Ad (Child, II, 203); 75 A, B, E, F, H, I; 76 A, C; 85 C (Child, V, 226) and *Giles Collins* (Child III, 515); 87 A, B; and 222 (Child, V, 262).

In American texts: 7, Campbell and Sharp, pp. 9 ff., A, C; 73, Louise Pound, *American Ballads and Songs*, p. 31; 74, *JAFL*, XIX, 281; XXIII, 381 f.; XXVIII, 154; XXX, 303 f.; Campbell and Sharp, pp. 62 ff., A, B, C, D; McGill, *Folk Songs of the Kentucky Mountains*, p. 70; Mackenzie, *op. cit.*, p. 124; 75, *JAFL*, XIX, 283 ff., a, b; XVIII, 291 ff., A, B; McGill, *op. cit.*, p. 10; Louise Pound, *op. cit.*, p. 7, B; Sharp, *One Hundred English Folksongs*, p. 60; 84, *JAFL*, VI, 133; XIX, 285 ff., a, b, c, f; XX, 256; XXII, 63; XXIX, 161; Campbell and Sharp, pp. 90 ff., A, B, C, E, F (in D, turtle dove and sparrow instead of plants); Lyman and Brockway, *Lonesome Tunes*, p. 5. This incident is not present in the Child versions of 84. Its occurrence in American texts and in English and Scottish texts since Child may be due to a borrowing from 75, which is a sort of companion piece.

In English and Scottish texts since Child: 7, Gavin Greig, *Folk-Song of the North-East*, Vol. I, art. 57; 73, Leather, *Folk-Lore of Herefordshire*, p. 200; *Journal of the Folk-Song Society*, II, 105 ff., 4th version; 74, *ibid.*, III, 64; 75, *ibid.*, p. 74, and texts, pp. 304 ff.; *ibid.*, I, 43 f.; *ibid.*, V, 136; Greig, *Folk-Song of the North-East*, Vol. II, art. 159; 84, *Journal of the Folk-Song Society*, I, 111; *ibid.*, II, 15; Sharp and Marson, *Folk Songs from Somerset* (1st. ser.), p. 45.

[2] On the sacred character of the birch in balladry see *infra*, pp. 155 ff.

[3] *Folk-Ballads of Southern Europe*, pp. 275 f.

[4] See Child, I, 96 ff., 489 f.; II, 205-6, 498; III, 498; IV, 443; and V, 491: Index of Matters and Literature.

Jewett, "that in the Southern ballads roses and lilies give place, for the most part, to firs, cypresses, olives, pines, and orange or lemon trees."[1] In certain American texts of the British ballads, as well as in a number of English and Scottish variants recovered since Child, the plants are usually a rose and a briar; a "green, green rose" and a "briar";[2] a "golden briar" and a "thorn";[3] a "damask rose" and a "sweet briar";[4] a "diamond rose" and a "sweet briar";[5] a "cherry-tree" and a "willow."[6]

What evidence, we may ask here, does balladry preserve of the superstition of the life-index or external soul? There is perhaps something of this superstition in the magic-ring incident in *Hind Horn* and *Bonny Bee Hom*. And there may be a vestige of it in those lines in *The Unquiet Grave* where the dead lover speaks of a flower that is withered to a stalk. It is noteworthy that in the Shropshire text of *The Unquiet Grave* (78 F)—a text which retains the old motif of setting tasks—there should be less of that sentimentalizing tone which characterizes the other versions of this ballad. After warning his sweetheart that one kiss of his lips will be fatal, the dead man says:

> *"O don't you remember the garden-grove*
> *Where we was used to walk?*
> *Pluck the finest flower of them all,*
> *'T will wither to a stalk."*

Or better yet, according to the Cornwall text: "The fairest flower that in the garden grew is witherd to a stalk."[7] This and the preceding reading are not incompatible with the notion that the lover's life was bound up with the flower. It is to be regretted that our ballads offer no such clear

---

[1] *Op. cit.*, p. 276. [2] No. 74, *JAFL*, XXVIII, 154.

[3] No. 73, Louise Pound, *op. cit.*, p. 31.

[4] No. 75, *Journal of the Folk-Song Society*, III, 74 f.

[5] No. 75, *ibid.*, I, 43.

[6] No. 74, *JAFL*, XXXV, 342. The plants are a "myrtle tree" and a "sweet briar" in a Greig text of *Earl Brand* (7), *Traditional Ballads and Ballad Airs*, p. 6, stanza 17.

[7] Child, III, 513.

evidence of the external soul as that yielded by a passage ascribed to Thomas the Rhymer. According to Thomas' prophecy, the fortunes of the Hays of Errol are bound up with the fate of an immemorial oak:[1]

> *"While the mistletoe bats on Errol's aik,*
> *And the aik stands fast,*
> *The Hays shall flourish, and their good grey hawk*
> *Shall nocht flinch before the blast.*

> *"But when the root of the aik decays,*
> *And the mistletoe dwines on its withered breast,*
> *The grass shall grow on Errol's hearth-stane,*
> *And the corbie roup in the falcon's nest."*

It is probable that in both *Hind Horn* (17) and *Bonny Bee Hom* (92) we have vestiges of the life-token.[2] In both songs the changing hue of a ring that the lady gives her lover indicates the state of the lady's affection. In *Bonny Bee Hom* (92 A) the color of the "ruby" stone serves, in addition, to show that the lady has died—an important matter in proving that we have to do here with the idea of the life-token:

> *"But gin this ring shoud fade or fail,*
> *Or the stone shoud change its hue,*
> *Be sure your love is dead and gone,*
> *Or she has proved untrue."*

The lover had been gone but a twelvemonth and a day when he found the stone to grow "dark and gray"—evidence that his lady is dead. Buchan's copy of the ballad (B) tells us that the stone not only changed color but that it burst "in three":

> *Time after this was not expir'd*
> *A month but scarcely three,*
> *Till black and ugly was the ring,*
> *And the stone was burst in three.*

[1] J. B. Pratt, *Buchan* (4th ed.; Aberdeen, 1901), p. 57 n.
[2] Cf. Hartland, *The Legend of Perseus*, II, 26, 27 n.

THE BIRD-SOUL

The belief in the bird- or animal-soul may be inferred from the ancient and widespread notion that birds and animals have the power of speech.[1] Birds talk and reveal or keep secrets in the following ballads: *Lady Isabel and the Elf-Knight* (4 C, D, E, F),[2] *Young Hunting* (68 A, B, C, etc.), *The Bonny Birdy* (82), *The Broomfield Hill* (43 A, C, D, E, F), *Child Waters* (63 C, E, F), *Mary Hamilton* (173 K), *The Rising in the North* (175, stanza 4), *Jamie Douglas* (204 J). The hero in *Hind Horn* (17) gives his mistress (A) a "silver wand with seven living lavrocks sitting thereon" or (B) "with three singing lavrocks set thereon." It is likely that the larks are of the helpful family of birds and are to keep the hero informed of events at home while he is away.[3] In *Lady Isabel and the Elf-Knight* (4 C) the bird, a parrot, is bribed by the promise of a cup of "flowered gold" to keep secret the doings of its mistress. That the bird is called a parrot is no doubt the result of rationalization of the early belief that all birds were able to speak and act like human beings:

Up then and spoke the pretty parrot:
"May Colven, where have you been?
What has become of false Sir John,
That woo'd you so late the streen?

"He woo'd you butt, he woo'd you ben,
He woo'd you in the ha,
Until he got your own consent
For to mount and gang awa."

[1] On helpful animals and talking birds in popular traditions, see Marian R. Cox, *Cinderella*, pp. 526 ff.; J. G. Frazer, "The Language of Animals," *Archaeological Review*, I, 81, 161.

[2] The talking-bird incident is well preserved in American variants of this piece.

[3] This interpretation is borne out by a Gavin Greig text, *Traditional Ballads*, p. 18. Here we find a "birdie sweet singin" in place of the artificial singing birds of the Child texts.

> *"O hold your tongue, my pretty parrot,*
> *Lay not the blame upon me;*
> *Your cup shall be of the flowered gold,*
> *Your cage of the root of the tree"* [C].

The Bonny Birdy (82) is given over to a dialogue between a bird and a knight. The bird, because of ill treatment at the hands of the knight's lady, reveals the secret of the lady's guilty love:

> *"Gin she had deen as ye her bade,*
> *I woudna tell how she has wrought."*

In *The Broomfield Hill* (43), a ballad of magic and witchcraft, there are talking and helpful animals as well as birds. The hero of the piece, enchanted by a soporific charm, has complained in turn to his greyhound, his berry-brown steed,[1] and his goshawk, because they have not wakened him. The reply of the hound will suffice here:

> *"I scraped wi my foot, master,*
> *Till a' my collars rang,*
> *But still the mair that I did scrape,*
> *Waken woud ye nane"* [C].

A wild boar speaks in *Sir Lionel* (18 C):

> *"O what dost thou want of me?" the wild boar said he;*
> *"O I think in my heart I can do enough for thee."*

The ballad of *The Gay Goshawk* likewise reflects the belief in talking and helpful birds, as do also the songs *Johnie Cock* and *Young Hunting*. *The Three Ravens* (26) details a conversation held by corbies.[2] In *The Gay Goshawk* (96) a bird acts as a messenger between lovers (A):

[1] For other unusual steeds in balladry see No. 30, stanzas 26 ff., and version of No. 15, Greig, *Traditional Ballads and Ballad Airs*, p. 16, stanza 6. The fairy steed is considered in our chapter on "The Ballad Fairy."

[2] Cf. an American variant, *JAFL*, XX, 154: a "gay little birdie" overhears the plans of the ravens.

"O well's me o my gay goss-hawk,
That he can speak and flee;
He'll carry a letter to my love,
Bring back another to me."

"O how can I your true-love ken,
Or how can I her know?
Whan frae her mouth I never heard couth,
Nor wi my eyes her saw."

"Birds," says Child, "are not seldom employed as posts in ballads. . . . . For a love-message of a general sort, not involving business, the nightingale is usually and rightly selected."[1] Child observes that the dove, the falcon, and the parrot are employed in ballad errands, and to this list Nigra adds the lark, the eagle, the raven, and the swallow.[2] There is a bird messenger in *Lord William* (254) and in *Johnie Cock*, a ballad to be considered shortly.

The idea of the bird-soul is borne out more explicitly in *Johnie Cock* and *Young Hunting* than in any of the songs just quoted. In *Young Hunting* (68) a jilted lady murders her false lover. That a bird reveals the deed points in all likelihood to an old superstition preserved in the original story,[3] according to which the bird must have been the dead lover, who, in order to denounce the murder, assumed this shape.[4] According to Herd's text of our ballad, the "bonny bird" addresses the murderess immediately after the crime, as also in Scott's versions (E, J):

Out an spake the bonny bird,
That flew abon her head:
"Lady, keep well thy green clothing
Fra that good lord's blood" [68 A].

---

[1] *Op. cit.*, II, 356 f.; see also "Birds," *ibid.*, V, 471.

[2] See Katharine Bates in notes to Sophie Jewett, *op. cit.*, p. 281.

[3] It is safe to assume here, as in the case of other ballads, that much has been lost in the course of oral transmission.

[4] Cf. T. F. Henderson, *The Ballad in Literature*, pp. 35 f.

In several texts (A, B, C, J, K) the bird divulges the guilty secret and tells the seekers how to find the drowned body by means of burning candles:

> *"Leave aff your ducking on the day,*
> *And duck upon the night;*
> *Whear ever that sakeless knight lys slain,*
> *The candels will shine bright"* [A].

The bird incident of the foregoing ballad is somewhat closely paralleled by a tale of the South African Bechuanas. A younger brother has been slain by an older, but he appears immediately as a bird and tells what has happened. Although the bird is twice killed—the last time burnt and its ashes scattered—yet it still reappears and announces that his body lies by a spring in the desert.[1]

The bird of our folksong is usually a "bonny bird," a "little bird," or a "wee birdie," but in certain texts is rationalized, Buchan-fashion, to a "small pyet," "pretty parrot," or "popinjay."[2] Among other crimes of which Buchan's blind beggar was guilty was that of making parrots of his talking birds. In his version of *The Gay Goshawk* (96 G) Buchan substitutes a parrot for the bird of other texts.

The substitution of a parrot in G, a bird that we all know can talk, testifies to the advances made by reason among the humblest in the later generations. A parrot, says Buchan, "is by far a more likely messenger to carry a love-letter or deliver a verbal message," . . . . The parrot goes well with the heroine swooning on a sofa (stanza 33) and the step-dame sitting on the sofa's end (stanza 36).[3]

But even Child may stop short of recognizing the early or primitive *raison d'être* of the talking bird in balladry. For instance, he regards the talking bird in *Child Waters* (63 C, E, F, H) as superfluous, but if, as there is good reason

[1] Grimm, *Kinder- und Hausmärchen*, III, 361.

[2] The talking bird is present in American variants of No. 68: *JAFL*, XX, 252; XXX, 297 ff., three texts; Campbell and Sharp, pp. 47 ff., A, B, D, E, F.

[3] Child, *op. cit.*, II, 357.

to think, this was originally a fairy ballad,[1] the bird may be a vestige of the supernatural elements of the song.

The belief in the passage of the soul into bird form is perhaps reflected in an American variant of *Bonny Barbara Allan* (84). Here a "turtle dove" and a "sparrow" are substituted for the usual plants which grow from the lovers' graves.[2] In another American variant of this piece, Barbara, upon the death of her lover, is accused by the "small birds" of cruelty, instead of by the bells in other texts.[3] In a Breton ballad, *Le Seigneur Nann et la Fée*, a song closely akin to the oldest Danish version of *Elveskud*, a Norse analogue of *Clerk Colvill* (42), there appears to be a combination of the bird-soul and the tree-soul:

> *Next morn from the grave two oak-trees fair,*
> *Shot lusty boughs high up in air;*
>
> *And in their boughs—oh, wondrous sight!—*
> *Two happy doves, all snowy white—*[4]

The white falcon of the Hays of Errol, a bird mentioned in a passage accredited to Thomas the Rhymer, was, it is possible, thought of as an ancestral spirit in bird form. The legend of the House of Errol held that it would be exceedingly unlucky for a Hay to kill a white falcon.[5]

The bird incident in *Johnie Cock* (114), that piece which won such high praise from Child,[6] represents "a faint and corrupted survival of the ancient superstition as to the reappearance of the human spirit in bird form."[7]

[1] See W. M. Hart, *Ballad and Epic*, p. 29.

[2] Campbell and Sharp, p. 94.

[3] *Ibid.*, p. 96; cf. McGill, *op. cit.*, p. 40.

[4] Tom Taylor, *Ballads and Songs of Brittany*, pp. 7 ff.; see also translation by Keightley, *Fairy Mythology*, p. 436.

[5] Cf. A. B. Cook, "The European Sky-God," *Folk-Lore*, XVII, 319 f.; see also Frazer, *Golden Bough*, XI, 283.

[6] " . . . . This precious specimen of the unspoiled traditional ballad . . . . " (*op. cit.*, III, 1).

[7] *Minstrelsy of the Scottish Border* (ed. Henderson), III, 140. The helpful bird (starling) incident is excellently preserved in a Greig text of our ballad, *Traditional Ballads*, p. 94.

The story briefly is that Johnie, a young outlaw, having slain the king's deer, is done to death in the greenwood by the king's foresters, and sends a bird to bid his mother come and fetch him away. The bird in version H, Buchan's text, turns out to be a parrot. But it is called simply a "bird" in B and K, a "bonnie bird" and a "starling" in F. The reading "boy" in A is evidently a corruption of "bird." That Johnie calls upon his mother and not upon his father to fetch him away is in keeping with the peculiar mother-son relationship in balladry.[1] In the opening stanza of one of the best versions of *Lady Isabel and the Elf-Knight* (4 B 1) a bird comes "out o a bush, on water for to dine." The bird in question may be the elfin-lover in disguise, and may represent for our ballads the tradition of the fairy-lover who assumes a bird shape in order to gain access to his mortal mistress.[2]

In connection with *The Death of Parcy Reed* (193) there is an interesting tradition which testifies to the popular belief in the bird-soul. In his letter to Sir Walter Scott concerning the foregoing ballad, Telfer says: "There is a place in Reed water called Deadwood Haughs, where the country-people still point out a stone where the unshriven soul of Parcy used to frequent in the shape of a blue hawk, and it is only a few years since he disappeared."[3] We may mention here those bird shapes through which Tam Lin (39) passes in the process of his escape from the fairies. In version C the hero is transformed into a "dove but and a swan"; in F, into an eagle. A text in the *Journal of the Irish Folk-Song Society* gives "a bird so wild" as one of his shapes.[4] The "bird," "fowl," and "owl" shapes in *The Cruel Mother* (20) have already been recorded. The lovers in *The Twa Magicians* (44) become two turtle doves. The youth in *The Earl of Mar's Daughter* (270) takes the form

[1] See Gummere, "The Mother-in-Law," *Kittredge Anniversary Papers*, pp. 15–24.

[2] Cf. T. P. Cross, "The Celtic Origin of the Lay of Yonec," *Revue celtique*, XXXI, 452 n.

[3] See Child, IV, 521.   [4] I, 47.

of a "turtle-doo." His mother is an enchantress and lives on "foreign isles"; hence the hero's shape-shifting powers:

> *"I am a doo the live-lang day,*
> *A sprightly youth at night;*
> *This aye gars me appear mair fair*
> *In a fair maiden's sight."*

The superstition that the soul may reside in a bird[1] is reflected clearly enough in certain Scandinavian versions of the ballad which is represented in Scotland by *Leesome Brand* (15). According to the Danish song *Redselille og Medelvold*, a girl dies in the wood from childbirth. Her lover, who has gone to find her a "draught of water clear," hears two nightingales singing at the spring:

> *"Deep in the dale he reach'd the spring,*
> *And there two nightingales heard sing:*

> *"With two small infants by her side*
> *Your lady in the grove has died."*[2]

But most of the Scandinavian songs have only a single nightingale, "and, as Grundtvig points out, the single bird is right, for the bird is really a vehicle for the soul of the dead Redselille."[3] A German variant of *Lady Isabel and the Elf-Knight* (4) likewise preserves the tradition of the soul in bird form. In his analysis of German J Child says: "There is no sense in the *two* doves. The single dove one may suppose to be the spirit of the last victim. We shall find the *eleven* appearing as doves in Q."[4]

The foregoing belief again occurs in Norse song.[5] The Danish ballad *The Maid on the Pyre* tells a story of a maiden who is wrongly accused by her brother of inconti-

---

[1] On ghosts as birds see Frazer, *The Golden Bough*, III, 33 ff., 177; Hartland, *Legend of Perseus*, I, 182–228; G. Henderson, *op. cit.*, pp. 89 ff.; Wentz, *Fairy-Faith in Celtic Countries*, pp. 240, 304 n., 355.

[2] Prior, *op. cit.*, III, 6.

[3] Child, I, 180.

[4] *Ibid.*, p. 33 n.   [5] See Prior, *op. cit.*, I, 352 ff.

nence and by him committed to the flames. But she is borne away as a dove to heaven; the wicked brother, as a raven to hell. Two doves come for the maiden:

> '*Twas two flew down, and home flew three,*
> *The fairest of all of them was she.*

> *There came two ravens from out of hell,*
> *And Ivar took with them to dwell.*

> '*Twas two flew up, and back flew three;*
> *The foulest of all of them was he.*[1]

One finds the same superstition as a motif in the hymn of Prudentius to St. Catharine's counterpart, St. Eulalia, a hymn written in the late fourth century. A pigeon rises from the dying body of Eulalia, seeming to leave by the martyr's mouth:

> *Emicat inde columba repens*
> *Martyris os nive candidior*
> *Visa relinquere, et astra sequi.*
> *Spiritus hic erat Eulaliae*
> *Lacteolus, celer, innocuus.*

Two other Danish ballads, *The Nightingale* and *The Maid as a Hind and a Hawk*, furnish first-rate examples of bird metamorphosis. A "hard stepmother" has, according to the former piece, turned a maiden into a nightingale, the maiden's brother into a "grisly wolf":

> "*Myself she shaped to a Nightingale,*
> *And drave me from my home,*
> *My brother a grisly wolf she made*
> *In forest wild to roam.*"[2]

Another stepmother works her black magic in the second of the foregoing songs. She transforms her stepdaughter into a "little white hind," her victim's seven maids into

---

[1] *Ibid.*, II, 65.
[2] Grundtvig, II, 171; trans. Prior, *op. cit.*, III, 120.

wolves. In order to escape the hounds the maiden changes from her deer form into a hawk:

> *The hounds they press'd the hind so sore,*
> *For covert she fain must fly;*
> *She shaped herself to a little wild hawk,*
> *And flew to the clouds so high.*[1]

Restoration to their original forms—a point to be considered in connection with the blood-soul[2]—is the happy fate of the enchanted mortals in both this and the preceding song.

In view of the foregoing bird-soul superstition as exemplified by folksong, a list of ballad birds is not without interest. Of the birds named below many are found again and again in our traditional poetry: robin, peacock, wren, parrot, swan, pheasant, blackbird, lavrock (lark), woodweele (wood-lark?), starling, magpie, popinjay, goshawk, (falcon), spier-hawk (sparrow-hawk), eagle, linnet, bunting, dove, turtle dove, sparrow, thristle-cock (thrush), mavosie (mavis), duck, drake, owl, carnal (crow), raven, corbie, crane, hen, cock, capon, jaye, maw (seamew), swallow, nightingale.

THE ANIMAL-SOUL

Under the general term "animal-soul" I include such forms of the soul as the deer, the wolf, the hare, the serpent, and the seal. From evidence supplied by a number of ballads we may claim for British folk-poetry the belief that the soul may at death pass into animal form or that a person through magic means and without the interposition of death may be so metamorphosed.[3] Such evidence is found in the excellent ballad of *Leesome Brand* (15), evidence rather fragmentary, to be sure, but which may be pieced out by reference through Grundtvig to Danish tradition.

[1] *Ibid.*, p., 158; trans. Prior, III, 127.

[2] *Infra*, pp. 75, 341 f.

[3] In the *Journal of the Folk-Song Society*, VII, 17–21, Miss A. G. Gilchrist has something to say of animal transformations in balladry.

Indeed, the "white hind" incident of our folksong, even when read alone without the aid of Scandinavian lore, seems hardly to be explained save as an example of the animal-soul superstition. One must, however, regret that "lost Scottish ballad" from which Grundtvig has suggested came the "hind" and the "blood" of *Leesome Brand*, neither of which incidents belongs, according to Child, to this latter piece. This lost ballad, thought Grundtvig, would resemble the Danish song *The Maid Transformed into a Hind*.[1]

Brought to her "grief and pain" in the forest,[2] the eleven-year-old mistress in *Leesome Brand* requests, according to a familiar ballad custom, that her lover refrain her "companie,"[3] and gives him instructions similar in part to those given the brother-lover in *Sheath and Knife* (16). In this latter piece, however, there is no mention of a hind. The former reads:

> *"Ye'll take your arrow and your bow,*
> *And ye will hunt the deer and roe.*

> *"Be sure ye touch not the white hynde,*
> *For she is o the woman kind"* [15 A].

The passage in text B of *Leesome Brand* is almost identical with that in *Sheath and Knife* (16 A, B, C):

> *"When ye hear me give a cry,*
> *Ye'll shoot your bow and let me lye"* [15 B].

The passage which in *Sheath and Knife* corresponds to the foregoing stanza was thought at first by Child to mean the shooting of an arrow to mark the grave, as in *Robin Hood's*

---

[1] See Child, I, 178.

[2] With respect to birth in the forest in another piece, No. 103, Child, *op. cit.*, II, 416, says: "The only part of the ballad which has the stamp of indubitably ancient tradition is the child-birth in the wood, and this scene is the rightful, and perhaps exclusive, property of 'Leesome Brand,' No. 15."

[3] On the custom of rejecting male assistance at childbirth as depicted in balladry, see the notes by David Rorie, M.D., in *Folk-Lore*, XXV, 383.

Death (120 B 16),[1] but later he says: ".... the idea seems rather to be, that the arrow is to leave the bow at the moment when the soul shoots from the body."[2] But to return to the "white hind." Such "pleasure in deer and roe" does the lover take that he forgets his "ladye" until reminded of her by the "milk-white hynde." He hastens to the greenwood tree only to find his mistress and her young son lying dead. All this occurs in such narrative sequence—if one may trust to plot arrangement in a ballad—as to bear out the interpretation that the soul of the dead lady has passed into the form of the hind. This interpretation is borne out additionally, of course, by the prevalence of the transformation belief, as well as by Grundtvig's above-mentioned suggestion that these lines belong to a "lost" Scottish ballad on the order of *The Maid Transformed into a Hind*. Child's analysis of the Danish song may be given here:

> In this ballad a girl begs her brother, who is going hunting, to spare the little hind that "plays before his foot." The brother nevertheless shoots the hind, though not mortally, and sets to work to flay it, in which process he discovers his sister under the hind's hide. His sister tells him that she had been successively changed into a pair of scissors, a sword, a hare, a hind, by her step-mother, and that she was not to be free of the spell until she had drunk of her brother's blood. Her brother at once cuts his fingers, gives her some of his blood, and the girl is permanently restored to her natural shape, and afterwards is happily married.[3]

The request of the maiden in both the Scottish and the Norse ballad that the huntsman refrain from shooting the hind finds an interesting parallel in a legend concerning the forester of the Fairy Corry. According to Mr. Duncan Whyte, a direct descendant of the forester, the hero of the story, when forced at the command of Argyll to fire at a white hind, falls dead on the spot. The white hind was none other than his sweetheart in fairy form.[4]

The incident of the white hind as related in *Leesome*

[1] *Op. cit.*, I, 185.   [2] *Ibid.*, III, 103 n.   [3] *Ibid.*, I, 178.
[4] See G. Henderson, *op. cit.*, pp. 124 f., citing *Glasgow Herald* (Aug. 20, 1910).

Brand is found also in *Willie and Earl Richard's Daughter* (102 B). But as Child observes, "The first part of B 4–18 is a variety of the wide-spread tragic ballad of 'Leesome Brand,' No. 15."[1] In this connection we may mention the ballad of *The Bonny Hind* (50), the symbolical "hind" of which is possibly traceable to the belief in animal transformation. This song may account for the hind in *Leesome Brand.*[2]

Another example of transformation into a deer is supplied by that "tender little English ballad" *The Three Ravens* (26). The rather symbolical character of the song is a thin disguise of what was actual belief in the animal-soul, the fallow doe in the story being none other than the faithful true-love metamorphosed.[3] Under his shield a knight lies slain, and three ravens know where to make their breakfast but for the dead knight's hawks and hounds, which guard him well. Then, to give her lover sepulture before she herself dies, comes his "leman" in the form of a "fallow doe." To interpret this animal form as a bit of allegory is only one way of saying that what was matter of fact for the early mind is for us nothing more than poetry:

> *Downe there comes a fallow doe,*
> *As great with yong as she might goe.*
>
> *She lift vp his bloudy hed,*
> *And kist his wounds that were so red.*
>
> *She got him vp vpon her backe,*
> *And carried him to earthen lake.*
>
> *She buried him before the prime,*
> *She was dead herselfe ere euen-song time.*

In another copy of *The Three Ravens*[4] the "leman" is called "a lady, full of woe," but this copy is one of those "tradi-

---

[1] *Op. cit.*, II, 412.

[2] See *ibid.*, I, 178. The white-hind incident occurs, however, in a recently recovered text of *Leesome Brand* (Greig, *Traditional Ballads*, pp. 16 f.).

[3] Cf. W. M. Hart, *English Popular Ballads*, p. 313.   [4] Child, V, 212.

tional copies, differing principally by what they lack."
There can be little question that one of the things lacking
here is the "doe" form of the mistress. It is worthy of note
that in a copy of *The Twa Corbies*, a "cynical variation" of
The Three Ravens, the knight has been hunting the "wild
deer."[1] It is very probable that our ballad reflects the tradition of beast marriage, a tradition preserved in popular
tales the world over, tales on the order of Perrault's story
of "Beauty and the Beast" and current among civilized,
barbarous, and savage peoples.[2]

In the Breton song *Le Seigneur Nann et la Fée*, an
analogue of *Clerk Colvill* (42), a fairy or korrigan, in the
shape of a white hind, insists that a young man marry her.
Keightley's translation from the collection of Villemarqué
may be given, though in this text we must infer, what is
made clearer in another copy, that the Otherworld mistress
is in the form of a hind:

> *When he unto the wood drew nigh,*
> *A fair white doe he there did spy,*
>
> *And after her such chase he made,*
> *The ground it shook beneath their tread.*
>
> *And after her such chase made he,*
> *From his brows the water copiously*
>
> *And from his horse's sides ran down.*
> *The evening had now come on,*
>
> *And he came where a streamlet flowed*
> *Fast by a Korrigan's abode;*
>
> *And grassy turf spread all around.*
> *To quench his thirst he sprang to ground.*
>
> *The Korrig at her fount sat there*
> *A-combing of her long fair hair.*

---

[1] *Ibid.*, I, 254.

[2] See MacCulloch, *Childhood of Fiction*, pp. 253–78.

She combed it with a comb of gold—
These ladies ne'er are poor, we're told.

"Rash man," cried she, "how dost thou dare
To come disturb my waters fair!

"Thou shalt unto me plight thy fay,
Or seven years thou shalt waste away,
Or thou shalt die ere the third day."[1]

The well-known French ballad *La Biche Blanche* tells how a brother was unwittingly the death of his sister, who was a maid by day, a hind by night. A popular tale of Thomas the Rhymer, as given by Scott, pictures two fairies in the forms of a hart and a hind.

Accordingly, while Thomas was making merry with his friends, in the Tower of Ercildoune, a person came running in, and told, with marks of fear and astonishment, that a hart and hind had left the neighbouring forest, and were, composedly and slowly, parading the street of the village. The prophet instantly arose, left his habitation, and followed the wonderful animals to the forest, whence he was never seen to return.[2]

In the course of his shapeshifting, the Otherworld knight of *Tam Lin* (39) becomes (G 55) a "deer sae wild." Janet (H 7) speaks of her child as being "to a wild buck rae," and calls her lover (G 21) an "elfin rae."

Danish balladry gives excellent examples of metamorphosis into deer form. The traditionally cruel stepmother of *Jomfruen i Linden* has changed her stepchildren into various shapes—"fleeting deer," "hawks," and "linden tree":

"She changed us, some to fleeting deer,
And some as hawks bade skim the air;

"Myself a linden tree she made,
And set to grow on a green-wood glade."[3]

---

[1] Keightley, *op. cit.*, p. 434; cf. translation by Tom Taylor, *op. cit.*, p. 9, and see Child's analyses of other texts (*op. cit.*, I, 378 ff.).

[2] *Minstrelsy* (ed. T. F. Henderson), IV, 83.   [3] Prior, *op. cit.*, III, 141.

Another girl in the Danish song *The Maid as a Hind and a Hawk* is the victim of a stepmother no less heartless:

> "*She shaped myself to a little white hind,*
> *And bade me to greenwood wend;*
> *My seven little maids she turn'd to wolves,*
> *And bade them my flesh to rend.*"[1]

The most common witch-familiars in the British Isles are cats, hares, and occasionally red deer. These animals have taken the place of wolves, which, having been eradicated, may no longer serve the purposes of the witch.[2] In view of this fact we may, on the strength of deer and wolf transformations, attribute to British balladry a relatively high antiquity.[3] It is chiefly in its supernatural character that the wolf appears in our folksong. *Kemp Owyne* (34), a song of pure magic and related to Icelandic saga, tells a story of spelling and unspelling. The kemp asks the lady who it was that had "misshapit" her (B):

> "*O was it wolf into the wood,*
> *Or was it fish intill the sea,*
> *Or was it man, or wile woman,*
> *My true love, that misshapit thee?*"

Instead of "wolf" and "fish," another text has "warwolf in the wood" and "mermaid in the sea."[4] Apparently the wolf was not yet extinct at the period of our ballad. Discussing at some length the werwolf or *lycanthropus* in connection with our ballad, Scott remarks: "The Editor presumes, it is only since the extirpation of wolves that our British sorceresses have adopted the disguise of hares, cats, and such more familiar animals."[5]

[1] *Ibid.*, p. 126.

[2] See Gomme, *Ethnology in Folklore*, p. 50; cf. Bugge, *op. cit.* (trans. W. H. Schofield), p. 118.

[3] Just as the oath by oak, ash, and thorn in *Glasgerion* (67 A 18) is a trait of high antiquity.

[4] Child, I, 311.

[5] *Op. cit.* (ed. T. F. Henderson), III, 307.

Lycanthropy seems to be in evidence in three texts of *Johnie Cock* (114 A, B, C). Johnie rebukes his treacherous enemies by telling them that he would have fared better at the hands of "the wildest wolf in aw this wood":

> *"The wildest wolf in aw this wood*
> *Wad not ha done so by me;*
> *She'd ha wet her foot ith wan water,*
> *And sprinkled it oer my brae,*
> *And if that wad not ha wakened me,*
> *She wad ha gone and let me be"* [A 17].

Obviously, Johnie's wolf belongs to the class of human-like animals.

Percy was struck with the occurrence of the wolf in A 17, found also in B 10, C 5. He considered, no doubt, that the mention of the wolf was a token of the high antiquity of the ballad. "Wolues that wyryeth men and children" are spoken of in Piers Plowman, C, Passus, X, v. 226, Skeat, 1886, I, 240, and the C text is assigned to about 1393. Holinshed (1577), I, 378, says that though the island is void of wolves south of the Tweed, yet the Scots cannot boast the like, since they have grievous wolves."[1]

There is a terrible wolf in *Young Andrew* (48):

> *Ffull soone a wolfe did of him smell,*
> *And shee came roaring like a beare,*
> *And gaping like a ffeend of hell.*

". . . . How the wolf comes into the story," says Child, "will probably never be known."[2] Tam Lin (39 G 52) passes through the form of a wolf in the course of his disenchantment.

Wolf metamorphosis is not uncommon in Danish ballads. The black magic of the cruel stepmother is operative in all three of the following examples. *The Maiden Transformed to a Wer-Wolf* tells of a girl who was changed to "a scissars small," "a sword-blade," and finally to a "werwolf":

---

[1] Child, III, 2; see also *ibid.*, IV, 495.

[2] *Ibid.*, I, 432. The wolf is mentioned also in No. 70 B 7: "As I came thro the woods this night, the wolf maist worried me; . . . ."

> *"As wer-wolf then by her cruel spell*
> *She drove me to roam the wood and dell.*
>
> *"Eight years no other home I knew,*
> *And many a gallant man I slew."*[1]

The following lines from *The Nightingale* have already been quoted in connection with the bird-soul:

> *"Myself she shaped to a Nightingale,*
> *And drave me from my home,*
> *My brother a grisly wolf she made*
> *In forest wild to roam.*
>
> *"In wolfish guise for seven long years*
> *He roam'd the murky wood;*
> *For bound he was in runic spell,*
> *Till he should drink her blood."*[2]

According to *The Maid as a Hind and a Hawk*, a girl is transformed into a "hind"; her "seven little maids" are shaped into "wolves."[3]

The wolf form, as well as those animal shapes now to be discussed, is probably in the first remove, at least, from the earlier or more basic belief that the soul at death may assume an animal form. Or, the werwolf superstition may have its origin in the allied belief that animals themselves have spirits. That is, the metamorphoses in *Tam Lin* and *Kemp Owyne*, for instance, like those in certain *Märchen*, illustrate the translation of more primitive and fundamental ideas into the lore of witchcraft. They find their *raison d'être* in the realm of magic.

Fish, eel, and whale transformations have already been discussed under transmigration beliefs. A familiar creature in witchcraft and found in fairy tales as a transformed human being, the toad may be mentioned here as one of Tam Lin's shapes (39 C 9):

[1] Grundtvig, II, 156; trans. Prior, *op. cit.*, III, 115.
[2] *Ibid.*, p. 171; trans. Prior, III, 120.
[3] *Ibid.*, p. 158; trans. Prior, III, 126.

"Next I'll grow into your arms
A toad but and an eel."

The toad shape is an expiatory metamorphosis in Lamb's
Laidley Worm, a poem allied to *Kemp Owyne* and based on
tradition. Here the witch queen becomes a "loathsome
toad":

> *Now on the sand near Ida's tower,*
> *She crawls a loathsome toad,*
> *And venom spits on every maid*
> *She meets upon the road.*[1]

Belief in the sacred character of the serpent is widespread and is illustrated, for example, by the notion that
the soul may take the form of a snake.[2] Denizens of the
Otherworld are often ophidian in character, and in folk-
tales and romance mortals frequently appear in serpent
guise.[3] Among the many transformation incidents[4] of balladry serpent metamorphosis holds an important place.
Tam Lin becomes in the course of his shape-shifting an
"esk and adder":

> *"They'll turn me in your arms, lady,*
> *Into an esk and adder;*
> *But hold me fast, and fear me not,*
> *I am your bairn's father"* [39 A 31].

The "ask" or newt-shape occurs also in texts C, F, and H.
The adder—usually "an adder and a snake"—is found in
all texts except two, and of all the shapes, in all the variants of the ballad, it is the most constant. In a version of
The Laidley Worm the enchanted lady is in the form of a
"laidley adder."[5]

[1] Child, I, 313; cf. *ibid.*, II, 505.

[2] See "Serpent-Worship," *Encyclopaedia of Religion and Ethics*, Vol. XI;
"Animals," *ibid.*, I, 525 ff.

[3] See W. H. Schofield, *Studies on the Libeaus Desconus*, "Harvard Studies
and Notes in Philology and Literature," Vol. IV (1895); Olrik, *Danske Studier*,
I, 1 ff.; Child, I, 306 ff.

[4] On transformations of all kinds see S. Prato, *Bulletin de folklore*, I, 316–35.

[5] Child, II, 504.

Kemp Owyne, Allison Gross, and *The Laily Worm and the Machrel of the Sea* offer further instances of serpent transformation. Dove Isabel of *Kemp Owyne* (34) is changed by her stepmother into a hideous shape:

> *Her breath grew strang, her hair grew lang,*
> *And twisted thrice about the tree,*
> *And all the people, far and near,*
> *Thought that a savage beast was she* [A 4].

That Dove Isabel's enchantment is broken by three kisses from the kemp places our ballad in a class with German tales of *Schlangenjungfrauen.*[1] The description of the serpent in a text closely resembling A is virtually that of the foregoing stanza. In B and Bb it is called a "fiery beast." Lamb's copy has a "poisonous worm";[2] Grow's, "laidley ask" and "laidley adder."[3]

Not less monstrous is the enchantment in *Allison Gross* (35). A young man has rejected the love of a witch:

> *"She's turnd me into an ugly worm,*
> *And gard me toddle about the tree."*

The Laily Worm (36), like *The Marriage of Sir Gawain* (31), instances a double transformation of brother and sister at the hands of a malicious stepmother:

> *"For she changed me to the laily worm,*
> *That lies at the fit o the tree,*
> *And my sister Masery*
> *To the machrel of the sea."*

Admirable examples of serpent metamorphosis are furnished by the Danish songs *Lindormen* and *Jomfruen i Ormeham,* both of which, like *Kemp Owyne,* tell how an enchanted mortal is freed by means of a kiss or kisses. In *Lindormen* a maiden thus releases from enchantment a

---

[1] See Child's many references, *op. cit.,* I, 307 f.; IV, 454; V, 289 f. On serpent births in popular fictions see *ibid.,* I, 339 n.

[2] *Ibid.,* I, 313.   [3] *Ibid.,* II, 504 f.

knight who in the form of a "lothely Lindworm" has besought her aid:

> *Soon as the cave he came within,*
> *He cast aside the Lindworm skin.*[1]

Jomfruen i Ormeham belongs likewise to the swan-maiden class of stories. The heroine of the song is a courtly maid by day, a "creeping snake" by night. Sir Jenus, like other legendary heroes, unspells the lady by kissing her while she is a snake:

> *Sir Jenus he went by a lonely road*
> *Along the mountain side,*
> *And there he beheld the creeping snake*
> *Through herbage and bushes glide.*
>
> *Sir Jenus over the saddle bent,*
> *The bright little snake he kiss'd*
> *And straight there was smiling a lovely maid*
> *Where even a snake had hiss'd.*[2]

Jomfruen i Ormeham, in the matter of the kiss, has close connections with both Icelandic saga and *Kemp Owyne*.[3]

The English song *The Queen of Scotland* (301), an insipid ballad, tells of a long-starved serpent which winds itself about Troy Muir's middle. A maiden who chances by allays the serpent's rage by cutting off her "fair white pap" for him. Two serpents "out of hell" serve in *Dives and Lazarus* (56) as guides to conduct Dives to the lower regions:

> *As it fell out upon a day,*
> *Rich Dives sickened and died;*
> *Then came two serpents out of hell,*
> *His soul therein to guide* [A 12, B 13].

[1] Grundtvig, II, 213; trans. Prior, *op. cit.* III, 133.
[2] *Ibid.*, p. 177; trans. Prior, III, 137.
[3] See Child, I, 307.

These serpent guides remind one of that gorgeous serpent which appeared as Aeneas was pouring libations on his father's tomb,[1] but one may go to much lower cults for the belief in the serpent-soul. Finally, with reference to the serpent, snake, or worm-soul in balladry we should not overlook that "channerin worm" in *The Wife of Usher's Well* (79 A 11) which "doth chide" at the absence of the ghost sons from the grave.

Known throughout Europe as a witch-familiar, the hare[2] figures, moreover, in the lore of primitive peoples and is a common character in myths and folktales.[3] As a transformation animal the hare, as well as the cat, an animal that rivals the hare in popular superstitions, appears in *Fair Annie* (62). The forsaken heroine of this piece voices the belief in animal metamorphosis when, in her despairing wish, she cries (A 23):

> *"Gin my seven sons were seven young rats,*
> *Running on the castle wa,*
> *And I were a grey cat mysell,*
> *I soon would worry them a'.*

> *"Gin my seven sons were seven young hares,*
> *Running oer yon lilly lee,*
> *And I were a grew hound mysell,*
> *Soon worried they a' should be."*

Texts B, E, and I give virtually the same reading as A, but in G 4 there are "gray-hounds" only; C 25, her sons "cats," herself a "blood-hound"; J, in addition to "hares" and "greyhound," has "brown rats" and "grey cat."[4] In *Hind Etin* (41 C 8) a woman who has borne seven bairns to a troll or hillman wishes, as does Annie, that her bairns

---

[1] *Aeneid* v. 90–93.

[2] Murray, *Witch-Cult in Western Europe*, p. 227; G. Henderson, *op. cit.*, p. 102; Gomme, *op. cit.*, pp. 49 f.; J. G. Campbell, *Witchcraft and Second Sight in the Highlands and Islands of Scotland*, pp. 30–45.

[3] See De Gubernatis, *Zöological Mythology*, II, 76–82.

[4] Cf. text, Greig, *Traditional Ballads*, p. 49: "tods" (foxes) and greyhound; seven rats and gray cat.

were "seven greedy rats," herself a "great grey cat to eat them ane and a'." The cat as a helpful and talking animal is found in one text of *The Elfin Knight* (2 K 5).

The sole ballad example of the goat in a supernatural rôle is found in *Willie's Lady* (6), a story about magically obstructed childbirth. Throughout medieval demonology the goat is associated with Satan and with witches.[1] But the devil in goat guise seems not to occur at all in Great Britain.[2] In our ballad the "master kid," which plays a part in the witch's spell, is, to all appearances, not to be taken as a form of the witch herself. Are we to understand, then, that the goat is here a form of the devil? That the "master kid" is slain would not, of course, invalidate this interpretation. Slaying the kid serves, among other counter activities, to break the witch spell:

> *And Willie's taen down the bush o woodbine*
> *That hang atween her bower and thine.*

> *And Willie has killed the master kid*
> *That ran beneath that ladie's bed.*

Willie's Lady is considered in full under the Otherworld spell. As an ordinary domestic animal the goat is found in other ballads: Nos. 99 B 28, "goat-horn"; 101 B 25, C 13, "goat-milk"; 225 A 13, C 19.

In the course of his transformations Tam Lin becomes (39 A 32) a bear and a lion, or (E 12) a "wood black dog to bite." In *Sir Lionel* (18) there is a terrible wild boar that belongs to a giant or to a "wild woman." A wild boar's head is proof against the knife of a cuckold in *The Boy and the Mantle* (29). Allusions to the wild boar occur in still other pieces (46 A 17, Bd 17; 93 R 1), and "wild-wood swine" is a stock phrase. References to the bear are found in *Young Andrew* (48, stanza 35) and *Queen Eleanor's Confession* (156 E 19, F 22). To his true love's wedding Lord Wayets will send "the nine hides o the noble cow" (66 C

[1] *Encyclopaedia of Religion and Ethics*, I, 517.
[2] See Murray, *op. cit.*, p. 68.

19). Lions and ravens appear in a dream of ill omen in *Young Johnstone* (88 D 11, 16 f.). The lion is mentioned in still other pieces (48; 55; 61; 101 A 14, B 12, 17). On lions in Scotland we may quote Holinshed: "Lions we have had verie manie in the north parts of Scotland, and those with maines of no less force than they of Mauritania are sometimes reported to be; but how and when they were destroied as yet I doo not read."[1] Swine also appear in dreams of ill omen (88 D, 69 E, 74 A, B, C; 259).[2] Some few other ballad animals not mentioned in the foregoing pages are sheep, rams, ewes, staghounds, slough-hounds, horses, oxen, bulls, cows, nouts (neat cattle), otters, squirrels, and rattlesnakes. With the exception of horses, which occur as fairy steeds, none of these animals figures in supernatural pieces. The talking dogs in *The Broomfield Hill* (43) have already been discussed.

TOTEMISM

Before taking up those ballad incidents which give evidence that the soul may reside in parts of the body, such as the hair, the bones, and the blood, we may digress for a moment to raise the question as to whether or not British folksong reflects in any way totemistic thought. According to N. W. Thomas in his study "Animal Superstitions and Totemism," the "survivals of Totemism in Europe must be sought in the animal superstitions . . . . of the uncivilised or little civilised European peasant."[3] To observe, then, certain of those superstitions listed by Mr. Thomas as evidential of totemistic belief,[4] we may say that the data contributed by English and Scottish traditional poetry strengthen the case for "Totemism in Europe." The ballads preserve the old notion of talking and helpful birds

[1] *Chronicles of England, Scotland, and Ireland*, I, 379.

[2] On dreaming of swine see W. Gregor, *Folk-Lore of the North-East of Scotland*, p. 29; W. Henderson, *op. cit.*, p. 327. On the swine-cult see MacCulloch, *Religion of the Ancient Celts*, pp. 210 f.

[3] *Folk-Lore*, XI, 227–67.

[4] Mr. Thomas' classification is based in part on that made by Gomme of Frazer's Totemism.

and animals, as in *The Broomfield Hill* (43). They illustrate the superstition of the witch-familiar—the werwolf, for instance, in *Kemp Owyne* (34) or the mermaid in the same piece. They give rather full depiction to the belief in soul-animals; the bird-soul in *Young Hunting* (68) and the deer-soul in *Leesome Brand* (15) are good examples. The latter piece seems also to preserve the primitive notion of the animal tabooed. Leesome Brand is forbidden to shoot the "white hind."[1] There are animal lovers and some hint even of animal parentage. Whether or not we see this last-named belief in Janet's statement (39 H 7) that her child is "to a wild buck rae," certainly it is clear enough in another of our excellent supernatural ballads, *The Great Silkie of Sule Skerry* (113):

> *Then ane arose at her bed-fit,*
> *An a grumly guest I'm sure was he:*
> *"Here am I, thy bairnis father,*
> *Although that I be not comelie.*

> *"I am a man, upo the lan,*
> *An I am a silkie in the sea;*
> *And when I'm far and far frae lan,*
> *My dwelling is in Sule Skerrie."*

"A photograph has been exhibited before the Folk-Lore Society," says Marian Cox, "of an old Scotch woman who proudly claims to be the grand-daughter of a seal, and tells the story of her grandfather's capturing and marrying the seal maid."[2] To return to the animal tabooed, it is possible that the prophecy of the seal-lover in the foregoing ballad is a case in point. The sealman predicts that his sweetheart will marry a gunner who will shoot him and his son:

> *"An it sall come to pass on a simmer's day,*
> *When the sin shines het on evera stane,*
> *That I will tak my little young son,*
> *An teach him for to swim the faem.*

[1] Mr. Thomas lists forty-seven animals which are or have been tabooed in various parts of Europe.

[2] *Introduction to Folk-Lore,* p. 101.

[67]

> *"An thu sall marry a proud gunner,*
> *An a proud gunner I'm sure he'll be,*
> *An the very first schot that ere he schoots,*
> *He'll schoot baith my young son and me."*

Is not this a reflection, however indirectly, of the belief that it is unlucky to kill a seal since it is a transformed human being? The foregoing evidence, then, in view of Mr. Thomas' thesis, may be said to show that balladry is not wanting in those animal superstitions which point to totemistic thought in Europe.[1]

THE BONE-SOUL

After our rather digressive inquiry into totemic thought we may turn to a survey of those ballad incidents that illustrate the belief that the soul may reside in parts of the body. Such shapes or vehicles of the soul, among them the blood and the kidneys, may be classified as examples of the corporeal soul.[2] But in connection with these corporeal vehicles we should bear in mind the corporeity of the ballad ghost as discussed in our chapter on the dead man.[3]

The singing-bone incident of *The Twa Sisters* (10), a song with excellent Norse analogues, illustrates the widespread and primitive belief that the soul resides in some particular part of the body, frequently a bone. Our ballad is representative of popular tales known throughout Europe and likewise in Asia and Africa.[4] Briefly, the ballad story is as follows: A maiden is drowned by her jealous sister, and through a viol or harp—a fiddle is the usual instrument in Norse ballads[5]—furnished by some part of her body,[6] she

[1] That the soul-animal superstition is evidential of totemistic thought is generally recognized. See Wundt, *Elements of Folk Psychology* (trans. E. L. Schaub), pp. 190 ff.; Durkheim, *Elementary Forms of the Religious Life* (trans. J. W. Swain), pp. 260 ff.; MacCulloch, *Religion of the Ancient Celts*, p. 360.

[2] Cf. Wundt, *op. cit.*, pp. 205 ff.   [3] *Infra*, pp. 229 ff.

[4] See Child, I, 124, 493; II, 498; III, 499; IV, 447; V, 208, 286; Hartland, *Legend of Perseus*, I, 192.

[5] See Child, I, 121 n.

[6] In certain texts the instrument is made altogether from her body.

reveals the identity of her slayer.[1] To Child's view on the original character of the ballad story Hartland takes exception. "Perhaps the original conception," says Child, "was the simple and beautiful one which we find in English B and both the Icelandic ballads, that the king's harper, or the girl's lover, takes three locks of her yellow hair to string his harp with."[2] Hartland thinks, however, that the "tradition supplied by the singer of one of the Swedish versions, though lost from the ballad itself, is much nearer the mark in relating that the drowned maiden floated ashore and grew up into a lime-tree, from whose wood the harp was made."[3] There is nothing of the tree idea in the English ballad unless Motherwell's copy (10 G 12) gives a hint of it in the "thorn" beneath which the drowned maiden lay "until Monday morn." The Jamieson-Brown version, among other texts, has the "hair" incident:

> An by there came a harper fine,
> That harped to the king at dine.
>
> When he did look that lady upon,
> He sighd and made a heavy moan.
>
> He's taen three locks o her yellow hair,
> An wi them strung his harp sae fair [B].

"Three tets" of her hair furnish the strings in D, E, I, V, and W; in F, "three links of her yellow hair" for a string; in H, "he buskit his bow in her bonnie yellow hair." The hair is also used for strings in C, L, P, and O.

In a broadside copy of 1656 the "violl" is made from the maiden's "brest-bone":

> What did he doe with her brest-bone?
> He made him a violl to play thereupon [A].

The use in this text of the fingers for "peggs," the "nose-ridge" for a "bridge," the "veynes" for "strings," and so

---

[1] See motives for the return of the dead, *infra*, p. 261.
[2] *Op. cit.*, I, 121.　　　　[3] *Op. cit.*, I, 194.

on, carries one into something of buffoonery, but in these matters the separation of chaff from wheat is not difficult.[1] Child gives in detail the parts of the body used in English and Norse versions.[2] In texts C, G, H, as well as in A and J, of the English piece, the instrument is fashioned from the breastbone. According to a Swedish text, the fiddle-frame is made from the maiden's skull; according to English Lb, from her "back-bone." The former may be taken as an example of the magic skull, the latter as a curious instance, perhaps, of the belief that the spine is the seat of life. Several tales analyzed by Child in connection with *The Twa Sisters* bear out the idea of the bone-soul: a herdsman finds a white bone and makes a pipe or horn of it; a bagpipe is made of the bones and skin of a murdered youth. A Chinese drama also illustrates the fundamental conception; a dish made of the ashes and bones of a murdered man speaks and denounces the murderers.[3] In an Esthonian ballad with some resemblance to our song a maiden comes up as a birch. In a Slovak song a maiden is turned into a maple, and in a Lithuanian poem a dead girl speaks through a linden tree.[4] These incidents illustrate the tree-soul idea and bear out Hartland's interpretation of our ballad story.

It is significant that in certain texts of *The Twa Sisters* the harp is said to speak.

The viol in A and the harp in H are expressly said to speak. The harp is laid upon a stone in C, J, and plays "its lone"; the fiddle plays of itself in Lb. B makes the harper play, and D F K O [likewise V], which say the fiddle played, probably mean that there was a fiddler, and so perhaps with all the Norse versions; but this is not very material, since in either case the instrument speaks "with most miraculous organ."[5]

[1] Cf. L.
[2] *Op. cit.*, I, 121.
[3] *Ibid.*, pp. 125 f.
[4] See Child's analyses, *ibid.*, p. 124.
[5] *Ibid.*, p. 122.

A text of our ballad in the *Journal of the Folk-Song Society* has "the harp began to play alone."[1]

In one Swedish version and in nearly all the Norwegian texts of the foregoing song the maiden is restored to life. The harp is dashed against a stone or upon the floor and the maiden stands forth disenchanted. "However this may be," observes Child, "the restoration of the younger sister, like all good endings foisted on tragedies, emasculates the story."[2] This good ending may have been, however, as Hartland remarks, "of the very essence and primitive matter of the plot." Hartland goes on to say that it does not occur once "in England and Scotland, where the influence of culture has been most decisive."[3] And yet this disenchantment may be suggested by the incident in certain of our English texts of laying the harp upon a "stone" where it plays "its lone" (C, J), when one recalls that the harp in the Norse ballads is dashed against a stone in order to break the spell. Moreover, the witch character of the elder sister which Lanstad sees in Scandinavian parallels[4] may well be borne out in an English text (I 8) by the "silver wand" with which the elder sister pushes the younger in. In G 8 she drives the younger from the land with a switch.

Considered in all its variants, foreign as well as British, *The Twa Sisters* is a striking embodiment of ancient beliefs concerning the soul. Whether the idea in the song was originally, as Hartland says, that of the tree-soul; whether it is the kindred notion of the soul in the bone; or whether, as Child thinks, the original idea was that the maiden's spirit manifested itself through the hair, the important fact remains that our little song carries us into the presence of primitive thought. With respect to Child's construction that the soul is to be thought of as residing in the hair, we should point out that hair plays a part in magic practices

[1] II, 285 f. Here we have the harp of the "breastbone," "harp-pins" of the fingers, strings of "golden hair." Cf. an American text, Campbell and Sharp, p. 16: "fingers so small" for "harp screws," "hair so long" for "harp strings."

[2] *Op. cit.*, I, 123.   [3] *Op. cit.*, I, 194.

[4] *Norske Folkviser*, p. 484; see Child, I, 123.

the world over. In Sarawak, for instance, we find a clear example of the hair-soul. When the soul is thought to have forsaken the body it may be restored in the shape of a bundle of hair.[1] The hair plays an interesting part in a number of ballads, some of them supernatural: In *Willie's Lady* (6) witch-knots in a woman's hair arrest childbirth. The elf-lover in *Hind Etin* (41 B) ties a captured maiden to a tree by her yellow locks. The hair of a maiden enchanted in monstrous form (34 A) is "twisted thrice about the tree."[2] A maiden dreams (69 D) of cutting her "yellow hair and dipping it in the wells o blood." Combing the hair is a ballad commonplace. Ghosts, as well as transformed mortals, have their hair combed.[3] In ballads and *Märchen* wonderful things are done with hair.[4] In *The Braes o Yarrow* (214) and *The Water o Gamrie* (215) a maiden ties her hair about her dead lover and drags him home.

THE BLOOD-SOUL

The blood is among the chief corporeal vehicles of the soul. The connection of the soul and the blood is a belief common to the Karens, the Papuans, the Jews, and the Arabs,[5] and is present in both Teutonic and Celtic traditions.[6] Nor is it absent from British lore as reflected in the ballads; that is, we may infer its presence from certain instances of blood magic found in our folksong.[7] Among such examples of blood magic are those of blood-drinking; catching the blood of the slain, especially that of a person of high rank, to keep it from being spilled upon the ground; the belief that the corpse of a murdered man will bleed

[1] A. Bastian, *Allerlei aus Volks- und Menschenkunde*, I, 401.

[2] See *infra*, pp. 124 f., 336, 366 f.   [3] See *infra*, pp. 195 ff.

[4] See Child, *op. cit.*, IV, 162 n.; I, 40, 486; III, 516; "Hair," *ibid.*, V, 482.

[5] Tylor, *Primitive Culture*, I, 431.

[6] See Gummere, *Germanic Origins*, pp. 175, 456; G. Henderson, *op. cit.*, pp. 29 ff.

[7] That many beliefs must be so inferred when dealing with folksong is simply to say that the ballad is purely narrative and seldom if ever enters into explanations.

upon the approach of, or upon contact with, the murderer; and indelible bloodstains. All these practices and superstitions, among others, are employed by folklorists to show that the blood is regarded as the body essence. And they are all found in the ballads. In the matter of the blood-soul the balladist agrees with those who, as Lactantius says, hold the soul to be the blood, for with the blood it passes away: "Alii animam ignem esse dixerunt, alii spiritum, alii sanguinem. Ignem dicunt, quia vivificat corpus, spiritum quia spirat per membra, sanguinem, quia cum sanguine migrat."[1]

The custom of drinking the blood of the slain is found in several copies of *The Braes o Yarrow* (214). A wife drinks her slain one's blood. This is "disagreeable, assuredly, and unnatural too," says Child. But one can press the unnaturalness of ballad custom too far:

> *She kissd his cheek, she kaimd his hair,*
> *As oft she did before, O;*
> *She drank the red blood frae him ran,*
> *On the dowy houms o Yarrow* [E 12].

This blood-drinking is found also in texts F, G, and M. The reading in A is "wiped." But, as Child observes, "It is 'drank,' probably, that is softened to 'wiped' in A 14. Scott, to avoid unpleasantness, reads 'She kissd them [his wounds] till her lips grew red'; which would not take long."[2] The fallow doe—a maiden transformed—in *The Three Ravens* (26) "lift" up the "bloudy hed" of her slain lover "and kist his wounds that were so red." This, too, is probably a case of euphemism.

In the practice of blood-drinking, as reflected in *The Braes o Yarrow*, there is undoubtedly in evidence some form of the blood covenant.[3] It is a means, perhaps, of effecting

[1] Wasserschleben, *Die irische Canonensammlung* (2d ed., 1885), p. 233.

[2] *Op. cit.*, IV, 162 n.

[3] See H. C. Trumbull, *The Blood Covenant*; Hartland, *Legend of Perseus*, II, 238 ff.; Frazer, *The Golden Bough*, III, 130; VIII, 69, 154 ff.

communion with the dead,[1] and is in accord, of course, with the widespread primitive belief that one may acquire another's qualities by, for instance, drinking his blood or eating his heart. In Saxo we are more obviously at home in savage custom. The traditions of Saxo tell how strength may be gained by drinking the blood of a lion that eats men and how like bodily vigor may come from drinking the blood of a bear.[2] A Gaelic song, *I'd Follow Thee, Follow Thee*, offers a much closer parallel to the incident in our ballad. A maiden would drink the blood of her drowned lover: "I could drink—though displeasing to my kindred— not of [fresh] water nor of brine, but of thy body's blood after having been drowned."[3] The displeasure of the kindred would arise, of course, not from the maiden's act of drinking the blood but from its being the blood of a lover unacceptable to them. Again, as illustrative of the blood-soul, we may give the following stanza from a poem on Gregor MacGregor, of Glenstrae, who was executed in 1570. The words are sung by Gregor's wife:

> On a block of oak they set his head,
>   They shed his blood with a will;
> On the ground they spilt it, and had I a cup
>   I would of it have quaffed my fill.[4]

Johny Cock and his hounds (114 A 8) take out "the liver bot and the tongue" of the deer they have slain, and "they eat of the flesh, and they drank of the blood." But apparently there is nothing here of the supernatural.

Blood-drinking in Norse balladry effects restoration of enchanted mortals to human form. A hint of this is given in *Leesone Brand*, but hagiolatry has probably obscured an originally pagan incident. A woman and her child are resuscitated by means of three drops of St. Paul's blood:

---

[1] Cf. swallowing the ashes of the dead (Frazer, *op. cit.*, VIII, 156 ff.) and drinking the blood of men to acquire their qualities (*ibid.*, pp. 148, 150 ff.).

[2] Elton-Powell, *Saxo*, pp. 29, 69.

[3] *Journal Folk-Song Society*, IV, 224 f.

[4] Translated from the Gaelic by G. Henderson (*op. cit.*, p. 31.).

He put his hand at her bed head,
And there he found a gude grey horn,
Wi three draps o' Saint Paul's ain blude,
That had been there sin he was born.

Then he drappd twa on his ladye,
And ane o them on his young son,
And now they do as lively be,
As the first day he brought them hame [15 A].

As we have already noted in connection with the deer-soul, Grundtvig suggests that the hind and the blood in *Leesome Brand* come from a lost Scottish ballad on the order of the Norse song *The Maid Transformed into a Hind*.[1] As portrayed in Norse balladry, unspelling by drinking the blood of human beings will be considered in detail under the Otherworld spell.[2] A single example from the Danish *Nattergalen* may be given here. A youth is changed to a wolf by his stepdame, but he regains his original shape when he tears out the heart and drinks the blood of the stepmother:

"*He griped her fast with wolfish claw,*
And then with deadly bite
Tore out her heart and drank her blood,
And so stood up a knight."[3]

It is probable that the marriage or betrothal ring is a survival of some ancient practice of binding the blood covenant upon the hand.[4] A custom preserved in *The Lass of Roch Royal* (76 A, D, G, H) goes as far as, or perhaps farther than, the ring in the direction of the original blood

---

[1] See *supra*, pp. 52 ff. It should be observed, however, that the three drops of blood with their restorative virtue are found in a text of our ballad recorded by Greig, *Traditional Ballads*, pp. 16 f. But here there is no mention of St. Paul. It is significant that the blood is found in both the Child and Greig versions at the "bed head" where it has been since the hero was born. It is probably the blood of childbirth; hence its "life-livin" power.

[2] *Infra*, pp. 341 f.

[3] Grundtvig, II, 171; trans. Prior, *op. cit.*, III, 121.

[4] Cf. George Henderson, *op. cit.*, p. 37.

covenant between lovers. Gregory has asked the heroine
for some token that she is his former sweetheart:

> "*Have you not mind, Love Gregory,*
> *Since we sat at the wine,*
> *We changed the smocks off our two backs,*
> *And ay the worst fell mine*" [A 15].

A ring is the token in versions B, C, E, and I.

The ceremony of swearing brotherhood implies the belief that the life or soul resides in the blood. The ballad of
Bewick and Graham (211) "is remarkable," says Scott, "as
containing probably the very latest allusion to the institu-
tion of brotherhood in arms, which was held so sacred in the
days of chivalry, and whose origin may be traced up to the
Scythian ancestors of Odin."[1] For Teutonic tradition the
Short Brunhild's Lay gives record of this bond of sworn
brotherhood and tells how it was entered into: "Ye twain
did let your blood run together in the footprint, ..."[2]
Saxo likewise alludes to the ancient ceremony: "Now the
ancients, when about to make a league, were wont to be-
sprinkle their footsteps with the blood of one another, so
to ratify their pledge of friendship by reciprocal barter of
blood."[3] Sworn brotherhood is found not only in *Bewick
and Graham* but also in *Adam Bell, Clim of the Clough, and
William of Cloudesly* (116, stanza 4):

> *They were outlawed for venyson,*
> *These thre yemen euerechone;*
> *They swore them brethen vpon a day,*
> *To Englysshe-wood for to gone.*

The foregoing blood-drinking incidents of balladry bring
to mind certain vestiges of cannibalism and human sacrifice that are found in British folksong.[4]

The practice of catching the blood to avoid spilling it

[1] *Op. cit.*, III, 75.

[2] Vigfusson-Powell, *Corpus poeticum boreale*, I, 308.

[3] Elton-Powell, *op. cit.*, pp. 28 f.   [4] See *infra*, pp. 323 ff., 392 ff.

upon the ground, a practice that implies the idea that the blood is the vehicle of the soul,[1] occurs in the songs *Lamkin*, *Little Musgrave*, *Sir Hugh*, and apparently in *Bonny Barbara Allan*, according to texts recovered since Child. Lady Wearie's murderer, in *Lamkin* (93 A), would draw but not defile his victim's blood:

> "*O scour the bason, nourice,*
> *and mak it fair and clean,*
> *For to keep this lady's heart's blood,*
> *for she's come o noble kin.*"

"That your lady's noble blood may be kepped clean"[2] is the reading in C 21; "For our lady's heart's blude is gentle to tine," in O 8. The words "kepped" and "tine" mean "caught" and "lose," respectively. Catching the blood is found in the following texts of *Lamkin*: A, C, D, G, I, N, O, R, T, V, and X. This incident occurs in only three of the Child versions of *Sir Hugh* (155 F, H, J), a poem based on the account of the alleged murder of Hugh of Lincoln in 1255. Our song tells a story similar to that of Chaucer's *Prioresses Tale*, and reflects in all likelihood the popular opinion that Jews were wont to kill children in order to get their blood for use in the Paschal rites.[3] The Jew's daughter has enticed little Sir Hugh into a "stone chamber" of her house:

> *She set him in a goolden chair,*
> *And jaggd him with a pin,*
> *And called for a goolden cup*
> *To houl his heart's blood in* [F].

According to H, she "called for a wash-basin, to spill his life blood in"; according to J, "I will scour a basin as bright

---

[1] Cf. Frazer, *The Golden Bough*, III, 247, 239 ff.

[2] Distinctions in ballad burials give the upper side of the grave to those who come of the "better kin." See No. 81 A 29, C 32, F 24, H 20, I 22, J 25, L 45. See also my study, *Death and Burial Lore in the English and Scottish Popular Ballads*, pp. 130 ff.

[3] See Child, III, 240.

as silver to let your heart-blood run in." In American variants the golden vessel becomes "tin."[1] In texts G, T, and Fb of *Lamkin* (93) the vessel is gold; in F and O it is silver. Variants, both British and American, later than Child have a "bason" or "silver basin."[2] The incident of catching the lady's blood, as related in *Little Musgrave* (81 G 28, 30), is probably borrowed from *Lamkin*. The vessel in the former piece is a "basin of pure silver." It is noteworthy that in all instances the vessel is of precious metal or is scoured clean. In texts B, D, and E of *Sir Hugh* (155) the murderess is said to dress her victim "like a swine." Is this a reminiscence of the disemboweling in the legend of Hugh of Lincoln as given by Matthew Paris?[3] The lady's blood in *Lamkin* (93 A 24) is "as clear as the lamer," that is, amber; the young son's is "the clearest ava." According to *Sir Hugh* (version A), as well as other texts,

> *And first came out the thick, thick blood,*
> *And syne came out the thin,*
> *And syne came out the bonny heart's blood;*
> *There was nae mair within.*

May one recognize in C 9 a hint of the belief implied in *Deuteronomy* (12: 23) that "the blood is the life"? The ballad reads: "Then out and cam the bonny heart's blude, where a' the life lay in." J 6 has a similar reading. The phrase "heart's blood" is of very frequent occurrence in balladry. "Where the innocent blood lies slain, the candles will burn fou bricht," says the bird in *Young Hunting* (68 H 8).

In certain texts of *Barbara Allan* (84) not included by, or recovered later than, Child, there is a passage which bears some resemblance to those in the foregoing ballads. The dying lover thus reproaches his false sweetheart:

---

[1] *JAFL*, XIX, 293 ff., texts a and b.

[2] *Rymour miscellanea*, II, 136 ff.; *Journal of the Folk-Song Society*, V, 82; Leather, *Folk-Lore of Herefordshire*, pp. 199 f.; *JAFL*, XIII, 117; *ibid.*, XXIX, 162.

[3] See Child, III, 235.

"Look down, look down, at my bed-side,
You'll see a bowl o'er flowing;
And in that bowl there's my heart's blood,
That's shed for Barbara Ellen."[1]

A text given in the *Journal of the Folk-Song Society* has "You'll see a basin standing; there's all the blood I shed for love."[2] Gavin Greig's variants read respectively: ". . . . Ye'll find my bloody shirt, that was bled for Bawbie Allan"; "A china basin full of tears." Miss Burne's text[3] has a "basin" filled with the lover's "heart's blood and tears."[4]

The idea that the soul is in, or identical with, the blood, lies back, unquestionably, of the superstition of the bleeding corpse. The motif of the bleeding corpse occurs in the *Nibelungenlied* and in the *Ivain* of Chretien de Troies and, for our balladry, in the song of *Young Hunting*. Upon this superstition rested the law of the bier—that the body of a murdered person will bleed upon the approach, or at the touch, of the slayer. The mere approach of the murderer suffices in the Harris and the Kinloch texts of our traditional poem (68):

> *O white, white war his wounds washen,*
> *As white as a linen clout;*
> *But as the traitor she cam near,*
> *His wounds they gushit out* [B 21].

"But sune's the traitor stude afore," reads the Harris text (C 23), "then oot the red blude sprang." Gloucester's presence has a like effect upon his victim in *King Richard III*, I, 2: ". . . . Dead Henry's wounds open their congeal'd mouths and bleed afresh." The bleeding corpse in *Young Hunting*, it should be noted, is in the nature of an

[1] *JAFL*, XXIX, 161.

[2] I, 111.

[3] *Op. cit.*, p. 544.

[4] This variant Child excluded from his collection because he supposed that it was derived from print (*op. cit.*, III, 514).

ordeal, the outcome of which is confirmed by the subsequent ordeal of fire.[1]

Blood magic in its various manifestations prevails at all cultural levels and has its source in the idea that the blood is a form or vehicle of the soul.[2] To obtain blood for magical purposes furnishes a motive for the murders in one of the three classes of ballads into which fall the German analogues of *Lady Isabel and the Elf-Knight* (4). In our ballad the murderous propensity of the elf knight seems virtually unmotivated. This lack of motive is characteristic, too, of certain Norse variants, as well as some of the German variants.[3] According to German P, however— this in keeping with a traditional story in the Swabian Oberland—the devil puts it into the head of a leper that he can be cured by "bathing in the blood of twelve [seven] pure maidens."[4] A "lazar" or leper in *Sir Aldingar* (59 A 53) is made whole by standing under "the gallow tree." Child does not show any disposition to restore to our ballad *Lady Isabel and the Elf-Knight* the curative-blood motive found in certain German texts. Nevertheless, he notes as "something horribly uncanny" the "bloody streams" in Danish variants: "The scenery of the halting-place in the wood—the bloody streams in Danish A, B, D, H, L, K, the blood-girt spring in German H, J, K, L, O, P, Q—is also, to say the least, suggestive of something horribly uncanny. These are undoubtedly ancient features, ..."[5] In connection with blood magic we must refer again to the "three draps o' Saint Paul's ain blude" (*Leesome Brand*, 15 A 47), with its life-restoring virtue. But as outside the present philosophy, perhaps, we must pass over blood omens and dreams.[6]

Two superstitions, other than the foregoing, are illus-

---

[1] The ordeal by battle is found in *Sir Aldingar* (59).

[2] See Frazer, *The Golden Bough*, III, 239 ff., 247, and *passim*.

[3] See Child, I, 49 f.

[4] *Ibid.*, p. 47; see also Kittredge's notes in *ibid.*, IV, 441; V, 285.

[5] *Ibid.*, I, 50 n.

[6] On omens and dreams see my study, *op. cit.*, chap. iii.

trative of the general view that the soul is bound up with the blood. The idea that bloodstains, when associated with crime, are indelible—one thinks of that "damned spot" in *Macbeth*—and the kindred notion of the "guilt of blood," as Scott describes it, are both present in British folksong. Indelible bloodstains are found in *Babylon* and *The Cruel Mother*. In the first of these, versions of which are common in Scandinavian tradition, "an outlyer bold" has slain, unwittingly, two of his sisters, but he cannot wipe their blood from his knife:

> *He wiped his knife along the dew;*
> *But the more he wiped, the redder it grew* [14 D].

The Cruel Mother (20 Q) reads:

> *She wiped the penknife in the sludge;*
> *The more she wiped it, the more the blood showed.*

An American variant of the foregoing piece retains this incident: "You wiped your penknife on your shoe, and the more you wiped it the bloodier it grew."[1]

"Popular superstition in Scotland," says Scott, "still retains so formidable an idea of the *guilt of blood*, that those ancient edifices, or castles, where enormous crimes have been committed, are supposed to sink gradually into the ground."[2] This belief that a blight or curse falls upon that spot where innocent blood has been shed occurs in *Jellon Grame* (90). A boy inquires of his mother's murderer why no grass grows "on that small spot":

> *"O how is this," the youth cried out,*
> *"If it to you is known,*
> *How all this wood is growing grass,*
> *And on that small spot grows none?"*

> *"Since you do wonder, bonnie boy,*
> *I shall tell you anon;*
> *That is indeed the very spot*
> *I killed your mother in"* [B].

[1] Campbell and Sharp, p. 30.   [2] *Op. cit.*, III, 419.

According to the story of Kullervo in the *Kalevala*, a story which has "striking resemblances with the ballads of the Bonny Hind class,"[1] grass or flowers will not grow on the spot where incest has taken place.

THE LIGHT-SOUL

In connection with blood superstitions we may illustrate here the peculiar notion that the blood of the slain may be transformed into a light or that a miraculous light may burn over buried bodies—phases, possibly, of the corpse-light superstition. The appearance of the soul as a light, or rather of the blood as a light, does not find very convincing exemplification in English balladry proper, but it occurs no farther away than in Faroese and Icelandic variants of *Babylon* (14). Katrine of the Faroese song, like the heroine of the British ballad, is beheaded by her murderer, and "wherever her blood ran a light kindled; where her head fell a spring welled forth; where her body lay a church was [afterwards] built."[2] According to the Icelandic versions, "a miraculous light burned over the place where the maids had been buried."[3] In the story of Oliva, or Sibilla, in the Charlemagne cycle of fictions, a story which has connections seemingly with *Sir Aldingar* (59), when Hugo cuts off the black man's head "every drop of his blood turns to a burning candle."[4] As a possible parallel to these instances of the soul as a light we may cite an incident in *Lamkin* (93), according to which a severed head, like other objects in balladry, gives off a supernatural light:

> *Then he cut aff her head*
> *fram her lily breast-bane*
> *And he hung't up in the kitchen,*
> *it made a' the ha shine* [B].

[1] Child, I, 445.   [2] *Ibid.*, 172.

[3] *Ibid.*, 173. The light is found also in a Norwegian version (see *ibid.*, V, 287).

[4] *Ibid.*, II, 39.

Other examples of this miraculous illumination will be considered presently in connection with the weapon-soul. Magic and talking heads are found in foreign ballads. The head of the false knight in foreign variants of *Lady Isabel and the Elf-Knight* (4) is struck off by the clever lass. That the tongue "talks after the head is off, ... is," says Child, "another mark of an unearthly being."[1] In the Danish ballad *Svend Ranild* the head of Thrude, severed by Ranild, rejoins its body on the sea floor.[2]

The identification of the spirit of the dead with a bluish light seems to be present in one of Miss Broadwood's texts of *The Unquiet Grave* (78):

> *"Oh! don't you see the fire, sweetheart,*
> *The fire that burns so blue?*
> *Whilst my poor soul's tormented here?*
> *Whilst I remain with you?"*[3]

A broadside variant of *The Braes o Yarrow* (214) likens the "sprite" of the slain lover to a "gleam."[4] One of the shapes through which Tam Lin (39) passes during his disenchantment is, according to different texts of the ballad, a "flash of fire," "a fire burning bold" or "wild," or a "burning gleed." Tam Lin's metamorphoses are considered in detail later in this study.[5]

Scott's ready assumption that the candles in *Young Hunting* (68) are those corpse-lights "which are sometimes seen to illumine the spot where a dead body is concealed"[6] is questioned by Child. "Sir Walter Scott supposed these candles to mean 'the corpse-lights . . . .' . . . . the meaning is as likely to be that a candle, floated on the water,

---

[1] *Ibid.*, I, 49; see also pp. 25, 26, 30, 485 f.

[2] Grundtvig, I, 372; see translation by Prior, *op. cit.*, I, 286. After the ax has fallen, Lord Derwentwater's head talks, according to a text (208) in C. J. Sharp, *Folk-Songs of England*, III, 5: "Now there lies the head of a traitor," he said, and it answered and said "No."

[3] *English Traditional Songs and Carols*, p. 120.

[4] *Rymour miscellanea*, I, 44.   [5] *Infra*, pp. 381 ff.

[6] See Scott, *op. cit.*, III, 240. On ghost lights see R. C. Maclagan, "Ghost Lights of the West Highlands," *Folk-Lore*, VIII, 203–56.

would burn brighter when it came to the spot where the body lay."[1]

THE NAME-SOUL

English balladry preserves something of the early and primitive belief that a man's personality or spirit is bound up with his name. Savage and semi-civilized people the world over believe that a strange power—"mana," it may be called—is present in the name, and evidences of this belief have been taken as lending weight to the "pre-animistic" theory.[2] We would not, from the ballad evidence, attempt to make out a case for this theory, but nevertheless the ballad hero may on occasion show himself just as mindful of his name as did the ancient Egyptian or as does the Kaffir or the Amerindian.[3] A number of ballads, *Riddles Wisely Expounded*, for instance, or *Earl Brand* and *Tam Lin*, make a point of this name philosophy in the story.

Our best example in balladry of magic in the name is the incident related in *Earl Brand* (7); that is, if one is permitted to restore to our British song the incident in full as it occurs in Norse analogues to this piece. Earl Brand, a representative, doubtless, of the primitive bride-stealer, is overtaken by the lady's father and brothers, her ever watchful guardians. The hero leaps from his steed, gives it in charge to his sweetheart, and, according to the Scottish ballad, enjoins her thus:

> *An bad her never change her cheer*
> *Untill she saw his body bleed.*[4]

The significance of the command is brought out more clearly in the Danish *Ribold og Guldborg*, a song with which the Scottish piece must have once agreed in all important par-

---

[1] *Op. cit.*, II, 143; see also *ibid.*, II, 512; III, 509; IV, 468.

[2] See Marett, *Threshold of Religion*, pp. 62, 66, 67; Clodd, *Magic in Names*, *passim*; "The Philosophy of Rumpelstiltskin," *Folk-Lore Journal*, VII, 135-61.

[3] On name taboos see Frazer, *The Golden Bough*, III, 349 ff.; on the name-soul in Celtic tradition see G. Henderson, *op. cit.*, pp. 19 f.

[4] Child, IV, 444, stanza 27; cf. texts A 22 f.; B 5; C 3 f.; D 3; E 4; A b, c.

ticulars. If she would save her lover from death the maiden must keep his name secret from her relatives:

> *"Now if in fight you see me fall,*
> *My name I pray you not to call.*

> *"And if you see the blood run red,*
> *Be silent, lest you name me dead."*[1]

Ribold lays low his sweetheart's father, likewise her betrothed. This the lady endures, but when the champion falls upon her "brothers with the golden hair," she cries out against any further blood-letting. Forgetful of the injunction not to speak, she unwittingly does her lover to death:

> *The moment Guldborg named his name,*
> *A fatal blow, the deathblow came.*

Like *Earl Brand*, to which it is closely related, the song of *Erlinton* (8 A, B, C) preserves the incident of dead-naming. It is interesting to find that an American text, in the matter, at least, of this dead-naming, is somewhat nearer the original telling than are the Child versions of *Earl Brand:*

> *She got down and never spoke,*
> *Nor never cheaped*
> *Till she saw her own father's head*
> *Come trinkling by her feet.*[2]

Or, according to another American text: "And never changed a word."[3] Dr. Cox's American variant has "And never shed a tear."[4] This is also the reading in a copy from Gavin Greig.[5]

Other ballad heroes, no less than Earl Brand and Ribold, are aware of the advantage of keeping one's name secret. In *The Hunting of the Cheviot* (162 A 16) Percy, it

---

[1] Grundtvig, II, 361; trans. Prior, II, 403.

[2] Campbell and Sharp, p. 11.

[3] *Ibid.*, p. 13; cf. text, *ibid.*, p. 15.   [4] *Folk-Songs of the South*, p. 18.

[5] *Folk-Song of the North-East*, Vol. I, art. lvii.

seems, proves himself to be well versed in the wizardry of the name. "Tell me whos men ye ar," demands Douglas. But Percy is not to be trapped in this fashion:

> *"We wyll not tell the whoys men we ar," he says,*
> *"nor whos men that we be."*

"The refusal to reply . . . . is characteristic of popular tradition," comments Walter Morris Hart, "and is doubtless based on the ancient notion that the knowledge of a name gave one power over the person of the bearer. Of course the men knew each other well enough,—see stanza 19."[1]

If we are to regard Percy and Earl Brand as "culture brothers" to the Fijian or the Omaha Indian, possibly we should include Child Waters of another ballad in the same fraternity. A prime qualification for a footpage—if we are to believe the hero of this piece—is the good sense not to divulge his master's name:

> *"You must tell noe man what is my name;*
> *My ffootpage then you shall bee"* [63 A].

In our sacred writings there is record of such name avoidance. "What is thy name," inquires Manoah of the angel of the Lord, "that when thy sayings come to pass we may do thee honour?" But the angel of the Lord, with abundant precedent for his answer, replies: "Why askest thou after my name, seeing it is secret?"[2] This is matched in Northern mythology. Woden, it may be remembered, keeps his real name under cover.

In his great collection of ballads Child notes the occurrence throughout various traditions of the belief that naming has an enfeebling or destructive effect on men engaged in fight, on the devil, on trolls, and nixies.[3] Ballads of the

---

[1] *English Popular Ballads*, p. 328. It has been pointed out to me, however, that this incident may have nothing to do with name magic; that, indeed, it is a commonplace in the romances, where knights encountered in armor without knowing the names of their antagonists, and often refusing to disclose their own.

[2] Judges 13: 17 f.

[3] *Op. cit.*, V, 489, under "Naming."

supernatural, such as *Riddles Wisely Expounded* and *Tam Lin* or, to turn to Norse song, the Danish *Rosmer* and *The Sword of Vengeance*, give striking examples of the magic properties of the name, examples which reflect the belief that the name is one form of the soul.

"Talk of the devil and you'll see his horns." But the devil may also be exorcised by the trick of piercing his disguise and saying his name. So it happens in our ancient ballad *Riddles Wisely Expounded*, a story of a clever lass who outwits a riddle-mongering fiend. The maiden is the youngest of three sisters. The devil has come a-wooing in knightly guise. The girl answers all his questions successfully and in her last reply calls him by his right name, Clootie. Like other goblins in similar circumstances, the demon vanishes, thoroughly mastered:

> *"The pies are greener nor the grass,*
> *And Clootie's waur nor a woman was."*
>
> *As sune as she the fiend did name,*
> *He flew awa in a blazing flame* [1 C].

This matter of sending a demon, gnome, or imp on his way by discovering his name is found in folktales of the Rumpelstiltskin type.

The Danish *Rosmer* tells a story similar to Jamieson's tale of Child Rowland. An undersea king or giant has carried to his realm of gold the lady Swanelille. The maiden's youngest brother seeks her out, but Rosmer, stalking in from the sea, swears that he smells the breath of a Christian man.[1] The hero remains a prisoner for fifteen years in the merman's sea cavern. But at the end of that time Rosmer gives him a chest of gold and agrees to carry him back home. Swanelille empties out the treasure, creeps into the chest, and goes along too. For his services the merman asks only a single boon, that the brother name not his sister, Swanelille:

---

[1] See Child, V, 201, on the *King Lear* fragment of what appears to be a Child Rowland ballad.

"And now I've borne thee to thy home,
The land of sun and moon;
I beg thee name not Swanelille,
And ask no other boon."[1]

By ignoring this name taboo the brother could, as Rosmer knows, recall the maiden to earth. During her sojourn in the subaqueous realm Swanelille was to all intents and purposes dead and, as the primitive man believes regarding his dead,[2] to name her would be to summon her.

Name magic not improbably enters into the shape-shifting process of the hero's recovery from fairyland in the ballad of *Tam Lin*, an important matter which seems to have escaped the notice of ballad scholars. According to a Motherwell text of this song, the lover says expressly that in fairyland he is known by the name of Tomlin:

"First they did call me Jack," he said,
"And then they called me John,
But since I lived in the fairy court
Tomlin has always been my name" [39 D 9].

The foregoing passage is, it is true, a ballad commonplace[3] and occurs in foreign as well as in British songs, but its possible significance in the present connection must not be overlooked. By giving him an "unearthly" name the elves have cut *Tam Lin* off from his earthly home. Moreover, Tam Lin is a naturalized member of the fairy community, and his elfin name suggests the initiation names adopted in savage ceremonies, in the manhood-initiation rites, for example, of native Australians.[4] As further proof that the above-quoted passage reflects the practice of concealing one's real name for this or that reason we may bring to bear an incident found in another Motherwell version of our ballad. It is noteworthy that in this text the hero's sweetheart, while rescuing her lover from the fairies, must hold him fast and cry "aye 'Young Tamlin,'" In thus

[1] Grundtvig, II, 82; trans. Prior, III, 56. [3] See Child, V, 474.
[2] See Frazer, *The Golden Bough*, III, 349 ff. [4] Clodd, *op. cit.*, p. 84.

calling his name she is carrying out the enchanted knight's previously given instructions (E 20):

> *They next shaped him into her arms*
> *Like the laidliest worm of Ind;*
> *But she held him fast, let him not go,*
> *And cried aye "Young Tamlin."*

To embrace a fairy or kiss a ghost is, in ballad story, as in popular traditions generally, to subject one's self to the Otherworld powers.[1] Magic works in contrary directions, however, and it is partly by holding him fast in her earthly embrace and showing herself possessed of his fairy name that Janet succeeds in saving her lover.

To be mentioned shortly as bearing out the idea of the soul in objects—in a sword, for instance—we may give here that excellent example of name magic found in the Danish song *The Sword of Vengeance*. Sir Buris of this ballad is blessed with one of those magic swords so common in popular fictions.[2] The supernatural power of such weapons, it has been suggested, may have been ascribed to them at the time when weapons of metal first proved their superiority over those fashioned of wood or bone—an interesting example of a myth in the making. But to return to the story. Sir Buris takes counsel with his faithful sword, than "whom" he has no other friend on earth. The sword promises vengeance on their common foes. Eight champions Sir Buris slays, and spares neither maid nor mother, prince nor king. A child in the cradle, like certain other precocious children in balladry, says that when he grows up he will take vengeance. The butchery reaches its climax when the hero, or rather his sword, cuts this child in twain. This is too much even for Sir Buris. He beseeches the sword to keep its "choler down." Bloodthirsty though it is, the weapon must yield to a master who can call it by name:

[1] See *infra*, pp. 282 ff.
[2] See Child, "Swords," *op. cit.*, V, 498.

Then spake the sword in sullen mood,
"Thee would I slay and taste thy blood.

"Hadst thou by name not call'd on me,
I would at once have slaughter'd thee."[1]

Further examples of magic in the name are found in ballad euphemisms for death and dying, for the devil and God, and for fairies. Death euphemisms occur in a number of songs.[2] The name of Christ as a charm against evil spirits is discussed under the Otherworld spell.[3] Belief in the power of the name extends in all parts of the world and throughout many traditions to the names of supernatural beings. The unwillingness of the Jews to pronounce the name of Jehovah and the reserve of Herodotus with respect to the name of Osiris are but two of countless instances.[4] The Irish and the Scotch speak of the fairies as "the good damsels" or "the good ladies," and modern Greek peasants, holding the Nereids in awe, call them "our Good Ladies" or the "Kind-Hearted Ones."[5]

Lady Isabel and the Elf-Knight (4 B) recounts a tale of a preternatural being who attempts to drown a clever lass in the "waters o Wearie's Well." Wearie is the devil himself, and his well an appropriate place for his evil designs. The devil is called an "auld, auld man" in *The Elfin Knight* (2 I 2) and replaces the Otherworld wooer of the somewhat better texts. The word "shame" is also used as an appellative of the devil. *Fair Annie* gives this euphemism in one of those ill wishes or curses so common in balladry:

"The shame scoup in his company,
And land whereer he gae" [62 A 15]!

---

[1] Grundtvig, I, 350; trans. Prior, I, 273.

[2] See Hart, *Ballad and Epic*, p. 22 n., and my study, *op. cit.*, pp. 81 f.

[3] *Infra*, p. 377.

[4] See Cox, *Introduction to Folk Lore*, pp. 204 ff.; Clodd, *op. cit.*, pp. 109 ff.; Frazer, *The Golden Bough*, Vol. III, chap. vi.

[5] See Lawson, *Modern Greek Folk-Lore and Ancient Greek Religion*, p. 131.

"Shame speed a your jesting, my lord," cries Dickie in *Dick o the Cow* (185, stanza 11).

A euphemism for God is found in the familiar salutation or wish "Weel met thee save." True Thomas thus addresses the fairy:

> *"Weel met thee save, my lady fair,*
> *For thou'rt the flower o this countrie"* [37 B 3].

With the same meaning, "weel" occurs also in *The Outlaw Murray* (305 B 9). For fairies *Tam Lin* gives "gude neighbours," a familiar euphemism for the "little folk":

> *"The night is Halloween, Janet,*
> *When our gude neighbours will ride"* [39 H 8].

The mermaid in *Sir Patrick Spens* (58 Q 2) is called a "wild woman."

In a study of early beliefs as depicted in balladry one has ever in mind, of course, Tylor's minimum definition of religion, a definition covered by the term "animism." The "pre-animistic" view that animism represents not the primary but rather a secondary stage in the development of religious ideas must also be recognized. The distinction between the two views, when we look for illustrations of either, is likely to be a hairsplitting one. Moreover, these two stages of religious thought may, it is obvious, be found side by side in actual experience. For example, the talking sword in the Danish ballad *The Sword of Vengeance* must, doubtless, be regarded as having a personal spirit or at least a personality. Its name, however, is a thing to conjure with, and it may illustrate, as other names in balladry seem to illustrate, that indefinable property or power known as "mana," a kind of plasmic force, let us say, from which have sprung our ideas of personal spirits.[1] Nor when looking for survivals of pre-animism in balladry need one confine himself to name magic. A more potent argument than the power of the name is to be found, perhaps, in the

---

[1] See Clodd, *op. cit., passim;* Marett, *The Threshold of Religion*, chap. i., and *passim.*

ghost of folksong. Our ballad revenant is decidedly corporeal. Its bodily characteristics are profusely illustrated in British folksong and seem to point to a time when the idea of personal spirits in the animistic sense had not yet evolved.[1]

THE OBJECT-SOUL

The ascription of personality to inanimate objects, such as a stone, a weapon, a ship, or a river, may well be taken as evidence that balladry has in store some of the most rudimentary forms of religious belief. Metamorphoses into a stone and a bell have already been considered under transmigration.[2] The rôles which stones play make an important chapter in primitive magic.[3] There is reason to think that the custom of swearing by the sword is indicative of the belief that spirits reside in weapons.[4] There is swearing by weapons in the following ballads: *A Gest of Robyn Hode* (117, stanza 202), "Thou shalt swere me an othe," sayde Robyn, "on my bright bronde"; *Queen Eleanor's Confession* (156 C 5); *The Bonnie House o Airlie* (199 B 4, C 7); *The Gypsy Laddie* (200 A 5), "by the hilt of my sword," or in the same piece (C 7), "by the top o my spear." Our folksong can boast, however, of still more primitive oaths than these, such as swearing by trees, the earth, the sun, the moon, and the stars, as well as by parts of the body.[5]

The notion preserved in balladry that weapons, rings, garments, and even a severed head have the power of giving off supernatural light may be considered in this connection. Listing specific ballad references in a footnote,[6] we

[1] See *infra*, pp. 229 ff.

[2] *Supra*, pp. 35 ff.

[3] See Frazer, *The Golden Bough*, XII, 475 f., under "Stone," "Stones."

[4] Cf. G. Henderson, *op. cit.*, p. 198.

[5] See *infra*, p. 362 and n. 4.

[6] A sword gives off light in No. 59 A 43; targe and sword in No. 234 B 13; armor in No. 251, stanza 37. Rings have like power in No. 71, stanza 20: "His goud rings showd him light"; and in Nos. 93 C 17; 80, stanza 17. Garments shine in No. 93 B 16, E 16, F 16; see also Nos. 73 E 24, 243 E 8. Cf. texts of

may quote here Professor Gummere's interesting account of this incident as it occurs in various traditions:

One of the most persistent echoes of an old idea is the mention in many ballads of a more or less supernatural light that is given out by some object. Weapons were once prone to this service; Valhalla was said to be lighted by the gleam of swords, and readers of the Beowulf remember how the magic brand throws radiance about that hall below the sea "even as when heaven's candle shines from the sky." In "Salomon and Saturn" light beams from the barrow of a dead warrior where still lies his sword, although in the Norse lay of Helgi it is the spears that shine. Magic, to be sure, is not far away; men were wont to read the future in their gleaming swords,—*im schwerte sehen;* but for the most part this illumination is contemporary. For ballads, the little champion's sword in "Sir Aldingar" casts light over all the field; but our singer's comment is feeble to a degree: "It shone so of gilding." A late Scottish ballad is quite as superfluously rational with Charlie Macpherson's sword and targe; and Lang Johnny More's armor is also bright in mere prose, dimming the king's eye. But the rings on the fingers of Old Robin's wife are better, and "cast light thorrow the hall;" and in "Young Lamkin" we are with good magic again. "How can I see without candle?" asks the lady; and her false nurse replies that there are two smocks in the coffer as white as the swan; "put one of them about you, it will show you light down." Lamkin cut off her head, and hung it up in the kitchen: "it made a' the ha' shine,"—a weird bit of folklore. The light from clothes became a commonplace, and very common at that, copied by vulgar songs. In a ribald piece about Charity the Chambermaid, her poet unexpectedly tells how "such a light sprung from her clothes, as if the morning-star arose,"—more than negligible stuff, were it not for its witness to the influence of good traditional ballads upon these outcast things.[1]

The marvelous light-giving glaives of Celtic popular tales and the mystical weapon of Arthurian romances belong to the same tradition as our gleaming weapons of balladry.[2]

Lamkin (93), *Journal of the Folk-Song Society,* II, 111 f.; V, 82 ff., first version: "silver mantles, as bright as the sun." Cf. two American texts of the same piece, Campbell and Sharp, p. 104: "Five golden mantles. . . . . You must come by the light of one." There is rationalization in the other text (*JAFL,* XXIX, 162 ff.): "Oh your seven bright lanterns, ... Oh, come down by one." Lanterns is a corruption of "mantles." The light-giving ring of No. 71 is found also in a Greig text (*Last Leaves,* p. 53).

[1] *The Popular Ballad,* pp. 302 ff.; see also Bugge, *op. cit.,* pp. 190 f.

[2] Cf. MacCulloch, *Religion of the Ancient Celts,* p. 292.

A striking argument for the weapon-soul in balladry is the attribution of human traits to weapons. Like birds and animals,[1] inanimate objects in folksong have the power of speech. A sword, a bed, blankets, and a sheet talk when questioned by the hero of *Gil Brenton* and reveal a momentous secret:

> *"Now speak to me, blankets, and speak to me, bed,*
> *And speak, thou sheet, inchanted web;*
>
> *"And speak up, my bonny brown sword, that winna lie,*
> *Is this a true maiden that lies by me?"*
>
> *"It is not a maid that you hae wedded,*
> *But it is a maid that you hae bedded"* [5 B].

In A 31, blankets, sheets, and cods give the same answer. In C 44, Billie Blin, a ballad household-familiar, takes the place of the foregoing objects. Child thinks the sword in B is "probably an editorial insertion," but he questions Jamieson's skepticism as to Billie Blin.[2]

Loath to bite was the Light-of-Battle in *Beowulf*, and there are swords in *King Estmere* which could "byte" well enough had not the prospective victim been made invulnerable by "gramarye" or magic. The hero is to have recourse to a certain "hearbe," with the following result:

> *"His color, which is browne and blacke,*
> *Itt will make redd and whyte;*
> *That sworde is not in all Englande*
> *Upon his coate will byte"* [60, stanza 38].

But King Estmere's enemies are not protected in like manner against the magic swords of our heroes (stanza 68):

> *And aye their swordes soe sore can byte,*
> *Throughe help of gramarye.....*

In *Young Orm and Bermer-Giant*, a ballad having certain features in common with *King Estmere*, a young champion

---

[1] See *supra*, pp. 44 ff.   [2] *Op. cit.*, I, 63.

prevails upon his dead father to give him from the tomb the magic sword "Birting."[1] With respect to the sword in *King Estmere*, Dr. W. M. Hart says: "The figure of speech goes back to an ancient belief that swords had personalities and wills of their own."[2] But such passages, even as they occur in the ballads, should not be thought of as mere metaphors. There is, for instance, a literalness in those lines which the hero in *Johnie Cock* addresses to his "trusty bow":

> *"O stand ye true, my trusty bow,*
> *And stout steel never fail!*
> *Avenge me now on all my foes,*
> *Who have my life i bail"* [114 H 19].[3]

A 18 has "O bows of yew, if ye be true" and "fingers five, get up belive." Johnie speaks to his "fingers five" and "silver strings" in B 11; to his bow and "golden string" in J 6; to his "trusty bow" and "stout steel" in H 19. In D 18 and E 16 he calls upon his "noble dogs."

Gummere remarks:

But we miss in English versions not only the horror and audacity of a piece like the Danish "Hævnersværdet," where the hero has to restrain his sword's avenging thirst for blood by naming its name, but also such vivid personifications as when in Beowulf a blade "sings eager war-song," and in the Finnsburg fragment "shield calls to shaft."[4]

The Danish incident of the avenging and talking sword has already been given under the name-soul and need not be repeated here.[5] Magical and invincible swords are found in the two Danish ballads *Ravengaard og Memering*,[6] a cousin to *Sir Aldingar* (59), and *Liden Grimmer og Hjelmer*

---

[1] Grundtvig, I, 160; trans. Prior, I, 132.

[2] *English Popular Ballads*, p. 318.

[3] Buchan's text. Here, as in many other ballads, Buchan, who is so often berated by Child, gives the best reading. On the traditional character of Buchan's texts see Greig, *Folk-Song of the North-East*, art. CVI; *Last Leaves of Traditional Ballads*, pp. xix ff.

[4] *Op. cit.*, p. 304.   [5] *Supra*, pp. 89 f.

[6] Grundtvig, I, 204; trans. Prior, *op. cit.*, I, 151.

Kamp,[1] a song paralleling in part *Sir Cawline* (61). To turn yet again to Norse folksong, there is an excellent example of sword metamorphosis in the Danish ballad *The Maiden Transformed to a Wer-Wolf*. A maiden is changed by her stepmother into a sword-blade:

> *She then to a sword-blade shaped my form,*
> *And bade me to toil in battle's storm.*
>
> *A sword-blade I was so keen and bright,*
> *And dear to squire and to gallant knight.*[2]

In the same song the maiden is also changed to "a scissars small." In view of the foregoing examples of the magic sword, let us again raise the question as to the presence in balladry of pre-animistic thought. The word "mana" is used in Maori with reference to a wooden sword that has wrought deeds so marvelous as to acquire for itself sanctity and power.[3]

As in its retention of plant- and animal-soul ideas, so in its imputation of human speech and action to weapons, implements, and even ships, ballad-lore is seen to spring from the heart of popular belief.[4] This is strikingly evidenced by the song of *Young Allan* (245). A "bonny boy" promises a ship gold for its hire if it will carry the crew safely to land:

> *"Spring up, spring up, my bonny ship,*
> *And goud sall be your fee!"*
> *Whan the bonny ship heard o that,*
> *That goud shoud be her fee,*
> *She sprang as fast frae the sat water*
> *As the leaf does frae the tree"* [A 17].

"By far the most interesting feature in this ballad," says Child, "is Allan's addressing his ship and the ship's intelli-

---

[1] Grundtvig, I, 353; trans. *Prior*, I, 277.

[2] *Ibid.*, II, 156; trans. Prior, III, 114.

[3] See Marett, *op. cit.*, p. 106, citing E. Tregear, *The Maori-Polynesian Comparative Dictionary* (Wellington, N.Z., 1891), *s.v.* "Mana."

[4] Cf. Gummere, *The Popular Ballad*, p. 304.

gent behavior, A 16, 17, B 12–15, C 21–22."[1] Among other
intelligent ships,[2] we have those in the excellent Danish
ballads *Svend Ranild* and *Hellig-Olavs Væddefart*. Having
slain Thrude, the king of Happy Isle, the hero of *Svend
Ranild* discovers that his ship has set sail. But upon hearing a blast from her master's gilded horn, the ship returns:

> *His gilded horn childe Ranild took,*
>   *And blew a blast so loud,*
> *A crack was heard from shore to shore,*
>   *For snapp'd was every shroud.*
> *"Come ye not back?" childe Ranild said.*
>
> *That good and faithful gilded ship,*
>   *So well his blast she knew,*
> *Asunder sailed her cables nine,*
>   *And back to Ranild flew.*
> *"Right welcome thou!" childe Ranild said.*[3]

In *Hellig-Olavs Væddefart*, a fine Danish ballad, there is an
even better personification of a ship. When sailed by St.
Olave, the "Ox" responds to his commands as though en-
dowed with consciousness. St. Olave strikes it on the ribs
and across the eye, and it goes faster and faster:

> *Saint Olave sat on the ship's prow;*
> *"Now, Ox, in name of Jesus go."*
>
> *Saint Olave seized his long white horn;*
> *"Now go, as if in fields of corn."*
>
> *Such strides the Ox began to make,*
> *That high with billows foam'd the wake.*[4]

---

[1] *Op. cit.*, IV, 376; see also text, *ibid.*, V, 276.

[2] For Child's references to talking and intelligent ships see *ibid.*, IV, 376 f.;
V, 275. The intelligent-ship incident is found in Greig's variant of *Young Allan*
(245) (*Folk-Song of the North-East*, art. LXIII).

[3] Grundtvig, I, 372; trans. Prior, *op. cit.*, I, 291 f.

[4] *Ibid.*, II, 134; trans. Prior, I, 359.

And then

> *A blow on the Ox's ribs he gave;*
> *"Put out thy strength and dance the wave."*
>
> *St. Olave struck him across the eye;*
> *"Now faster still to harbour hie."*
>
> *The Ox began to plunge and leap,*
> *Their legs the crew no more could keep.*

An instance of ship metamorphosis occurs in *The Twa Magicians* (44), a transformation-conflict ballad:

> *She turnd hersell into a ship,*
> *To sail out ower the flood.*[1]

Finally, we may mention here the superstition that a ship will not sail if fey folk or a sinful person is aboard. The heroine of *Bonnie Annie* (24) is fey, that is, doomed to die, and the ship will not sail until Annie is thrown overboard. Brown Robyn (57) is thrown overboard because his sin, that of incest, prevents the ship from going. This latter ballad, *Brown Robyn's Confession*, has excellent Scandinavian analogues.

The Mother's Malison (216) gives a rather poor example of the personification of a river, but it may serve to illustrate for balladry the universal notion of river spirits. The mother's curse, which dooms Willie to death, is, however, convincing enough and lends weight to the personification of Clyde's water:

> *"O spare me, Clyde's water,*
> *O spare me as I gae!*
> *Mak me your wrack as I come back,*
> *But spare me as I gae"* [A 8]!

C 10 gives virtually the same reading.

[1] Cf. text, Greig, *Last Leaves*, p. 33: "She became a ship, a ship, an' sailed upon the sea; . . . ."

Chapter II

THE GRAVE OR BARROW WORLD

❦

THE conception that the Otherworld does not extend beyond the grave-mound or barrow, an idea familiar, for example, to Eddic poetry,[1] and so common among early and primitive peoples as scarcely to need illustration, is clearly in evidence in British traditional poetry, in foreign analogues of our ballads, and in other continental songs. That this notion of continued existence in the grave is co-present in balladry with the belief in a general realm beyond the tomb is not out of keeping with popular thought. The two general conceptions, as illustrated again in the ideas of the barrow and of Hel in Teutonic tradition,[2] represent in all probability different strata of belief. It should be borne in mind, of course, that interment may be practiced with the most diverse ideas of the destiny of the soul. Among the early Hebrews, for instance, we find that Sheol was regarded now as identical with the grave and now, apparently, as separate therefrom. A like confusion characterized early Roman eschatology.[3]

That the future life is thought of in our traditional poetry as being intimately connected with the grave is shown by the following practices and ideas: the burial of belongings with the dead, as in *Robin Hood's Death* (120),

[1] See Vigfusson-Powell, *Corpus poeticum boreale*, II, 704; Elton-Powell, *Saxo*, pp. lxvi f.

[2] See Vigfusson-Powell, *op. cit.*, I, 420; and see a reconcilement of the two views (Rydberg, *Teutonic Mythology*, p. 505).

[3] See the various articles under "State of the Dead," *Encyclopaedia of Religion and Ethics*, Vol. XI.

The Twa Brothers (49), and *Sir Hugh* (155);[1] the custom of binding the limbs of the dead or otherwise barring the ghost;[2] the corporeality of the ballad revenant;[3] and, finally, the idea, found in virtually all the revenant pieces, that the ghost comes directly from the grave and returns to it. All these matters will be discussed in one connection or another in the following chapters, and it is only necessary at this point to emphasize somewhat the last two ideas— the materiality of the ballad ghost and the grave as the dwelling place of the dead.

Notwithstanding that the revenant in certain texts of *Sweet William's Ghost* (77) has knowledge of the far-off regions of paradise and hell, yet it is because of restlessness in the grave that it returns—a motive more explicitly stated in *The Unquiet Grave* (78) and *The Twa Brothers* (49), as in several texts of *Proud Lady Margaret* (47).[4] In texts B, D, and E, Sweet William mentions heaven and hell. In B 8 he says that he will be missed from heaven, but, according to the following stanzas, he returns to his grave. In E 13 he speaks of suffering "the pains of hell." C 10 reads:

> *She followed him high, she followed him low,*
> *Till she came to yon church-yard;*
> *O there the grave did open up,*
> *And young William he lay down.*

Descriptions, grimly realistic, of life after death, bear witness to the popular notion that the dead live on in the tomb. "Down among the hongerey worms I sleep," says Sweet William (77 B 14); and the revenant in *Proud Lady Margaret* (47 A 19) cries, "For the wee worms are my bedfellows, and cauld clay is my sheets." Virtually the same reading occurs in B 24, C 17. Texts B 26, C 18, D 12, and E 8 hint at a land beyond the grave. The ghost sons of *The Wife of Usher's Well* (79 A 6) got their hats of birch at

---

[1] In *Sir Hugh* the evidence has been somewhat Christianized. On the burial of belongings with the dead see my study, *Death and Burial Lore*, pp. 126 ff.

[2] See *infra*, pp. 253 ff. [3] See *infra*, pp. 229 ff. [4] See *infra*, pp. 230 ff., 256 ff.

the "gates o Paradise," but (A 11) they must return to
their place in the mold, for the "channerin worm doth
chide." Miss Burne's Shropshire text[1] gives the sons a sort
of "resurrection" body, but there is obviously Christian
editing here. Clerk Saunders (77 F 6) accounts as follows
for the absence of his arms: "By worms they're eaten, in
mools they're rotten." And the lips of the ballad shade are
usually "clay-cold," its breath "earthy strong," as in *The
Unquiet Grave* (78 A 5).[2] These lines and phrases, attesting
as they do the corporeity of the ghost, show that the dead
of balladry have a bodily immortality in the grave or at
least that the ghost or "body" lives in the tomb until the
complete decomposition of the corpse. Tylor discusses the
well-known belief, current, for example, among the New
Zealanders and the Iroquois Indians of America, that the
ghost remains near the body until the corpse is buried, exposed, burned, or otherwise disposed of, according to the
accepted custom of the land.[3] But this, after all, if Tylor
has interpreted primitive thought aright, implies a distinction or separation between the dead body and the ghost, a
distinction which, in the main, does not hold for the revenants of balladry. The ghost of folksong does not remain
near or hover about the corpse. It is the corpse. Hans
Naumann's view that revenants of this type point to pre-
animistic thought is considered later in our study.[4]

The reticence of traditional poetry warns one, of course,
against overinterpretation, but the evidence for the grave
world may be strengthened by reference to the habit which
the ballad ghost, in vampire fashion, has of issuing directly
from the grave and returning as directly to it. In this it recalls the revenants of Saxo's stories—that, for example, in
the tale of Asmund and Aswit, though we have no ghost
whose deeds match in horror those of Aswit, who not only
devours Asmund's horse and hound[5] but sets upon Asmund

[1] Child, *Ballads*, III, 513.　　　[3] *Primitive Culture*, II, 27 ff.
[2] On this commonplace see *infra*, p. 289.　　[4] *Infra*, pp. 229 ff.
[5] But cf. the terrible appetite of the monster, a transformed lady, in *King
Henry* (32), *infra*, p. 201.

himself. To end his fight with the dead man or with the spirit Asmund cuts off his head and impales "his guilty carcase with a stake."[1] In Miss Burne's copy of *The Unquiet Grave* (78 F 3) "this young man he arose" from his tomb, questioned his true-love as to her grief, and was thus answered by her:

> *"One kiss, one kiss, of your lily-white lips*
> *And return back to your grave."*

E 4 gives nearly the same reading. If the idea underlying this piece has to do, as Baring-Gould thinks, with the carrying off of the maiden by her dead lover to the world of shadows unless she can solve his riddles,[2] one would like to know just what this world of shadows is, whether the grave itself or an extension of the grave.

The lady in *Proud Lady Margaret* (47 A 17, B 22, C 15) would accompany the dead to the "clay," but, like the maiden in *Sweet William's Ghost* (77), is refused admittance to the grave. The revenant of the latter piece gives reasons which attest his materiality and exclude any idea of his being an incorporeal shade:

> *"There's no room at my head, Margret,*
> *There's no room at my feet;*
> *There's no room at my side Margret,*
> *My coffin's made so meet"* [A 13].

Although in both the foregoing ballads there is the notion of a general realm of the dead, it seems that this realm is thought of in connection with the grave or at least is reached by way of the grave. Certain stanzas of Motherwell's version of *Sweet William's Ghost* (77 C 11 ff.) provide the lover with three maidens at his head, three babes at his side, and three hell-hounds at his feet, a company reminiscent of the household of the Scandinavian barrow.[3]

[1] Elton-Powell, *op. cit.*, p. 201; see also *ibid.*, pp. 32, 54.

[2] See *infra*, p. 306.

[3] See Elton-Powell, *op. cit.*, pp. lxvi f.; Vigfusson-Powell, *op. cit.*, II, 704, under "Burial"; Gummere, *Germanic Origins*, pp. 310 f., 317.

The Danish ballad *Fæstmanden i Graven,* which closely parallels *Sweet William's Ghost* and which accords in many points with the conclusion of the second lay of Helgi Hundingsbani in the older *Edda,*[1] presents a picture—more complete than does our ballad—of life in the barrow or grave. Else's tears become blood in her hero's coffin—one thinks of the rivers of blood in the subterranean Otherworld of *Thomas Rymer* (37)[2]—but when she sings, his grave is hung with rose leaves. The English ballad has transported the flowers to a somewhat Christianized paradise.[3] In the Norse piece ideas of heaven and hell are not prominent, although the ghost must show itself a spirit of health by speaking the name of Jesus. We cannot dismiss the Danish song without giving it generous quotation:

> *"Now hear me, dear Sir Ogey,*
> *The truth I pray thee tell,*
> *How under ground thou farest*
> *Down in thy cell."*

> *" 'Tis so down in that earth-house,*
> *Where I must tarry now,*
> *'Tis as the joys of heaven,*
> *If happy thou."*

> *"Then hear me, knight Sir Ogey,*
> *And grant the boon I crave,*
> *To go with thee, my dearest,*
> *And share thy grave."*

> *" 'Tis so down in that earth-house,*
> *My narrow lonely cell,*
> *'Tis like to hellish torture,*
> *O cross thyself well!*

> *"So oft as thou art weeping,*
> *And grievest thee so sore,*
> *Is brimming full my coffin*
> *With blood and gore.*

[1] Cf. Child, II, 228.   [2] See *infra,* pp. 109 f.   [3] See *infra,* p. 149.

> *"Above my head is growing*
> *The grass so sweet,*
> *But lothely snakes are twining*
> *About my feet.*
>
> *"Yet when I hear thee singing,*
> *And thou art glad,*
> *Then is my grave's small chamber*
> *With roses clad."*[1]

The revenant hears the crowing of the white, the red, and the black cock, a signal for the departure of the dead from middle-earth. "Home I must go below," he says. "Unlock'd are all the portals, and I too must go." "For the gates o heaven will be shut, and I'll be mist away," complains the ghost in the English analogue (77 D 12). If the "portals" of the Danish piece are the "gates o heaven" of the English ballad it is clear that in both songs there is present the conception of an "earth-house" along with the notion of a land beyond the grave.[2]

The Eddic lay of Helgi and Sigrun, as already observed, closely resembles in part the foregoing Norse ballad, and presents an equally striking picture of the barrow ghost. Every night, ere she sleeps, Sigrun sheds bitter tears over the death of Helgi, who was slain by her brother. Discommoded by the tears of the living, Helgi, like the lover in *The Unquiet Grave* (78), returns from the barrow to comfort and reprove his beloved. Sigrun kisses Helgi, who has already proclaimed himself "no mere phantom," and cries: "Thy hair, my Helgi, is thick with rime, thy whole body is drenched with gory dew, thy hands are cold and dank. How shall I deliver thee from this, O my lord?"

---

[1] Grundtvig, II, 495; trans. Prior, *op. cit.*, III, 78.

[2] The editors of the *Danske Viser*, notes Prior (*op. cit.*, III, 79), paraphrase the line "Unlock'd are all the portals" as follows: "Nu aabnes Himmeriges Porte," "Now the gate of the kingdom of heaven opens." This means, says Prior, that "the day dawns," but for balladry this interpretation seems too metaphorical. Folksong, we may say, almost without reservation, is not given to figurative language.

Helgi answers: "It is thine own doing, Sigrun from Sevafell, that Helgi is drenched with deadly dew. Thou weepest cruel tears, ... before thou goest to sleep: every one of them falls bloody, dank cold, chilly, fraught with sobs, upon my breast. . . . . Let us drink costly draughts, though we have lost both love and land! Let no man chant wailing dirges, though he see the wounds on my breast. Now are maidens, royal ladies, shut up in the barrow with us dead men!"

Then says Sigrun: "I have made thee a bed here, Helgi, a very painless bed, thou son of the Wolfings. I shall sleep in thine arms, O king, as I should if thou wert yet alive."

To which Helgi: "Now I swear that there shall never be a greater marvel, early or late, at Sevafell: for thou, the white daughter of Hogni, art sleeping in the arms of the dead; thou, a king's daughter, art come down alive into the barrow."[1]

The Danish ballad *Orm Ungersvend og Bermer-Rise*, a song which, according to Bugge, has possible connections with *King Estmere* (60),[2] yields important evidence of life in the barrow. In order to make sure of victory in his coming fight with the giant Bermer, young Orm goes to his father's tomb, awakens his dead sire, and secures from him an irresistible sword. The dead man yields the weapon only upon condition that Orm avenge his death. That the sword is buried with its owner is only another instance of the old practice of burying belongings with the dead. The wealth of the barrow ghost in this piece is noteworthy:

> *"And is it thou art come, childe Orm,*
> *My youngest son so dear?*
> *And is it gold, or silver plate,*
> *Or coin, thou seekest here?"*

[1] Vigfusson-Powell, *op. cit.*, I, 143 f.

[2] See Child, II, 49, on Bugge's affiliation of *King Estmere* with various stories.

"I want nor gold, nor silver plate,
  Nor coin from out thy grave,
But all to win a lovely maid
  Sword Birting come to crave."

"Birting, my sword, thou shalt not get
  To win for thee the bride,
Till thou hast venged thy father's blood
  In Iceland, where he died."

"And if I Birting cannot get,
  And win the boon I crave,
With massive rock I'll pound thy tomb,
  And crush thee in the grave."

He gave him Birting from out his tomb,
  The hilt into his hand;
"Grasp it with firm and dauntless mood,
  And thee shall none withstand."[1]

According to another Danish ballad, *Young Swennendal,*[2] a youth, bent upon freeing a spell-bound maiden, goes to Goliat cave to seek counsel of his dead mother. He beats upon the grave-mound and arouses his mother, who furnishes him with magic equipment for his adventure: a marvelous steed, a magic sword, and a wonderful key and tablecloth.

Other evidence that the after-life may be confined in part, at least, to the gravehouse is furnished by the incident of mourning the dead from the grave, a motif treated in our chapter on "The Ballad Ghost."[3] The analogous incident of harping the dead—Orpheus-like—from the tomb is found in *The Twa Brothers* (49 B 10), but in the ballad Pluto's domain has shrunk, apparently, to a narrow grave world. In bringing to a close our discussion of the barrow, we should observe that in balladry life under the ground is not a life of bliss. It is comparable, perhaps, in this re-

[1] Grundtvig, I, 160; trans. Prior, *op. cit.*, I, 135.

[2] *Ibid.*, II, 248; trans. Prior, II, 333 f.   [3] *Infra*, pp. 230 ff., 256 f.

spect to the Hebrew Sheol; does not afford the dead even the shadowy company which Achilles endured; and is, at best, a sound slumber undisturbed by the grief or the affairs of the living. The dying boy in *The Twa Brothers* (49 B 6) says that he will sleep soundly if his "bible," "chaunter," and bow and arrows are buried with him.[1] An unhappy abode is the gravehouse, and the ballad revenant, in most instances, refuses his mortal mistress admittance to his side. In the Danish ballad *Fæstmanden i Graven*, for example, Sir Ogey describes his grave as like to heaven, but upon his true-love's desiring to share it with him he says it is a place of hellish torture.

[1] Cf. D 9, F 10, and *Sir Hugh* (155 E 20).

Chapter III

THE OTHERWORLD JOURNEY

❧

AS IN classic myth, medieval romance, or saga, or,
again, as in savage tradition, so also in balladry we
find a number of stories which tell how mortals are
enticed away to the Otherworld or make journeys thereto
more or less voluntarily.[1] The ballads depict, however, no
such eventful journey to the Otherworld as that experienced by Bran and his comrades,[2] but we may parallel this
and other such *imrama* in one respect, at least; namely,
that in traveling to the land of spirits or of fairies ballad
Otherworld itinerants must cross some sort of water barrier, a river or the sea. Crossing a river as a means of entering the world of spirits is a commonplace of literature, as
in Homer, Vergil, and Dante, but it is a commonplace
which rests ultimately, of course, upon primitive belief.

The custom of boat burial, a custom which implies the
belief that one must cross the sea in order to reach the
country of spirits,[3] seems to be reflected in the ballads
Edward (13 A 9, B 4) and *Lizie Wan* (51 A 11, B 13). As
a Northern parallel to the practice of boat or canoe burial
among the Oceanians[4] we may venture to quote the lines
from *Edward* (13 A 8 f.):

[1] On Otherworld journeys among primitive races see Tylor, *Primitive Culture*, II, 44 ff.; Frazer, *The Belief in Immortality*, I, 286 f., 361 f., 462 ff.; Rosalind
Moss, "Journey to the Afterworld," *Life after Death in Oceania*, chap. ix.

[2] See Meyer-Nutt, *The Voyage of Bran*.

[3] See Cox, *Introduction to Folk-Lore*, pp. 184 ff.

[4] See Moss, *op. cit.*, pp. 15 ff.; cf. Gummere, *Germanic Origins*, p. 325. See
also Axel Olrik, *The Heroic Legends of Denmark* (trans. L. M. Hollander), pp.
405 ff.

"What death dost thou desire to die,
Son Davie, son Davie?"

"I'll set my foot in a bottomless ship,
Mother lady, mother lady:
I'll set my foot in a bottomless ship,
And ye'll never see mair o me."

A slightly different reading of this passage occurs in *The Twa Brothers* (49 D 19). Nothing can be made, perhaps, of the revenant's saying in *Sweet William's Ghost* (77 A 9, E 11) that his "bones are buried in yon kirk-yard, afar beyond the sea."[1] The burial spot of the ghost in *Proud Lady Margaret* (47 B 25) is likewise "far beyond the sea." But C 14 of this piece reads: "I am William . . . . that died beyond the sea."

The rivers of "red blude" through which Thomas and the fairy queen (37 A 7, C 15 f.) wade or ride on their Otherworld journey are clearly evidential of some sort of water barrier to the land of spirits.

For forty days and forty nights
He wade thro red blude to the knee [A 7].

Scott's version, C 16, explains the "blude":

And they waded thro red blude to the knee;
For a' the blude that's shed on earth
Rins thro the springs o that countrie.

Campbell's copy, B 6, has simply "water clear" instead of the "red blude" of A and C. Commenting on the reading in Scott's text, Gummere says that this "is perhaps popular lore, too, with a glimpse of the old Scandinavian 'water-hell'; Professor J. A. Stewart aptly compares with this verse the mention in Dante of those infernal rivers which are fed by human tears."[2] Persian traditions offer an elaboration of the widespread tear-motif, present in

[1] Ballad lovers not infrequently come from over the sea.
[2] *The Popular Ballad*, p. 302.

[109]

The Unquiet Grave (78), that the tears of the living disturb the repose of the dead. According to the Persian belief, the tears of the living become rivers that hinder the passage of the departed to the Otherworld.[1] In the romance of Thomas of Erceldoune (stanza 45) the fairy queen speaks of her earthly captive as having come from beyond "the see."[2]

The water barrier to the land of shades is found again in *Johnie Cock* (114). For a single drop of his heart's blood Johnie's enemies would "ride the fords of hell":

> "*And for a drop of thy heart's bluid*
> *They wad ride the fords of hell*" [A 3].

The demon-lover in the ballad of that name (243) takes his earthly love out over the sea and within sight of the mountains of heaven and hell. These hills or mountains are found in only texts E and F, but in all versions the lover, "mariner" that he is, carries his mistress across the sea. The forsaken lady in *The Lass of Roch Royal* (76), a ballad with something of fairy-lore in it, must sail over the sea to find her lover. But certain of these matters have to do largely with the position and nature of the Otherworld and will be treated in detail farther on in this work. We may give here, however, those lines from Buchan's copy of *The Unquiet Grave* (78 D 8) which seem to imply that the dead cross the sea on their return to the realm of spirits: "But hoist up one sail to the wind," says the ghost to his truelove; "your ship must sail away." These lines are, to be sure, not very ballad-like.

The belief that the dead in journeying to spiritland must pass over a bridge, which, as a rule, is exceedingly narrow, is found in Aubrey's version of *The Lyke-Wake Dirge*,[3] a song which one would be glad to claim for British balladry. "The Lyke-Wake Dirge, the not yet forgotten funeral chant of the North Country, tells," remarks Tylor, "like some savage or barbaric legend, of the passage over

---

[1] See Child, *Ballads*, II, 235 f., 513.

[2] See *ibid.*, I, 328.

[3] *Remaines of Gentilisme and Judaisme* (ed. James Britten), pp. 31 f.

the Bridge of Death and the dreadful journey to the other world."[1] But the version of the song quoted by Tylor makes no reference to the narrowness of the bridge, an important feature which is found in a marginal addition to Aubrey's manuscript.[2] Before giving the dirge we may quote from a manuscript letter of the late sixteenth century in which Ritson found an illustration of the song:

When any dieth, certaine women sing a song to the dead bodie, recyting the journey that the partye deceased must goe; and they are of beliefe (such is their fondnesse) that once in their lives, it is good to give a pair of new shoes to a poor man, for as much as, after this life, they are to pass barefoote through a great launde, full of thornes and furzen, except by the meryte of the almes aforesaid they have redemed the forfeyte; for, at the edge of the launde, an oulde man shall meet them with the same shoes that were given by the partie when he was lyving; and, after he hath shodde them, dismisseth them to go through thick and thin, without scratch or scalle.[3]

The dirge, as Aubrey gives it, is as follows:

> This ean night, this ean night,
>   every night and awle:
> Fire and Fleet and Candle-light
>   and Christ recieve thy Sawle.
>
> When thou from hence doest pass away
>   every night and awle
> To Whinny-moor thou comest at last
>   and Christ recieve thy silly poor sawle.
>
> If ever thou gave either hosen or shun
>   every night and awle
> Sitt thee downe and putt them on
>   and Christ recieve thy sawle.
>
> But if hosen nor shoon thou never gave nean
>   every night, &c:
> The Whinnes shall prick thee to the bare beane
>   and Christ recieve thy sawle.

[1] Op. cit., I, 495.   [2] See Aubrey, op. cit., p. 220.
[3] See Scott, Minstrelsy (ed. Henderson), III, 163 f.

[III]

> *From Whinny-moor that thou mayst pass*
> *every night &c:*
> *To Brig o' Dread thou comest at last*
> *and Christ &c:*
>
> *From Brig of Dread that thou mayest pass*
> *no brader than a thread*
> *every night &c:*
> *To Purgatory fire thou com'st at last*
> *and Christ &c:*
>
> *If ever thou gave either Milke or drinke*
> *every night &c:*
> *The fire shall never make thee shrink*
> *and Christ &c:*
>
> *But if milk nor drink thou never gave nean*
> *every night &c:*
> *The Fire shall burn thee to the bare bene*
> *and Christ recive thy Sawle.*

The belief reflected in the foregoing song that the dead must walk a bridge on their journey to the Otherworld is present in such traditions as those of the North American Indians, the Teutons, the Mohammedans, and the Jews.[1] Among the Oceanians the crossing of the bridge—tree-trunk or log bridge—to the Otherworld is in the nature of an ordeal, as with the Solomon Islanders and the natives of Kwato in Southeast British New Guinea.[2]

As paralleling the "Brig o' Dread" in *The Lyke-Wake Dirge*, Britten gives the following passage from Sale's Preface to the Koran:

The trials being over, and the assembly dissolved, the Mohammedans hold that those who are to be admitted into paradise will take the right-hand way, and those who are destined to hell-fire will take the left;

[1] See Cox, *op. cit.*, pp. 189 f. On the Otherworld bridge in medieval literature, see Patch, "Mediaeval Descriptions of the Otherworld," *PMLA*, XXXIII, 634 ff.

[2] See R. Moss, *op. cit.*, pp. 110 f.

but both of them must first pass the bridge, called in Arabic al Sirât, which they say is laid over the midst of hell, and described to be finer than a hair and sharper than the edge of a sword, so that it seems very difficult to conceive how any one shall be able to stand upon it; for which reason most of the sect of the Motazalites reject it as a fable, though the orthodox think it a sufficient proof of the truth of this article that it was seriously affirmed by him who never asserted a falsehood, meaning their Prophet, who, to add to the difficulty of the passage, has likewise declared this bridge is beset on each side with *briars and hooked thorns*, which will, however, be no impediments to the good, for they shall pass with wonderful ease and swiftness, like lightning or the wind, Mohammed and his Moslems leading the way; whereas the wicked, what with the slipperiness and extreme narrowness of the path, the entangling of the thorns, and the extinction of the light, which directed the former to paradise, will soon miss their footing and fall down headlong into hell, which is gaping beneath them. This circumstance Mohammed seems to have borrowed from the Magians, who teach that, on the last day, all mankind will be obliged to pass a bridge, which they call Pûl Chînavad, or Chînavar: that is, the straight bridge, leading directly into the other world, on the midst of which they suppose the angels, appointed by God to perform that office, will stand, who will require of every one a strict account of his actions, and weigh them in the manner we have already mentioned. It is true the Jews speak likewise of the bridge of hell, which they say is *no broader than a thread*, but then they do not tell us that any shall be obliged to pass it, except the idolaters, who will thence fall into perdition.[1]

The most minute description of the "Brig o' Dread" occurs in the manuscript legend of Sir Owain.[2] Here the bridge is placed between purgatory and paradise. Those two stanzas which particularly describe the bridge may be given:

> *And Owain seigh ther ouer ligge*
> *A swithe strong naru brigge:*
> *The fendes seyd tho;*
> *"Lo! Sir Knight, sestow this?*
> *This is the brigge of paradis,*
> *Here ouer thou must go."*

[1] Aubrey, *op. cit.*, pp. 221 f.
[2] Cf. Scott, *op. cit.*, III, 165 ff.

The brigge was as heigh as a tour,
And as scharpe as a rasour,
And naru it was also;
And the water that ther ran under,
Brend o' lightning and of thonder,
That thocht him michel wo.

The "Brig o' Dread"—possibly a corruption of "the Bridge of the Dead"—"Whinny-moor," and the "Hell-shoon" of our dirge have parallels in many traditions.[1] The shoes bring to mind, of course, the *Todtenschuh* with which the dead in heathen days were provided for their journey. These hell-shoes, which facilitate the passage of Whinny-moor or its equivalent, are secured in various ways, as in the dirge, for example, by the charitable gift of "hosen and shoon" during life. Primitive funerary practices supplied the dead with all manner of things for the life after death.

The Bitter Withy, a traditional ballad,[2] tells how our Savior, in order to show his power and to punish three scornful "jolly jerdins," builds a bridge of sunbeams. The Savior goes over the bridge and is followed by the three jerdins, who, however, fall off and are drowned:

Our Saviour built a bridge with the beams of the sun,
And over He gone, He gone He,
And after followed the three jolly jerdins,
And drownded they were all three.

Mr. Percy Zillwood Round accounts for the sunbeams in our ballad, but regards a Norse origin for the bridge as problematical. Says Mr. Round:

I have identified the sunbeams, but not the *bridge* of sunbeams, nor the drowning. But a Norse origin seems problematical. The bridge and

[1] On these matters see Sidgwick, *Popular Ballads of the Olden Time* (2d ser.), pp. 241 f.

[2] Communicated by Frank Sidgwick to *Notes and Queries* (10th ser.), IV, 84 f., with information respecting the carol's origin and traditional character. For other texts see *Journal of the Folk-Song Society*, II, 205 ff.; 303 ff.; IV, 31 ff. On *The Bitter Withy* as a ballad see also G. H. Gerould in *PMLA*, XXIII, 141–66; Gummere, *op. cit.*, pp. 227 ff.

the burning flood over which the spirits pass to Paradise is found in Persian (bridge of Chinwat) and Arabic (bridge of Al Sirat), see E. G. Browne's *Literature of Ancient Persia*, p. 107. It seems to be the "Brig o' Dread" in Aubrey's Yorkshire "Lyke-wake Dirge" (see F. Sidgwick's *Ballads*, Vol ii, p. 88, 238), besides occurring in Norse Mythology, and "Riding the Moonbeams" is referred to in a story in Doni's *Moral Philosophie*, which is of Eastern origin, ...[1]

What may one make of the "bridge of steel" which the demon-lover in *James Harris* (243) promises to build for his mistress preparatory to carrying her over the sea? The phrase is possibly a kenning for ship, although the lover has already spoken of his "seven brave ships upon the sea."

> "*Have you any place to put me in,*
> *If I with you should gang?*"
> "*I've seven brave ships upon the sea,*
> *All laden to the brim.*
>
> "*I'll build my love a bridge of steel,*
> *All for to help her oer;*
> *Likewise webs of silk down by her side,*
> *To keep my love from the cold*" [E].

The German ballad *Die schöne Agniese*, an analogue of *Hind Etin* (41), tells of a merman who plates a bridge with gold. Over this bridge walks the King of England's daughter, and it sinks with her into the water, that is, down to the realm of the merman.[2] In Saxo's story of King Gormo's visit to Guthmund's giantland there is a gold bridge for the use of spirits,[3] and in the same writer's account of Hadding's voyage underground we find a bridge over the River

---

[1] See *Journal of the Folk-Song Society*, II, 302; IV, 37 ff. Cf. the suggestion offered by Professor Gerould (*op. cit.*, XXIII, 161) that the source of the sunbeam bridge is in the oriental story—a story known in Europe before the end of the eleventh century—of the thief who made use of a moon ray as a means of conveyance into and out of the houses he robbed. Professor Gerould's suggestion finds support in the fact that the foregoing legend is given briefly in the Laurentian MS of Pseudo-Matthew.

[2] See Child, I, 365.

[3] Elton-Powell, *Saxo*, pp. 346 f., lxx.

of Blades.[1] The Norse ballad *Sir Bosmer in Elfland* relates
how a knight goes to meet a lovely maiden at the bridge.
The maiden is none other than an "elfquean":

> *But while he was crossing the bridge of stone,*
> *His horse tripp'd up on his golden shoon.*
>
> *His horse tripp'd up on the nails of gold,*
> *And into the torrent Sir Bosmer roll'd.*
>
> *Sir Bosmer he swam the eddying flood,*
> *To where on the bank an elfquean stood.*
>
> *"O welcome, Sir Bosmer! come home to me,*
> *I've brew'd the mead and the wine for thee."*[2]

The diffuseness of romance or epic would be welcomed
in that passage in *Proud Lady Margaret* (47) where the
revenant threatens the proud lady with the "roads" which
he has come:

> *"Leave pride, Janet, leave pride, Janet,*
> *Leave pride an vanitie;*
> *If ye come the roads that I hae come,*
> *Sair warned will ye be"* [D 12].

But *Thomas Rymer*, with the aid of romance, is less disap-
pointing—even though, perhaps, less ballad-like—and provides a not unsatisfactory cosmographical compromise
between Christianity and pre-Christianity, especially in
those lines where the fairy queen gives Thomas the power
to see the roads to heaven, hell, and fairyland. The most
interesting stage of the journey, however, the wading of
underground waters or "thro red blude to the knee," has
already been considered, and, in the story, is covered before Thomas views the "fairlies three." The ballad depiction of the roads to heaven, hell, and elfland will be given
after we have quoted Child's excellent abstract of Thomas'
journey as it occurs in the ballad texts and in the romance.

[1] *Ibid.*, pp. 38, lxviii.   [2] Prior, III, 319 f.

Before giving Child's analysis we may note by way of introduction that in the romance, as in Scott's text (C) of the ballad—in this latter, however, in a very corrupted form—Thomas, having embraced the queen of elfland, must accompany her to fairyland. Mrs. Brown's version, which, like Campbell's (B), omits the important incident of contact with the fairy,[1] goes on with the story. Like the Otherworld adventurer in the story of Lanval as told by Marie de France in one of her *Lais*,[2] Thomas is taken up on the fairy steed behind his elfin love. In the same way a mortal in *The Wee Wee Man* (38) and in *Hind Etin* (41 C 4) rides to the land of the trolls. But to give the stanzas from Mrs. Brown's copy of *Thomas Rymer* (37 A):

> *She turned about her milk-white steed,*
> *And took True Thomas up behind,*
> *And aye wheneer her bridle rang,*
> *The steed flew swifter than the wind.*

> *For forty days and forty nights*
> *He wade thro red blude to the knee,*
> *And he saw neither sun nor moon,*
> *But heard the roaring of the sea.*

> *O they rade on, and further on,*
> *Until they came to a garden green:*
> *"Light down, light down, ye laaie free,*
> *Some of that fruit let me pull to thee."*

At this point we may give Professor Child's abstract:

He must go with her for seven years, A, B; only for a twelvemonth, R. She takes him up behind her, A; she rides and he runs, B; she leads him in at Eldon hill, R; they cross a water, he wading up to the knee, B, R. The water is subterranean in R, and for three days naught is heard but the soughing of the flood. Then they come to an orchard, A, B, R, and Thomas, like to tyne for lack of food, is about to pull fruit, but is told that the fruit is cursed, A 9, B 8; if he plucks it, his soul goes to the fire of hell, R 35. The fairy has made a provision of safe bread

---

[1] See the Otherworld spell, *infra*, pp. 283 f.

[2] See "Die *Lais* der Marie de France," *Bibliotheca Normannica*, III, 86–112.

and wine for him in the ballad, A 10, B 9, but he has still to fast a while
in the romance. C, which lacks this passage, makes them ride till they
reach a wide desert, and leave living land behind, 9; and here (but in
A, B, and R in the vicinity of the orchard) the fairy bids Thomas lay
his head on her knee, and she will show him rare sights. These are the
way to heaven, A 12, B 11, R 38; the way to hell, A 13, B 10, R 41; the
road to Elfland, whither they are going, A 14. . . . . . Now follows in
A 15 (as recited, here 7), C 15, 16, the passage through the subterranean
water, which should come before they reach the orchard, as in B 6, R
30, 31. There is much exaggeration in the ballad: they wade through
rivers in darkness and hear the sea roaring, C 15, A 7, as in R, but they
also wade through red blood to the knee, A 7, C 16, and the crossing
occupies not three days, as in R 31, but forty days, A 7. In C they *now*
come to the garden.[1]

According to certain stanzas of our ballad given by Scott
in one of his copies of *Tam Lin* (39), Thomas and the fairy
"raid on and on'ard mair, oer mountain, hill and lee," until
they "came to a hie, hie wa, upon a mountain's bree."[2]

In the several texts of the ballad, as well as in the romance, the elf queen gives Thomas the power to see the
paths to heaven, hell, and fairyland. The Christianization
of the fairy queen's cosmography is noteworthy:

"O see not ye yon narrow road,
   So thick beset wi thorns and briers?
That is the path of righteousness,
   Tho after it but few enquires.

"And see not ye that braid braid road,
   That lies across yon lillie leven?
That is the path of wickedness,
   Tho some call it the road to heaven.

"And see not ye that bonny road,
   Which winds about the fernie brae?
That is the road to fair Elfland,
   Where you and I this night maun gae" [A].

B 11 describes the road to heaven as "yon narrow way,
that leadeth down by yon lillie lea"; the way to hell, 10, as

[1] *Op. cit.*, I, 320 f.   [2] *Ibid.*, IV, 458.

"yon broad broad way, that leadeth down by yon skerry fell." The descriptions of the paths to heaven and hell are in C 11, 12, identical with those in A. The road to elfland is not described in B. The lines in C 13 are the same as those in A 14. In the romance, 42, the elf queen does not point out the way to fairyland but shows Thomas her castle on a "heghe hill." However, she points out, 38, the "faire waye" to heaven; 39, the way to "paradyse"; 40, the way to purgatory; 41, the way to the "fyre of helle."[1] "Purgatory is omitted in the Cotton MS of the romance, as in the ballad."[2]

Tam Lin (39) gives some description of fairyland but nothing concerning his journey thereto; however, in order to visit him Janet goes to "Carterhaugh,"[3] an enchanted place. The journey to the fairy castle in *The Wee Wee Man* is briefly recounted:

> *On we lap, and awa we rade,*
> *Till we came to yon bonny green;*
> *We lighted down for to bait our horse,*
> *And out there came a lady fine* [38 A 5].

> *On we lap, and awa we rade,*
> *Till we came to yon bonny ha,*
> *Where the roof was o the beaten gould,*
> *And the floor was o the cristal a'* [stanza 7].

B, C, and F give virtually the same reading, but in D and E there are not two stages in the journey.

One would like to include among ballad Otherworld journeys such an adventure as that related of Thorkill in the old story preserved by Saxo, a parallel to which York Powell finds in *Thomas Rymer*.[4] But for British balladry proper nothing much remains to be said of such journeys. Jamieson's story of Child Rowland, it is true, tells how a brother seeks out his sister in the land of giants, but this

---

[1] See *ibid.*, I, 328.   [2] *Ibid.*, p. 321 n.

[3] On "Carterhaugh" see *ibid.*, p. 340.

[4] Elton-Powell, *op. cit.*, pp. lxxiii ff. See also the voyage of Hadding, *ibid.*, p. lxviii, and that of Eric the Speech-wise, *ibid.*, p. lxxvi.

will be reserved for discussion under the locality and the nature of the Otherworld. In *Sweet William's Ghost* (77 B 11) Margret follows her dead lover "untill she came to a green forest" where she "lost the sight of him." In A, where the bones of the dead lover are "far beyond the sea," she followed the "dead corp" "a' the live-lang winter night." According to C 10, "She followed him high, she followed him low, till she came to yon church-yard." With this should be compared the incident in Burne's text of *The Wife of Usher's Well* (79). The ghost sons lead their mother along "a green road" "until they came to some far chaperine" where Jesus is.[1] The dead man, again, in *Sweet William's Ghost* (77 C 5) says that he has come "oer many's the rock and hill."

Reference should not be omitted here to the belief that the soul is accompanied or guided to the land of spirits, an idea current in savage eschatology.[2] This notion is borne out, possibly, by the "three hell-hounds" which in *Sweet William's Ghost* (77 C 13) are "waiting" the dead lover's "soul to keep."[3] In connection with the incident of the hound's licking the blood of the knight in the traditional medieval carol *Over Yonder's a Park*, G. R. S. Mead observes that "the dog is the sacred animal of death and guide to the underworld."[4] Medieval imagination in *Dives and Lazarus* (56 A 10, 12; B 11, 13), though not accountable for the "two angels out of heaven" which guide Lazarus to the better world, probably supplies the "two serpents out of hell" which lead Dives to his place in torment. In the Danish ballad *The Maid on the Pyre* two doves guide Eline, in dove form, to heaven; two ravens guide Ivar, in raven shape, to hell.[5] The same incident is found in the Danish song *The Murdered Wife*.[6] *True Thomas* (37), as we have observed, is conducted to the Otherworld by the fairy queen.

[1] Child, III, 514.
[2] See, for example, Moss, *op. cit.*, pp. 72 ff.
[3] On the dog as a guide to the land of spirits see Cox, *op. cit.*, p. 50.
[4] *Journal of the Folk-Song Society*, IV, 66.
[5] See translation, Prior, II, 62.   [6] See *ibid.*, p. 66.

Chapter IV

LOCALITY OF THE OTHERWORLD

⚜

THE ballad geography of spiritland is decidedly puzzling if one thinks of fixing a specific locality for the Otherworld of traditional song.[1] He who would map out this sphere of souls, fairies, and demons is confronted on every hand with only fragmentary descriptions. Moreover, these descriptions are likely to represent not a single faith but to give evidence of the rival claims of various beliefs. Some confusion arises, for example, from a frequent merging of Christian and pre-Christian ideas. Is the abode of the departed, or the land of elves and demons, associated with the forest; is it on a hill or mountain; is it subterranean, submarine, over the sea, or on an island; is it far away; is it terrestrial or celestial? A phrase, a line, a stanza, here and there in the ballads, occasionally several stanzas, enable us to answer all these questions in the affirmative but scarcely make us sure of our cosmographical bearings.

Nor is the situation improved by an allusion now and then to middle-earth. "Ancient myth from Germanic days still lurks in the reference to middle-earth, an alliterative phrase of 'Sir Cawline,'" says Gummere.[2] The eldrige king's lady grants (61, stanza 25) the superior prowess of Christian arms:

> "And hees neu_er_ come vpon Eldrige [Hill],
>> Him to sport, gamon, or play,
>> And to meete noe man of middle-earth
>> And _that_ liues on Christs his lay."

[1] On the locality of the Otherworld see Tylor, *Primitive Culture*, II, 59 ff.
[2] *Popular Ballad*, p. 302.

[121]

We find the same shred of myth in the "merry midd-larf" of Herd's *Sweet William's Ghost* (77 B 8), thanks to Professor Ker's explanation of this phrase as meaning "merry middle-earth":[1] "O cocks are crowing a merry midd-larf." Again we meet with it in the "medill-erthe" of the romance of *Thomas of Erceldoune* (stanza 27).[2] And the hero of Jamieson's story of Child Rowland is warned not to eat or drink in elfland, otherwise he will "never see middle-eard again."[3]

THE FOREST

To leave for a while the larger cosmic implications of the phrase "middle-earth," is there anything in balladry of the belief that the dead live on in the forest? We should, perhaps, distinguish here between ideas which attribute spirits to trees and the belief in tree metamorphosis, and should further recognize a distinction, on the one hand, between both these beliefs and, on the other hand, the notion that the forest—regardless, possibly, of animistic thought—is the Otherworld of departed spirits and is populated partly, at least, by emigration from the land of living men.[4] Tree-soul ideas have already been canvassed in this study, ideas illustrated, for instance, by the commonplace of plants that grow from the graves of lovers.[5] But at this point we may turn our attention to certain other vestiges in our traditional poetry of ancient tree cults. There are signs of tree worship in the old practice of swearing by trees. In point of sanctity the oak tree stood first in Europe, and something of its sacred character is evidenced by Glasgerion's oath "by oake and ashe and thorne." Such an oath meant that the sacred tree was touched by him who swore.[6] Let us give the passage in full (67 A 18):

---

[1] See *infra*, p. 250.   [2] Child, *Ballads*, I, 327.

[3] *Northern Antiquities*, p. 399.

[4] For primitive examples see Moss, *Life after Death in Oceania*, pp. 6, 19, 56, and *passim*.

[5] See *supra*, pp. 37 ff.   [6] See Child, II, 137.

Glasgerryon swore a full great othe,
By oake and ashe and thorne,
"Lady, I was neuer in your chamber
Sith the time that I was borne."

The murderess in *Young Hunting* (68 A 16 f.) turns right
and round about and swears now by the "corn" and now
by the "moon."[1] Like the oak and the thorn, the birch is
a sacred tree in balladry. It grows by the gates of paradise,
according to *The Wife of Usher's Well* (79).[2]

According to certain ballads—*Hind Etin* (41 A 4, B 3)
or *Tam Lin* (39), in many texts of this latter piece—the
forest is a tabooed place. Mortals who invade its sacred
precincts summon, by a peculiar form of trespass,[3] an enchanted person or some other power of the wood. Upon
the lady's having pulled a nut or broken the tree, to give
the episode as it occurs in *Hind Etin*, her supernatural
lover accosts her thus:

"O why pu ye the nut, the nut,
Or why brake ye the tree" [A 4]?

Andrew Lang finds a classic parallel for this incident in the
breaking of the bough in the grove of Diana.[4] But with
more of an eye to the ballad plot we may suggest another
explanation. There is a widespread belief, reflected in popular fictions, that smelling flowers or eating the fruit of
certain trees may cause pregnancy,[5] and our ballad instances, perhaps, a kindred notion in the incident of Margret's pulling the nuts in Hind Etin's wood, clearly a sacred
domain. It is interesting that under like circumstances the
maiden in *Tam Lin* plucks roses.[6]

Further evidence of an old tree cult may be adduced
from the parallel that our ballads afford to the practice

[1] For further instances of swearing by trees or other objects see *infra*, pp. 362 f.
[2] See *infra*, pp. 155 ff.   [3] See *infra*, pp. 314 ff.
[4] "Breaking the Bough in the Grove of Diana," *Folk-Lore*, XVIII, 89-91.
[5] See Hartland, *Perseus*, I, 95 ff.; cf. Gummere, *Popular Ballad*, p. 387.
[6] See *infra*, pp. 150 f., 314 f.

among Swedish women of twining their arms about the "guardian-tree" in order to insure easy delivery in the pangs of childbirth.[1] The practice in question occurs in *The Cruel Mother* (20):

> *She leaned her back unto a thorn,*
> *Three, three, and three by three*
> *And there she has her two babes born.*
> *Three, three, and thirty-three* [C 1]

B 1 reads: "down below a thorn"; D 3: "set her back untill an oak, first it bowed and then it broke"; E 3, 4: "unto a tree," "unto a thorn" (cf. F 3, 4; G 2); H 2, 3: "foot to a tree," "to a stone"; I 4, J 1: "her back against a thorn"; O 4, 5, 6: "against a tree," "an oak," "a thorne." At the expense of digressing we must mention in this connection the sole instance of the couvade in British balladry. The heroine of *Fair Janet* (64 F 7) undergoes strange travail at the "top o yon greenwood tree." She directs her lover as follows:

> *"Ye'll do me up, and further up,*
> *To the top o yon greenwood tree;*
> *For every pain myself shall hae,*
> *The same pain ye maun drie."*

There is a hint of the couvade in B 6. Fair Margret in one text of *Tam Lin* (39 D 5) is said to "climb . . . . the tree" in the enchanted wood.

The enchanted forest brings to mind the "Silver Wood" in *Jellon Grame* (90 A 1) and *Child Maurice* (83 A 1), in both of which songs there is a hint of the supernatural.[2] And one thinks, too, of certain ballads in which metamorphosed beings are associated in one way or another with a tree. The hair of the enchanted girl in *Kemp Owyne* (34) is

---

[1] See Bugge, *Studien über die Entstehung der nordischen Götter- und Heldensagen* (trans. O. Brenner), p. 543.

[2] A number of ballads that do not pass for ballads of the supernatural are found, under careful scrutiny, to have traces of fairy machinery; for example, Nos. 63 and 76.

"twisted thrice about the tree." The youth in *Allison Gross* (35) is turned into an "ugly worm" and must "toddle about the tree." Another youth, in *The Laily Worm* (36), becomes a "laily worm" and must lie "at the fit o the tree." *The Marriage of Sir Gawain* (31) tells of an enchanted lady who sits "betwixt an oke and a greene hollen." The lady in *Sir Lionel* (18 A, C), a song which sings of supernatural doings, is found in the top of a tree, but the tree in this instance may be merely a place of refuge.

But superstitions about guardian trees, wood spirits or demons, and sacred groves should not be too confidently adduced as evidence of the belief that the future life is connected with the forest. There are spirits and spirits, and so it is well to furnish what looks like more direct proof of the idea in question. Confusion of beliefs in *Sweet William's Ghost* grants the dead a future life in as well as beyond the grave,[1] and in addition, to come to the matter in hand, offers a hint of a forest Otherworld. The revenant disappears in "a green forest":

> *It's hose an shoon an gound alane*
> *She clame the wall and followed him,*
> *Untill she came to a green forest,*
> *On this she lost the sight of him* [77 B 11].

The next stanza shows her at the grave. As in the foregoing ballad, the revenant in *Clerk Saunders* (69 G 35) vanishes in the forest:

> *And in the midst o gude greenwood,*
> *'T was there she lost the sight o him.*

But the incident of the ghostly visit at the end of this version is a blending of *Proud Lady Margaret* with *Sweet William's Ghost*.[2] Of more significance here is that "green road" spoken of in a Shropshire text of *The Wife of Usher's Well*. Along this road the ghost sons lead their mother.

[1] See *supra*, p. 100.
[2] Cf. Child, II, 156.

The white cock has crowed, so has the red, and it is "high time for the wicked to part from their dead":

> *Then they laid* [=*led*] *her along a green road,*[1]
> *The greenest that ever was seen,*
> *Until they came to some far chaperine,*[2]
> *Which was builded of lime and sand;*
> *Until they came to some far chaperine,*
> *Which was builded with lime and stone.*[3]

> *And then he opened the door so big,*
> *And the door so very wide;*
> *Said he to her three sons, Walk in!*
> *But told her to stay outside* [79 C].

In *Hind Etin* (41 C 12) the son requests his mother, who has been the bride of an elf, to go with her children to some kirk: "You say they are built of stane."

The "far chaperine" and the "green road" of *The Wife of Usher's Well* bring to mind the "hall" "down in yon forest" of a Derbyshire version of the traditional medieval carol *Over Yonder's a Park*, or the "hall" and the "park" of another copy of this song, the park symbolizing, it is very probable, a paradise of trees.[4] The Derbyshire text reads:

> *Down in yon forest there stands a hall,*
> (*The bells of paradise I heard them ring.*)
> *It's covered all over with purple so tall*
> (*And I love my Lord Jesus above any thing.*)[5]

---

[1] *Ibid.*, III, 514.

[2] In *ibid.*, V, 322, Child says: "would make some sense as chapel, but the form is unaccountable except as a popular diminutive." "The West and South Shropshire folk say *far* for *fair*," observes Burne (*Shropshire Folk-Lore*, p. 541).

[3] Miss Burne (*loc. cit.*) refers, respecting the "lime and stone" of our ballad, to a note (*ibid.*, p. 427) which reads in part: "Dwellings of masonry, 'well builded with stone and lime,' are still called 'white houses' in the islands of Lewis and Harris, as distinguished from the 'black houses' of unhewn 'dry-stone' work and sods." There is a house of "lime and stone" in No. 108, stanza 15.

[4] *Journal of the Folk-Song Society*, IV, 66.

[5] *Ibid.*, p. 63.

Corpus Christi, preserved "in a late 14th to early 15th century MS. in Balliol College Library," has "In that orchard
there was an halle." Into this orchard "brown," according
to preceding stanzas, "the faucon hath born my make
away."[1]

These few hints of a ghost realm in the forest have, perhaps, received undue consideration, but we should not dismiss the subject without recalling that ballad elves and
other supernatural folk dwell in the forest. This has already
been indicated by the sacred-tree superstitions given in the
preceding pages, and we have also made reference to the
"Silver Wood" of *Jellon Grame* (90 A) and *Child Maurice*
(83 A). The elf-lover in *Hind Etin* (41 A) carries his bride
into "Elmond's (Elfman?) wood"; according to B, into
"Mulberry wud"; C, "wood o Amonshaw"; according to a
Gavin Greig variant, into "Elwin's wood."[2] In *Tam Lin*
(39) the heroine meets her fairy-lover in the sacred or enchanted wood. A giant and a terrible boar dwell in the
"wood o Tore" or "forrest" in *Sir Lionel* (18 B, A). The
witch stepmother in *Kemp Owyne* (34 B 17 f.) is changed
into a monstrous, four-footed beast, and "in Wormie's
Wood she sall ay won." "Like a feend of hell" the transformed lady in *The Marriage of Sir Gawain* (31, stanza
47) has had to live in the "greene forrest." The home of
the elves, according to various texts of *The Wee Wee Man*
(38), is on a "bonny green" or in a "bonny glen." The
association of the apple tree with fairy capture is discussed
in detail in our chapter on modes of enchantment. The
forest habitation of these supernatural folk is worthy of
mention in connection with ghostland by reason of the
widespread confusion of ghost and fairy beliefs. It is well
known that in Scandinavia the dead were formerly called
"elves."

THE UNDERGROUND REALM

However problematic the forest realm of spirits, the
ballads, if we may again consult *Thomas Rymer*, give clear

[1] *Ibid.*, p. 53. [2] *Folk-Song of the North-East*, art. CLVII.

evidence of a subterranean Otherworld. It is a land sunless and moonless, with underground rivers of blood or water, a land where is heard the roaring of the sea, a country which answers in important particulars to Guthmund's realm of Saxo's story.[1] Belief in a subterranean Otherworld is, of course, prevalent among lower races.[2] Such an underworld Thomas and the fairy queen traverse until they come to a "garden green" or, according to the romance, a "faire herbere." But the garden is a sort of paradise and must await discussion with other ballad Elysiums.[3] The ballad picture of this lower world is gloomy enough:

> *For forty days and forty nights*
> *He wade thro red blude to the knee,*
> *And he saw neither sun nor moon,*
> *But heard the roaring of the sea* [37 A 7].

The crossing takes only three days in the romance (stanza 31).[4] The river of "blude" is found in version C also, but is found neither in text B nor in the romance, which have "water" simply. The romance reads (stanza 31): "herd bot swoghynge of" the flood. C 15, like A, describes the region as being without sun or moon, and in addition (stanza 16) says: "It was mirk mirk night, and there was nae stern light." The romance (stanza 30) reads: "dirke as mydnyght myrke."

So far as Germanic fancy pictured an underworld of sorrow and gloom,—not, of course, of pain or of punishment,—it was a world of cold and cheerless waters: a "water-hell," men have named it. In the Old English ballad of Thomas the Rymer, or Thomas of Ercildoune, we hear of these chill and gloomy waters.[5]

The "devil's mere" in *Beowulf* belongs to the same tradition.[6] Like Thomas' underworld, the enchanted wood in

---

[1] Elton-Powell, *Saxo*, pp. 344 ff.; see also Thorkill's second voyage, *ibid.*, pp. 351 ff.

[2] See Tylor, *op. cit.*, II, 65.   [3] *Infra*, pp. 153 ff.

[4] On Thomas' journey see *supra*, pp. 109, 116 ff.

[5] Gummere, *Popular Ballad*, pp. 36 f.

[6] Cf. Gummere's note in his *The Oldest English Epic*, p. 59 n.

Tam Lin (39 G 10)—a Buchan text—is without either sun
or moon:

> *Seven days she tarried there,*
> *Saw neither sun nor meen.*

So, too, the realm of the giant in the Danish song *Rosmer*
is lighted neither by sun nor moon. To the hero, whom he
has carried back to earth, the giant says:

> *"And now I've borne thee to thy home,*
> *The land of sun and moon."*[1]

Of this underground realm, we catch, after leaving the
foregoing ballads, only a hint here and there in British
folksong. In the incident of the ballad revenant's return
to the grave,[2] English and Scottish folksong makes record,
perhaps, of the first stage of the belief in a general subterranean abode of the dead. And the heathen point of view
is insistent enough—to fall back again upon *Thomas Rymer*
—in this ballad's indiscriminate localization underground
of the old Norse water-hell, the oversea paradise of trees
and birds, elfland itself, and the Christian heaven and
hell.[3] Again, through the crowing of the cock in *Sweet William's Ghost* (77) and *The Wife of Usher's Well* (79), a signal
for the departure of the dead to the world of spirits, we may
perhaps restore to our tradition a land of gloom comparable
to, if not identical with, the Norse Niflheim or Hel.[4] The
practice of cave-burial, which is reflected in the Danish
ballad *Young Swennendal*, a piece which also illustrates
definitely the idea that the dead live on in their barrows, is
interesting in view of the belief in an underground or cave

[1] Prior, III, 56.

[2] See *supra*, pp. 101 ff.; *infra*, pp. 251 ff.

[3] On the Christian and pagan elements in *Thomas Rymer* (37) see Meyer-
Nutt, *Voyage of Bran*, II, 226; Andrew Lang, *A Collection of Ballads*, p. 232;
Josephine M. Burnham, "A Study of Thomas of Erceldoune," *PMLA*, XXIII,
393, 411, and *passim*.

[4] See *infra*, pp. 248 ff.

afterworld.[1] To consult his dead mother, the hero goes to Goliat cave where she lies buried.[2]

The underground or cave Otherworld is, of course, strikingly evidenced by the hill-haunting proclivities of elfin folk. "The elphin knight sits on yon hill," according to numerous texts of *The Elfin Knight* (2). Tam Lin (39 A 23) goes to dwell in a "green hill." In foreign analogues of *Hind Etin* (41) it is to a hill that the dwarf king lures a mortal woman.[3] The home of the elves in these pieces is obviously within rather than on the hill. The fairies of Scotland "inhabit the interior of green hills, chiefly those of a conical form, in Gaelic termed *Sighan*, ..."[4] In the romance of *Thomas of Erceldoune* the fairy guide leads Thomas "in at Eldone hill";[5] and Sir Cawline (61, stanza 25) fights the elf king on Eldrige Hill. The "gyant" (18 A 35) lies under "yond low." In *The Broomfield Hill* (43) magic is practiced on a hill. The Norse ballad *Peter Gudmanson and the Dwarfs* sings of trolls who live in a mountain cave:

> *The knight Sir Peter Gudmanson*
> *Enter'd the mountain cave,*
> *And up to meet him rose the dwarf*
> *And a hearty welcome gave.*[6]

Searching for his sister in the Otherworld or the land of dwarfs, Child Rowland of Jamieson's tale finds her within a green hill.[7] Likewise, the hero of the analogous Danish ballad *Rosmer* discovers the object of his quest in a mountain cave, but the cave here is to be thought of, apparently, as beneath the sea.[8] *King Orfeo* (19) tells a story of fairy capture. The king goes to find his stolen queen:

[1] See, for example, Cox, *Introduction to Folk-Lore*, p. 182; Moss, *op. cit.*, pp. 34 ff.

[2] See *supra*, p. 106.

[3] See Child, I, 361 ff.

[4] Scott, *Minstrelsy* (ed. Henderson), II, 352.

[5] Child, I, 327.   [6] Prior, III, 201.   [7] *Op. cit.*, p. 398.

[8] See translations, Prior, III, 52 ff.

And aifter dem da king has gaen,
But whan he cam it was a grey stane.

Our ballad, whether or not it be a *précis* of the medieval romance of Sir Orpheo, gives, at least, the chief incident of that story. And the "grey stane" of the ballad is unquestionably the "roche" of the romance. Into this roche Sir Orpheo follows the fairy train:

In then at the roche the ladies ryde,
He went sone after, he nolde not byde,
When he was into the roche ygo.[1]

The earthly mistress in *Hind Etin* (41) dwells in a cave "monie fathoms deep," a cave "howkit" by her fairy-lover (B 7), or (C 9) for ten long years she dwells with her elfin husband in "the cave of stane." With this may be compared the "vault o stone" in which Prince Heathen (104 B 7) confines his mistress, though it is not certain that the lover here is supernatural. The mountain dwarfs or elves in the Danish song *Trolden og Bondens Hustru* question the right of the farmer to lay waste their wood:

He hew'd him balks, he hew'd him beams,
With eager toil and haste;
"Who," ask'd the Elves in the mountain cave,
Who's come our wood to waste?"[2]

Another Danish ballad, *Hr. Tönne af Alsö*, tells a story of a dwarf maiden who, with her parents, lives in a mountain cave:

"My father dwells in mountain cave
His courtiers round him stand;
My mother dwells there too and plays
With gold in lily hand."[3]

[1] Ll. 333. For a discussion of the matters in this romance see the article by G. L. Kittredge, *American Journal of Philology*, VII, 176 ff.

[2] Prior, III, 166.

[3] *Ibid.*, p. 11. Cf. Keightley's translation of the better Swedish version (*Fairy Mythology*, p. 97).

The dwarf king of the Norse song *Jomfruen og Dvaerge-kongen* carries a mortal maid into his mountain cavern. We have already taken note of the cave in the analogous British piece *Hind Etin* (41 B, C).

> *She lived in his cave eight years or more,*
> *And there to the Dwarf seven sons she bore.*[1]

So, too, in the related Scandinavian ballad *Agnete og Havmanden* Agnes goes to live in a mountain cave with her supernatural lover.[2] In other versions of this piece, however, the lover, like the giant in *Rosmer*, dwells beneath the sea.[3]

THE MOUNTAIN OTHERWORLD

In both *Thomas Rymer* (37) and *The Daemon Lover* (243) the Otherworld seems to be thought of as situated on a mountain or hill. In the former, as well as in the latter piece, we find an ethical division of the Otherworld.[4] Carried out over the sea by her demon- or ghost-lover, the earthly mistress in *The Daemon Lover* (243 F 12 f.) is promised a sight of "the lilies" that "grow on the banks of Italy"; she ceases her weeping to ask:

> *"O what hills are yon, yon pleasant hills,*
> *That the sun shines sweetly on?"*
> *"O yon are the hills of heaven," he said,*
> *"Where you will never win."*
>
> *"O whaten a mountain is yon," she said,*
> *"All so dreary wi frost and snow?"*
> *"O yon is the mountain of hell," he cried,*
> *"Where you and I will go."*

A sort of Zoroastrian dualism—this in a Motherwell text (E)—pictures the hill of heaven as "bright," that of hell as "black, dark." These descriptions accord with those in American variants, although in one American text, at

---

[1] Prior, III, 339.   [2] *Ibid.*, pp. 335 ff.   [3] See *ibid.*, pp. 332 ff.

[4] " . . . . It may be urged that dualism is foreign to the spirit of Germanic heathendom" (Gummere, *Germanic Origins*, p. 479).

least, the hills have vaporized into clouds. A version in the *Journal of American Folk-Lore*[1] makes the hills of heaven as "white as snow"; the hills of hell "low and dark." A Campbell and Sharp variant reads: "banks of Heaven" as "white as any snow"; "banks of hell" as "black as any crow."[2] Another Campbell and Sharp text gives "cloud" instead of "hill": "Yon light cloud arising as light as any snow" is the "place called heaven"; "yon dark cloud arising as dark as any crow" is the "place called hell."[3]

The more impressive "mountain" of hell, "so dreary wi frost and snow"—as pictured in Child's version F—is in all probability a creation of the Norse imagination. It recalls, of course, the thick-ribbed ice of the innermost circle of Dante's Inferno, but as an arctic hell is akin also to those icy regions traversed by Thorkill in Saxo's story of Gormo's visit to Guthmund.[4] There is, perhaps, observes Gummere, "a shred of myth left in the description of a 'mountain . . . . dreary wi' frost and snow' which the Demon Lover declares to be his proper abode."[5] But British balladry itself, through one of Scott's versions of *Thomas Rymer* (37), offers us something of a parallel to the arctic hell of *The Daemon Lover*. That road which leads "straight to the pit o hell" lies "out-owr yon frosty fell" or hill:

> "*But do you see yon road, Thomas,*
> *That lies out-owr yon frosty fell?*
> *Ill is the man yon gate may gang,*
> *For it leads him straight to the pit o hell.*"[6]

"That leadeth down by yon skerry fell" (rocky hill) is the reading in B 10. In the romance of *Thomas of Erceldoune* the road to heaven (stanza 38) leads over yon "heghe mountayne"; the fairy's castle (stanza 42) is on a "heghe

---

[1] XX, 257.

[2] *English Folk Songs from the Southern Appalachians*, p. 121.

[3] *Ibid.*, p. 120.

[4] See Elton-Powell, *op. cit.*, p. 353.

[5] *Popular Ballad*, p. 302.   [6] Child, IV, 455, stanza 15.

hill." According to one of Scott's texts of *Tam Lin* (39 M 4 f.), eight stanzas of which (4–12) belong to *Thomas Rymer*, the Otherworld orchard is within a wall "upon a mountain's bree."[1]

THE UNDERSEA REALM

Analogous to the subterranean Otherworld is the land under the waves. Merfolk, both male and female, assure for British popular song the tradition of a submarine region peopled with beings who ascend now and then to the upper world for commerce with mortals. Mermaidens play a rôle in *Clerk Colvill* (42), *Sir Patrick Spens* (58), *The Mermaid* (289), *Kemp Owyne* (34), and *The Laily Worm* (36).[2] *The Great Silkie of Sule Skerry* (113) furnishes an excellent example of the seal-lover superstition. A copy of this piece—a version better than Child's—is recorded by Frank Sidgwick in his *Popular Ballads of the Olden Time:*

> *In Norway lands there lived a maid,*
> *"Hush, ba, loo lillie," this maid began;*
> *"I know not where my baby's father is,*
> *Whether by land or sea does he travel in."*
>
> *It happened on a certain day,*
> *When this fair lady fell fast asleep,*
> *That in cam' a good grey selchie,*
> *And set him doon at her bed feet,*
>
> *Saying, "Awak', awak', my pretty fair maid,*
> *For oh! how sound as thou dost sleep!*
> *An' I'll tell thee where thy baby's father is;*
> *He's sittin' close at thy bed feet."*
>
> *"I pray, come tell to me thy name,*
> *Oh! tell me where does thy dwelling be?"*
> *"My name it is good Hein Mailer,*
> *An' I earn my livin' oot o' the sea.*

---

[1] On medieval conceptions of the mountain Otherworld see Patch, "Mediaeval Descriptions of the Otherworld," *PMLA*, XXXIII, 611.

[2] On the character and activities of merfolk see *infra*, pp. 286 f., 326 f.

"I am a man upon the land;
I am a selchie in the sea;
An' whin I'm far frae every strand
My dwellin' is in Shool Skerrie."[1]

Another important supernatural ballad, *The Queen of Elfan's Nourice* (40), places the home of the "elf man" under the sea—this according to a version recovered since Child:

"Come, nurse an elf child, elf child, elf child,
Come an' nurse an elf child,
Down 'neath the sea."[2]

It is noteworthy that the elf man of this story is said to be little, a matter for discussion under the attributes of the ballad fairy.[3] Again, as evidential of the undersea Otherworld, we may cite the Danish ballad *Agnete og Havmanden*, a song analogous in certain of its principal features to our *Hind Etin* (41). An earthly maiden bears seven children to her sea-lover beneath the waves:

Her ears he stopp'd, and her mouth he stopp'd,
And down to the bottom of ocean dropp'd.

Eight years she dwelt with the Merman there,
And under the sea seven children bare.[4]

The story of Agnes and the merman occurs also in Swedish and Norwegian balladry, as well as in German songs, from which the Norse forms of the tale were derived. It is found, moreover, in a Wendish song and, with modifications, in a Slovenian ballad.[5]

Prior thinks that the British ballad *The Daemon Lover* (243) has the "same tale" as the Danish song *Agnete og*

---

[1] *Op. cit.* (2d ser.), pp. 235 ff., from R. Menzies Fergusson, *Rambling Sketches in the Far North and Orcadian Musings* (1883), pp. 140 f.

[2] See *infra*, pp. 326 f.   [4] Prior, III, 332.

[3] *Infra*, pp. 172 f.   [5] See Child, I, 364 ff.

Havmanden,[1] but Child says nothing to this effect. The British song is not, however, clear as to the exact nature of the Otherworld lover,[2] nor does it give us a satisfactory idea of the land to which the ghost, demon, or ordinary seaman transports his mistress. It may be that Prior is right. It is true that the demon, by reason of some intrusion of Christian belief, carries his lady within sight of the hills of heaven and hell, but that he then (E 18, F 15) sinks his ship in "a flash of fire" to the "bottom of the sea" seems to bear out Prior's conclusion. In D 8 the lover promises to show his mistress "whare the white lillies grow, in the bottom of the sea." It is interesting that in certain points *The Daemon Lover* resembles *Thomas Rymer* (37). According to each ballad, a human traveler, conducted by an Otherworld guide, comes within sight of heaven and hell or the roads thereto. In the latter song the fairy shows Thomas "ferlies three"; in the former ballad (E 18) the demon takes the maiden "up to the topmast high, to see what she could see." First-rate evidence of an under-the-ocean realm comes from the Danish *Rosmer*, a ballad which closely parallels Jamieson's tale of Child Rowland.[3] In the Danish song the hero's ship sinks to the undersea realm of merfolk, and the hero gropes his way from the wreck to begin his submarine adventure:

> *Childe Roland left the sunken wreck,*
> *And groped along the ground,*
> *And leading towards Eline's bower*
> *A little pathway found.*[4]

THE NORTH AS THE ABODE OF EVIL SPIRITS

The oversea or island Otherworld, evidence of which we have already given in the chapter on the Otherworld journey,[5] will be further illustrated in the following chap-

---

[1] *Ancient Danish Ballads*, III, 329 f.

[2] See *infra*, p. 258.

[3] Jamieson, *op. cit.*, pp. 398 ff.

[4] Prior, III, 57.

[5] *Supra*, pp. 108 ff.

ter on characteristics of the fairy realm and so need not detain us here. In concluding our discussion of the localization of the land of souls and of fairies, we may raise the question as to whether or not balladry reflects the belief that the north is the abode of evil spirits. The north, it seems, became a place of devils rather than of gods after the introduction of Christianity among Germanic people. In the *Freres Tale* of Chaucer the fiend (in disguise) says that he dwells "in the north contree."[1]

Brand observes that burial on the north side of the church is unlucky: "It is that that is the part appropriated for the interment of unbaptised infants, of persons excommunicated, or that have been executed, or that have laid violent hands upon themselves."[2] The foregoing superstition is possibly reflected in certain Norse ballads which preserve the incident of the loving plants. In these songs the graves of the sweethearts are made north and south in the churchyard.[3] Like Chaucer's fiend, the supernatural wooer in *Lady Isabel and the Elf-Knight* (4 E 1) is an "outlandish knight" from the "north lands." In other versions, however, he is said to come (D 1) from the "south country," (D c) from the "west countrie."[4] But, again, according to version F, he hails from the "north land." So, too, in texts recorded in the *Journal of the Folk-Song Society* he is "an outlandish Knight from the northlands."[5] His home is in the same quarter, according to a version given in *Folk-Songs from Somerset*.[6] In a variant which I recovered recently from a Nebraska singer[7] the false knight promises

---

[1] For Chaucer's fiend and other instances as pointing to the north as the abode of evil spirits, see Gummere, *Germanic Origins*, p. 418 n.

[2] *Popular Antiquities*, II, 292.

[3] See Child, I, 96; II, 498.

[4] *Ibid.*, I, 62.

[5] II, 282.

[6] *Op. cit.* (4th ser.), p. 14.

[7] Mrs. Mary Bruun, Humboldt, Nebraska; heard when a child in Pennsylvania.

to carry "Polly" "down to the merry green lands." Miss Gilchrist gives an interesting account of the false knight's character:

> Though the main idea of the "Outlandish Knight" is founded upon an oral tradition widely spread in many European countries, the knight himself, in these English forms of the story, seems to be a lineal descendant—divested of supernatural attributes—of the malevolent water-spirit ("havmand") of Scandinavian ballads, who in the enchanted guise of a white knight weds a young girl that he may drag her down to his home beneath the sea-waves. When the supernatural character of this water-spirit became lost, the conception of his submarine dwelling would also be lost, and the girl engulfed beneath the waves would naturally be supposed to be drowned. But a suggestion of the northern source of our ballad survives, I think, in the "north lands" from which the "outlandish" stranger comes forth on his evil quest.[1]

The riddle-mongering wooer—a fiend disguised—in *Riddles Wisely Expounded* (1 A 2) "lived in the North."[2] *Allison Gross* (35, stanza 1) is "the ugliest witch i the north country." And it is interesting that the demon-lover's (243 F 14) "mountain of hell" is "dreary wi frost and snow,"[3] another possible vestige of the belief that evil spirits dwell in the north lands:

> *"O whaten a mountain is yon," she said,*
> *"All so dreary wi frost and snow?"*
> *"O yon is the mountain of hell," he cried,*
> *"Where you and I will go."*

[1] *Journal of the Folk-Song Society*, IV, 123. On the supernatural traits of the knight in No. 4 see my article, "Two Traditional Ballads," *American Speech*, III, 114–18.

[2] On the preternatural character of the knight in this song see *infra*, pp. 301 f.

[3] See *supra*, pp. 132 f.

Chapter V

DESCRIPTIONS OF THE OTHERWORLD

THE preceding chapters on the Otherworld journey and the locality of the land of spirits as beneath the earth, under the waves, in a hill, or on a mountain have anticipated in part certain of the following descriptions of the Otherworld. This chapter will concern itself chiefly with the realm of spirits as an abode of bliss, an Elysian state, which seems to derive its elements from, or finds, at least, a close analogue in, the oversea paradise of Celtic tradition, and answers in general to medieval depictions of the realm of happiness[1] or, for that matter, to aspects of the Otherworld as portrayed in savage beliefs.[2] The ballads depict, too, a cheerless and gloomy Underworld, a land without sun or moon, and they also give a hint of an arctic hell, but these realms have been considered in the foregoing pages.

Ballad traditions instance, as we have already observed, the usual confusion in the localization of Elysium or fairyland, placing it underground, under the sea, over the sea, or picturing it as coextensive with this world.[3] One would not be overconfident in evaluating the ballad evidence, but it appears likely that *Thomas Rymer* (37) has combined the idea of an oversea land of bliss with that of a subterranean paradise. Thomas' entire journey, it seems, is confined to an underground sphere, but before reaching the

[1] See Patch, "Mediaeval Descriptions of the Otherworld," *Publications of the Modern Language Association*, XXXIII, 604 f.

[2] See "Blest, The Abode of the," *Encyclopaedia of Religion and Ethics*, Vol. II.

[3] Cf. Celtic traditions, MacCulloch, *Religion of the Ancient Celts*, pp. 362 ff., and medieval traditions generally, Patch, *op. cit., passim.*

"garden green" of the ballad or the "faire herbere" of the romance the hero has to wade through rivers of blood or water. The ballad of *The Daemon Lover* (243) seems to confuse its oversea mountains of heaven and hell with a land beneath the waves.[1] According to different versions of the Danish *Rosmer*—a piece with Scottish affiliations through Jamieson's story of Child Rowland—the home of the troll is beyond or beneath the sea.[2]

We are rid of such confusion, however, in the opening stanza of *Leesome Brand* (15), one of our finest traditional songs, in which appears very distinctly the island paradise of the Danish *Ribold and Guldborg*, a ballad to be considered presently. Again, by virtue of certain foreign parallels to our *Lady Isabel and the Elf-Knight* (4) and *The Fair Flower of Northumberland* (9), English balladry may be said to hold proprietary rights in the Elysian fields. We might, of course, rest the case strictly with our own folksong and find that *Thomas Rymer* (37), *Sweet William's Ghost* (77), *The Wife of Usher's Well* (79), *The Daemon Lover* (243), and other supernatural pieces go no little way toward furnishing those elements which characterize the pagan abode of bliss, those features of a happy Otherworld which answers in part, at least, to the Celtic oversea paradise with its flowers, its trees, its birds, its music, and its beautiful women.

Tam Lin, an "elfin grey," vouches for the joys of elfland:

> "*Full pleasant is the fairy land,*
> *And happy there to dwell*" [39 C 4].

Or D 15: "The Elfins is a pretty place in which I love to dwell"; G 28: "O Elfin it's a bonny place, in it fain woud I dwell"; I 32: "Then would I never tire, Janet, in Elfish land to dwell."[3] He gives similar testimony in A 24, B 23, but in all variants says that the fairies, according to cus-

[1] See *supra*, pp. 135 f.

[2] *Supra*, p. 136.

[3] On the activities of fairies see *infra*, pp. 189 ff.

tom, must at the end of every seven years pay a tithe to hell.[1]

The Danish ballad *Ribold and Guldborg*, "a jewel that any clime might envy,"[2] gives depiction to an island paradise, a hint of which is found in *Leesome Brand* (15):

> *My boy was scarcely ten years auld,*
> *Whan he went to an unco land,*
> *Where wind never blew, nor cocks ever crew,*
> *Ohon for my son, Leesome Brand* [A 1].

The fairy in *Thomas Rymer* (37 B 4) calls herself "a lady of an unco land," and the heroine in a Greig text of *The Lass of Roch Royal* (76)[3]—a ballad containing supernatural traits—would seek her love in "an unco lan'." *Ribold and Guldborg* gives us more than a mere glimpse of this strange country. Ribold, a king's son, has sought Guldborg's love in secret. He promises to bear her to a land where enters neither death nor sorrow, a land where all the birds are cuckoos, the grass is leeks, and all the streams run wine:[4]

> *"Guldborg, will ye plight your troth to me,*
> *And I'll till a better land bring thee.*

> *"Till a better land I will thee bear,*
> *Whare there never comes or dule or care.*

> *"I will bring thee untill an öe*
> *Whare thou sall live and nagate die."*[5]

Guldborg, with, perhaps, Christian compunction, fears that her true-love cannot bear her to such an "öe" or

---

[1] See *infra*, pp. 323 ff.

[2] Child, *Ballads*, I, 88.

[3] Greig, *Last Leaves*, p. 61 (version B).

[4] Cf. Child, *op. cit.*, I, 89; see also Bugge, *Home of the Eddic Poems*, pp. 315 f.

[5] Translation by Jamieson, *Northern Antiquities*, pp. 324 f. Danish G is also translated by Prior, *Ancient Danish Ballads*, II, 400.

island, for to God she owes that she "should die." To this
Ribold responds by describing certain other pleasures of
his paradise:

> *"There leeks are the only grass that springs,*
> *And the gowk is the only bird that sings;*

> *"There a' the water that rins is wine:*
> *Ye well may trow this tale o' mine."*[1]

The several features of Ribold's paradise, with its perpetual spring, will be considered farther on in connection with
the streams, the flowers, and the birds of the Otherworld.[2]

At this point it will be well to give Child's conclusions
respecting the presence of the wonderland in *Leesome
Brand* and that in *Ribold and Guldborg*. It should be observed to begin with that the latter song finds its British
analogue in *Earl Brand* and not in *Leesome Brand*. Child
says:

> Though the paradise has not been transmitted in any known copy
> of "Earl Brand," it appears very distinctly in the opening stanza of
> "Leesome Brand" A. This last has several stanzas towards the close
> (33–35) which seem to belong to "Earl Brand," and perhaps derived
> these, the "unco land," and even its name, by the familiar process of
> intermixture of traditions.[3]

Then, as regards the origin of the paradise in *Ribold and
Guldborg*, Child remarks:

> The paradise promised Guldborg in all the old versions of 82 disap-
> pears from the recited copies, except K, M. It certainly did not original-
> ly belong to "Ribold and Guldborg," or to another Danish ballad in
> which it occurs ("Den trofaste Jomfru," Grundtvig, 249 A), but rather
> to ballads like "Kvindemorderen," Grundtvig, 183 A, or "Líti Kersti,"
> Landstad, 44, where a supernatural being, a demon or a hillman, seeks
> to entice away a mortal maid. See No. 4, p. 27.[4]

The "No. 4" to which Child refers is our *Lady Isabel and
the Elf-Knight*. This song with its continental analogues
we may now take up.

[1] This ballad land of immortals recalls Ódáinsakr in the Hervarar saga (cf.
Prior, *op. cit.*, II, 405).

[2] *Infra*, pp. 153, 159 f.   [3] *Op. cit.*, I, 90 n.   [4] *Ibid.*, p. 90.

As we have already observed, there are other foreign ballads which, like *Ribold and Guldborg*, tell of a far-come lover who offers to bear his mistress to a paradise exempt from death and sorrow. Certain of these songs, by virtue of their affiliation with English and Scottish traditional poetry, bring within the domain of our ballads the conception of a happy Otherworld. The lover in *Lady Isabel and the Elf-Knight*, as well as in the continental variants of this piece, is clearly supernatural.[1] "Though the lady is not lured away in the Scandinavian ballads by irresistible music, Danish A, E, Norwegian A, B, and Swedish D present to her the prospect of being taken to an elf-land, or elysium, and there are traces of this in Danish G and D also, and in Polish Q."[2] In Polish Q the lover tells the maiden that in his country "the mountains are golden, the mountains are of gold, the ways of silk, ..."[3] In Magyar D "reappears the very important feature of the wonderland: 'Come, let us go, Anna Miller, a long journey into the wilderness, to a place that flows with milk and honey.'" According to Magyar A, the knight has seven palaces; according to C, six stone castles and is building a seventh.[4] Golovatsky has a ballad in which the wonderland is similar to that in the Polish version of *Lady Isabel and the Elf-Knight*. A Cossack invites a maid to accompany him to the Ukraine. "Our land," he says, "is not like this: . . . . with us the willows bear pears and the girls go in gold."[5]

English and Scottish folk-poetry may be said to have further acquaintance with the happy Otherworld conception by reason of the connection of *The Fair Flower of Northumberland* (9) with the Danish *Den trofaste Jomfru* and with the Swedish and Norwegian variants of this latter piece.[6] The similarity between the Scandinavian

[1] *Ibid.*, pp. 49 f.
[2] *Ibid.*, p. 49.
[3] *Ibid.*, p. 41.
[4] *Ibid.*, p. 46.
[5] *Ibid.*, p. 487. Cf. other Russian variants cited by Child at the foregoing reference; cf. also II, 496 f.

[6] The Norse ballads treat briefly the theme of the English romance *The Nutbrown Maid*, and resemble only in part *The Fair Flower of Northumberland*.

ballads and our *Child Waters* (63) must not be overlooked, a matter to be discussed shortly. As in the foreign analogues of *Lady Isabel and the Elf-Knight*, so in these Norse songs, a knight woos a maiden by making her splendid promises of a land of gold castles, an incident which recalls the demon-lover's promise (243) to show his mistress where the lilies grow on the banks of Italy or his promise to give her (B 7 f.) slippers of "beaten gold" and a "gilded boat."[1] The gold castles of the Norse songs bespeak more clearly, however, a land of wonders, a land which in certain texts proves to be a reality:

A knight carries off a maid on his horse, making her magnificent promises, among which are eight gold castles, Dan. C, D, E, H, I; one, K, L, M; eight, Norw. A; nine, Norw. B; seven, Swed. B; seven gold mountains, Swed. A., perhaps, by mistake of ber*gen* for bor*gar*.[2]

The possibility that *Child Waters* (63) may have been originally a fairy ballad is discussed briefly by Dr. W. M. Hart in his *Ballad and Epic*. Dr. Hart does not mention, however, or may have overlooked, the fact that Child remarks upon the resemblances between the foregoing Norse ballads and *Child Waters*. Child says:

There is a similarity, which is perhaps not accidental, between these Scandinavian ballads and "Child Waters." Child Waters makes Ellen swim a piece of water, shows her his hall—"of red gold shines the tower" —where the fairest lady is his paramour, subjects her to menial services, and finally, her patience withstanding all trials, marries her.[3]

Child traces the resemblances between *The Fair Flower of Northumberland* (9) and the Polish ballads of the class of *Lady Isabel and the Elf-Knight* (4),[4] which resemblances, through the interrelationships of these several pieces, may argue a supernatural character for the lover in *Child Waters*. Were the knight in those Norse ballads which resemble in part *The Fair Flower of Northumberland* unquestionably an Otherworld character like the wooer in *Lady Isabel and the Elf-Knight*, then Dr. Hart's suggestion as to

[1] Cf. A 26, C 13, D 4, E 6, G 2, H 1.   [3] *Ibid.*, p. 112 n.

[2] Child, I, 112.   [4] *Ibid.*, p. 113.

the supernatural nature of *Child Waters* would be even
more plausible than it is. Something of his analysis of the
possible supernatural elements of this ballad is, at any rate,
too significant to be omitted here as supplying, it may be,
additional evidence of an elfland or Elysium of gold castles
and fair women:

> In Child Waters we have what looks like a case of earthly wife and
> fairy husband from which the supernatural element has completely
> disappeared. It is pleasanter, certainly, to think of Child Waters as
> acting not voluntarily, but in obedience to the conditions of his being.
> It has been pointed out that the name *Waters* suggests something of
> this kind. Child Waters and Burd Ellen cross the wan water as one does
> on the journey to the other world; and the hall with its towers and gates
> of red gold, and the four-and-twenty ladies, can be roughly paralleled
> from the glimpse of the other world in the Wee Wee Man,

> > *Whare the roof was o the beaten gould,*
> > *And the floor was o the cristal a'.*

> It is obviously impossible, however, to prove that Child Waters was
> originally a fairy prince; at the same time it is impossible to prove that
> he was not.[1]

Professor Hart goes on to say that the ballad of *Fair Annie*
(62) "may be open to the same sort of explanation."[2]
Child describes as "superfluous and meddling" the parrot
or "wylie bird" which in certain texts of *Child Waters* (63 C
12, E 15, F 6, H 5) corrects the false statements of the
man,[3] but this incident of the talking and helpful bird may
be taken as further evidence that our song was originally
a fairy ballad. It recalls, moreover, the helpful cuckoo in
a Russian ballad, a folksong illustrative of the wonderland
encountered in ballads of the type of *Lady Isabel and the
Elf-Knight:* "In one version of this ballad a cuckoo flies up
and bids the maid not listen to the Cossack's tales: 'I have
flown all over the world, and I have never seen golden
mountains, nor eaten pears from willow-trees, nor beheld
maidens clad in gold.'"[4] It may be worthy of note, too,
that Ellen (63 A 16) crosses the water by the aid of "our

[1] *Ballad and Epic*, p. 29.   [3] *Op. cit.*, II, 84.
[2] *Ibid.*, p. 29.   [4] See *ibid.*, pp. 496 f.

Ladye." In *Young Beichan* (53 M 28) a lady, setting out upon the sea, strokes round about with a wand and takes God to be her pilot.

But let us turn from the general notion of an Otherworld of bliss to a brief examination of the Elysian elements—golden castles, flowers, birds, streams, and music. The inhabitants of the Otherworld will be considered in the following chapter. The golden castles or golden mountains which the wooer in ballads of the type of *Lady Isabel and the Elf-Knight* (4) promises a mortal maid have already been taken into account.[1] Additional descriptions of the Otherworld castle are found in *The Wee Wee Man* (38), *Tam Lin* (39), and *Hind Etin* (41), as well as in *Child Waters* (63), if we concede a supernatural character to the knight in this piece. The exceptional wealth of ballad fairies will be further illustrated in the chapter on Otherworld beings.[2] Of gold and crystal is the bonny hall in *The Wee Wee Man*:

> *On syne we past wi wondering cheir*
> *Till we cam to a bonny ha;*
> *The roof was o the beaten gowd,*
> *The flure was o the crystal a'* [38 B 7].

A 7 and C 7 have the same description. According to F 6, the "rafters were o the beaten gold, and silver wire were the kebars all"; according to G 5, the "kipples ware o the gude red gowd, the reef was o the proseyla." Crystal is a common feature of the Otherworld.[3] The term "proseyla" is not clear.[4] The fairy castle in a Scott version of *Tam Lin* (39 M 9)[5] stands between the roads to heaven and hell:

> *"O dinna ye see yon castle, Tamas,*
> *That's biggit between the twa,*
> *And theekit wi the beaten goud?*
> *O that's the fairies' ha."*

[1] *Supra*, pp. 143 f.
[2] *Infra*, pp. 180 ff.
[3] See Patch, *op. cit.*, XXXIII, 609 f.
[4] See Child, V, 366. [5] *Ibid.*, IV, 458.

But this stanza, among others, belongs to *Thomas Rymer* (37) and furnishes for this ballad a description to match that in the romance of Thomas of Erceldoune, where (stanza 42)[1] the castle stands on a high hill: "Of towne and towre" it takes the lead, "in erthe es none lyke it vn-till." The elfin-lover in *Hind Etin* (41 A 7 f.) builds for his mortal mistress a bower which is invisible to earthly eyes, a bower made secure with "carbuncle and stane":

> *The highest tree in Elmond's wood,*
> *He's pu'd it by the reet,*
> *And he has built for her a bower,*
> *Near by a hallow seat.*

> *He's built a bower, made it secure*
> *Wi carbuncle and stane;*
> *Tho travellers were never sae nigh,*
> *Appearance it had nane.*

The "hallow seat" of the first stanza is a saint's place. The "bowers and lofty towers" in *Lady Isabel and the Elf-Knight* (4 D 11) are clearly reminiscent of the paradise to which in foreign analogues of this piece the false knight promises to bear the heroine:

> *"Is this your bowers and lofty towers,*
> *So beautiful and gay?"*

This is given more effectively in a Gavin Greig variant:

> *"Is this your bowers and lovely towers,*
> *So costly, rich, and gay?"*[2]

The gates and the tower of Child Waters' hall (63 A 19 f.) are of "redd gold." J 16 reads: "And gowd towers stand sae hie"; C 14: "yon bonnie castle, lies on yon sunny lea"; B 13: "yon castle, Ellen, that shines sae fair to see." In *Lord Thomas and Fair Annet* (73 B 31)—a ballad with hints of the supernatural—the heroine speaks of a "bouer

---

[1] *Ibid.*, I, 328.   [2] *Folk-Song of the North-East*, art. CVI.

o bane" (bower of ivory?).[1] More fully than any of the foregoing ballads, the Danish song *Elveskud*, a parallel to *Clerk Colvill* (42), reveals the riches of fairyland in those promises which the elfin lass makes Sir Olave:

"The benches and chairs, whereon you sit,
   You'll see them of golden chain-work knit.

"And wrought of the gold each drawbridge stands,
   As pure as the rings that grace your hands."[2]

"The enchanting garden of the Otherworld," writes Mr. Patch, "is at once the most definitely marked and the vaguest of the Otherworld features. We always find the lovely meadows, the beautiful flowers with their subtly strange perfumes, the sparkling fountains and streams, and the tree of life."[3] It is not within the province of Mr. Patch's paper to refer these matters to the Otherworld of savages, but it may be well to note here those "shrubs and flowers of undying fragrance" found in the Polynesian land of bliss, and the "lakes and rivers, gardens with fruit-trees and flowers" of the Sea-Dyak's Elysium, or that Otherworld land of plenty, "sunshine and perpetual summer" of the Greenland Eskimos, not to mention similar features present in the eschatological beliefs of other primitive peoples.[4] We may say here what we have already implied in the general Introduction to this work, that citation of savage parallels is not meant to raise any question one way or the other as to the origin of our ballads. Such citation— whatever the origin of folksong—shows simply that certain ideas embodied in balladry are of a primitive character. Scholars are too prone, perhaps, where the ballads are concerned, to rest the case with medieval literature, as though the fact that a ballad incident is present in a romance should end all discussion. The matter of the romances, as well as that of the ballads, often has a basis in popu-

[1] See "bane" (Child, V, 313).

[2] Prior, II, 302.

[3] *Op. cit.*, XXXIII, 619.   [4] See "Blest, The Abode of the," *op. cit.*, II, 682 ff.

lar belief and custom, belief and custom which in turn not infrequently find their counterparts in savage thought and practice.

But let us return to the ballad depiction of Otherworld flowers and trees. Gillyflowers and roses blossom in the Christianized Elysium of *Sweet William's Ghost* (77). Margret has asked her dead lover what becomes of women "that dy's in strong traveling." The revenant replies:

> *"Their beds are made in the heavens high,*
> *Down at the foot of our good Lord's knee,*
> *Well set about wi gilly-flowers,*
> *A wat sweet company for to see"* [B 7].

"And it's a' clad ower wi roses red," he says in the Robertson version (D 8). There is little question, though Child makes no observation to this effect, but that the roses here should be thought of in connection with the rose-leaves which in the analogous Danish song *Aage og Else* are said by the ghost to line his grave cell when his mistress sings and is happy. In the English ballad (D 6) hell is described as "clad ower wi burnin pitch"; in the Danish piece the revenant says, when his true-love would follow him, that his grave is like blackest hell.[1]

As for the gillyflowers in Sweet William's paradise, Scott observes in his notes on *Clerk Saunders*[2] that "from whatever source the popular ideas of heaven be derived, the mention of gillyflowers is not uncommon."[3] Gillyflowers are among the flowers which adorn the fields about the "city faire" in Ritson's *Dead Men's Song*:

> *"The fields about this city faire,*
> *Were all with roses set;*
> *Gillyflowers, and carnations faire,*
> *Which canker could not fret."*[4]

[1] See Child, II, 228, and Prior's translations, *op. cit.*, III, 76 ff.

[2] *Clerk Saunders* as given by Scott (*Minstrelsy*, III, 222 ff.) is a combination of *Clerk Saunders* proper (69) and *Sweet William's Ghost* (77).

[3] *Minstrelsy*, III, 230.   [4] Ritson, *Ancient Songs*, p. 283.

From the legend of *Sir Owain* Scott gives a passage which describes a plenteously beflowered terrestrial paradise:

> *"Fair were her erbers with flowres,*
> *Rose and lili divers colours,*
>   *Primros and parvink;*
> *Mint, feverjoy, and eglenterre,*
> *Colombin, and mo ther wer*
>   *Than ani man mai bithenke.*
> *It berth erbes of other maner,*
> *Than ani in erth groweth here,*
>   *Tho that is lest of priis;*
> *Evermore thai grene springeth,*
> *For winter no somer it no clingeth,*
>   *And sweeter than licorice."*

The subterranean and over-the-water paradise of *Thomas Rymer* (37) has, according to the several variants of the ballad (A 8, B 7, C 17),[1] a "garden green" wherein is a tree or trees, the fruit of which is forbidden, but no mention is made of flowers. Nor are flowers mentioned in those two stanzas which in the romance of *Thomas of Erceldoune* describe the garden or "faire herbere." The forbidden fruit of the ballad and the romance and the birds of the romance will be considered shortly. There are roses or flowers in the enchanted wood of *Tam Lin* (39); roses: A 5, B 5, C 2, E 5, F 8, G 5, I 7, K 2, L 4; "flowers" simply: H 5; "flowers" "both red and green": D 4. The elfin knight forbids Janet to pluck the roses:

> *She had na pu'd a double rose,*
>   *A rose but only twa,*
> *Till up then started young Tam Lin,*
>   *Says, Lady, thou's pu nae mae* [A 5].

In his discussion of the derivation of *Tam Lin* T. F. Henderson, in his edition of Scott's *Minstrelsy*, says: "One remarkable similarity is the connection of Tom a Lin with

[1] As also in texts, Child, IV, 454 f.; cf. the *Thomas Rymer* stanza in Scott's *Tam Lin* (39 M 5), Child, IV, 458.

the rose, not otherwise associated with fairy-tales."[1] But Friend observes that the "Rose used to be regarded as being under the special protection of elves, dwarfs, and fairies, who were ruled by the lord of the Rose-garden. The name of this King was Laurin.

"Four portals to the garden lead, and when the gates are closed,
  No living wight dare touch a Rose, 'gainst his strict command opposed."[2]

Hind-Etin (41), like *Tam Lin*, preserves the incident of the tabooed forest, but in the former ballad we find "nuts" instead of "roses." "This reading, *nuts*," says Child, "may have subsequently made its way into A instead of *rose*, which it would be more ballad-like for Margaret to be plucking, as the maid does in 'Tam Lin,' . . . ."[3]
  We may make something of the demon-lover's promise (243) to show his earthly mistress how the lilies grow on the banks of Italy:

  "O hold your tongue, my sprightly flower,
    Let a' your mourning be;
  I'll show you how the lilies grow
    On the banks o Italy" [C 16].

F 12 and G 6 have virtually the same reading; D 6: "I'll show whare the white lillies grow, on the banks of Italie." An American variant has "On the banks of old Tennessee."[4] May the lilies be the flowers of an undersea paradise? D 8, C 21, and E 16, 17, possibly bear out this idea, though the lover's promise in these passages carries something of a threat. D 8 reads: "I'll show whare the white lillies grow, in the bottom of the sea." But in E 16 the banks of Italy

---

[1] II, 387.

[2] *Flowers and Flower Lore*, pp. 287 f. Child takes note (*op. cit.*, I, 360 n.) of Grimm's suggestion that the dwarf Laurin, with his rose-garden, offers a parallel to Tam Lin. There are roses in Tam's wood according to Greig (*Traditional Ballads*, p. 27).

[3] *Op. cit.*, I, 360 n., citing Grimm, *Deutsche Mythologie*, III, 130.

[4] Child, IV, 361.

where "the leaves grow green" is offered as an alternative
to the bottom of the sea where "the fishes swim."[1] On the
foregoing passage Scott gives this note in Sharpe's *Ballad
Book:*

> I remember something of another ballad of diablerie. A man sells
> himself to the fause thief for a term of years, and the devil comes to
> claim his forfeit. He implores for mercy, or at least reprieve, and, if
> granted, promises this:

> *"And I will show how the lilies grow*
> *On the banks of Italy."*

Satan, being no horticulturist, pays no attention to this proffer.[2]

"Scott's memory," says Child, "seems to have gone quite
astray here."[3] One would like to know the geography of
that "Rose Isle" at which, in text C 19 of our ballad, the
Otherworld lover says they will stay before going on to see
a "far countrie."

We may list in this connection the most important
flowers of balladry: primrose, in Nos. 11 A, E; 195 A, 219
A; blossom of broom, No. 43 A, B, C, employed in witchcraft; broom, associated with fairies, No. 39 A, B; gilly-
flower, Nos. 14 C; 219 A, B; 298; cowslip, No. 81 C; mary-
gold, No. 112 C, 219 A; violet, No. 112 C; sweet-william,
No. 219 A;[4] gowans or daisies, Nos. 4 A; 233 A, B; 235 D;
heather-bell, No. 214 Q; see the flower-burden, "Parsley,
sage, rosemary and thyme," No. 2 G 1. References to
flowers of various kinds are to be found in ballad refrains.[5]
The foregoing list is not exhaustive, but we may say without hesitation that the rose and the lily are the most popular flowers in our ballads. A "rose garland" is found in
Young Benjie (86 B 12). The lily and the rose are occasionally mentioned together, as in Nos. 5 C 5, 60, and 195

---

[1] Cf. C 21.

[2] C. K. Sharpe, *op. cit.* (1880), p. 158.

[3] *Op. cit.*, IV, 361 n.

[4] Several other flowers and herbs are mentioned in this unimportant piece.

[5] For plant burdens see *Journal of the Folk-Song Society*, III, 309 f.; IV, 326;
V, iv ff. On magical plants in the ballads see *infra*, pp. 352 ff.

B 2, and the lily, especially, occurs many times in stock descriptive phrases, such as "lily-white hands" and "lily feet."

In the paradise pictured in the Danish song *Ribold and Guldborg* "leeks are the only grass that springs":

> *"There leeks are the only grass that springs,*
> *And the gowk is the only bird that sings."*[1]

The leek was of old held in high esteem by Germanic peoples as contributing to manly vigor and was regarded as a plant of decidedly magical properties.[2] Among the Arabs and the Chinese it was employed as a charm against witchcraft.[3]

Without reference to ancient tree cults, sacred groves, and tree-haunting spirits or tree-souls, all of which are considered earlier in this work,[4] we find in *Thomas Rymer* (37) and in *The Wife of Usher's Well* (79) direct allusion to Otherworld trees. The former ballad (37 A 8, B 7, C 17) and the allied romance (stanzas 32 f.) tell of a "garden green" or "faire herbere," the fruit of which Thomas is forbidden to touch:

> *O they rade on, and further on,*
> *Until they came to a garden green:*
> *"Light down, light down, ye ladie free,*
> *Some of that fruit let me pull to thee."*

> *"O no, O no, True Thomas," she says,*
> *"That fruit maun not be touched by thee,*
> *For a' the plagues that are in hell*
> *Light on the fruit of this countrie"* [A].

The tree from which, according to B 7, Thomas is about to pluck fruit is evidently the Forbidden Tree, for in the following stanza the fairy warns him thus: "It was a' that cursed

---

[1] Translated, Jamieson, *op. cit.*, pp. 324 f.

[2] See Jamieson, *ibid.*, p. 330; Gummere, *Germanic Origins*, pp. 67 f.

[3] Friend, *op. cit.*, p. 543.　　　　[4] *Supra*, pp. 37 ff., 122 ff.

fruit o thine beggared man and woman in your countrie."[1]
Concerning the nature of the fruit tree or trees in texts A
and B of the ballad and in the romance, Child says: "It was
not that Thomas was about to pluck fruit from the For-
bidden Tree, though B understands it so: cf. R 32, 33.
The curse of this tree seems, however, to have affected all
Paradise."[2] According to the romance (stanza 35), Thomas
will send his soul to the "fyre of helle" if he plucks the fruit.
The tree, according to the "entirely perverted" stanza of
Scott's copy (C 17), is an apple tree.

In C they *now* come to the garden. Stanzas 15, 16 are out of place
in C, as just remarked, and 17 is entirely perverted. The cursed fruit
which Thomas is not to touch in A 9, B 8, R 35, is offered him by the
elf-queen as his wages, and will give him the tongue that can never lie,
—a gift which is made him in the romance at the beginning of the
second fit, when the fairy is preparing to part with him.[3]

In two other of Scott's texts, as well as in stanzas from one
of his versions of *Tam Lin* (39 M), stanzas which belong
to *Thomas Rymer*, the tree is an apple tree, and in all three
of the foregoing texts, as in B 8, it is thought of as the
Forbidden Tree. In one text the apple is called "the evil
fruit o hell, beguiled man and women in your countrie."
In another of the three texts "it's the very fruit o hell."[4]
According to the *Thomas Rymer* stanzas in *Tam Lin* (39 M
5 f.), "The apples hung like stars of goud out-our that wa
sa fine." Thomas would pluck one, but the fairy says: "O
let that evil fruit now be! It was that apple ye see there
beguil'd man and woman in your country."[5]
In the Brown copy (A) and in the Campbell text (B)
the fruit is not named. We have simply in both versions a
"garden green" and "fruit." The romance, however, speci-
fies the kinds of fruit—the pear, the apple, the date, the
plum, the fig, and the wineberry; the "damasee" is the
damson plum:

[1] See Child, I, 321 n.

[2] *Ibid.*, p. 322 n.

[3] *Ibid.*, p. 321.

[4] For this and the preceding text see *ibid.*, IV, 454 f.   [5] *Ibid.*, p. 458.

Scho lede hy̲m in-till a faire herbere,
  Whare frwte was g[ro]wan[d gret plentee];
Pere and appill, bothe ryppe þay were,
  The date, and als the damasee.

þe fygge, and alsso þe wyneberye,
  The nyghtgales byggande on þair neste.[1]

One is reminded here of the extensive lore of the apple tree. In our balladry, for example, this tree is associated with the fairy capture of mortals.[2] *Thomas Rymer*, like certain other folksongs, represents a confusion of Christian and pagan beliefs, and it is possible that the tree of the subterranean, paradisaic orchard was originally the tree of life, a universal conception.[3] Of course, so far as the ballad story goes, the tree or the fruit gives us the well-known incident of the eating taboo to which mortal visitants to the Otherworld are subject.[4]

The excellent traditional song *The Wife of Usher's Well* (79), like *Thomas Rymer*, has not escaped the influence of Christian eschatology. But at the very gates of its paradise flourish something of heathen ideas in the form of the birch tree, a tree which has furnished the ghost sons with their "hats o birk":

It fell about the Martinmass,
  When nights are lang and mirk,
The carlin wife's three sons came hame,
  And their hats were o the birk.

It neither grew in syke nor ditch,
  Nor yet in ony sheugh;
But at the gates o Paradise,
  That birk grew fair eneugh [A].

[1] *Ibid.*, I, 327.

[2] See *infra*, pp. 311 ff.

[3] See Patch, *op. cit.*, XXXIII, 624 f.; J. H. Philpot, *The Sacred Tree*, pp. 131, 142, 170.

[4] See *infra*, pp. 275 ff.

"Wi their hats made o the bark," is the reading in Kinloch's text (B 1). Scott finds an interesting parallel for our birch of paradise in a rabbinical tradition as given in the *Maasebook*, according to which an apparition says, respecting the garland it wears, that it "consists of excellent herbs of Paradise." "I wear it," says the apparition, "to the end the wind of the world may not have power over me; . . . ."[1] Analogous to our paradisaical birch is that Otherworld angelica which the fairy woman in Saxo's story brings to Hadding.[2]

The sacred nature of the birch is well known,[3] and in our ballads this tree is not infrequently associated with death. To dream of pulling the "birk sae green" portends death in *The Braes o Yarrow* (214 O 1). A "wand o bonny birk" is laid on the breast of the dead in *Sweet William's Ghost* (77 G 1).[4] A living mother in *Sir Hugh* (155 C 16) makes an appointment to meet the "corpse" of her son at the "birks of Mirryland town," though "birks" here may be a corruption of "back" in B 13. The corruption may well, however, be the other way about. Of love-animated plants which spring from the graves of lovers, one is a birch, as in *Fair Janet* (64 A 30): "Out of the tane there grew a birk, and the tither a bonny brier." The birch is again one of the love-animated plants in *Lord Thomas and*

---

[1] *Op. cit.*, III, 324 f.

[2] Elton-Powell, *Saxo*, p. 37; cf. *ibid.*, p. lxviii.

[3] The birch was anciently regarded as especially sacred and was placed in houses at Easter and St. John's Eve (Aubrey, *Gentilisme and Judaisme*, p. 119). In Shropshire the churches were decorated on Whit Sunday with birch boughs (Burne, *Shropshire Folk-Lore*, p. 350). The birch is sacred to a Mordwin goddess (*Folk-Lore Journal*, VII, 106). In Ainu folklore the birch is of sacred significance (*JAFL*, XXV, 73). Sacred images were made of birch by the Lapps (*Folk-Lore*, XXI, 78). The Bhurja, a species of birch, is sacred in India (W. Crooke, *Popular Religion and Folk-Lore of Northern India*, II, 114; see also *ibid.*, p. 86). The "birch-bark tray" has a part in magical ceremonies in British Columbia (*JAFL*, XXIII, 205). On the birch as a prevention against witchcraft see Frazer, *Golden Bough*, II, 54; IX, 162; XI, 20 n., 162. "Buds of the birch-tree" figure in folk-medicine (*JAFL*, XVII, 117). According to Canadian folklore, lightning will never strike a birch-tree (*ibid.*, XI, 161). An account of the origin of the birch relates that it sprang from the tear of a girl (*Folk-Lore*, I, 337).

[4] Also in text, Child, IV, 474, stanza 1.

Fair Annet (73 A, B, E, F, G); *Lord Lovel* (75 I); *The Lass of Roch Royal* (76 A); *Prince Robert* (87 A, B); and in *Bonny Baby Livingston* (222).[1] A coffin is made of birch in *Sir Hugh* (155 N); biers, of "byrch and haysell graye" in *Otterburn* (161 A 67) and in *The Hunting of the Cheviot* (162 57).[2] Childe Viat's "nexten stroke" (66 D 8) sends Lord Ingram's head "fifty feet oer a burken buss." According to *Charles Graeme*, the first stanzas of which belong to *The Unquiet Grave* (78), the ghost lover pulls up a "birken bow" and places it in the maiden's right hand.[3] But this incident occurs in that part of the song which reads, observes Child, "as if some contributor had been diverting himself with an imposition on the editor's simplicity."[4] In view of the foregoing association of the birch with death, the grave, and the Otherworld, however, this incident takes on something of importance. In *Clerk Saunders* (69 G 13) the third of those brothers, the seventh of whom "gard" Clerk Sandy die, is said to be standing "on the birk." Child thinks this reference to standing on the birch is nonsense,[5] but again, we may point out, as in the case of the *Charles Graeme* piece, that there may be some connection here between the birch and death. Bearing still in mind the generally sacred character of the birch, we may venture to see an Otherworld forest in the Silver Wood of *Child Maurice* (83 A 1, G 1) and *Jellon Grame* (90 A 1, 5, 6, 17; D 5), for there is a hint of myth in it.[6] It has been suggested that there is meant here a "wood of silver firs or of birches."[7] *Child Maurice* (83 A 1) reads:

> *Childe Maurice hunted ithe siluer wood,*
> *He hunted itt round about.*

[1] *Ibid.*, V, 262; see the tree-soul, *supra*, p. 41.

[2] The bier is usually of red gold and silver clear, as in No. 96 A.

[3] Child, IV, 476.

[4] *Ibid.*, p. 475.

[5] *Ibid.*, V, 316.

[6] Cf. Gummere, *The Popular Ballad*, p. 328; see *supra*, p. 124.

[7] Hart, *English Popular Ballads*, p. 315.

That Child Maurice's steed (B 1, C 1) is shod with silver and gold argues a supernatural character for the hero.[1] The "silver wood" appears in the story from the "traditions of Galloway" sketched by Child in connection with *Jellon Grame*.[2] Not associated with death, the birch is found in Nos. 5 D; 47 B, C; 65 J; 81 L; 96 A, E, G; 195 A, B; and 240 C.

The wood to which the Otherworld lover in *Hind Etin* (41) entices his earthly sweetheart is "Elmond's wood" (Elfman's?), according to text A. Buchan's copy (C 4) calls it "the wood o Amonshaw"; Kinloch's version (B 2), "Mulberry wud." "Amonshaw" may be a corruption of Elmond-shaw (Elfman-shaw?).[3] I have found no evidence to the effect that the mulberry is an Otherworld tree. Friend records the superstition, however, that the mulberry, like the classic hyacinth, "was red with the blood of living hearts."[4] Black cites the *Medicina de Quadrupedibus* of Sextus Placitus on the magical or medicinal virtues of the mulberry tree.[5] The mulberry tree is mentioned in the refrain of *Babylon* (14 C 1). Other ballad woods associated with supernatural beings and mentioned specifically by name are the "wood o Tore" in *Sir Lionel* (18 B 6) and "Wormie's Wood" in *Kemp Owyne* (34 B 18). Other places of enchantment, such as hills, banks, wells, and streams, will be considered under the Otherworld spell,[6] and the forest as a locality for the Otherworld has been discussed in connection with the position of the land of spirits.[7]

At this point we may devote a moment to the streams of paradise, bearing in mind, of course, a distinction between these happy waters and those which are crossed to reach the Otherworld.[8] Already quoted at some length, the ballad of *Ribold and Guldborg*—the paradise in this

---

[1] See fairy steeds, *infra*, p. 187.

[2] *Op. cit.*, II, 302 f.

[3] See *ibid.*, I, 360.

[4] *Op. cit.*, p. 316.

[5] *Folk-Medicine*, p. 189.

[6] See *infra*, pp. 316 ff.

[7] See *supra*, pp. 122 ff.

[8] See *supra*, pp. 108 ff.

song is mentioned in *Leesome Brand* (15 A 1)[1]—provides Norse and Scottish tradition with an Elysian stream. Ribold describes the land of immortality to which he would bear Guldborg:

> *"There a' the water that rins is wine;*
> *Ye well may trow this tale o' mine."*[2]

Prior's translation of the same text reads: "For water run the brooks with wine."[3] According to Russian ballads which depict a paradise similar to that in the Polish version of *Lady Isabel and the Elf-Knight*, the water is mead or the rivers are of honey.[4] In a Magyar text of the foregoing English ballad the land is said to flow with milk and honey.[5]

Mead flows plentifully in fairyland, and the food is delectable. Cromek records a story of a mortal woman who suckles a fairy child, as in our *Queen of Elfan's Nourice* (40). Out of gratitude the fairy mother gives the earthly nurse meat of a most delicious flavor. "This food tasted, says tradition, like loaf mixed with wine and honey."[6] The Norse ballad *Peter Gudmanson and the Dwarfs* tells a story of a knight who is bespelled in elfland by drinking the nut-brown mead and the sparkling wine:

> *"The nutbrown mead we'll pour for you,*
> *The sparkling wine as well,*
> *But here, Sir Peter Gudmanson*
> *A twelvemonth you must dwell."*[7]

But Child Rowland of Jamieson's tale refuses to taste of the golden bowl of bread and milk which is offered him in the giant's cave.[8] In the beautiful Danish song *Elfin Hill*

[1] See *supra*, p. 141.

[2] Jamieson's translation, *op. cit.*, p. 324.

[3] *Op. cit.*, II, 401.

[4] See Child, I, 487; II, 496 f.

[5] *Ibid.*, I, 46.

[6] R. H. Cromek, *Remains of Nithsdale and Galloway Song*, p. 302; see Child, I, 359.

[7] Prior, III, 201.   [8] Jamieson, *op. cit.*, p. 402.

another mortal man, advised by his enchanted sister, avoids capture by letting the elfin wine flow down his bosom.[1]

We may still remain within ballad tradition for a brief study of the widespread conception of paradisaical birds. In balladry we cannot find those birds of Bran's paradise which "call to the Hours,"[2] or match the soft-voiced songsters of the Cuchulinn story,[3] but in the Norse *Ribold and Guldborg* we are clearly enough in touch with the general idea of Otherworld birds, as also in the romance of *Thomas of Erceldoune*, not to mention the bird-soul conception, which is amply illustrated in balladry and which, as Mr. Patch observes, may be the basis of the belief in paradisaical birds.[4] The cuckoo, Scotch *gowk*, is the ideal bird of spring, and no other bird sings in Ribold's realm of eternal bliss:

> "*There leeks are the only grass that springs,*
> *And the gowk is the only bird that sings.*"[5]

The lore of the cuckoo is very extensive. Its name has been given to flowers. Rhymes about it abound in the British Islands and on the Continent. Portents are drawn from its cry. It is the harbinger of spring and is thought to be the cause of summer.[6]

Elysian birds are not found in the ballad of *Thomas Rymer*, but in the romance they are several in number and are mentioned by name—the nightingale, the popinjay, and the thrush:

> *The nyghtgales byggande on þair neste;*
> *þe papeioyes fast abowte gane flye,*
> *And throstylls sange, wolde hafe no reste.*[7]

---

[1] See Prior's translations, *op. cit.*, III, 243 ff.

[2] See Meyer-Nutt, *Bran*, I, 6.

[3] See *ibid.*, p. 155.

[4] *Op. cit.*, p. 627.

[5] Jamieson, *op. cit.*, p. 324.

[6] See Charles Swainson, *The Folk-Lore of British Birds*, pp. 109–22.

[7] See Child, I, 327, stanza 33.

The foregoing birds are common in the ballads, and the nightingale figures prominently in folklore.[1]

But the birds are not alone in furnishing the music of paradise or elfland. The seductive strains of elfin music are heard here and there in balladry, for it is often by their magic notes that Otherworld folk lure mortals to fairyland. In their wooing of mortal maidens the fairy knights in *The Elfin Knight* (2), *Lady Isabel and the Elf-Knight* (4), and in *Hind Etin* (41) all have recourse to magical music. This is a matter, however, which will be taken up in detail under the Otherworld spell.[2] The music and dancing in the elf castle of *The Wee Wee Man* (38) and in the romance of *Thomas of Erceldoune* will be considered in the following chapter on "Otherworld Beings."[3] Those interesting "psalms o heaven" in *Sweet William's Ghost* (77), as well as the "bells o heaven" in this same piece, may await discussion in connection with the Christian Otherworld,[4] although they occur in a ballad which is replete with non-Christian lore.

[1] On the nightingale, the popinjay, and the thrush see Swainson, *op. cit.*, pp. 18–22; 100; 1, 3, 8, 73.

[2] See *infra*, pp. 293 ff.

[3] See *infra*, pp. 191 ff.

[4] See *infra*, pp. 410 ff.

PART II
PAGAN OTHERWORLD BEINGS

INTRODUCTORY

❧

U NDER the head of Otherworld beings I shall consider the fairy, the witch, and the ghost—the term
"fairy" embracing, of course, various kinds of legendary creatures, among them elves, trolls, dwarfs, mermaids, mermen, and household-familiars. The chapter on
the fairy may be regarded as a continuation of the foregoing chapter on the nature of the Otherworld. In the
fact that fairy, witch, and ghost beliefs are closely allied I
have found justification for grouping here my chapters on
the witch and the ghost. Time and again throughout this
work, particularly in the present section and in that on
the Otherworld spell, we are confronted with striking resemblances between the ballad ghost and the ballad fairy,
and we find, moreover, that witches and fairies, especially
in the matter of their supernatural powers, are often
indistinguishable.[1]

[1] For European witchlore see Margaret A. Murray, *The Witch-Cult in Western Europe*, p. 238 and *passim*. On the resemblances between the dead and fairies
see, for example, Wentz, *The Fairy-Faith*, pp. 218 ff., 436 ff., Pineau, *Les vieux
chants populaires scandinaves*, pp. 222–38; Vigfusson-Powell, *Corpus poeticum
boreale*, I, 413 ff.

Chapter VI

THE BALLAD FAIRY

❧

MANY of the beliefs relating to the physical attributes, the activities, and the powers of fairies are found in English and Scottish balladry. It should be said, however, that the fairy-lore of our folksong illustrates, in all probability, a commingling of various traditions—the Celtic and the Teutonic chiefly. But no attempt will be made here to determine the specific tradition to which a given preternatural creature belongs. That Tam Lin (39) is called an "elfin grey" may be sufficient reason for thinking of him as a Teutonic dwarf,[1] but that he is captured by the fairies while sleeping beneath an apple tree (G 26) may imply that he is a Celtic fairy. "That Tam Lane was taken by the fairies while sleeping under an apple-tree," remarks Kittredge, "certainly seems to be . . . . a Celtic survival."[2] So, too, in the fairy ballad of *The Wee Wee Man* (38) we might point out the presence side by side of Celtic and Teutonic fairy-lore. But such an ethnological distinction is not particularly germane to our purpose here. Moreover, as regards their basic characteristics the Celtic fairies differ little from Teutonic or Norse elves, dwarfs, and trolls—so little, indeed, that the same cycle of *Märchen* and superstitions is common to both.[3]

These pages are not concerned with the various theories that have arisen respecting the origin of the belief in fairies, such theories as the mythological, the naturalistic,

[1] See *infra*, p. 176.

[2] "Sir Orfeo," *American Journal of Philology*, VII, 190. On the commingling of the Celtic and the Teutonic "fairy" traditions see A. Maury, *Les Fées du Moyen Age.*

[3] Cf. "Fairy," *Encyclopaedia of Religion and Ethics*, V, 678.

[167]

the pygmy or ethnological, and the psychological.[1] I shall be content here with a simple portrayal of the non-human folk of British popular poetry, paying especial attention to fairies, elves, and dwarfs—their size, their color, their wealth, their occupations, and their government. Before passing to the ballad evidence, however, we should point out that the belief in fairies, or in fairy-like creatures, is universal; that such a belief is at home not only in Celtic and Teutonic countries, but flourishes in all parts of Europe, in Asia, in Africa, in Central Australia, and among the Amerindians.

PHYSICAL ATTRIBUTES OF THE FAIRY

One of the most important characteristics of the fairy is its size. Except in the notable instance of *The Wee Wee Man* (38) and in the case of a recently recovered version of *The Queen of Elfan's Nourice* (40), the evidence yielded by our ballads does not square with the general view that fairies are tiny creatures. This general opinion meets with criticism in serious studies on the nature of fairies, as in MacCulloch's observation on the dimensions of these supernatural beings. This scholar says:

> Frequently fairies are regarded as a diminutive folk, but there is much contradiction on this subject, and many fairies (the *fées* of S. Europe, the Slavic *vilas*, and the *síd* folk of Ireland) are hardly to be distinguished in size from mortals. In the same region some groups of fairies may be tall, others pygmies, but the varying size is sometimes due to their power of changing their form. Once fairies were regarded as small, their smallness would tend to be exaggerated.[2]

Shakespeare's elfin folk are for the most part diminutive, but it is probable that they owe their characteristics, in some degree, at least, to poetic fancy.[3] In such ballads as

---

[1] For an exposition of these several views see Wentz, *The Fairy-Faith*, pp. xxi ff.

[2] "Fairy," *Encyclopaedia of Religion and Ethics*, V, 679; see also Wentz, *op. cit.*, pp. 242 f.

[3] See H. B. Wheatley, "Folklore of Shakespeare," *Folk-Lore*, XXVII, 380; cf. Drayton's fairies, "The Folk-Lore of Drayton," *Folk-Lore Journal*, III, 134 ff.

Tam Lin (39), *The Elfin Knight* (2), and *Lady Isabel and the Elf-Knight* (4) there is little or nothing to indicate that the elf differs in size from mortals. Certainly there is no reason to think that the fairy queen in *Thomas Rymer* (37) is diminutive.

The apparently human stature of many of our ballad fairies may indicate the influence of Celtic tradition,[1] but it is noteworthy that in this matter of size our fairies correspond to the elves of Danish balladry—elves which, one might suppose, would resemble the diminutive folk so common in German popular tales. In his remarks on the Danish ballad *Sir Olave*, Prior observes: "Under the name of Elves are comprised several very different beings. In general, they seem, as in this ballad, and Sir Tonne, No. 102, and many more, to be of human shape and size, and only in some copies of the 'Elf and the Farmer's Wife,' No. 124, are they represented as diminutive beings."[2] And even with respect to this last-named piece, which describes the elf as being (stanza 5) like "an emmet small and slim," he says: "This is quite inconsistent with the subsequent part of the ballad, see st. 23."[3] Again, on the size of fairies, Prior remarks that it "is to be observed that in Danish ballads fairies are full grown women and not the diminutive beings of our English tales, ..."[4] But he fails to note that in this respect the fairy women of English ballads resemble those in Danish folksong.

Certain stanzas of Scott's *Tam Lin* (39) are to the effect that fairies can convert their "shapes and size" at will to "either large or small," but of these stanzas Child is suspicious and relegates them to an appendix. It is on the strength of these "suspicious" stanzas, however, that Prior, commenting yet again on the size of elves, makes a significant observation concerning verses in *The Elf and the Farmer's Wife*, verses resembling those in another text of

[1] Cf. Kittredge on *Sir Orfeo* (*op. cit.*, VII, 188).

[2] *Ancient Danish Ballads*, II, 298 f.

[3] *Ibid.*, III, 166 n.   [4] *Ibid.*, pp. 249 f.

this piece referred to a moment ago. The lines in question read:

> *Out came the very smallest Elf,*
> *An ant were scarcely less.*[1]

Farther on in the ballad this elf seems to be of human stature. With reference to the second of the foregoing verses, "An ant were scarcely less," Prior says: "This, as remarked above, must have crept into the ballad by some accident, for in Danish ballads we find no trace of the Scotch belief that Elves could assume different sizes, as in *Young Tamlane.*"[2] Following this comment, Prior quotes from Scott's copy of *Tam Lin* those stanzas which, as we have pointed out, Child regarded with suspicion.[3]

Of course, we must bear in mind with respect to the ability of fairies to change their size and form that this very ballad of *Tam Lin* illustrates the shape-shifting powers of the Otherworld folk. But as concerns the size of ballad fairies and the transmutation of that size, Prior is thinking, as we are thinking, of the fairy in its human-like shape. It is true that in taking the ballad evidence we must always make allowance for the reticence of folksong. Nevertheless, it seems, even after making such allowance, that the fairies of British balladry are, as a rule, of human stature. In this respect they are like the fairies of romance. Andrew Lang says:

> There seems little in the characteristics of these fairies of romance to distinguish them from human beings, except their supernatural knowledge and power. They are not often represented as diminutive in stature, and seem to be subject to such human passions as love, jealousy, envy and revenge. To this class belong the fairies of Boiardo, Ariosto and Spenser.

[1] *Ibid.,* p. 173.

[2] *Ibid.,* p. 174.

[3] In his study of our ballad fairy Görbing unfortunately makes a great deal of these same suspicious stanzas. See his *Die Elfen in den englischen und schottischen Balladen,* p. 7.

In this same connection Lang comments upon the stature of the *Daoine Shie* of Ireland and Scotland: "The 'people of peace' (*Daoine Shie*) of Ireland and Scotland are usually of ordinary stature, indeed not to be recognized as varying from mankind except by their proceedings. . . . ."[1] To return to our ballads, Tam Lin in one text of the song of that name (39 C 4) thus describes himself: "I am a fairy, lyth and limb," that is, joint and limb, but there is no indication that he is other than human in size.[2]

With respect to the size of fairies, *The Wee Wee Man* (38), unlike the foregoing ballads, is specific enough. On the whole, it bears out—as regards stature, at least—the general view that fairies are mannikins. Of course, we are dealing in this piece with a particular kind of fairy, a being ugly and misshapen and on the order of such creatures as the dwarf, the gnome, and the kobold. The hero of our ballad, although possessing the strength of a giant, is a dwarflike, ill-proportioned being of midget stature, with a frame—according to certain variants of the song—which in thickness and breadth is of gigantic bulk. Two versions (B 2, D 2) picture him, however, as tiny in nearly every dimension:

Thick and short was his legs,
And sma and thin was his thie,
And atween his een a flee might gae,
And atween his shouthers were inches three [D 2].

B 2 reads: "His legs were scant a shathmont's length, and sma and limber was his thie; atween his shoulders was ae span, about his middle war but three." Both A 2 and C 2 describe him as having legs scarce a "shathmont" (six inches) in length, but as being broad browed and thick thighed:

[1] "Fairy," *Encyclopaedia Britannica* (11th ed.), X, 134 f.

[2] Görbing (*loc. cit.*), commenting on the size or stature (*Gestalt*) of our ballad fairies, says, "Sie sind lyth und limb (Tam Lin II, 39, C, 4)." He mistakes the dialectal "lyth," meaning member or joint, for "lithe." It is true that in I 7 Tam is called a "wee wee man," but this is, no doubt, an intrusion from *The Wee Wee Man* (38).

> *His legs were scarce a shathmont's length*
> *And thick and thimber was his thigh;*
> *Between his brows there was a span,*
> *And between his shoulders there was three* [A 2].

The expression "thimber," meaning "heavy and massive,"
is corrupted in C 2 to "umber"; in E 2, F 2, to "nimble";
and in G 2 to "nimle." But the proportions of the dwarf,
except in height, are gigantic in E 2, F 2, and G 2:

> *His legs they were na a gude inch lang,*
> *And thick and nimble was his thie;*
> *Between his een there was a span,*
> *And between his shouthers there were ells three* [F 2].

All texts, however, speak of him as a tiny or wee wee man,
as in A 1:

> *As I was wa'king all alone,*
> *Between a water and a wa,*
> *And there I spy'd a wee wee man,*
> *And he was the least that ere I saw.*

Or F 1: "a wee wee mannie, the weeest mannie that ere I
saw."[1] There is a giant, though not of a supernatural character, in *Johnie Scot* (99). Version L 18 describes him thus:
"Between his brows three women's spang, his shoulders
was yards three."

The fairy ladies of *The Wee Wee Man* are "jimp and
sma," and in the elfin hall of gold they dance with "wee
wee knichts" (B 8):

> *When we cam there, wi wee wee knichts*
> *War ladies dancing, jimp and sma.*

The elfin ladies are accorded the same description in A 8,
C 8, E 7, G 6.[2] In D 5 the fairy queen is called a "dainty
dame." In a version of *The Queen of Elfan's Nourice* (40),

---

[1] Cf. the "litel man" in the analogous fourteenth-century poem (Child, *Ballads*, I, 333).

[2] So in Cunningham's copy (*ibid.*, p. 333, stanza 8).

recovered from Scotland within recent times by Mr. Claude
Eldred, we again find the tradition of the little elf:

> *An' the little elf man, elf man, elf man,*
> *An' the little elf man*
>   *Said unto me:*

> *"Come, nurse an elf child, elf child, elf child,*
> *Come an' nurse an elf child,*
>   *Down 'neath the sea."*[1]

But nothing in Child's version of this piece indicates that
the elfin characters are diminutive.

All sorts of supernatural powers are attributed to
fairies. In physical prowess the Wee Wee Man (38) compares favorably with the elf-lover in *Hind Etin* (41) or
with the eldrige king in *Sir Cawline* (61). A "meikle stane"
is as nothing in the hands of the Wee Wee Man, who, according to all but one text (F) of the ballad, hurls such a
stone a great distance:

> *He took up a meikle stane,*
>   *And he flang 't as far as I could see;*
> *Though I had been a Wallace wight,*
>   *I couldna liften 't to my knee* [A 3].

B 3, C 3, D 3, E 3, have virtually the same reading. According to G 3 he throws "a stane sax feet in hight" over
fifty yards. The elfin king of *Sir Cawline* (61) is a "ffuryous
king and a ffell," "mickle of might"; his "eldryge sword"
is as "hard as any fflynt"; and his "ringes fiue" are "harder
then ffyer, and brent." "The etin of the Scottish story,"
Hind Etin (41), "is in Norse and German a dwarf-king,
elf-king, hill-king, or even a merman."[2] In the Scottish
ballad (A 7) he shows his supernatural power by plucking
up the "highest tree in Elmond's wood" and building
thereof an invisible bower for his earthly mistress. His
strength is seen to be even more prodigious in B 7:

[1] See *JAFL*, XX (1907), 155.   [2] Child, I, 361.

> *He pu'd a tree out o the wud,*
> *The biggest that was there,*
> *And he howkit a cave monie fathoms deep,*
> *And put May Margret there.*

A common trait of fairies is their power to make themselves invisible. This characteristic is illustrated in several ballads. Hind Etin (41), as we have already noted, builds his mortal mistress an invisible bower:

> *He's built a bower, made it secure*
> *Wi carbuncle and stane;*
> *Tho travellers were never sae nigh,*
> *Appearance it had nane* [A 8].

Tam Lin (39) has the faculty of vanishing and appearing at will. When Janet goes to meet him at the well of Carterhaugh he is there and yet not there:

> *When she cam to Carterhaugh,*
> *Tam Lin was at the well,*
> *And there she fand his steed standing,*[1]
> *But away was himsel* [A 18].

But, according to the next stanza, he starts up suddenly when she plucks a rose:

> *She had na pu'd a double rose,*
> *A rose but only twa,*
> *Till up then started young Tam Lin,*
> *Says Lady, thou pu's nae mae.*

B 17, I 6, and L 3 have much the same reading as A 18. According to F 2, H 5, J 2, K 2, L 4, Tam Lin starts up from nowhere:

> *Till up there startit young Tam Lane,*
> *Just at bird Janet's knee* [H 5].

---

[1] Cf. the following reading from a text in Greig, *Traditional Ballads*, p. 27: "She turned her richt an' roon aboot to ask her true-love's name; but she nothing heard, an' she nothing saw, but a' the woods grew dim." The dimming of the woods implies, probably, the troll mist. See *infra*, p. 321.

Janet's trespass on the fairy domain is discussed under the Otherworld spell. In *The Wee Wee Man* (38) the fairies and their castle disappear in the twinkling of an eye:

> *There war pipers playing on ilka stair,*
> *And ladies dancing in ilka ha,*
> *But before ye coud hae sadd what was that,*
> *The house and wee manie was awa* [D 7].

B 8 reads: "But in the twinkling of an eie, baith green and ha war clein awa"; C 8: "But in the twinkling o an eye, they sainted clean awa"; A 8: "But in the twinkling of an eye, my wee wee man was clean awa"; G 7: "Out gat the lights, on cam the mist, ladies nor mannie mair coud see"; Cunningham's copy: "He clapped his hands, and ere I wist, he sank and saunted clean awa."[1] It is noteworthy that the ghost of balladry does not, as a rule, disappear in this magical fashion. Like an ordinary mortal of flesh and blood he betakes himself to the land of the living and therefrom back to the grave.[2] Other magical powers of the Otherworld folk, such as their ability to enchant earthly people by means of music, runes, gifts, and the fairy kiss or the fairy dart, and their ability to transform mortals, will be considered later under the Otherworld spell and need not detain us here.[3]

To resume our discussion of the physical attributes of fairies, what have the ballads to say concerning the color of elves? "Like the *feld elfen* of the Saxons, the usual dress of the Fairies is green," says Scott, "though, on the moors, they have been sometimes observed in heath-brown, or in weeds dyed with the stoneraw, or lichen."[4] Virtually all the elfin folk of Britain and Ireland dress in green,[5] a color, indeed, that is pretty generally characteristic of fairies.[6]

---

[1] Child, I, 333.
[2] See *infra*, pp. 251 ff.
[3] *Infra*, pp. 275 ff.
[4] *Minstrelsy* (ed. Henderson), II, 354.
[5] See Wentz, *op. cit.*, pp. 312 f., and *passim*.
[6] See Keightley, *Fairy Mythology*, p. 290 and *passim*.

For romance there is the notable case of the green knight in *Gawain and the Green Knight*—his face, hair, his coat and mantle, even his horse and its accouterments are green.[1] The association of green with the dead and with witches, and the familiar superstition that green is unlucky, will be illustrated later in this study.[2] Wherever described in our balladry, female fairies are dressed in green.

With the exception of Thomas Rymer and the fairy leman in *Tam Lin* (39) there is no reference in our ballads to the color of elfmen. Tam is called an "elfin grey" in texts A 15, B 15, I 21:

> *"If my love were an earthly knight,*
> *As he's an elfin grey"* [A 15].

Because of his gray dress Tam Lin has been regarded as a Teutonic elf.[3] True Thomas in the ballad of *Thomas Rymer* (37)—a ballad with certain of its features conspicuously Celtic—wears a green costume during his sojourn in the fairy realm. Since he is virtually a naturalized member of the elfin community, Thomas should be regarded, along with Tam Lin, as a fairy man. In texts A 15 and C 20 Thomas is provided with shoes of velvet green:

> *He has gotten a coat of the even cloth,*
> *And a pair of shoes of velvet green,*
> *And till seven years were past and gone*
> *True Thomas on earth was never seen* [A 15].

Green men and even green dogs and horses are not uncommon in folk-traditions.[4] The "grateful dead man" in Douglas Hyde's version of this widespread story is in the guise of a green dwarf[5] and recalls the green ghosts of our bal-

---

[1] Cf. Kittredge, *Gawain and the Green Knight*, p. 5 and *passim*.

[2] In his *Zauber und Aberglaube in den englisch-schottischen Volksballaden* Georg Rüdiger offers a slight treatment of color symbolism, *Farbensymbolik*, in our ballads.

[3] See MacCulloch, "Fairy," *Encyclopaedia of Religion and Ethics*, V, 679.

[4] For a number of instances see Kittredge, *op. cit.*, pp. 195 f.

[5] *Beside the Fire*, pp. 18–47.

ladry.[1] Sir Bredbeddle of *King Arthur and King Cornwall* (30) is called the "Greene Knight" (stanzas 53, 55, etc.) and, like the Sir Bredbeddle[2] in Percy's version of the romance of the Green Knight, has certain magical powers. The mantle that the witch in *Allison Gross* (35) offers her prospective leman is of "red scarlet." The dwarf in a fourteenth-century poem on the order of *The Wee Wee Man* (38) is richly dressed. But his robe is "noithere grene na gray"; it is all of "riche palle" and "alle golde bigane."[3]

The elfin ladies in *The Wee Wee Man* (38) are (B 6) all "comely cled in glistering green"; according to A, C, D, E, F, they are clad simply in "green." The second of the fairy courts in one text of *Tam Lin* (39 D 19) is "clad in robes of green." It is the chief court of all:

> "*The next court that comes along*
> *Is clad in robes of green,*
> *And it's the head court of them all,*
> *For in it rides the queen.*"

The fairy in *Thomas Rymer* (37) is likewise clad in green:

> *Her skirt was of the grass-green silk,*
> *Her mantel of the velvet fine* [A 2].

C 2 has the same reading with the substitution of "shirt" for "skirt." Another text reads: "Her mantle was o velvet green."[4] Buchan's text of *Young Beichan* (53 M 15) has a woman—probably a fairy—who is "clad in green." The "four-and-twenty maids" who, according to one copy of *Tam Lin* (39 M 15),[5] dwell with the fairies, have gowns as "green as grass." The mermaid's sleeve in *Clerk Colvill* (42 A 6) is "sae green." The witch of *Allison Gross* (35)

---

[1] See *infra*, pp. 240 ff.

[2] On the name "Bredbeddle" see Child, I, 280.

[3] *Ibid.*, pp. 333 f., stanzas 1, 5.

[4] *Ibid.*, IV, 455.

[5] *Ibid.*, p. 458; cf. L 8 (*ibid.*, pp. 457 f.): "An some war blue an some war green, but Janet was like the gress." The color "blue" seldom occurs in the ballads. An interesting instance is the "blue bonnet" of the "auld man" or devil in No. 2 I 2.

[177]

blows thrice "on a grass-green horn." We should observe here that although green is a fairy color and of ill omen, and is, moreover, associated with witches and the dead, yet it is the favorite ballad color for the dress of women as well as of men. Descriptive of dress, it occurs some three hundred times in our folksongs, counting all the Child variants. Transformed into a monstrous shape, the lady in *The Marriage of Sir Gawain* (31, stanza 15) sits "betwixt an oke and a greene hollen" and is "cladd in red scarlett." The color red, in one shade or another, occurs with reference to the dress of men and women something over a hundred times in the Child ballads, all versions included. Though regarded as a lucky color, blue is seldom found in the ballads.[1] In connection with dress it occurs only about a score of times.

Female fairies are usually described as beautiful, but certain classes of the "good people," such as dwarfs and kobolds, are ugly and malformed to the point of frightfulness. We have already noted the ill proportions of the Wee Wee Man (38). According to the Danish song *Trolden og Bondens Hustru*, elfmen are foul and loathsome:

> *Seven hundred Elves from out the wood,*
> *And foul and grim they were,*
> *Would at the farmer's hold a feast*
> *His meat and drink to share.*[2]

Tam Lin (39) seems, on the other hand, to be a comely knight. But in the main, just as supernatural strength and frightful mien may be attributes of ballad elfmen, surpassing loveliness is a characteristic of our fairy ladies, as in old Irish stories—the story, for example, of the *Voyage of Teigue, Son of Cian* in which we find a wealth of feminine beauty.[3] The worst of the fairies, according to several

---

[1] On blue as lucky see Child, II, 182, 512; III, 479, stanza 6; 481, stanza 6; in these two last instances, however, as symbolic of good faith.

[2] Prior, III, 167, stanza 10; cf. stanza 25.

[3] On the appearance of the fairy women in the Teigue story and in other Irish stories see Wentz, *op. cit.*, p. 350 and *passim*.

texts of our ballad *The Wee Wee Man* (38 A, B, C, D, E, F), might have been Scotland's queen:

> *Four and twenty at her back,*
> *And they were a' clad out in green;*
> *Though the King of Scotland had been there,*
> *The warst o them might hae been his queen* [A 6].

True Thomas, like his near-analogue in the romance of Ogier le Danois or like Jean Cate in a Breton story, *La Fleur du Rocher*, pays the fairy queen the compliment of mistaking her for the Queen of Heaven:[1]

> *"All hail, thou mighty Queen of Heaven!*
> *For your peer on earth I never did see"* [37 A 3].

Or, according to another text of the ballad: "O save ye, save ye, fair Queen o Heaven."[2] "Marye, moste of myghte" is the reading in the romance of Thomas of Erceldoune.[3] The beauty of the fairy is, in the romance, reflected in the rich caparison of her steed. Elfin horses will be considered presently.

After Thomas and the fairy—according to the romance —have reached the elfin hall, "lufly ladyes, faire and free," sit and sing "one riche araye"—sing, it seems, to the dancing of the fairy "knyghtis" (stanza 52). "The Elfins is a pretty place," says Tam Lin (39 D 15), but he does not describe the fairy queen. Nor is this Otherworld being described in *The Queen of Elfan's Nourice* (40), nor yet in *Allison Gross* (35), save that in this latter piece her hand is said to be "milk-white." Clerk Colvill's heartless sea-fay has skin "whiter than the milk" (42 A 5). "Lady fair" and "lady bright" are descriptive of the fairy in two texts of *Thomas Rymer* (37 B 1, C 1). As shines the "sonne" on a summer's day, so shines the "faire lady" in the related romance (stanza 5). And if an Elysian character be con-

---

[1] On the Ogier instance and that in the Breton story—the latter furnished by Kittredge—see Child, I, 319; III, 504.

[2] *Ibid.*, IV, 455, stanza 4.

[3] *Ibid.*, I, 327, stanza 11.

ceded to the gold-shining towers of Child Waters' home,[1]
then we may match the lovely damsels of *The Wee Wee
Man* (38) with the "four and twenty ffaire ladyes" of the
Child Waters story (63), the fairest of whom is the knight's
"paramoure" (A 19).[2] With reference to ladies alone, the
epithet "fair" is used in the Child pieces—all texts included—something like a thousand times. Beauteous ladies
there are, too, in those fairylands of gold portrayed in foreign analogues of *Clerk Colvill* (42).[3] The loveliness of the
dwarf maiden in the Danish song *Hr. Tönne af Alsö* is in
keeping with the traditional beauty of the woman fay:

> *"All hail, Dwarf's daughter, lovely maid!*
> *Of flowers the peerless rose!*
> *No mortal man thy beauty sees,*
> *But straight with passion glows."*[4]

The elfin girl in another Danish piece, *Elvehöj*, is likewise
"a lovely and peerless maid."[5]

FAIRY WEALTH

Fairies in general, the Tuatha De Danann, for example,[6]
or the dwarfs of German tradition,[7] are accredited with
wealth—gold, silver, and precious stones—beyond the
dreams of mortals. This belief has already been illustrated
for balladry in our discussion of the fairy castle, which
reveals great luxury and splendor.[8] The elves display their
wealth, moreover, in their rings and other ornaments.
"Stones of oryente" in "grete plente" adorn the saddle of

---

[1] On the supernatural character of Child Waters see *supra*, pp. 144 f.

[2] Cf. B 19, C 17 f., G 11, H 7, J 19 f. The number "four-and-twenty" is a
favorite in our balladry (see Child, V, 490).

[3] See *ibid.*, I, 373 ff.

[4] Prior, III, 11; cf. Swedish version, Keightley, *op. cit.*, p. 98.

[5] Prior, III, 247.

[6] See Wentz, *op. cit.*, pp. 291 ff.

[7] See Keightley, *op. cit.*, p. 217.   [8] *Supra*, pp. 143 ff.

the fairy steed in the romance of *Thomas of Erceldoune*,[1] a
steed shortly to be considered in detail. In one text of the
related ballad (37) the fay's "velvet green" mantle is "a'
set round wi jewels fine," and "her bugle-horn in gowd did
shine."[2] The elf king's hand, according to the Harris version of *Sir Cawline* (61), "was set aboot wi chains a' goud."[3]
And the Percy copy (stanza 27) speaks of "ringes fiue."
Because of his earthly lineage, Tam Lin is next to the fairy
queen in "renown" and wears a "gold star" in his crown
(39 D 20, G 35). The sorceress in *Allison Gross* (35), like
the enchantress in *The Laily Worm* (36), has a silver wand.
In *King Arthur and King Cornwall* (30, stanza 66) there is
a magic wand of gold.

In order to win the love of mortals, or for other reasons,
the preternatural folk of balladry promise them, or provide them with, splendid gifts, a matter to be stressed in
connection with the Otherworld spell. The witch in *Allison
Gross* (35) tries to prevail over a young man by offering
him a series of rich articles, thus instancing for balladry
the belief that witches, like fairies, are opulent beings. In
Danish balladry fairies offer similar gifts, and in view of
the similarity between the dead and fairies it is interesting
that certain Norse songs tell of gifts, such as wondrous
weapons and steeds, furnished the living by the barrow
ghost. The dwarf wife in *Hr. Tönne af Alsö* provides the
earthly knight with a horse and saddle, spurs of gold, and
a shield inlaid with jewels, besides other magical equipment
for his adventure.[4] But the dead, as well as fairies, have
like power to accouter earthly men. The hero in *Young
Swennendal* would unspell a beauteous maid. He goes to
Goliat cave to ask his mother rede. The ghost mother
gives him a wondrous steed, a marvelous sword of gold, a

---

[1] Child, I, 326, stanza 7.

[2] *Ibid.*, IV, 455, stanza 3.

[3] *Ibid.*, II, 62, stanza 16.

[4] See translation, Prior, III, 14 f.; cf. the Swedish version (trans. Keightley,
op. cit., pp. 100 f.).

golden key, and a magic tablecloth.[1] The riches housed in ancestral graves suggest, of course, an origin for the belief that underground fairies are wealthy. In Scotland, Ireland, Wales, and Brittany the dead, like fairies, are guardians of hidden treasure.[2] Childe Orm in another Danish piece, *Childe Orm and the Berm Giant*, goes to his sire's barrow to secure the sword Birting. Barrow riches are strikingly in evidence here; witness the barrow ghost's questioning of the hero:

> *"And is it thou art come, childe Orm,*
> *My youngest son so dear?*
> *And is it gold, or silver plate,*
> *Or coin, thou seekest here?"*[3]

The fay in *Le Seigneur Nann et la Fée,* a Breton analogue of *Clerk Colvill* (42), combs her hair with a comb of gold:

> *She combed it with a comb of gold—*
> *These ladies ne'er are poor, we're told.*[4]

Bound to a stone by means of a runic spell, a sea fairy in the Danish ballad *Sir Luno and the Mermaid* would buy her freedom with seven tons of silver and eight of gold:

> *"Seven tons of silver and eight of gold;*
> *Have mercy, Sir Luno, and loose thy hold!"*[5]

To further his love for an earthly maiden, the hill king in a Swedish version of *The Maid and the Dwarf King* offers his mother the "ruddiest gold":

> *"Thee will I give the ruddiest gold,"*
> *Time with me goes slow.—*
> *"And thy chests full of money as they can hold."*
> *But that grief is heavy I know.*[6]

---

[1] See Prior's translation, *op. cit.*, II, 333 f. Silver keys are mentioned occasionally in our ballads, as in Nos. 77 D 13; 81 A 18, B 9; 89 A 7.

[2] Cf. the excellent survey of resemblances between the dead and fairies (Wentz, *op. cit.*, pp. 218 ff.).

[3] Prior, I, 135.

[4] Keightley, *op. cit.*, p. 434.

[5] Prior, III, 258.

[6] Keightley, *op. cit.*, p. 104.

With gold and pearls and precious stones a mermaid tries
to tempt a young man in the Swedish ballad *Duke Magnus
and the Mermaid:*

> *"To you will I give as much of gold*
> *As for more than your life will endure;*
> *And of pearls and precious stones handfuls;*
> *And all shall be so pure."*[1]

But from the rich mines of Norse balladry we might furnish
innumerable instances of the wealth of fairies. A few more
examples must suffice. According to a Swedish version of
Hr. Tönne af Alsö, the hill king plays merrily at "gold
tables," the dwarf mother counts among her household
duties that of laying "gold in the chest," while the dwarf
daughter makes music on a "gold harp."[2] A Danish version
of the same ballad pictures the dwarf mother as playing
"with gold in lily hand."[3] In the elfland of Norse folksong
chairs are of gold. The dwarf mother of the Swedish ballad
mentioned above has a "red-gold chair."[4] According to the
Danish piece *Elvehöj*, the "Elfin queen" sits on a golden
chair.[5] If he will but plight his troth to the elfin maid, the
mortal knight in *Elveskud* may sit thereafter on benches
and chairs of gold:

> *"The benches and chairs, whereon you sit,*
> *You'll see them of golden chain-work knit.*
>
> *"And wrought of the gold each drawbridge stands,*
> *As pure as the rings that grace your hands."*[6]

The underwater mountain dwarf in the Danish *Rosmer*
gives the brother of his earthly mistress a "chest of gold"
from out his "treasured store."[7] In British balladry,
whether in songs of the supernatural or not, there
are, as we shall see presently, innumerable references to

---

[1] *Ibid.*, p. 154.
[2] *Ibid.*, p. 98.
[3] Prior, III, 11.
[4] Keightley, *op. cit.*, p. 99.
[5] Prior, III, 244.
[6] *Ibid.*, II, 302.
[7] *Ibid.*, III, 55.

gold and silver. One would like to know what fairy god-
mother it was who provided poor Annet, who has neither
"gowd" nor "gear," with her wondrous apparel, her golden-shod steed, and her splendid retinue. Commenting on
the foregoing ballad, *Lord Thomas and Fair Annet* (73),
Professor Hart says: "The magnificence of Fair Annet's
apparel is thoroughly characteristic of ballads. It is here
all the more striking in that it was precisely because she
had neither gowd nor gear that Lord Thomas was forsaking
her."[1]

Before discussing the fairy steed, which is usually white
and which is caparisoned quite in keeping with its elfin
rider, we may devote a moment or so to the remarkable
display of gold and silver in balladry. This display of
wealth and ornamentation has been commented on at some
length by Andrew Lang. He remarks:

A more curious note of primitive poetry is the lavish and reckless
use of gold and silver. M. Tozer, in his account of the ballads in the
Highlands of Turkey, remarks on this fact, and attributes it to Eastern
influences. But the horses' shoes of silver, the knives of fine gold, the
talking "birds with gold on their wings," as in Aristophanes, are common to all folk-song. Everything almost is gold in the *Kalewala* (*q.v.*), a
so-called epic formed by putting into juxtaposition all the popular songs
of Finland. Gold is used as freely in the ballads, real or spurious, which
M. Verkovitch has had collected in the wilds of Mount Rhodope. . . . .
If the horses of the Klephts in Romaic ballads are gold shod, the steed
in *Willie's Lady*[2] is no less splendidly accoutred,—

> Silver shod before,
> And gowden shod behind.

Readers of Homer, and of the Chanson de Roland, must have observed
the same primitive luxury of gold in these early epics, in Homer reflecting perhaps the radiance of the actual "golden Mycenae."[3]

A dozen or more pages might be devoted to a mere
listing of the gold and silver objects, the jewels and precious stones, the garments of costly material, which enrich

---

[1] *English Popular Ballads*, p. 318.

[2] No. 6, stanza 14; cf. stanza 15: "And at ilka tet of that horse's main,
there's a golden chess and a bell ringing."

[3] "Ballads," *Encyclopaedia Britannica* (11th ed.), III, 266.

the ballad story and shine in sharp contrast to the dark
fatalism of folksong. There is no little import in this parade
of magnificence. As Lang points out, it is a primitive trait,
just as the fondness of the ballads for bright colors and
certain mystic numbers reflects a background of life which
belongs to an early and pagan philosophy. We cannot forego an enumeration of a few of the golden objects: Gold
combs (58 A 10, H 25; 62 J 23); "gowden" fans (10 E 6;
11 A 23, C 18, etc.); gold chairs (5 A 19, C 29, D 21;
261, stanza 11; 65 E 6, F 10; 155 F 5); shoes of gold
(10 O 12; 53 H 30; 243 B 7, C 13, G 2); "gowden knife"
(15 A 36); coffin of gold (24 A 16), bier of "guid red goud"
and "silver clear" (73 G 27); collar of greyhound "flour-
ishd with gold" (43 F 13); "gowd pins" (47 B 28, D 13);
as much gold on "horse's neck" as would buy an earldom
of land (53 B 16); the "bierly bride" was "a' goud to the
chin" (53 C 29, M 39); "the talents of golde were on her
head sette hanged low downe to her knee" (60, stanza 17);
another lady "wore gold" to her toe (63 J 31); gold cradle
(54 B 12, C 11, D 8); basin of gold (93 G 14); cup of gold
(6, stanza 6; 35, stanza 6; 155 F 5); ship-masts "tappd wi
gold" (53 H 29; cf. 58 L 1); gold "beak" of ship (5 C 16);
mantle of "burning gowd" (94, stanza 3); girdle of "red
gowd" with "fifty silver bells and ten" hanging at every
"silver hem" (6, stanza 23); gold key (95 F 2); gold ball
(95 H 3); tower of gold (96 G 12); talking bird to get a cup
of "flowered gold" or a cage of "glittering gold" with the
door of the "best ivory" (4 C 15, E 18); helpful bird to
have "one wing of the beaten gowd, and another of the
silver clear" (96 B 3; cf. 68 A 10, B 13, C 12, D 15, E 9,
F 10, G 4, J 9; 248, stanza 6; 255, stanza 9); smith's ham-
mer "o the beaten gold," hammer-shaft "o gude red
gowd" (98 A 2, C 3); his "studie was o the beaten gowd"
(B 2); golden bowstrings, silver strings (114 J 6, B 11); of
"redd gold shine the yates" of the castle (63 A 18); ship,
chair, shoes, veil of gold (243). Gold is mentioned much
more frequently than silver, but the two often go together.
The Lass of Roch Royal (76 B 5), a ballad with some-

thing of fairy machinery in it, has a "bonny ship" "a' cored oer with pearl"; or, according to another text, the mast of the ship is of beaten gold, the anchor of silver.[1] Sir Andrew's ship (167 A 75) is "besett with pearles and precyous stones."[2] We find diamonds in Nos. 4 D 29; 10 E 11, W 2; 17 A 4, B 2; 76 D 17, E 14; 93 O 1; 213, stanza 19; 235 E 2. The foregoing list is in no sense exhaustive, nor have I given the complete ballad references for any specific use of gold, such as gold chairs, gold girdles, and so on. But lack of space forbids additional references.

THE FAIRY STEED

As already indicated in Lang's remarks, something of the ballad love for ornamentation is found in descriptions of the fairy steed, to which we may now direct our attention. Elfin steeds are splendidly accoutered. Beautiful is the fairy in *Thomas Rymer* (37), and at "ilka tett of her horse's mane" hang "fifty silver bells and nine" (A 2, C 2), or, according to another text, nine "gowden bells."[3] In the related romance there are "bellys three" on each side of the bridle.[4] Whenever "her bridle rang, the steed flew swifter than the wind" (A 6, C 8). The fairy bridles ring at the midnight procession of the elves in *Tam Lin* (39 A 37). Such bridles are often ascribed to fairies, and, as we find in Cromek, the horses' manes may be "hung wi whustles that the win played on."[5] But this accouterment of golden bells is found not only in fairy ballads; it occurs in other songs as well, and, indeed, is not to be taken as distinctive of fairies.[6] In *Willie's Lady* (6), a song of witchcraft, there is a golden-shod horse and "at ilka tet of that horse's main, there's a golden chess and a bell ringing." The heroine in *Lord Thomas and Fair Annet* (73) seems, as we have already noted, to have been magically equipped

---

[1] Child, IV, 472.

[2] On splendid ships see *ibid.*, V, 285.

[3] *Ibid.*, IV, 455.

[4] *Ibid.*, I, 327, stanza 9.

[5] *Remains of Nithsdale and Galloway Song*, p. 299.

[6] See Child, I, 320 n.; V, 290, 470.

to outshine her rival. Her steed is shod with silver and gold, and at its mane hang silver bells (A 17, B 24, E 23, G 15,[1] H 27). According to H 27, a silver bell did hang "on every tait o her horse's mane, an on every tait o her horse's tail a golden bell did ring"; A 16: "He amblit like the wind"; so, too, in No. 94, stanza 4.

In the fairy ballad of *Tam Lin* (39 A) and in two other pieces, *Lord Thomas and Fair Annet* (73 A 16, B 23) and *Child Maurice* (83 B, C), both of which contain traces of the supernatural, the steeds are no less swift than the elfin steed in *Thomas Rymer* (37 A, C) and, in addition, are shod with silver and gold:

> *"The steed that my true-love rides on*
> *Is lighter than the wind;*
> *Wi siller he is shod before,*
> *Wi burning gowd behind"* [39 A 16].

Steeds are shod in similar fashion in Nos. 6, stanza 14; 11 A 21; 76 A 4; 91 E 5; and 94, stanza 4. The fairy steed in the poem of Thomas of Erceldoune is resplendent with saddle of "roelle bone," "stefly sett with precyous stones, and compaste all with crapotee; stones of oryente, grete plente." Its girths are of "nobyll sylke," "bukylls" of "berelle stone," "payetrelle" of "irale fyne," "cropoure" of "orpharë,"[2] and "brydill" of "clere golde" with "bellys three" on "aythir" side.[3]

In certain Norse ballads fairies and ghosts provide mortals with wondrous steeds. The dead mother in the Danish song *Young Swennendal* equips her living son with an elfin horse which "tramps as well on ocean wave as on the solid ground."[4] The dwarf wife in both Swedish and Danish versions of *Hr. Tönne af Alsö* furnishes the earthly

---

[1] Cf. text (*ibid.*, V, 224, stanza 14).

[2] See *ibid.*, V, Glossary, for explanation of these terms.

[3] *Ibid.*, I, 326 f.

[4] Prior, II, 333. Cf. the steed with like powers in the Swedish ballad *Duke Magnus and the Mermaid* (trans. Keightley, p. 154); Danish text (trans. Prior, III, 344).

knight with a horse which will always keep its rider from losing the way.[1] In an effort to seduce Sir Olave, the fairy maiden in *Elveskud* offers him a marvelous horse:

> *"I'll give you a horse to ride, a dun,*
> *To Rome and back in an hour will run."*[2]

Fairy horses—that is, those of the first order—are, in British balladry, usually milk white. In his Introduction to *Tam Lin* (39) Child comments on this color. I omit Child's references to his sources:

The fairy in the Lai de Lauval, ... rides on a white palfrey, and also two damsels, her harbingers . . . . ; so the fairy princess in the English Launfal, ... The fairy king and all his knights and ladies ride on white steeds in King Orfeo, ... The queen of Elfland rides a milk-white steed in Thomas Rymer, A, C; in B, and all copies of Thomas of Erceldoune, her palfrey is dapple gray. Tam Lin, A 28, B 27, etc., is distinguished from all the rest of his "court" by being thus mounted; all the other horses are black or brown.[3]

In British ballads—songs of the supernatural or not—the white horse is the one which will bring the rider to his destination, after the black and the brown have failed (65 B 20 ff.; 91 B 23 ff.).[4] Buchan's copy of *Tam Lin* (39 G 36, 48) gives us a fire-breathing fairy steed, and there is a seven-headed fire-breathing fiend in *King Arthur and King Cornwall* (30, stanza 56).

That the fairy steed is usually white and that the ballads prefer, as a rule, this color for the horse, is possibly a survival of a belief in the sanctity of the white horse or of white animals generally. The white hind as a soul and as a fairy animal has been considered under ideas of the soul.[5] White swine figure in a dream of ill omen in *Fair Margaret*

[1] Swedish text (Keightley, p. 101); Danish (Prior, III, 14).

[2] Prior, II, 302.

[3] *Op. cit.*, I, 339 f. But Tam's steed is "bluid-red" in J 5 (*ibid.*, p. 508), as also in a Greig text, *Last Leaves*, p. 28.

[4] Cf. Nos. 65 C 14 ff., D 15 ff., E 13 ff., F 17, H 28; 75 I 10; 76 A 3, B 23, G 25 ff.; 81 I 7; 91 A 24, G 26 ff.; 222 A 28 ff., B 23 ff. See note, Child, II, 309.

[5] *Supra*, pp. 53 ff.

and Sweet William (74 B 11), though "white" may be a corruption of "wild." Descriptive of animals and fowl and of the complexion of both men and women, and with reference to money, bread, flowers, wine, and so on, the epithet "white" occurs about seven hundred times in the Child ballads.

ACTIVITIES OF FAIRIES

What have the ballads to say concerning the time of day for the appearance of the elfin folk; what of their interest in the chase, in music, and in dancing? The magical powers of fairies will be taken up in detail in our chapters on the Otherworld spell. According to *Tam Lin* (39 A 26), the fairies ride at the "mirk and midnight hour":

> *"Just at the mirk and midnight hour*
> *The fairy folk will ride."*

D 17 and G 32 read: "Between twall hours and ane"; I 47: "the dead hour o the night"; G 31: "they begin at sky setting, rides a' the evening tide." Sir Cawline (61, stanza 18) meets the hill king on Eldrige Hill at "midnight" when "the moone did rise." By the "lee licht o the moon" Clerk Colvill (42 C 5) pays his fatal visit to the mermaid. The doomed sailors in *Sir Patrick Spens* (58 L 2 f.) see the mermaid at night. It was on "a misty night, whan summer was in prime," that Hind Etin (41 A 15), an elf-lover, captured his earthly sweetheart. On a "cauld day and a snell," as he comes from hunting, Tam Lin is taken prisoner by the fairies (39 A 23, B 22).

The belief that fairies roam about on the eve of All Saints' Day is reflected in two of our best ballads, *Tam Lin* and *Allison Gross*. According to every Child variant of the former piece, Tam Lin's fairy friends ride on Hallowe'en. In D 16 they are said to ride "throw all the world wide":

> *"The morn at even is Halloween*
> *Our fairy court will ride,*
> *Throw England and Scotland both,*
> *Throw al the world wide."*

[189]

But according to an Irish text of *Tam Lin*, the fairies ride on the "first of May."[1] Traditions throughout Europe assign Hallowe'en as a time for the wandering of goblins of all sorts. As in *Tam Lin*, so, too, in *Allison Gross* (35, stanza 12) the elves are abroad at this time: "But as it fell out on last Hallow-even, when the seely court was ridin by." With respect to Tam Lin's escape from fairyland in order to avoid being offered by the elves as payment of their "teind to hell," T. F. Henderson observes: "Hallowe'en was the last night of the Celtic year; the 'teind to hell' would become due every seventh Hallowe'en; and apparently escape from fairyland was only possible when the old and new year met."[2] It is noteworthy that the disenchantment of the youth in *Allison Gross* (35) is effected by the fairy queen on Hallowe'en.

Fairies, like ghosts, lose their power over mortals and vanish at cockcrow.[3] In unspelling her lover, the heroine in *Tam Lin* (39 G 56) "held him fast, let him not go, till she saw fair morning." According to D 34, Tam's disenchantment is brought about at "early morn." It is to the crowing of the cock that the young swain in the Danish song *Elvehöj* owes his escape from the "Elfin queans":

> *If God had not help'd me in time of need*
> *With crowing of cock so shrill,*
> *I surely had stay'd with these Elfin queans*
> *In cavern beneath the hill.*[4]

Or as in a Swedish variant: "Had not . . . . the cock his wings clapped then, I had slept within the hill that night, all with the Elve-women."[5] Bound by a runic charm, the

---

[1] *Journal of the Irish Folk-Song Society*, I, 47 f. On fairies and May see Keightley, p. 354. What is the significance of the "bludy month of May" in No. 11 M 13?

[2] Scott, *op. cit.* (ed. Henderson), II, 407.

[3] On the dead and cockcrow see *infra*, pp. 248 ff.

[4] Prior, III, 246.

[5] Keightley, p. 87.

mortal knight in the Danish *Hr. Tönne af Alsö* does not awake from his trance until cockcrow:

> *For o'er a chair she spread for him*
> *A costly silken cloak*
> *And on it sat the knight in trance,*
> *At cockcrow first awoke.*[1]

According to a Swedish version, "she cast Sir Thynnè into a sleep until that the cock he crew."[2]

Aside from their activity in carrying off mortals for this or that reason,[3] the principal occupations of the elves of folksong are dancing, hunting, and riding. Widespread superstitions ascribe to fairies an inordinate love for music and the dance.[4] English and Scottish ballads furnish instances of the elfin dance, and there are excellent examples in Norse folksong. In the British songs—a noteworthy point—this pastime is found indoors. Thus, according to all versions of *The Wee Wee Man* (38), the fairy revels take place in the hall of gold. The dance is accompanied, in certain texts (D, E, G), by the music of pipers:

> *There war pipers playing on ilka stair,*
> *And ladies dancing in ilka ha,*
> *But before ye coud hae sadd what was that,*
> *The house and wee manie was awa* [D 7].

A Motherwell copy (F 7) affords a possible example of vocal accompaniment:

> *And there was mirth in every end,*
> *And ladies dancing, ane and a,*
> *And aye the owre-turn o their sang*
> *Was "The wee wee mannie's been lang awa."*

---

[1] Prior, III, 13.

[2] Keightley, p. 99.

[3] See *infra*, pp. 321 ff.

[4] See Keightley, pp. 351, 363, and *passim;* Wentz, *op. cit.*, pp. 175, 181 f., 207 f., and *passim.*

The romance of Thomas of Erceldoune seems likewise to give evidence of singing to the fairy dance:

> *Knyghtis dawnesede by three and three,*
> *There was revelle, gamene and playe;*
> *Lufly ladyes, faire and free,*
> *That satte and sange one riche araye.*[1]

A preceding stanza (49) lists, however, a number of musical instruments which Thomas finds in the fairy castle. Earlier in the poem (stanza 7) the elfin queen is seen riding over the lea and awhile she "blewe," another she "sange." But elfin music must await discussion in connection with the Otherworld spell.[2]

In the Danish ballad *Elveskud*, an analogue of *Clerk Colvill* (42), the elves dance, not within doors, but on a hill at nightfall, the scene illumined by the magic glow of fairyland:

> *Sir Olave a journey at nightfall rode,*
> *It seem'd as if round him daylight glow'd.*

> *The hill he had trodden, where all by night,*
> *The dwarfs were tripping their dance so light.*[3]

With respect to the magic light in the foregoing ballad, Child has this note: "So, also, Swedish A, F, Norwegian A, C. This is a cantrip sleight of the elves. The Icelandic burden supposes this illumination, 'The low was burning red;' and when Olaf seeks to escape, in Norwegian A, C, E, G, I, K, he has to make his way through the elf-flame, elvelogi."[4] According to our Danish version, Sir Olave is slain by the elves because he refuses to dance with them or accept their rich gifts.[5] In a number of Danish texts of

---

[1] Child, I, 328, stanza 52.

[2] See *infra*, pp. 293 ff., 332 ff.

[3] Prior, II, 301.

[4] *Op. cit.*, I, 375 n.

[5] On the fatal effect of accepting gifts from fairies see *infra*, pp. 290 f.

this piece and in a Swedish copy the hero dances with the fairies—obviously, however, under compulsion.[1]

The dancing scene, given more at length in a Danish copy other than the one we have just quoted, is still in the open, beneath the greenwood tree, with the elf king's daughter leading the dance:

> *Sir Olave he speeds his lonely way*
> *To bid his friends to his wedding day.*
>> *The Elves in chorus with mirth and glee*
>> *Are dancing beneath the greenwood tree.*
>
> *And four he saw dance, and five saw dance,*
> *The Elf-king's daughter herself advance.*
>> *The Elves etc.*
>
> *She tripp'd from out of the Elfin band,*
> *And smiling she held him forth her hand.*
>
> *"O welcome, Sir Olave, but why such speed?*
> *Come hither with me the dance to lead."*[2]

Nothing can tempt Sir Olave to take part in the revels, for tomorrow is his wedding day. But the elf king's daughter will not be thus scorned by an earthly knight:

> *"And dost thou refuse to dance with me?*
> *Then sickness of death shall follow thee."*

According to the Danish song *Elvehöj*, the fairies dance in a ring to the accompaniment of singing:

> *"O do as I bid thee, my pretty young swain,*
>> *And join in the dancers' ring;*
> *My maiden shall time it with sweetest strain,*
>> *Lips ever were heard to sing."*[3]

---

[1] See Child, I, 375 ff.

[2] Prior, II, 306 f.   [3] *Ibid.*, III, 244.

The dancers are said to join hands, according to another text of this ballad: "Join hands in our dancer's ring, and tread to the time of the cheerful strain, my maiden for thee shall sing."[1]

Playing "at the ba' "[2] and "at the chess," and flying "o'er hill and dale" are among the pleasures of the enchanted mortals in one of Scott's texts of *Tam Lin*:

> *There was four-and-twenty earthly boys*
> *Wha all played at the ba,*
> *But Tamas was the bonniest boy,*
> *And playd the best amang them a'.*
>
> *There was four-and-twenty earthly maids,*
> *Wha a' playd at the chess,*
> *Their colour rosy-red and white,*
> *Their gowns were green as grass.*
>
> *"And pleasant are our fairie sports,*
> *We flie o'er hill and dale;*
> *But at the end of seven years*
> *They pay the teen to hell"* [39 M].

The hill king in a Swedish version of *Hr. Tönne af Alsö* sits within the hill and "at gold tables plays merrily." The dwarf king's betrothed should be—so scolds her mother in the same song—in the hill finishing her bride-dress instead of sitting in the rosy grove playing on her gold harp.[3] Overthrown by an earthly knight, the eldrige king in *Sir Cawline* (61, stanza 25) will, so his lady promises, come no more to Eldrige Hill to "sport, gamon, or play."

In addition to riding in procession the fairies are given to hunting.[4] The fairy queen, whose embrace means the

---

[1] *Ibid.,* p. 247.

[2] The game of ball, in various forms, is one of the favorite pastimes of balladry. See Gummere, *Old English Ballads*, pp. lxxxi f.; Broadwood, *Journal of the Folk-Song Society*, IV, 46 n.

[3] Keightley, pp. 98 f.

[4] See Scott, *op. cit.*, II, 354.

loss of seven years of earthly life for True Thomas, calls herself a huntress:

> *"For I'm but a lady of an unco land,*
>   *Comd out a hunting, as ye may see"* [37 B 4].

Another text pictures her with "hawks and hounds" and a "bugle horn" which "in gowd did shine."[1] So, too, in the romance she rides a-hunting, with her *"three* grehoundis in a leesshe," seven "raches" or scenting dogs running beside her, a horn about her neck, and under her belt full many an arrow (stanza 10). Thus equipped, she hunts (stanza 16) the "wylde fee" or animals. Tam Lin was coming from the hunt (39 A 23, B 22, D 13, I 29, I b 47) when he was captured by the "Queen o Fairies."[2]

In virtually all our fairy ballads (35, 37, 38, 39) the elves ride, whether it be for pleasure, in the chase, in the fairy procession, or to carry off or do battle with mortals. The steed of Sir Cawline's Otherworld antagonist is led by a beautiful elfin lady:

> *And a ladye bright his brydle led,*
>   *That seemlye itt was to see* [61, stanza 19].

In both *The Wee Wee Man* (38) and *Thomas Rymer* (37), stories of abduction, the fairy steed is made to carry double:

> *She turned about her milk-white steed,*
>   *And took True Thomas up behind* [37 A 6].

Tam Lin (39), as we have already observed, rides with the fairy courts on Hallowe'en.

According to the ballads, combing the hair is a favorite occupation with both sexes, and with fairies as well as with mortals. There is probably no reason to think that the comb in folksong is employed in supernatural procedure, but it is interesting to note that in primitive life the comb has value not only for ordinary uses but in magic practices

---

[1] Child, IV, 455.

[2] The elf in *Hind Etin* (41 A 21) goes "hynd-hunting"; cf. B 12, C 5.

as well.[1] The witch in *Allison Gross* (35, stanza 2) begins her blandishments by combing the hair of her intended victim. Mermaids are, of course, provided with combs. The sea-fay who dooms Sir Patrick Spens and his sailors to a watery grave starts up by the ship (58 L 2) "wi the glass and the comb in her hand." In other copies she has a fan (P 2) or a "siller cup" (Q 1). All save one of the Child texts of *The Mermaid* (289) are consistent in picturing the water-witch with "a comb and a glass in her hand." For the mermaid with her comb and glass text F 4 substitutes "the kemp o the ship, wi a bottle and a glass intil his hand." "On ilka Saturdays night," says the enchanted youth in *Allison Gross* (35, stanza 10), "my sister Maisry came to me, wi silver bason an silver kemb, to kemb my heady upon her knee." An even more remarkable instance of hair-combing is that in *The Laily Worm* (36, stanza 8). On "every Saturday at noon" a maiden, transformed as a "machrel" of the sea, combs the hair of her brother, who, under a similar spell, is a "laily worm." It is probable that both sister and brother regain their human shapes on Saturday, a point lost from the story. In the Breton ballad *Le Seigneur Nann et la Fée*, an analogue of *Clerk Colvill* (42), a korrigan sits by a spring and combs her hair with a gold comb.[2] According to the British song, the mermaid washes her "sark o silk" at the "wall o Stream" (A 5); washes "silk upon a stane" (C 6). In the latter text she asks her lover to come with her and "fish in flood."

Another interesting case of combing the hair is found in the Danish ballad *Aage og Else*, a probable parallel of *Sweet William's Ghost* (77). The maiden in the story combs the hair of her lover's ghost:

> *She took her comb, fair Elsey,*
> *She comb'd his tangled hair,*
> *And every lock she straighten'd,*
> *She dropp'd on it a tear.*[3]

---

[1] Cf. MacCulloch, *Childhood of Fiction*, p. 180 n.

[2] Trans. Keightley, pp. 433 ff.   [3] Prior, III, 77.

"This image of a lady combing her lover's hair," says Prior, "and dropping a tear on every lock is one of those common to the ballad poetry of the period."[1] May Margret, a soon-to-be enchanted lady (41 B 1), combs "doun her yellow hair." Child Maurice (83 A 2), probably an Otherworld knight, combs "his yellow lockes." "O wha will kemb my yallow hair, wi the new made silver kemb?" cries Anny in *The Lass of Roch Royal* (76). Her brother (D4, E 4; cf. B 4) takes upon himself this important duty. The bereaved maiden in *The Braes o Yarrow* (214 A, E, F, G, I, L) performs a like service for her drowned lover, and in certain texts (A, B, etc.) she ties her long hair about his neck or middle and drags him home.

FAIRY GOVERNMENT

As for their social life—evidenced in their occupations and pastimes and in their dealings with mortals—ballad fairies belong to popular tradition generally. Nor do they depart from this tradition in their government, which is aristocratic. The fairies, says Kirk, are "said to have aristocraticall Rulers and Laws, ..."[2] The British ballads *King Orfeo* (19), *Tam Lin* (39 G 33), Eldred's copy of *The Queen of Elfan's Nourice* (40),[3] Jamieson's story of Child Rowland,[4] and *Sir Cawline* (61) give us a "king of Ferrie," an elf king, or an "eldridge king."[5] And the supernatural lover in *Hind Etin* (41) is—to judge from Norse and German analogues of this piece—a dwarf king, elf king, or hill king. The Otherworld lover in a Gavin Greig variant of *The Elfin Knight* (2) is called the "Laird o' Elfin."[6] Otherworld kings are common in Danish balladry, as in the song *Hr. Tönne af Alsö*:

[1] *Ibid.*, p. 81.

[2] *Secret Commonwealth* (ed. Andrew Lang), p. 15.

[3] *JAFL*, XX, 155.   [4] *Northern Antiquities*, p. 398.

[5] "The eldrige king has something of the character of the ellor-gást family in Beówulf . . . ." (Child, V, 331).

[6] *Folk-Song of the North-East*, art. C.

> *"The King of Dwarfs didst thou betrothe,*
> *To him thine honour plight."*[1]

We find a fairy queen in *Allison Gross* (35), *Thomas Rymer* (37), *The Wee Wee Man* (38), *Tam Lin* (39), and *The Queen of Elfan's Nourice* (40). There are fairy knights and ladies in *The Wee Wee Man*, *Tam Lin*, and in the romance of *Thomas of Erceldoune;* a knight in *The Elfin Knight* (2) and *Lady Isabel and the Elf-Knight* (4). In *Tam Lin* the fairy court, in three companies, rides in procession on Hallowe'en. According to a Motherwell copy of the ballad (39 D 18 ff.), the elfin queen rides in the "head court of them all," and Tam himself, by reason of his earthly lineage, rides next to the queen with a "gold star" in his crown. In J 4, 5, Tam rides in the "thirden court" on "a bluid-red steed, wi three stars on his crown." Buchan's version mentions four courts (G 33 ff.):

> *"Then the first an court that comes you till*
> *Is published king and queen;*
> *The next an court that comes you till,*
> *It is maidens mony ane.*

> *"The next an court that comes you till*
> *Is footmen, grooms and squires;*
> *The next an court that comes you till*
> *Is knights, and I'll be there.*

> *"I Tam-a-Line, on milk-white steed,*
> *A goud star on my crown;*
> *Because I was an earthly knight,*
> *Got that for a renown."*

The black, brown, and white steeds which the fairies ride (A, C, E, F, H, I, J) are in keeping, it seems, with the rank or station of the riders. Thus in the Glenriddell text (B 27):

[1] Prior, III, 12.

"Some ride upon a black, lady,
And some ride on a brown,
But I ride on a milk-white steed,
And ay nearest the town:
Because I was an earthly knight
They gae me that renown."

Tam Lin says (D 20) that he is "next to the queen in renown," because he is an "earthly knight." It is probable
that the fairy queen and her immediate retinue ride white
horses, though this is not expressly stated in any of the
Child versions of our ballad. The dwarf king and his courtiers are found in *Hr. Tönne af Alsö*, a Danish song to which
we have already referred:

"My father dwells in mountain cave
His courtiers round him stand;
My mother dwells there too and plays
With gold in lily hand."[1]

Of all the pages, "gude knights'-sons," that are obliged to
dwell in fairyland, Tamas (39 M 13) is the elf queen's
pride. But let us conclude these remarks on the fairy court
by quoting one of the most beautiful passages in balladry.
Tam Lin has just been rescued from the elves by his sweetheart (39 D 32):

Then sounded out throw elphin court,
With a loud shout and a cry,
That the pretty maid of Chaster's wood
That day had caught her prey.

OTHER PRETERNATURAL BEINGS

Besides portraying elves or fairies proper, the ballads contain many references to supernatural creatures of various
kinds. Monsters, both male and female, were not beyond
the imagination of our ballad-makers. Or rather, we should
say, the balladist simply took over such characters from
popular superstition or indirectly therefrom through ro-

[1] *Ibid.*, p. 11.

mance, saga, and folktales. A giant and a terrible boar[1]
range the "wood o Tore" in *Sir Lionel* (18), a ballad which
"has much in common with the romance of 'Sir Eglamour
of Artois,'" and which "has also taken up something from
the romance of 'Eger and Grime.'"[2] The ballad of *Sir
Cawline* (61), which has remote resemblances to the Danish
Liden Grimmer og Hjelmer Kamp,[3] portrays a "gyant" no
less formidable than the one in *Sir Lionel*, with "fiue heads"
"vpon his squier," but who is no match for the "eldrige
sword" of the hero. A six-headed giant, borrowed from
romances, falls before the valor of another hero in the poor
ballad of *Young Ronald* (304). A Burlow-Beanie or Billy-
Blin, usually found in British balladry as a beneficent
household demon, is in *King Arthur and King Cornwall*
(30)—a ballad which treats of matters known to romance
—a seven-headed, fire-breathing fiend in the service of
Cornwall, but which even here, when once subdued, has
his good points.[4] In *Earl Brand* (7) "Odin in his malicious
mood" is found "masking as Old Carl Hood, 'aye for ill and
never for good.'"[5] The name "Fin" in *The Fause Knight
upon the Road* (3) is "diabolical," says Child, "by many
antecedents."[6]

The Marriage of Sir Gawain (31), another ballad of
minstrel origin, tells the story, very nearly as related in
Arthurian romance,[7] of a brother and sister witched by a
stepmother to dwell in the forest—the one as a carlish
baron with a "great club vpon his backe," the other as the

---

[1] "A terrible swine is a somewhat favorite figure in romantic tales" (Child,
I, 209 f.).

[2] See *ibid.*, p. 209.

[3] See *ibid.*, II, 57.

[4] The Billie Blin is found also in Nos. 5 C 35 f., 44; 6, stanzas 29 ff.; 53 C
14–23; 110 D 15 f., F 60, G 31, N 29. On the derivation of Billie Blin see Child,
I, 67.

[5] Child, I, 67; see also *ibid.*, pp. 95 and nn., 283, 404 f.; Bugge, *Home of the
Eddic Poems* (trans. W. H. Schofield), pp. 313 ff.

[6] Child, I, 21.

[7] *Ibid.*, p. 289.

"worse formed lady" that man ever saw "with his eye."
"Most like a feend of hell" is the sister, a good match for
her brother "soe foule":

> Then there as shold haue stood her mouth,
> Then there was sett her eye;
> The other was in her forhead fast,
> The way that she might see.

> Her nose was crooked and turnd outward,
> Her mouth stood foule a-wry;
> A worse formed lady than shee was,
> Neuer man saw with his eye.

Like nothing so much as the "fiend that wons in hell" is the
even more monstrously formed lady in *King Henry* (32),
the story of which is a variety of that found in the foregoing
piece, and which has a parallel in an episode in Hrólfr
Kraki's saga.[1] A "griesly ghost" of gigantic dimensions,
this foul specter, with her enormous appetite, devours
King Henry's "berry-brown steed," his "good gray-
hounds," his "gay gos-hawks," and then drinks a "punch-
eon o wine" poured into the horse's "sewd up," bloody
hide. That she finally regains her original and lovely shape
scarcely atones for her hideousness as described early in
the story:

> Her teeth was a' like teather stakes,
> Her nose like club or mell;
> An I ken naething she 'peared to be,
> But the fiend that wons in hell.

Kempy Kay's mistress, in an offensive ballad (33), is,
with her vulgar dimensions, a fitting partner for her giant
lover, but, as Child says, she "does not comport herself
especially like a giantess":[2]

[1] See Scott, *op. cit.*, III, 339 f.

[2] *Op. cit.*, I, 301.

Ilka nail upon her hand
Was like an iron rake,
And ilka tooth intil her head
Was like a tether-stake [A 12].

The "wild woman" of two texts of *Sir Lionel* (18 C, D), with her "pretty spotted pig," should not be forgotten,[1] nor the "savage beast" of *Kemp Owyne* (34) and the ugly "worms" of *Allison Gross* (35) and *The Laily Worm* (36), these latter so many transformed mortals. Metamorphosed mortals are not, however, strictly speaking, creatures of the Otherworld, but the dividing line is hardly to be drawn, especially in view of the kindred tradition of mer-folk, a tribe of supernatural characters which are taken into account here and there in this work. Furthermore, it is often difficult to distinguish between fairies and witches, beings who play occasional rôles in balladry and whom we shall consider in the following chapter. To return for a moment to the preternatural folk of the present chapter, it is noteworthy that giants, fire-breathing fiends, and other monsters appear chiefly in ballads which have connections with romance. And I think it is safe to say that such fabulous creatures are not at home in those ballads which seem to be markedly independent of longer, more diffuse, and more literary forms.

[1] The mermaid in *Sir Patrick Spens* (58 Q 2) is called a "wild woman." On the wild women of German tradition see Keightley, *op. cit.*, pp. 234 ff.

Chapter VII

THE BALLAD WITCH

THIS chapter will give some account of those characters in balladry who practice the magic art—
something as to the nature of the sorceress, her
appearance, her apparatus, and her activities, such as
transforming others or herself, producing sleep, causing
the dead to speak, and arresting childbirth. These magical
operations will be treated here, however, with all possible
brevity and largely for the purpose of characterizing the
witch of folksong. Various supernatural practices recorded
in balladry, those of the fairy magician as well as those of
the witch, will be considered at length in our section on the
Otherworld spell.

He who would look for the remote, if not the immediate, antecedents of the witch or enchantress of balladry
will recognize that it is not possible to set even the most
general date for the origin of the belief in sorcery. Moreover, he will recognize that such a belief is not peculiar to
any particular people. It is prevalent among Australians,
Africans, and Amerindians, and may be traced upward
from the level of primitive thought into the life of the bar-
barian and civilized worlds. And it is significant that this
demonism prevailing at the lowest levels of culture does
not differ materially from the witchcraft of civilization—
this as regards the powers of the magician: power over the
elements, over wild beasts, and over man himself. To draw
near to our folksong, it is a commonplace of ethnology and
folklore that the witchcraft of Europe, or, more specifically,
of the British Islands, exemplifies all the basic features of
that of the Solomon Islanders or the natives of Ceylon.[1]

[1] Cf. Gomme, *Ethnology in Folklore*, pp. 48, 52.

And something of that terror occasioned by the worker of evil spells in savage life today or in ancient Teutonic life is reflected in the English ballads just as it is reflected in Icelandic sagas[1] or in fairy tales.[2]

The ballad practitioners of magic—black magic or white—are not, as a rule, to be thought of as members of the "professional" order of sorcerers; that is, they are not pictured in folksong as "official" or public magicians, such as witch doctors or medicine men. Nor do our best ballad witches seem to be akin to those women who formerly in Europe set up as consultants in matters of sorcery. Moreover, the ballads give no evidence of organized witch cults, and there is no indication of those witches who acted concertedly, as in the gangs Scott speaks of.[3] That the ballads do not more fully delineate the witch and her background of life is due probably to the brevity of folksong and to the exigencies of its dramatic character. In the main, then, the ballad witch, or, better, simply the worker in magic, may be regarded as a "lay" magician—one who is acquainted with magical procedure but who, so far as the ballad story goes, has recourse to the black art merely as a means of gaining her own private ends. There is, to be sure, an occasional example of an old crone or "witch-wife" who—somewhat, say, as do old women among the Agariyas of Bengal[4]—imparts her supernatural knowledge to another, but this need not imply witch cults or organizations.

In English and Scottish folksong the practitioners of the malefic art are women, almost without exception. This is to be expected, since in Europe magical powers are almost exclusively in the hands of woman.[5] In Danish folksong Prior finds confirmation of the statement of Tacitus that the Germanic nations ascribed superior wisdom to

[1] Cf. Elton-Powell, *Saxo*, p. lxxx.

[2] Cf. MacCulloch, *Childhood of Fiction*, p. 19 and *passim*.

[3] *Letters on Demonology and Witchcraft* (2d ed.), p. 332.

[4] See Crooke, *Popular Religion and Folk-Lore of Northern India*, II, 264 f.

[5] Cf. "Witchcraft," *Encyclopaedia Britannica* (11th ed.), XXVIII, 755.

women.[1] Says Tacitus: "Inesse quin etiam sanctum aliquid et providum putant, nec aut consilia earum aspernantur aut responsa neglegunt."[2] Our folksong makes occasional mention of the male witch or wizard, and of course fairies work their spells and charms, just as ghosts exert certain powers over the living; but as a general thing the worker in evil magic is a female magician. Without reference to malefic magic, there is many a clever lass in balladry, such as the maiden in *Lady Isabel and the Elf-Knight* (4) and the girl in *The Elfin Knight* (2) or in *Riddles Wisely Expounded* (1), who belongs, perhaps, to the same tradition as the shrewd lass in the Danish song *Childe Ranild:*

> *The King he has a daughter fair,*
> *And young and shrewd is she,*
> *Knows all that in the world is wrought,*
> *And all that e'er shall be.*
> *"Were I as wise!" childe Ranild said.*[3]

The rôle of the man's mother is, in this connection, significant. Witness the part she plays in *Gil Brenton* (5), *Willie's Lady* (6), *Lord Randal* (12), *Edward* (13), *Prince Robert* (87), or in *The Mother's Malison* (216), to give only some of the notable instances. In the ballad household the man's mother holds a position of authority, and it is to her rather than to his father that the son appeals in times of crisis. How much this is the result of the ballad plot and how much the result of the reflection of actual custom, it is hard to say. But it is noteworthy, as in the ballad *Lizie Wan* (51) or the song *Willie o Winsbury* (100 A), that we may in some measure offset this mother-son relationship by the close relationship between father and daughter. In the former case we have, of course, the mother-in-law motif to contend with. However, Gummere's remarks on

[1] *Ancient Danish Ballads*, I, 292.

[2] *Germania* (ed. Furneaux), p. 54.

[3] Prior, I, 287. Cf. the king's daughter in *Sir Cawline* (61, stanza 8): "Ffeitch yee downe my daughter deere, shee is a leeche ffull ffine; . . . ."

the supremacy of the man's mother may well be given here. He says:

> In the case of the mother-in-law, as in the case of the mother's brother, of the sister's son, there is direct historical evidence of ancient power and dignity now unknown; and faint as the traces are in the ballads of this old supremacy of the man's mother, and of the reaction against her pride of place, by cumulative proof they help one to visualize her as a beneficent and authoritative member of the primitive household.[1]

Black magic is, according to our balladry, resorted to by such malevolent characters as the traditionally wicked stepmother, the cruel mother-in-law—the husband's mother, that is—"old women," and "witch-wives." Benevolent magic is usually confided to the hands of the hero or the heroine, as in *Kemp Owyne* (34) and *Tam Lin* (39). In the former piece the man, however, acts under instructions from the enchanted maiden; in the latter, the maiden performs her magic according to the directions of the enchanted hero. But white or benevolent magic will be reserved, on the whole, for discussion under modes of disenchantment.[2]

The rôle of enchantress is played by the malignant stepmother in several of our best ballads—*The Marriage of Sir Gawain* (31), *King Henry* (32),[3] *Kemp Owyne* (34), *The Laily Worm* (36), and *Tam Lin* (39 G). Of these pieces, the first three, at least, have affiliations with romance. The witch stepmother in *The Marriage of Sir Gawain* (31, stanza 46) is "a younge lady," who transforms her stepson and stepdaughter into monstrous shapes. According to the much-abused heroine in *Kemp Owyne* (34 A 1), the enchantress is "the warst woman that ever lived in Christendom." No less wicked is the stepdame in *The Laily Worm* (36): "My father married the ae warst woman the warld

---

[1] "The Mother-in-Law," *Kittredge Anniversary Papers*, p. 24; see also Albert W. Aron, *Traces of Matriarchy in Germanic Hero-Lore*, "University of Wisconsin Studies in Language and Literature," No. 9.

[2] See *infra*, pp. 331 ff.

[3] See Scott's copy (Child, *Ballads*, I, 300, stanza 20).

did ever see." This last-named piece, though "somewhat mutilated, and also defaced, ... has certainly never been retouched by a pen, but is pure tradition."[1] Tam Lin's stepmother (39 G 25), like other malevolent workers of magic, who reverse benevolent charms, exposes Tam to the power of the fairies by "ill-saining" him, just as the cruel mother in *The Mother's Malison* (216) withholds her blessing and pronounces upon her son a curse which drowns him in Clyde's water.

In all the foregoing ballads, save *Tam Lin*, the step-dame transforms her victims into monstrous shapes. And we should say here that the witch of folksong is seen meta-morphosing others rather than herself, although in the traditions of all countries we find instances of self-metamor-phosis by sorceress, fairy, wizard, or medicine man. "She witched me," says the lady in *The Marriage of Sir Gawain* (31), "to the greene forrest to dwell, and there I must walke in womans likenesse, most like a feend of hell. She witched my brother to a carlish b[aron] . . . . that looked soe foule, and that was wont on the wild more to goe." The words of the lady in *King Henry* (32) do scant justice to the maleficent art of her stepdame: "For I was witched to a ghastly shape, all by my stepdame's skill, till I should meet wi a courteous knight wad gie me a' my will." No less horrible are the enchantments in the other ballads, but these are treated in connection with the Otherworld spell and must not detain us here.[2] The power of the witch over the animal world is well illustrated in *The Laily Worm* (36, stanza 14):

> *She has taen a small horn*
> *An loud an shrill blew she,*
> *An a' the fish came her untill*
> *But the proud machrel of the sea.*

In romance, saga, and folktales, as well as in foreign ballads, the stepmother has the rôle of a wicked enchant-

---

[1] Child, I, 315.   [2] See *infra*, pp. 335 ff.

ress.[1] In the Danish *Nattergalen* a harsh stepdame transforms her stepson into a wolf, his sister into a nightingale.[2] The stepchildren in another Danish piece, *Jomfruen i Linden*, suffer a similar fate. One is changed to a linden, the others to deer and hawks.[3] A stepmother poisons her stepson in certain texts of *Lord Randal* (12 J, L, M, N, O); in *Lady Isabel* (261) a maiden meets the same death at the hands of her jealous stepdame. The stepmother in *Kemp Owyne* and in *The Laily Worm* is, like her prototype in certain fairy tales, completely worsted. In the former piece (34 B 17 f.) she is punished by being metamorphosed into a terrible creature—rough-haired, long-toothed, and four-footed. Death by burning, one of the most common penalties for witchcraft in savage, as well as in civilized countries, is the fate of the wicked enchantress in *The Laily Worm* (36).

Our best picture of magic procedure of the black variety is found in *Willie's Lady* (6), where the man's mother casts a wicked spell over the household. The husband's mother, as we have already observed, occupies a commanding position in ballad society, and we should bear this in mind when considering her in the rôle of witch.[4] In *Gil Brenton* (5) the magic powers of the authoritative mother are exercised in behalf of the son and have a semblance of the benefic sort of wizardry, but as a general thing, in balladry and out, the husband's mother, directing her spells, as she often does, against the young wife, takes on a wicked character.[5]

It is this long-standing enmity of the young wife toward the husband's mother that, no doubt, foists upon the moth-

[1] Cf. Child, I, 178, 290 ff., 297, 307, 336 f.

[2] Trans. Prior, III, 119.

[3] *Ibid.*, III, 140; see also *ibid.*, pp. 114, 125.

[4] Cf. Gummere, *Popular Ballad*, p. 173: "Matriarchy in the background or not, the ballads give vast preference to the maternal as compared with the paternal relation."

[5] The position of the mother in balladry is excellently surveyed by Gummere ("The Mother-in-Law," *Kittredge Anniversary Papers*, pp. 15 ff.).

er-in-law in *Willie's Lady* the character of witch. The entire plot of our poem has to do with the arresting of childbirth through the magical devices of the wicked mother-
in-law. Willie's lady can never be "lighter" until the
witch spells are broken. That they are undone by the help
of "Belly Blind," our familiar ballad household-fairy,
brings the song to an interesting conclusion. The fairy
queen in *Allison Gross* (35), a ballad to be considered presently, likewise breaks the charms of a witch. *Willie's
Lady* (6) paints the mother-in-law sorceress in no flattering
colors:

> *And to his mother he has gone,*
> *That vile rank witch of vilest kind.*

The character of our witch's Norse prototype is well portrayed in Danish analogues of *Willie's Lady*. Child's synopsis, in part, of the Norse variants will suffice to picture
the powers of the sorceress:

> She had thought she could twist a rope out of flying sand, lay sun
> and moon flat on the earth with a single word, turn the whole world
> round about! She had thought all the house was spell-bound, except
> the spot where the young wife's chest stood, the chest of red rowan,
> which nothing can bewitch![1]

The various witch charms, as well as the countercharms,
in *Willie's Lady* must be deferred for detailed discussion in
connection with the Otherworld spell.[2]

"Stark and strang" is the husband's mother in the old
ballad of *Gil Brenton* (5), a song with Scandinavian and
French parallels, but she is a practitioner of white rather
than of black magic. That is, she exerts her art in behalf
of her son and at the expense of his bride. By means of a
golden chair she has tested the chastity of each of the
"seven king's daughters" whom, from time to time, her
son has wedded, and in our story she subjects an eighth
bride to the same proof. The point is that none but a "leal
maiden" will sit down in the chair of gold until bidden:

[1] *Op. cit.*, I, 83.   [2] See *infra*, pp. 355 ff.

Was she maiden or was she nane,
To the gowden chair she drew right soon.

Was she leman or was she maiden,
She sat down ere she was bidden.

Out then spake the lord's mother;
Says, "This is not a maiden fair.

"In that chair nae leal maiden
Eer sits down till they be bidden" [5 C].

The same test is found in version D, but the significance
of the chair has been lost in A. In an excellent version of
Leesome Brand recorded in Greig's *Last Leaves of Tradition-*
al Ballads (IX) we again encounter the "golden chair"
test of maidenhood. Apparently, it is to avoid this test
that the heroine elopes with her lover:

"The morn is the day," she said,
"I in my father's court maun stan',
An' I'll be set in a chair o gold,
To see gin I be maid or nane."

In texts A, B, and C of *Gil Brenton* the unchaste bride
induces her bowerwoman to take her place in the marriage-
bed. But in A the imposture is detected through the
agency of magical sheets, blankets, and pillows, which talk
to the husband and divulge the truth. In B, blankets,
sheets, and sword perform the same office:

"Now, speak to me, blankets, and speak to me, bed,
And speak, thou sheet, inchanted web;

"And speak up, my bonny brown sword, that winna lie,
Is this a true maiden that lies by me?"

"It is not a maid that you hae wedded,
But it is a maid that you hae bedded."

Billie Blin, the household-familiar, exposes the same fraud
in C. Standing on a stone is a test whereby the father in

Willie o Winsbury (100 A 4) inquires into the progress of his daughter's amour. Whether or not we have here some kind of stone magic, it is interesting that the father and not the mother, as in *Gil Brenton*, superintends matters. In a Norwegian tale, *Vesle Aase Gaasepige*, a stepping-stone at the side of the bed talks and tells the prince, with respect to each of three successive brides, that he has chosen an impure woman.[1] According to our ballad *The Boy and The Mantle* (29), a minstrel piece affiliated with Arthurian story, the wearing of a magic mantle, the carving of a "bores head," and drinking from a horn serve as divinatory means to prove who among the lords and knights is a "cuckolde."

Again, in *The Lass of Roch Royal* (76) we encounter the man's mother in a sinister rôle. Traces of fairy-lore in this piece justify us in attaching no little significance to Lord Gregory's "witch-mother." Sailing over the sea in search of her lover, the heroine finds him at last in a bonny bower (B 10). Her sailing the bower round about (B 11, F 8), riding the castle "round about" (A 9), and her cry (F 8), "Now break, now break, ye fairy charms," point clearly enough to magic procedure. But our heroine's counter-charms avail naught against the wiles of the man's mother. Long the forsaken maiden stands at her lover's door and tirls at the pin (D 9), but she cannot awaken her lover, who, if we do not discount the supernatural element in the story, is probably sleepbound beneath his mother's magic. In another text Lord Gregory denounces his dame as a "witch-mother":

> *"It's woe be to you, witch-mother,*
> *An ill death may you die!*
> *For you might hae set the yet open,*
> *And then hae wakened me"* [C 10].

The general trend of the story forbids that we regard the hero's epithet as a mere term of opprobrium. Nor, in all probability, is it simply a matter of calling names when the

---

[1] Trans., Dasent, *Popular Tales from the Norse* (2d ed.), p. 478.

[211]

mother, in another copy (D 11 f.), accuses her son's sweetheart of being a "witch, or wile warlock, or mermaid o the
flude." A fragmentary version (G 14) puts this accusation
into the mouth of the hero.

An excellent example of the female magician, a witch
with the various appurtenances of witchcraft, occurs in
the fine ballad *Allison Gross*. The enchantress here is
wealthy; tries, like fairies, to seduce a mortal; and, like
fairies, has the power of transforming human beings. She
is provided with a grass-green horn, exemplifies in her
magical procedure the efficacy of the number "three," has
a "silver wand," and mutters a witch incantation. Like
fairies, she punishes mortal men who reject her love. And
it is significant that she lives in the "north country" as
does the fairy or Otherworld wooer in *Lady Isabel and the
Elf-Knight* (4 E 1, F 1):[1]

> O *Allison Gross, that lives in yon towr,*
> *The ugliest witch i the north country,*
> *Has trysted me ae day up till her bowr,*
> *An monny fair speech she made to me* [35].

The name "Allison" is among the most common witch
names.[2] Failing to seduce the hero by the offer of rich
gifts, Allison vents her fury by changing him into an "ugly
worm."[3] But her malefic spell is undone by the fairy queen,
who, with her "seely court," comes riding by on Hallow-
e'en.[4] The striking resemblance between witches and fairies is illustrated by our ballad. According to a Greek tale,
a variety of "Beauty and the Beast," a youth upon his
refusal to espouse a fairy is turned by her into a snake,[5]
just as the youth in our song is metamorphosed for a similar offense. An elf, a hill-troll, or a mermaid, according

---

[1] See *supra*, pp. 136 ff.

[2] See Murray, *The Witch-Cult in Western Europe*, pp. 255 f.

[3] See the Otherworld spell, *infra*, pp. 290 f.

[4] See *infra*, pp. 343, 396.

[5] B. Schmidt, "Die Schönste," *Griechische Märchen*, No. 10 (cited, Child,
I, 313).

to different versions of the Norse ballad *Elveskud*, attempts—as does our witch—to win a leman by the offer of splendid gifts. But death, as in the analogous *Clerk Colvill* (42), not transformation, is the hero's punishment for rejecting the fairy's suit.[1] This close similarity between witch and fairy will be further illustrated in our chapters on enchantment and disenchantment.[2] Commerce between fairies and witches and even the identification of the Devil with a fairy are instanced in the witchcraft of Western Europe,[3] and the cases of such historic witches as Katherine Carey and Isobel Gowdie in seventeenth-century witch trials likewise exemplify this mingling of fairy and witch beliefs.[4]

Interesting examples of witchcraft or magic, though not altogether of the black variety, are found in three excellent traditional ballads—*The Gay Goshawk*, *The Broomfield Hill*, and *Young Benjie*. The wise woman or "witch-wife" in all these songs is conveniently near at hand and seems, in the first two, to be a member of the household. She is an important figure and offers her services in crises where ordinary human beings are at a loss. According to *The Gay Goshawk* (96), the central idea of which is found in a ballad widely known in France, an "auld witch-wife" (B 12 ff., C 22 ff.) puts into operation an ordeal or test whereby a maiden, who is feigning death, may be proved dead or alive. In texts D and F the mother performs the rite; in E, the "cruel step-minnie";[5] in G, the "auld stepdame." But the "witch-wife" has charge in the better versions, and it is altogether probable that she is the original character and that the mother and stepmother are substitutions. In one version (D 7, 8) the test for death

[1] See Child, I, 314, on *Elveskud* and other Norse pieces. See translations of *Elveskud* (Prior, II, 301 ff.); Swedish texts (Keightley, pp. 82 ff.).

[2] See *infra*, pp. 275, 331.

[3] See Murray, *The Witch-Cult*, pp. 238 ff.

[4] See MacCulloch, "The Mingling of Fairy and Witch Beliefs in Sixteenth and Seventeenth Century Scotland," *Folk-Lore*, XXXII, 236 ff.

[5] See Child, II, 367*b*.

consists in rubbing "red, red lead" on the chin and on the toe of the clever maiden. Considering that the red lead "is to be *rubbed on*," says Child, "one may ask whether some occult property of minium may have been known to the mother."[1]

The Broomfield Hill (43) gives us still another witch, and tells a story of sleep-producing charms. Concerning this ballad and its survival in Somerset and Dorset, Lucy Broadwood observes:

> That a ballad so full of magic should have survived in Somerset and Dorset is not surprising in the light of Miss M. A. Murray's anthropological study *The Witch-Cult in Western Europe* (1921), where a mass of documents prove how wide-spread the cult was in those counties throughout long centuries, and how persistent and organized it still was, there, in the latter part of the seventeenth century.[2]

By carrying out a witch woman's instructions, the heroine of our ballad, wholly without injury to her honor, keeps an appointment with her lover. Wrought upon by the witch spell, a kind of circle magic coupled with the strewing of broom flowers, the lover falls asleep on the hill, and is not aware that his sweetheart has kept her tryst until (C 17 ff.; cf. A, B, D, E, F) he is so informed by his "berry-brown steed," his "gay goss-hawk," his "guid grey hound," and his "merry men." Needless to say, the testimony of the "merry men" is superfluous in a good ballad where horse, hawk, and hound have the power of speech.[3] The soporific spell is paralleled in Scandinavian ballads, where, however, the sleep is produced by runes.[4] Let us give those passages in the British song which serve to introduce the witch. The maiden, after having agreed to meet her lover, is in a quandary, but she is directed aright by (A 4) a

---

[1] *Ibid.*, p. 357 n. See the "burning lead" (*ibid.*, p. 367*b*). In the story of Child Rowland the king of elfland employs a "bright red liquor" in reviving the hero's two brothers from their magic sleep. He anoints their lips, nostrils, eyelids, ears, and finger-ends (Jamieson, *Northern Antiquities*, p. 403).

[2] *Journal of the Folk-Song Society*, VII, 32.

[3] On speaking and helpful animals, see *supra*, pp. 44 ff.

[4] See *infra*, p. 300.

"witch-woman, ay from the room aboon"; or (C 6) by "an auld witch-wife, sat in the bower aboon." A tale in the *Gesta romanorum* has a similar incident of sleep-producing magic. The "witch-woman" in the British folksong plays the rôle of the philosopher in the *Gesta*.[1]

The fine ballad of *Young Benjie* (86) preserves the superstition that if certain ceremonies are observed a corpse can be made to speak—a belief considered at some length later in this study in connection with the return of the dead.[2] Two brothers seek their sister's murderer. On the night of her wake, the slain maiden, brought back to life by magic rites (A), speaks to her brothers and tells who her slayer is. These rites are lacking in B. In lieu thereof we find an "auld woman" who happens along after the elder brother has expressed a wish that he might consult a conjurer in some country:

> "O if I were in some bonny ship,
>   And in some strange countrie,
> For to find out some conjurer
>   To gar Maisry speak to me!"
>
> Then out it speaks an auld woman,
>   As she was passing by:
> "Ask of your sister what you want,
>   And she will speak to thee."

Our ballad incident may in a general way be classed with the universal feat of raising corpses as instanced in the Witch of Endor story and in the "phenomena" of the modern spiritistic *séance*. It is possible that in some unknown variant of our song the "auld woman" of B appears as conductress of the ceremonies found in A, although Scott's account of the superstition, as current in Scotland, makes no mention of witch or wizard.[3]

The number of ballad witches is not unimposing and might be far larger yet, were it not that the ballad-maker

[1] Cf. Child, I, 393.

[2] See *infra*, pp. 262 f.   [3] See *infra*, p. 262.

so often fails to specify the agents of that magic which
permeates folksong. Nevertheless, several good examples
of the witch remain to be surveyed. A notable ballad witch
is the "old woman" who bans bold Robin in that song
which tells how the outlaw hero meets his death at the
hands of his kinswoman, the false prioress. Robin Hood is
ailing, and, with Little John, is on his way to Kirklees pri-
ory for "blooding." They come to black water, crossed by
a plank. On the plank an old woman is kneeling, and curs-
ing Robin Hood:

> *They two bolde children shotten together,*
>   *All day theire selfe in ranke,*
> *Vntill they came to blacke water,*
>   *And over it laid a planke.*
>
> *Vpon it there kneeled an old woman,*
>   *Was banning Robin Hoode;*
> *"Why dost thou bann Robin Hoode?" said Robin* [120 A].

. . . .

"Robin Hood asks why," comments Child, "but the answer
is lost, and it is not probable that we shall ever know: out
of her proper malignancy, surely, or because she is a hired
witch, for Robin is the friend of lowly folk."[1] Despite the
fragmentary evidence, we must believe that the designs
of the guilty prioress on Robin's life were made more certain of their effect by the old woman's curse. Witches of
old were wont thus to vent their vituperative magic upon
many a hapless victim, and of course their services were
greatly in demand when the business of vengeance was to
be accomplished. That the old woman in the ballad is
kneeling above the water as she bans Robin and that the
water is black may not be without significance, though we
should not venture to say that we have to do here with a
water demon of some sort. In *The Mother's Malison* (216)
a maternal curse dooms a young man to death in Clyde's
water, and, incidentally, gives the song its name.

[1] *Op. cit.*, III, 102.

[216]

The ballad of *Northumberland Betrayed by Douglas* tells, among other things, of a lady whose mother was a "witch woman" and who has the power of second sight—the ability, in this instance, to discern events occurring at distant places. The period of our ballad was one of witchcraft, and the imputation of practicing the black art was directed not altogether at crones of lowly life but at ladies of rank as well, among them the Countess of Athole, the Lady Buccleuch, and the Lady Foullis.[1] Mary Douglas of the ballad has, like certain other ballad characters, learned the art of sorcery from her mother:

> "My mother, shee was a witch woman,
>   And *part* of itt shee learned mee;
> Shee wold let me see out of Lough Leuen
>   What they dyd in London cytye" [176, stanza 26].

This confession Mary makes after she has shown the chamberlain, through the "weme" or hollow of her ring, the English lords who are waiting for his master "thrise fifty mile" distant. During the procedure, the chamberlain stands at Mary's right hand. But he, well aware of the ill repute in which witchcraft is held, has already disclaimed any love for the profession:

> Saies, I neuer loued noe witchcraft,
>   Nor neuer dealt with treacherye [stanza 19].[2]

Parallels to Mary's divinatory feat are numerous in European traditions,[3] and, to return to our own folksong, we have in *Hind Horn* (17) and *Bonny Bee Hom* (92) incidents that are probably related to that preserved in the *Northumberland* ballad. In ballad and romance a ring, by changing color or by rusting, reveals the infidelity or the death of an absent loved one.[4] Such a ring we find in *Hind Horn* (17 A):

[1] See *ibid.*, p. 410.

[2] Cf. variant stanza (*ibid.*, p. 415, stanza 19).

[3] See *ibid.*, p. 411; V, 299.

[4] See *ibid.*, I, 201, 269; IV, 450; Hartland, *Perseus*, II, 1 ff.

He's gien to her a silver wand,
With seven living lavrocks sitting thereon.

She's gien to him a diamond ring,
With seven bright diamonds set therein.

"When this ring grows pale and wan,
You may know by it my love is gane."

The ring is also present in texts B, C, D, E, F, G,[1] and H. The wand and the larks are found in only two texts besides A—versions B 3, F 4. The significance of the wand is not clear, but we may suppose it was to perform some such function as that of the ring. It may represent a combination of motifs—that of talking and helpful birds with that of magic rings and other ornaments.[2] The magic ring in *Bonny Bee Hom* has the power to make a man invulnerable, and, in addition, by the discoloration of its stone, to indicate that his love is dead or untrue. Both here and in the *Hind Horn* piece we may have vestiges of the life-token motif:[3]

"Weell, take this ring, this royal thing,
Whose virtue is unknown;
As lang's this ring's your body on,
Your blood shall neer be drawn.

"But if this ring shall fade or stain,
Or change to other hue,
Come never mair to fair Scotland,
If ye're a lover true" [92 B].

According to A, it is a "chain of the beaten gold" that gives invulnerability; the ring with a ruby stone, by changing its hue, proves "your love is dead and gone, or she has

---

[1] Cf. variant of G (Child, V, 210).

[2] Cf. Gummere, *Popular Ballad*, p. 294 n.; Child, III, 501; IV, 450. Cf. the bird in a Greig version, *Last Leaves of Traditional Ballads and Ballad Airs*, p. 18.

[3] See *supra*, p. 43.

proved untrue." A common ill omen in balladry is that
—as in *Lamkin* (93 B 23)— of rings breaking in twain.[1]
But let us return to more obvious instances of witchcraft.

The male witch, conjurer, or wizard, as we have already
observed, seldom appears in our balladry. So far as the
ballad story goes, when we do find the man working in
magic he is acting under instructions from the woman, as
in *Kemp Owyne* (34). After the knight in this piece has restored the maiden to her human form, it is the maiden,
and not he, who retorts the black magic upon the witch
stepmother (B 17 f.). Adler Yonge in *King Estmere*, a ballad to be considered shortly, owes his knowledge of "gramarye" to his mother. Whether or not old Carl Hood,
Odin in malignant guise,[2] defeats the plans of Earl Brand
and his sweetheart (7) by some sort of evil spell or whether
he merely plays the part of a telltale, it is certain that the
eloping lovers owe their misfortune to him, who "comes for
ill, but never for good":

> They have ridden oer moss and moor,
> And they met neither rich nor poor.

> Until they met with old Carl Hood;
> He comes for ill, but never for good.

> "Earl Bran, if ye love me,
> Seize this old carl, and gar him die."

> "O lady fair, it wad be sair,
> To slay an old man that has grey hair" [A 7].

In still other texts of our ballad Carl Hood appears: A c 7;[3]
G 4, 5; H 7, 8; and in two copies not numbered by Child.[4]

---

[1] For other ballad instances see Nos. 93 H; 208 B, D, E, F, H, I. Cf. buttons
that fly off: Nos. 65 J (Child, IV, 466), 90 D; 93 D, H. See my study, *Death and
Burial Lore*, chap. iii.

[2] On Carl Hood as Odin see Child, I, 67, 95.

[3] *Ibid.*, p. 104.   [4] *Ibid.*, IV, 443 ff.

In all these versions, except H, the maiden asks her lover to kill Carl Hood, but he, usually out of respect for gray hairs, refuses to do so. In one version it is the "auld palmer Hood" who gives Earl Brand his deathblow.[1] Concerning Carl Hood's counterpart in Norse ballads, Child says:

For "old Carl Hood," . . . . Danish 82 X and Norwegian A, C have an old man, Danish C a crafty man, T a false younker, and Norwegian B and three others "false Pál greive." The lady's urging Earl Brand to slay the old carl, and the answer, that it would be sair to kill a gray-haired man, sts. 8, 9, are almost literally repeated in Norwegian A, Landstad, No. 33. The knight does slay the old man in Danish X and Norwegian C, and slays the court page in Danish Z, and the false Pál greive in Norwegian B,—in this last *after* the battle.[2]

In only one of the Child texts of the English song does Carl Hood play a part in the battle.[3] In *Johnie Cock* (114) another malignant old man plays the rôle of informer, not a supernatural rôle, to be sure, but these wicked old men of our ballads should not go unnoticed. In A 10, B 4, he is called an "old palmer"; in D 10, E 9, G 9, J 3, a "silly auld man"; in F 9, a "silly auld carle"; in H 11, a "stane-auld man."

Adler Yonge, the brother of King Estmere in the ballad of that name (60), is, as we have already said, versed in "gramarye," knowledge of which he, like Mary Douglas of *Northumberland Betrayed by Douglas* (176), has acquired from the maternal side of the house. Adler employs his magic by way of making King Estmere, his brother, proof against any sword in England. Invulnerability to the deadliest arms is a common feature of folktales.[4] Our ballad, according to Bugge, has important affiliations with Norse balladry, *Young Orm and Bermer-Giant* and *Olger the Dane*[5]—the latter based on the romance of *Ogier le Danois*—as well as with the Faroese ballad *Arngrim's*

---

[1] *Ibid.*, p. 445, stanza 20.

[2] *Ibid.*, I, 92; see also *ibid.*, p. 95 n.

[3] *Ibid.*, IV, 445, stanza 20.

[4] Cf. MacCulloch, *Childhood of Fiction*, p. 19.

[5] For translations of these two songs, see Child's references (*op. cit.*, II, 50 nn.)

Sons.[1] In all these pieces an irresistible sword plays a part. Taught by his mother, who, like all witches, understands the magic properties of plants, Adler Yonge knows an herb which will give his royal brother protection against his foe:

"Now hearken to me," sayes Adler Yonge,
"And your reade must rise at me;
I quicklye will devise a waye
To sette thy ladye free.

"My mother was a westerne woman,
And learned in gramarye,
And when I learned at the schole,
Something shee taught itt mee.

"There growes an hearbe within this field,
And iff it were but knowne,
His color, which is whyte and redd,
It will make blacke and browne.

"His color, which is browne and blacke,
Itt will make redd and whyte;
That sworde is not in all Englande
Upon his coate will byte."

Magic flowers and plants are discussed at length under the Otherworld spell.[2]

According to Lord Scroope in *Kinmont Willie* (186, stanza 46), bold Buccleuch, by his daring feat of plunging through Eden Water, proves himself of diabolical lineage. "He is either himsell a devil frae hell," cries Lord Scroope, "or else his mother a witch maun be." For a similar accomplishment, Dicky Ha (188 A 42) wins like questionable praise: "I think some witch has bore the, Dicky, or some devil in hell been thy daddy"; or (B 28):

[1] See *ibid.*, pp. 49 f., Bugge's conclusions and Child's criticism thereof.

[2] See *infra*, pp. 349 ff.

"Surely thy minnie has been some witch,
Or thy dad some warlock has been;
Else thow had never attempted such,
Or to the bottom thow had gone."

Or yet again (C 31): "Your mither's been some wild rank witch, and you yoursell an imp o hell." That Donald (226 B 20) may be a "witch or a warlock, or something o that fell degree," does not deter Lizie Lindsay from eloping with him. Andrew Lammie (233 C 17) denies that he has employed the "wicked art" in winning bonny Annie.

The foregoing pages will suffice to show the general character of the practitioner of magic as portrayed in the English ballads. Such matters as the apparatus of the witch—the horn, the wand, the magic circle, magic plants, incantations, and so forth—are treated more in full in the following chapters on the Otherworld spell. The witch-familiar is also considered in that connection, as well as in the chapter on ideas of the soul. In concluding the present section, let us glance for a moment at whatever evidence the ballads hold of those books that are associated with witches and conjurers. We shall find a hint, possibly, of that book or manuscript from which the devil instructed his votaries—such a volume as the *Red Book of Appin*, a book in existence up until the beginning of the last century.[1] One thinks of Prospero's book in *The Tempest*, though the deposed duke is, of course, a white magician. Concerning the expression "gramarye" or magic in *King Estmere* (60, stanzas 36, 41, 55, 68), Child has this glossarial note:

Gramery=grammar, learning, occurs three times in the Towneley Mysteries, but strangely enough seems not to have been heard of in the sense of magic till we come to Percy's Reliques. Percy suggests that the word is probably a corruption of the French *grimoire*, a conjuring book. Grimoire, however, does not appear until the 16th century and was preceded by gramoire (Littré). Gramaire in the 13th–15th centuries has the sense of magic: see the history of grimoire in Littré. Godefroi interprets gramaire savant, magicien.[2]

[1] See J. G. Campbell, *Superstitions of the Highlands*, pp. 293–94.
[2] *Op. cit.*, V, 340; see also "Gramarye," *New English Dictionary*, IV.

In connection with her power of second sight, instanced in her ability to see London through the "weme of her ring," Mary Douglas (176), who has been tutored by her mother, a "witch-woman," speaks of a "booke."[1] But her "booke" may or may not be a book of magic. The "Booke of Mable" in *The Earl of Westmoreland* (177, stanza 61; cf. 39) is a book of prophecies. With a "litle booke" Sir Bredbeddle, in *King Arthur and King Cornwall* (30, stanza 46), subdues a fire-breathing, "lodly feend, with seuen heads, and one body."[2] In the Danish ballad *Hr. Tönne af Alsö* the dwarf's wife calls for the "book" and releases the earthly knight from the spell of the "runic strain."[3] A Swedish version reads:

> *And it was Thora, the little Dwarf's wife,*
> *The five rune-books she took out;*
> *So she loosed him fully out of the runes,*
> *Her daughter had bound him about.*[4]

Lady Livingston's mother (262, stanza 30) "got it in a book" that her daughter would suffer misfortune:

> *"My mother got it in a book,*
> *The first night I was born,*
> *I woud be wedded till a knight,*
> *And him slain on the morn."*

In this same piece Lord Livingston has been warned by a "witch-woman" that disaster is imminent.

Throughout this chapter we have seen that it is usually the woman who shows herself possessed of supernatural powers and who is acquainted with magical procedure. As another instance of the wise woman of British balladry we may cite the case of Leesome Brand's mother (A 15). Leesome has lost both his lady and his young son, but his

---

[1] See Child, III, 412, stanza 25; 415, stanza 25.

[2] On the character of this "litle booke" see *infra*, p. 379.

[3] See translation (Prior, III, 13, stanza 23).

[4] Keightley, p. 99.

mother tells him how to restore them to life with "three draps o' Saint Paul's ain blude."[1] The lover in *The Earl of Mar's Daughter* (270) owes the convenience of his bird shape to his mother who lives on "foreign isles" and is "skilld in magic spells":

> *"Likewise well skilld in magic spells,*
> *As ye may plainly see,*
> *And she transformd me to yon shape,*
> *To charm such maids as thee."*

From someone the clever lass in *The Elfin Knight* (2 I 15) has learned riddlecraft. Upon this teacher the "auld man" —outwitted by the maiden—pronounces a curse:

> *"My curse on those wha learnëd thee;*
> *This night I weend ye'd gane wi me."*

---

[1] Cf. an excellent version of this ballad in Gavin Greig, *op. cit.*, pp. 16 f. In this text the three drops of blood are not said to be Saint Paul's.

with stones, orientation, burial of belongings with the
dead, distinctions in burial, double burial, heart burial, and
burial at sea. Dreams, premonitions, omens, auguries of death,
occur here and there, and are treated in the kindred field of
that empty the entire folk ballad and its sustaining catalogue.
The ballads furnish material enough for a chapter on barbarous practices—various forms of mutilation, such as severing the hands and feet, the head, and the breasts, pluck

Chapter VIII

THE BALLAD GHOST

❧

THE term "ballad," even when applied to the traditional poem or Child type of song, not infrequently carries with it a connotation of humor and
jesting of that variety which in the past drew down ecclesiastical anathema upon both ballad and balladist. If the
British ballads, however, as illustrated in Professor Child's
cyclopedic work, merit churchly reproof, it is not—with
the exception of a few pieces—because of their being characterized by unseemly levity or gross fun. Offensive
enough, to be sure, is the ballad of *Kempy Kay* (33), and
perhaps also *The Twa Magicians* (44), a "base-born cousin
of a pretty ballad known over all Southern Europe." Inoffensive comedy there is in songs like *Hind Horn* (17) and
Tom Potts (109), but it is tragedy, heavy and somber,
which, on the whole, serves as the inspiration of the Northern ballad at its best. "A round hundred of ballads," computes Professor Gummere, "the longest list, are purely and
simply tragic; and to these must be added 'Otterburn' and
'Cheviot' from the chronicles."[1]

This tragic character of the British ballads suggests at
once that our popular poetry holds a wealth of superstitions and practices centering about the subject of death.
Nor is one disappointed who looks thoroughly into the
matter. The ballads have a great deal to say about mourning, about the wake, and about related matters, such as
the "dead-bell," doles for the dead, laying out the corpse,
and making the graveclothes, the bier, and the coffin. They
speak, too, of modes of burial—the heaping of the grave

[1] *The Popular Ballad*, pp. 339 f.; cf. W. M. Hart, *English Popular Ballads*,
p. 13.

with stones, orientation, burial of belongings with the dead, distinctions in burial, double burial, boat burial, and burial at sea. Dreams and omens, premonitory of death, occur here and there in our folksong, and the kinds of death that empty the ballad stage make an interesting catalogue. The ballads furnish material enough for a chapter on barbarous practices—various kinds of mutilation, such as severing the hands and feet, the head, and the breasts, plucking out the eyes, or cutting out the tongue and the heart. In folksong one finds no inadequate depiction of judicial procedure, especially as exemplified in capital crimes and punishments, in private as well as collective justice.[1] But these matters, even those relating to funerary customs, lie somewhat outside the scope of this work. We shall here consider the ballad actor after he has passed from the mortal stage, or as he returns thereto in the character of a dead man.

THE BALLAD TREATMENT OF THE SUPERNATURAL

The ballad grave, as well as any other, knows how, on occasion, to let "forth his sprite." But it is perhaps a mistake to introduce the ghost of popular song with a literary allusion, even though that allusion be to Shakespeare, who knew his folklore. The dead in balladry are, in the main, not "literary," are not meant to lend an atmosphere, nor do they need an atmosphere to set them off. To the ballad folk and to the folk-ballad they were entirely plausible and matter of fact. Not yet vulgarized to the modern spook nor yet refined to the discarnate soul, the revenant of traditional poetry can, as in *The Unquiet Grave* (78), feel the tears of the living. Not unsubstantial and airy, it can touch and be touched, and its kiss is fatal.[2] Dr. Otto Böckel and Dr. Walter M. Hart have pointed out the naïve belief of ballad folk in the supernatural and the special fitness of the ballad

---

[1] See my study, *Death and Burial Lore in the English and Scottish Popular Ballads*, "University of Nebraska Studies in Language, Literature, and Criticism" (1927), No. 8.

[2] See *infra*, pp. 289, 330 ff.

to treat this belief. Innumerable, and met with in all literatures of the people, are those folksongs in which the dead speak with the living and hunt them out in order to carry them away. But, says Dr. Böckel, "Das alles wird nicht etwa als wunderbar empfunden, sondern durchweg als selbstverständlich und wohl begreiflich naiv berichtet."[1] Dr. Hart observes:

They [the ballads] illustrate implicit belief in the existence of such beings, of mermen and mermaids, elves and fairies, witches and ghosts. And this belief is so complete that the balladist seems to take the supernatural quality for granted and to feel under no obligation to make his story seem probable by means of some special way of telling it. It is altogether by accident that the ballad art is peculiarly fitted for the representation of the supernatural. The brevity of the ballad, its tendency to proceed by allusion and suggestion, its omission of essentials, its love of the unmotived and unexplained, combine to give a special charm and effectiveness to its stories of fairies or ghosts. Yet the method of the ballad is quite other than that of the literature of art.[2]

Professor Hart's statement as to the "method of the ballad" and the ready acceptance by the ballad-singing folk of the supernatural, disposes one to ask whether or not the ballad revenant, with its unquestionable corporeity and objectivity, may not be described as non-literary, or, at least, as being one or more removes nearer the revenant of early thought than is the ghost of the literature of art— the ghost, say, of Shakespeare's art.[3] The ballad ghost, as will be seen shortly, is decidedly a corporeal revenant. It has not suffered displacement by the "mere ghost," a displacement which was, as the result of a literary convention, the fate of the bodily revenant of Greek tradition.[4] An instance of modernization of the ballad ghost was readily detected by Professor Child. At the expense of anticipa-

[1] *Psychologie der Volksdichtung*, pp. 209 f.

[2] *English Popular Ballads*, p. 26; see also the same author, *Ballad and Epic*, pp. 21 f.

[3] On Shakespeare as a folklorist see H. B. Wheatley, "The Folklore of Shakespeare," *Folk-Lore*, XXVII, 378.

[4] See J. C. Lawson, *Modern Greek Folk-Lore and Ancient Greek Religion*, p. 432.

tion it may be noted here. The vanishing of the lover's
spirit, or rather the lover's corpse, is thus described in the
Ramsay text of *Sweet William's Ghost* (77 A 15):

> *Evanishd in a cloud of mist,*
> *And left her all alone.*

But there can be no doubt, as Child says, that this stanza
and the one which follows it "are modern."[1] Such a passage is on a par with those ballad texts or lines in which
Buchan makes parrots of his talking birds, and is almost
as unballad-like as the following stanza from a text of
Tam Lin (39). The would-be balladist offers a description
of the fairies:

> *They sing, inspired with love and joy,*
> *Like skylarks in the air;*
> *Of solid sense, or thought that's grave,*
> *You'll find no traces there.*[2]

The ballad ghost does not vanish in the spectacular
manner described in Ramsay's text of *Sweet William's
Ghost*, for the revenant of folksong—this even in Ramsay's
text—is obviously an animated or living corpse, is in most
cases thought of as not separated from the body at all, and
is at times, indeed, designated as the "corpse." There is
little or nothing in our best supernatural ballads to indicate that the ghost of folksong is the breath—*anima, spiri-
tus*—in keeping with the shades of Greek, Roman, or Hebrew traditions.[3] Of course it should be borne in mind
that the belief in a bodily revenant may exist alongside
the belief in a more immaterial ghost. But the materiality
of the ballad revenant is a primitive or early trait,[4] and our
songs seem to reflect a period or stage of thought when

---

[1] *Ballads*, II, 226.   [2] *Ibid.*, I, 357.

[3] I may call attention here to a study of our ghost ballads by Konrad Ehrke:
Das Geistermotiv in den schottisch-englischen Volksballaden (Marburg, 1914). Dr.
Ehrke recognizes the corporeal nature of our revenants.

[4] On Celtic traditions see MacCulloch, *Religion of the Ancient Celts*, pp.
336 f., 339.

mankind had not yet grasped the idea of the separation between soul and body or, it is very possible, had not yet
conceived the idea of the soul. We should urge at this
point, moreover, that there is little doubt as to the objectivity of the ghosts of folksong, however much there may
be as to that of Shakespeare's revenants.[1] The ballad
ghost seldom appears in dreams and may present itself to
more than one person at a time.

THE LIVING DEAD MAN

As introductory to our evidence that the ballad revenant is a living corpse, I shall, at the risk, perhaps, of too
generous quotation, call attention to Hans Naumann's
important study of the "pre-animistic" significance of the
living corpse. In his illuminating work *Primitive Gemeinschaftskultur* Dr. Naumann observes:

> Totenkult und Seelenglaube sind keineswegs etwa identisch, und
> der eine bedingt nicht den andern. Dass Totenkult notwendig auf eine
> dualistische Auffassung hinweisen müsse, ist eine Voreingenommenheit.
> Dass er aber auf den Glauben an ein Weiterleben nach dem Tode
> hindeutet, darf wohl als sicher gelten. Nur ist die Form dieses Weiter-
> lebens mitunter und zunächst eine andere, als man bisher annahm,
> nämlich die körperliche, unseelische.[2]

And, warning against the tendency to impose upon primitive thought the outlook or interpretation of a late culture,
Naumann says that the walking of the living corpse is not
to be explained by holding that the disembodied soul was
in this event thought by primitive man to have rejoined
the dead body:

> Dieses Umgehen des lebendigen Leichnams aus einer Wiederverei-
> nigung der Seele mit dem Körper zu erklären, wie Brunner und andere
> das tun, erscheint uns heute mindestens für die primitive Zeit gleich-
> falls viel zu kompliziert. Ich möchte aber meinen, dass der Volksglaube
> überhaupt niemals auf diese Erklärung verfällt, sondern nur der mo-
> derne Interpret, der an die Dinge mit dem Animismus wie mit einem
> Postulat heranzutreten gewöhnt ist.[3]

[1] See E. E. Stoll, "Objectivity of Ghosts in Shakespere," *PMLA*, XXII,
201–33.

[2] P. 25. [3] P. 27.

The substance of Naumann's essay is that the conception of the living corpse did not in the primitive mind necessarily carry with it the conception of a soul or spirit. The animistic interpretation erroneously ascribes to early thought a belief which, as in the case of the material revenant, had, in all probability, no existence. We need not go beyond the pre-animistic view in order to explain the animated corpse.

We may now survey those ballad incidents which reflect the conception of the bodily revenant. Among a mass of convincing evidence which he assembles to support his view that the vitalized dead man is a pre-animistic notion, Naumann includes the belief that the dead man is disturbed by the tears of the living, a belief widely spread, and preserved in folksong, tale, and saga, as in the German ballad *Der Vorwirt*, and so, too, in the lay of Helgi Hundingsbani. Having commented upon the decidedly corporeal nature of the returned Helgi—a matter to be considered farther on—Naumann points out that the *Tränenmotiv* of the Helgi lay is present also in the foregoing German ballad:

Situation und Motiv (der Tote beklagt sich, dass ihn im Grabe die täglichen Tränen der Gattin benetzen) begegnen gleichfalls in Balladenform auch in dem deutschen Volkslied "Der Vorwirt," d. h. der erste Gatte (der wieder verheirateten Frau). Der Tote lässt ihr sagen:

> *Sie soll auf den Abend kommen hieher,*
> *wenn alle Leute schlafen schwer,*
> *wenn alle Türen verschlossen sein,*
> *wenn alle Gräber weit offen sein.*

(Vergl. im Helgiliede: Auf ist der Hügel geschlossen. Helgi ist gekommen die Wunden bluten, es bittet dich der Fürst usw. Str. 42.)

> *Sie soll mir bringen alleine,*
> *ein Hemd von weissem Leinen;*
> *das erste ist mir von Tränen so nass,*
> *was weint sie immer, was tut sie das?*

(Vergl. dazu Helgilied Str. 44: Du selber, Sigrun, bist schuld, dass Helgi nass ist. Du weinst bittere Tränen, bevor du schlafen gehst; blutig, feucht, kühl fällt jede auf meine Brust.)

Wir können dieses häufige, besonders aus Grimm, *Kinder- und Hausmärchen* No. 109 bekannte Tränenmotiv hier nicht weiter verfolgen; seine präanimistische Natur ist klar.[1]

The widespread belief that the dead feel and are disturbed by the tears of the living, that such tears, according to Irish tradition, actually pierce a hole in the dead,[2] may be taken as part of our evidence that the ballad revenant is a material or bodily ghost. That excessive grieving for the dead will destroy their rest is a notion which is, or has been, prevalent in Scotland, England, and Ireland, as well as in other countries.[3] The grief of the living causes the dead to return in *The Unquiet Grave* (78), *The Twa Brothers* (49), and in certain American variants of *The Wife of Usher's Well* (79), as well as in the Danish *Aage og Else*, an analogue of *Sweet William's Ghost* (77). The Latham text of *The Unquiet Grave* (78 A) reads:

> *The twelvemonth and a day being up,*
> *The dead began to speak:*
> *"Oh who sits weeping on my grave,*
> *And will not let me sleep?"*

This reason for the return of the dead is present also in texts B, D, E, F, and is implied in C, G, and H, and is again given explicitly in texts not included by Child.[4] The reply of the maiden in Child's B is not found in other texts, but, giving evidence as it does of the ancient practice of burying belongings with the dead—gold, jewels, weapons, and so on[5]—it throws additional light on the material nature of the revenant in this song. The maiden says:

> *"It is not your gold I want, dear love,*
> *Nor yet your wealth I crave"* [B 4].

---

[1] *Op. cit.*, p. 34.   [2] Karl Killinger, *Erin*, VI, 65, 449.

[3] For Child's many references to the occurrence of this superstition see *op. cit.*, II, 228, 234 ff., 512 f.; III, 513; IV, 474; V, 62 f., 294.

[4] For example, Sharp and Marson, *Folk Songs from Somerset* (1st ser.), p. 15; Leather, *Folk-Lore of Herefordshire*, pp. 202 f.; Sharp, *One Hundred English Folk-Songs*, p. 56.

[5] See *supra*, pp. 99 f., 105 f.

Again, in one text of *The Twa Brothers* (49 C), weeping, as does harping in another copy (B), brings the dead from the grave. The same incident occurs in many tales which tell the story found in our ballad of *The Suffolk Miracle* (272).[1]

The foregoing superstition is given a more realistic portrayal in the Baring-Gould text of *The Unquiet Grave* (78), in the McGill and Belden American versions of *The Wife of Usher's Well* (79), and in somewhat corrupted verses found in three other American copies of this latter piece. In all these texts the tears of the living are said to wet the winding sheet of the dead. According to Baring-Gould's version of *The Unquiet Grave* (78 Hb),[2] the lover's "body straight arose." Our revenant is no thin apparition but is a living dead man with all the materiality of Helgi's "ghost":

> *"What is it that you want of me*
> *And will not let me sleep?*
> *Your salten tears they trickle down*
> *And wet my winding-sheet."*

Child remarks that in the Scott and Kinloch texts of *The Wife of Usher's Well* "there is no indication that the sons come back to forbid obstinate grief, as the dead often do."[3] But this motive, as we have already indicated, is supplied by American variants of this piece. Josephine McGill's variant reads:

> *"Green grass grows over our heads, mother,*
> *Cold clay is under our feet;*
> *And ev'ry tear that you shed for us*
> *It wets our winding sheet."*[4]

H. M. Belden's Missouri text has virtually the same reading.[5] Walter M. Hart's variant from North Carolina,[6] however, and Louise Pound's text from Nebraska[7] have it

---

[1] See Child's analysis of these tales (*op. cit.*, V, 62).

[2] *Ibid.*, IV, 475.   [3] *Ibid.*, II, 238.

[4] *Folk Songs of the Kentucky Mountains*, p. 4.

[5] *JAFL*, XXIII, 429.

[6] *Ibid.*, XXX, 306.   [7] *American Ballads and Songs*, p. 21.

that the tears are those of the babes, an obvious corruption. Dr. Pound's version reads: "The tears we have shed for you, mother, have wet these winding sheets." The Danish song *Aage og Else*, a Norse analogue of our *Sweet William's Ghost* (77), tells of a dead man who cannot rest in his grave while his beloved weeps for him; indeed, Lady Elsey's tears cause her lover's coffin to fill with blood and gore:

> "*So oft as thou art weeping,*
> *And grievest thee so sore,*
> *Is brimming full my coffin*
> *With blood and gore.*"[1]

So, too, in the closely related lay of Helgi and Sigrún the dead Helgi, no mere phantom, complains that Sigrún's tears fall bloody on his breast.[2]

By virtue of the living-corpse motif certain of our ballad incidents may lay claim to high antiquity.[3] In British folksong the ghost is frequently not even called a ghost. There is, in a sense, nothing "supernatural" about the ballad revenant, for it conducts itself in every way—in voice, movements, and actions—exactly like a human being. The ghost babes in *The Cruel Mother* are seen one day playing ball, and they talk with their mother in the most matter-of-fact manner. The mother does not recognize them as her own babes, nor does she suspect that they are dead until so informed by the children themselves. In one of the best versions of *Sweet William's Ghost* (77 B) the

[1] Prior, *Ancient Danish Ballads*, III, 78. The breath of the dead man in No. 78 (Child) D 5 is "as the sulphur strong."

[2] See Vigfusson-Powell, *Corpus poeticum boreale*, I, 143. On the relation between the Eddic lay and the Norse ballad see Bugge, *Home of the Eddic Poems* (trans. Schofield), pp. 222 ff.; Child, II, 228. On the revenant motif in the two foregoing stories and in the English ballads Nos. 77, 78, see Konrad Ehrke's tabular analysis, *op. cit.*, p. 26.

[3] Cf. Hartland, Introduction to E. M. Leather, *op. cit.*, p. viii: "The belief in the possibility of corpses becoming reanimated and returning among living men, ... was widely spread in the Middle Ages. It is still current in some parts even of Europe. Its roots are to be sought in savage doctrines concerning death and the dead."

dead man is not spoken of as a ghost. The three dead sons in *The Wife of Usher's Well* (79) come home and meet a reception at the hands of their mother that in no way indicates that they are other than human.[1] We have already seen that in Baring-Gould's text of *The Unquiet Grave* (78 Hb) the "body" of the dead lover is said to come from the grave.

That the ballad revenant is a living corpse can hardly be questioned, for not only does our ghost share in the attributes of the dead and reflect its condition, but appears in certain instances to be identical with it. Indeed, in *Sweet William's Ghost*, *Proud Lady Margaret*, and *Sir Hugh* the ghost is a veritable "corpse o clay," and is so designated in the first of these pieces (77 F 7):

> *But dowie, dowie was the maid*
> *That followd the corpse o clay.*

"The dead corp followed she," is the reading in another copy (A 11). The ghost or dead man is likewise called a "dead corpse" in *Sir Hugh* (155 A 16):

> *And at the back o merry Lincoln*
> *The dead corpse did her meet.*

In versions A, B, C, E, and F of this ballad the murdered boy talks to his mother from the depths of the well.[2] The dead mother in the Danish song *Svend Dyring* rises bodily from the grave:

> *Out from their chest she stretch'd her bones,*
> *And rent her way through earth and stones.*[3]

Like the mother in the Norse ballad the revenants in Celtic popular tales are to be called "ghosts" only in the sense that they are dead. There is nothing shadowy or airy about them. They appear in the flesh, so many living

[1] Cf. Hart, *Ballad and Epic*, p. 22.

[2] Cf. G, N, and T.

[3] Prior, I, 369.

corpses.[1] And in Irish sagas—the story of Cuchullin, for instance—we find the same striking evidence of the corporeal revenant. Cuchullin is as material as Helgi in the Eddic lay, and his chariot and horses are corporeal.[2]

Further proof that the connection between the soul and the body—granting the conception of the soul—is not broken at death is furnished by the familiar ballad commonplace in which the lips of the revenant are described as "clay-cold" and its breath "earthy strong." Thus in *The Unquiet Grave* (78 A):

> *"You crave one kiss of my clay-cold lips;*
> *But my breath smells earthy strong;*
> *If you have one kiss of my clay-cold lips,*
> *Your time will not be long."*

This commonplace is found in Child's other texts of *The Unquiet Grave* as well as in texts of this piece recovered since Child. It occurs also in *Sweet William's Ghost* (77 A, B, C) and in one Child text (B) and two American variants of *The Twa Brothers* (49).[3] The habitation of the ballad ghost is usually the grave[4]—further evidence of our revenant's remoteness from the vapory and unsubstantial type of ghost. The German ballad *Der todte Freier* tells a story of a dead man who returns, smelling of the mold, after eight years under the ground—a story somewhat analogous to *Sweet William's Ghost* (77). The dead man in *Proud Lady Margaret* (47 D 10) comes back after having been buried "mair than years is three."

Jamieson's copy of *Sweet William's Ghost* (77 F) offers striking evidence of the materiality of the ballad revenant. The incident of the dead man's returning without his arms, which, he says, have rotted off, may be explained by saying that the ghost simply reflects the condition of the dead

---

[1] See, for example, W. Larminie, *West Irish Folk-Tales and Romances*, p. 31; A. Le Braz, *La Légende de la Mort chez les Bretons armoricains*, II, 146, 159, 161, 184, 257.

[2] E. Hull, *The Cuchullin Saga*, p. 277.

[3] See modes of enchantment, *infra*, p. 289.   [4] See *supra*, p. 99.

body. But does not such an interpretation proceed from the "animistic" assumption of the existence of soul ideas?[1] Is it necessary in explaining the following passage to grant the existence of a belief in the soul or in personal spirits?

> *"Gin ye be Clerk Saunders, my true-love,*
> *This meikle marvels me;*
> *O wherein is your bonny arms,*
> *That wont to embrace me?"*

> *"By worms they're eaten, in mools they're rotten,*
> *Behold, Margaret, and see,*
> *And mind, for a' your mickle pride,*
> *Sae will become o thee."*

It is possible, of course, that there is a survival here of the savage belief that a man is not dead until the flesh has completely disappeared,[2] and that our ballad reflects the belief in a secondary or grave ghost which may exist alongside the conception of the soul in spiritland.[3] But even though our revenant is a secondary or grave ghost, it is still clear that it is a decidedly corporeal revenant. It is true that the dead Sweet William (A 9) does make a distinction between "body" or "bones" and "spirit," but this stanza, like the concluding stanzas of this text, has a modern ring. Sweet William speaks entirely out of character, for it is not in the true manner of the ballads to enter into such explanations. That we may not, however, slight the ballad evidence, we should point out, too, that although our dead man returns to his grave, which (C 10) "did open up," and lies down therein, yet he speaks (B, D, E) of heaven and hell. But his references to heaven and hell and the "Saviour" represent nothing more, probably, than the intrusion of Christian thought into an otherwise pagan story.

[1] See *supra*, pp. 229 f.

[2] See, for example, Moss, *Life after Death in Oceania*, pp. 97 ff., 108.

[3] See *ibid.*, pp. 58 ff.

The corporeal revenant is found again in Scott's text of *The Wife of Usher's Well* (79 A). If in this case we grant the belief in spirits or souls, it is nevertheless clear that the spirits of the dead sons are thought of as inhabiting their corpses at will or are regarded as being never dissociated therefrom. Or the dead sons are thought of as leading a sort of dual existence, that of the corporeal "soul" and that of the shadow soul, a notion entirely consonant with savage conceptions of the soul.[1] At any rate, however, the following passage, which shows that the dead sons may suffer bodily pains inflicted, apparently, by the "channerin worm," offers unmistakable evidence of a belief in the corporeal revenant:

"The cock doth craw, the day doth daw,
The channerin worm doth chide;
Gin we be mist out o our place,
A sair pain we maun bide."

The ballad revenant's concern over being "mist away"—from the grave or from heaven—is illustrated also in *Sweet William's Ghost* (77 B 8, D 4). In Miss Burne's text (C) of *Usher's Well*[2] the mother bids Jesus "go rise up" her "three sons" and put "breath in their breast, and clothing on their backs." "Down among the hongerey worms I sleep," says the dead man in *Sweet William's Ghost* (77 B). And the words of the revenant in *Proud Lady Margaret* (47 A) carry the same idea of the corporeal ghost: "The wee worms are my bedfellows, and cauld clay is my sheets."

The beautiful and celebrated Norse ballad *Aage og Else*, which has much in common with *Sweet William's Ghost* and with the lay of Helgi Hundingsbani, gives notable depiction to the conception of the living corpse. Unable to rest in his gravehouse because of the weeping of Lady Elsey, Sir Ogey staggers toward her chamber with his

[1] Cf. Wundt, *Elements of Folk Psychology*, pp. 206 f. Wundt is thinking here, it is true, of the "corporeal" soul in the sense that the soul may reside in some part of the body, the blood, the kidneys, etc.

[2] Child, III, 513.

coffin on his back—reminiscent in this of our Sweet William (77 C 5), who comes wearing his winding-sheet:

> *He rose, the knight Sir Ogey,*
> *With coffin on his back,*
> *And stagger'd towards her chamber*
> *A dismal weary track.*

He taps her door with his coffin, and, after having proved himself a reputable revenant by naming Lord Jesus, is admitted by his true-love. Prior's translation proceeds:

> *Uprose the Lady Elsey*
> *And bitter tears she shed,*
> *And let him in to her chamber,*
> *The cold buried dead:*

> *She took her comb, fair Elsey,*
> *She comb'd his tangled hair,*
> *And every lock she straighten'd,*
> *She dropp'd on it a tear.*[1]

But we need not quote the ballad further in order to show how earthy and material is Sir Ogey's ghost. The term "ghost" is, of course, hardly the word to use when speaking of the ballad revenant, for it conveys the idea of a disembodied spirit. Such an expression as "living" or "vitalized corpse" is much to be preferred. The dead Sir Ogey is, as Naumann says of the dead Helgi, "ein Wiedergänger jedenfalls rein körperlicher, völlig unseelischer Natur!"[2] The returned dead man in *The Suffolk Miracle* (272) complains that "his head did ake," and is said to be as cold as "any clay." He is no less material than those dead men in the analogous continental stories, so profusely cited by Child in his Introduction to our ballad. Wrought upon by magic, the dead maiden in another ballad, *Young Benjie* (86), speaks and gives the name of her murderer. In *The Twa Sisters* (10) a harp, fiddle, or viol, made from a

[1] *Op. cit.*, III, 76 ff.　　　[2] *Op. cit.*, p. 34.

drowned maiden's body, speaks and denounces the maiden's slayer. This latter incident impels us to say that the ballad ghost may be thought of as material or corporeal in the sense that the soul is thought to reside in the blood, in the hair, or in the bones.[1]

OBJECTIVITY OF THE BALLAD REVENANT

That the ballad revenant is a living dead man or a vitalized corpse goes no little way to attest its objectivity. It is true that the dead of folksong appear, as a rule, to one person only, but this is due in part to the condensed character of the ballad story. It is noteworthy, too, that few of our ballad revenants are dream ghosts. The "ghaist sae green" of the drowned maiden in *The Twa Sisters* (10 Q) seems to make itself known both to the miller and his daughter. And the corpse of that other drowned maiden in *Young Benjie* (86) speaks to the two brothers. The harp made from the dead girl's body in the former piece sings or speaks in the presence of the king's court. In balladry there is no "mind diseased" to conjure up a Banquo's shade, and our revenant seldom appears in dreams. Dreams do not account for the returned dead in the best ghost ballads: *The Unquiet Grave* (78), *Sweet William's Ghost* (77), *The Cruel Mother* (20), *The Twa Sisters* (10), and *The Wife of Usher's Well* (79). Where a dream does supply the *raison d'être* of the revenant or the spirit, as in a Massachusetts text of *Fair Margaret and Sweet William* (74)[2] and in two Campbell and Sharp variants of *The Wife of Usher's Well*, we are safe in saying, especially in the latter instance, that rationalization has been at work. It is pretty clear that the revenant is no dream ghost or thin apparition, and that so far as balladist, actor, and audience are concerned it may be said to have had an objective reality.

In the present connection and before taking up other attributes of our revenant—color, clothes, size, voice, movements—we should examine some, at least, of those

[1] See *supra*, pp. 68 ff., 72 ff.   [2] Child, V, 293.

phrases or epithets that are occasionally used in describing
the ballad revenant but that seem to be the result of modern accretion and to belong in no sense to the genuine stuff
of balladry. As we have already observed, the balladist
seldom uses the term "ghost", and when he does employ
it he is inclined to let it stand alone without epithetization.[1]
We recognize something of the modern touch in the epithet "pale" that describes the revenant in Motherwell's
copy of *Sweet William's Ghost* (77 C):

> *By her came a pale, pale ghost,*
> *With many a sich and mane.*

The use of "pale" seems to be a striving for effect or atmosphere and is altogether foreign to the ballad manner. Such
accessories are likely to be found in the poorer texts of
a given ghost ballad.[2] The revenant, it is true, is called a
"spirit" in certain versions of our ghost ballads (74 A, 77
A, 78 G), and in one copy of *Sweet William's Ghost* (77 C
13) the dead man speaks of his "soul," but these expressions
do not have the genuine ballad ring. In an inferior ballad,
Willie's Fatal Visit (255), the "ghost" is described as "wan
and weary," and in the Laing text of *Proud Lady Margaret*
(47 E 4) the dead man is said to wear a "white scarf"—
neither of which descriptions is especially convincing.

COLOR, CLOTHES, SIZE, VOICE, MOVEMENTS

In British folksong the color green is occasionally associated with the dead or with death. The fairies and witches
of balladry likewise favor this color,[3] and it is possible that
here again we encounter a significant resemblance between
the dead and fairies. Greenness as a trait of supernatural
beings—fairies, dwarfs, ghosts, and even animals—occurs
in the folktales of many lands.[4] Green is an unlucky color

---

[1] Cf. Hart, *Ballad and Epic*, p. 22.

[2] Cf. *ibid*. [3] See *supra*, pp. 175 ff.

[4] For a number of examples see Kittredge, *Gawain and the Green Knight*,
pp. 195 f. See also E. K. Chambers, *The Mediaeval Stage*, I, pp. 185 f.; Wentz,
Fairy-Faith, pp. 312 f. and *passim*.

for a bride in *Lord Thomas and Fair Annet* (73 B 20): "I'll na put on the grisly black, nor yet the dowie green." This is illustrative of the ill omen that in general attaches to green.[1] For each of three times that a well-educated Hull lady wore a green dress she lost someone dear to her.[2] Dreaming of pulling green heather, green apples, or green "birk" is premonitory of death in *The Braes o Yarrow* (214 A, C–F, I–M, O, R, S).

This association in British balladry of the color green with death and the dead has already attracted the attention of Annie G. Gilchrist in the *Journal of the Folk-Song Society*.[3] In connection with a study of *The Lady Drest in Green*, a children's singing game, Miss Gilchrist presents something of the ballad evidence. The foregoing song of the green lady, it should be noted, is in theme closely related to our ballad of *The Cruel Mother* (20). The singing game presents the story of a lady dressed in green who slays her baby with a penknife down by the greenwood side. Three babes ("bobbies") knock at her door (these correspond to the three ghost-children in certain texts of *The Cruel Mother*), accuse her of having killed her only son, and announce her punishment. Miss Gilchrist refers also to the English folktale of *Green Lady*, which tells of a green lady who dances in a basin of blood, and to Jenny Greenteeth, an evil water spirit, as well as to *Jenny Jo*, a singing game in which green is symbolic of grief. But in her survey of our ballad evidence she fails to mention two striking examples of the association of green and the dead, examples found in *The Cruel Mother* and *The Twa Sisters*.

One of the ghost babes in a Motherwell copy of *The Cruel Mother* (20 H) is clad in green:

> *The neist o them was clad in green,*
> *To shew that death they had been in.*

---

[1] See Henderson, *Northern Counties*, pp. 34 f.; Black, *Folk-Medicine*, pp. 114 f.; Child, *op. cit.*, II, 182.

[2] *County Folk-Lore*, VI, 81.

[3] VI, 82–84.

The drowned girl in the Campbell text of *The Twa Sisters* (10 Q) has a "ghaist sae green":

> *Then up and spak her ghaist sae green,*
> *"Do ye no ken the king's dochter Jean?"*

According to N 20, "Pale was her cheik and grein was her hair." In Fife the ghost of a lady was styled "Green Jean" and always appeared in a "long gown of green."[1]

"Death is greener than the gress," says Captain Wedderburn (46 B 17), in answer to one of his lady's riddles. The same question put in *Riddles Wisely Expounded* (1 A) is answered in somewhat similar fashion: "And poyson is greener than the grass." In a Shropshire version of *The Wife of Usher's Well* (79 C) the ghost sons lead their mother along a green road, "the greenest that ever was seen." And Sweet William's ghost (77 B 11) vanishes in a "green forest." In connection with Robin Hood's grave of "gravel and green" (120 B 17)—"grauell and of greete" (A 26)—Miss Gilchrist discusses the ring game of *Green Gravel* and notes that the color green may here be of ill omen, since the game still retains "the motif of a death and its attendant ceremonies."[2] With respect to the supposed funeral origin of the green-grass game, Alice Gomme remarks that the game was thought to have been originally "a child's dramatic imitation of an old burial ceremony."[3] This conclusion is arrived at by an identification of the game rhyme with a rhyme which occurs in a burial ceremony depicted in Henderson's *Folk-Lore of the Northern Counties:*

> *A dis, a dis, a dis,*
> *A green griss;*
> *A dis, a dis, a dis.*[4]

The practice in balladry of laying a green sod on the breast of the dead (49 F 16, H 6), or under the head (120 B

---

[1] *County Folk-Lore*, VII, 36 ff.

[2] *Op. cit.*, VI, 83.

[3] *Traditional Games of England, Scotland, and Ireland*, I, 169.   [4] P. 54.

17), or, again, a turf at the head (16 A 4), may, as does possibly the "gravel and green" of Robin's grave (120 B 17), furnish evidence of the symbolism of green in relation to death and burial. It is not improbable that the gravel "whose grass is so green" of the *Green Gravel* game is identical with the "gravil green" with which Janet in *Tam Lin* (39 G 18) would destroy her babe.[1] In County Wexford certain family graves were lined with green sod. The body was taken out of its coffin and "lowered into its green receptacle."[2] Our ballad incidents may point to the same color symbolism as that evidenced by certain prehistoric, primitive, and ancient funerary practices, those of the Cro-Magnons, the pre-Columbian Americans, and the ancient Egyptians, according to which green stones or pebbles were placed in the mouths of the dead or in the grave as symbolizing the principle of life.[3]

The dress of the ballad revenant receives little or no portrayal. The ancient belief in the sacredness of the birch has, however, provided the dead sons in *The Wife of Usher's Well* (79 A) with "hats o the birk":

> *It fell about the Martinmass,*
> *When nights are lang and mirk,*
> *The carlin wife's three sons came hame,*
> *And their hats were o the birk.*

> *It neither grew in syke nor ditch,*
> *Nor yet in ony sheugh;*
> *But at the gates o Paradise,*
> *That birk grew fair eneugh.*

The sacred character of the birch and the marked association in our folksong of the birch with the dead have been considered in detail earlier in this work.[4]

In the matter of its size there is nothing to lead one

---

[1] Cf. A. Gilchrist, *op. cit.*, VI, 83.   [2] *Folk-Lore Journal*, VII, 39.

[3] See Donald Mackenzie, "Colour Symbolism," *Folk-Lore*, XXXIII, 139 f.

[4] *Supra*, pp. 155 ff.

to think that the ballad revenant is of other than human dimensions. Our ghost or dead man is, indeed, as we have already seen, a corporeal revenant and has of course the form and size of the living man. Two apparent exceptions to this may be noted for what they are worth. In the poor ballad of *Willie's Fatal Visit* (255, stanza 13) the ghost is described as follows: "Great and grievous was the ghost . . . ., would fear ten thousand men." More convincing is the revenant in the Harris copy of *Proud Lady Margaret* (47 D). This returned dead man rides a steed which is "winder sma":

> *There cam a knicht to Archerdale,*
> *His steed was winder sma.*

It is barely possible that we have something here of the widespread belief that the soul is diminutive.[1]

The voice of the ballad revenant and its movements require only brief discussion. The ghost of our folksong usually conducts itself in speech, as in other matters, exactly like a living man, nor is there any particular evidence that it always waits to be spoken to before speaking.[2] Most of our ghost ballads (10, 20, 47, 49, 78, 79) give no indication of a ghostlike voice on the part of the revenant. Occasionally, however, the ballad dead man announces his presence by the traditional groaning, moaning, or sighing. Thus in the Ramsay text of *Sweet William's Ghost* (77 A):

> *There came a ghost to Margret's door,*
> *With many a grievous groan.*

"Mony a sad sigh and groan" is the reading in B; "with many a sich and mane" is the reading in C. And the supposed ghost in *Child Waters* (63 A) "greiuouslye doth groane." But throughout the rest of the former ballad the revenant speaks in the voice, or at least converses in the language, of the living.

[1] See Cox, *Introduction to Folk-Lore*, p. 60.

[2] ". . . . A ghost has not the power to speak until it has been first spoken to" (Brand, *Popular Antiquities*, III, 70).

The movements and activities of the ballad revenant are, as a rule, not at all unearthly or ghostlike. In one version of *Fair Margaret and Sweet William* (74 B 7) the ghost is, it is true, described as gliding:

> *In glided Margaret's grimly ghost,*
> *And stood at William's feet.*

The narrator's attempt here to create a supernatural atmosphere is not, however, in keeping with the true ballad manner. The specific verb "glided" of this version when compared to the more general term "came" in version A is seen at once to instance a conscious striving for effect.[1] It betrays a studiedness that is foreign, on the whole, to the best ballads, and is scarcely less objectionable than the "gloomy clouds and sky" of a Buchan text of another ghost ballad (47 B 32). Other texts of the former piece retain more of the simplicity of version A. "There walkd a ghost" is the reading in C; "something appeared," in an American text;[2] or "Lady Margret she rose and stood all alone,"[3] or, again, "Lyddy Margret's ghost came," according to still another "New World" variant.[4]

In *Sweet William's Ghost* (77 A 1) the revenant comes tirling "at the pin," or in the related Norse ballad *Aage og Else* raps on the door with his coffin.[5] The ghost babes in *The Cruel Mother* (20 C, D, E, H, etc.) are seen playing ball by a "castle wa." The dead boy simply rises from the grave in *The Twa Brothers* (49 B, C), as does the dead lover in *The Unquiet Grave* (78). "Clark Sanders came to Margret's window," according to the Herd text of *Sweet William's Ghost* (77 B), and in the same natural manner comes the ghost in *James Harris* (243 A 16). The dead man appears "in a lady's hall" (47 B), comes "waukin oer the wa"

[1] Cf. Hart, *Ballad and Epic*, p. 22.

[2] Campbell and Sharp, *English Folk Songs from the Southern Appalachians*, p. 63.

[3] *Ibid.*, p. 67.

[4] McGill, *op. cit.*, p. 69.   [5] See *supra*, p. 238.

(77 F 2), or shows himself in Lady Margaret's "wearie room" (77 D). A maiden's ghost appears beside her drowned body in *The Twa Sisters* (10 O, P). In both the foregoing texts the ghost gives the fiddler instructions as to making a fiddle from the dead body. In Q the ghost sends a lock of yellow hair to the lover. In *Sir Hugh* (155) the corpse of the murdered boy meets the mother (A 16) "at the back o merry Lincoln," or, according to other texts (B, E, C), "at the back o Mirry-land toun," "at the back of Maitland town," "at the birks of Mirryland town." The ghost appears at the "bed's feet" (74 A, B, C; 73 E).[1] Ballad fairies occasionally appear in the same place. Billy Blin (53 C 14, 110 G), for example, or the "green" woman (53 M 15), stands "at her bed-feet." In *Willie's Fatal Visit* (255) the ghost starts up in the churchyard. The dead babe in *The Cruel Mother* (20 B 5) is seen in the church porch. "It was believed [in Wiltshire] that if one stood in the church porch on the last night of the year he would see the shadows of those among his friends and relations who were doomed to die during the coming year."[2] The ballad revenant does not depart from the living in some weird and spectacular fashion, but simply returns to the grave and lies down therein—as we shall presently see—in the most matter-of-fact manner.

THE DEAD MAN ACTIVE AT NIGHT

Like ghosts in general and like fairies or other supernatural creatures, the revenant of folksong confines its activities chiefly to the nighttime.[3] "In the middle of the night" walks the spirit of the jilted maiden in *Fair Margaret and Sweet William* (74 C), and at the same hour the dead man returns in *The Suffolk Miracle* (272). Midnight is the customary time for the dead to make

[1] Cf. texts of No. 74 in Campbell and Sharp, pp. 63, 66, 67.

[2] *Folk-Lore*, XI, 345.

[3] The ghosts of savage tradition are active at night; see, for example, Rosalind Moss, *op. cit.*, pp. 6, 51, 74, 150.

their appearance.[1] Thus, it is "at the very parting o midnicht" that May Margret in *Sweet William's Ghost* (77 E) hears "a mournfu moan." At mirk midnight the corpse of a drowned maiden (86 A) speaks to two brothers. And in an Irish version of *Lord Thomas and Fair Annet* (73)[2] the plants from the lovers' graves grow "to a true lover's knot" at "twelve o'clock every night." Night is the time, according to *Proud Lady Margaret* (47 A, B) and *Clerk Saunders* (69 G 37), for the dead to be abroad. This is true also for the revenants in other pieces (73 E; 74 A, B; 77 A; 79; 243 A; 255). In one text of *The Unquiet Grave* (78)[3] the "ghost began to peep" at the "hour o one o'clock."

Neither in *The Cruel Mother* (20) nor in *The Twa Sisters* (10) is the time for ghost-walking specified—this with the exception of one text of the latter ballad (N 15). In texts B, F, and L of *The Cruel Mother* the murderess buries her babes by the light of the moon, but there is no indication that the dead children return after dark. On the contrary, it seems more likely that they come back in the daytime. When the mother sees them they are playing ball, as in C, D, E. F 10 reads: "It fell ance upon a day, she saw twa babies at their play." In *The Twa Sisters* (10 N 15) the wraith does appear at "deid of nicht," but in versions O, P, and Q the appearance seems to occur in the light of day. As for the time of year when ghosts wander abroad we have no hint save in *The Wife of Usher's Well* (79 B, A), and this may be without significance:

> *The hallow days o Yule are come,*
> *The nights are lang an dark,*
> *An in an cam her ain twa sons,*
> *Wi their hats made o the bark.*

A reads: "It fell about the Martinmass." In *Hamlet* (I, i) Shakespeare bears witness to the belief that on Christmas

---

[1] Brand, *op. cit.*, III, 69.

[2] Child, II, 198.

[3] *Ibid.*, IV, 475.

Eve "the bird of dawning singeth all night long" and that then "no spirit dare stir abroad." In two American texts of our ballad the babes return as Christmas is drawing near.[1] According to a Berwickshire tradition relative to the enchanted queen in *The Laidley Worm*—a poem allied to *Kemp Owyne*—unspelling can be effected only at the end of seven years, on Christmas Eve.[2]

THE RETURN TO THE GRAVE AT COCKCROW

A widespread and ancient superstition holds that ghosts, demons, and fairies cannot endure the light of day, and vanish at cockcrow.[3] A ghost's paradise must have been that "unco land" in *Leesome Brand* (15 A 1) "where wind never blew, nor cocks ever crew." But most of the ballad country comes within earshot of cockcrow, and it is at this signal that our revenants make their departure. The crowing of the black cock, especially efficacious in driving away evil spirits and ghosts, though present in Norse balladry, is not heard in English and Scottish folk-song. In the Danish ballads *Svend Dyring* and *Aage og Else*, this latter an analogue of *Sweet William's Ghost* (77), there is a color triad of cocks—the white, the red, and the black.[4] First crows the white cock, next the red, and last the black, thus announcing that it is time for the dead to part from the quick. Says the dead man in *Aage og Else*:

> *"The white cock now is crowing,*
> *And down must I below;*
> *To earth wend all my fellows,*
> *And with them I must go.*

---

[1] *JAFL*, XXIII, 429; Louise Pound, *op. cit.*, p. 20. Cf. Cox, *Folk-Songs of the South*, p. 90; *ibid.*, p. 89: "about the New Year's time."

[2] See Child, I, 311.

[3] In his *Ancient Danish Ballads*, III, 86 ff., Prior has noted the occurrence of this incident in Norse ballads, in Anglo-Saxon and Eddic poetry, in Prudentius and elsewhere. See also Brand, *op. cit.*, II, 52; Child, II, 228; V, 294.

[4] See R. Köhler, "Der weisse, der rothe und der schwarze Hahn," *Germania*, XI, 85 ff.

"The red cock now is crowing,
And down must I below;
To earth must wend all dead men,
And I too must go.

"And now the black cock's crowing
Home I must go below;
Unlock'd are all the portals,
And I too must go."[1]

So, too, in *Svend Dyring* crow the "rooster red," "the black cock," and the "white."[2] The lore of the black cock is extensive. In the Outer Hebrides the crow of a black cock is especially effective against evil spirits.[3] In an Irish fairy tale three drinks of water out of a black cock's skull restores to a mortal maiden her speech, of which she had been deprived by the fairies.[4] The black cock is in France used for raising the devil.[5] A cock with black and white feathers is a sacrificial fowl in India.[6] In County Clare there was a superstition, surviving in 1869, to the effect that the druids offered black cocks to the devil.[7] In a song recovered by the present writer from Mariana Cummings, of Lincoln, Nebraska, a lover's ghost vanishes at the crowing of the black cock:

The black cock crew, the spirit fled;
Nae more o' Sandy could she see,
But soft the passing spirit said,
"Sweet Mary, weep no more for me."

Cockcrow is the signal for the departure of the revenants in *Sweet William's Ghost* (77) and *The Wife of*

[1] Prior, III, 79.
[2] See *ibid.*, I, 370.
[3] *Folk-Lore*, X, 263.
[4] *Ibid.*, IV, 354.
[5] Henderson, *op. cit.*, p. 147 n.
[6] Crooke, *Popular Religions and Folk-Lore of Northern India*, I, 284.
[7] *Folk-Lore*, XXII, 51.

Usher's Well (79), but in neither of these pieces does the black cock appear. There are only two cocks in Ramsay's copy of the former ballad (77 A):

> *Then up and crew the red, red cock,*
> *And up then crew the gray:*
> *"Tis time, tis time, my dear Margret,*
> *That you were going away."*

In G 3 the cocks are "milk-white" and "grey." C 9 does not give the colors, but has the effective lines: "The cocks they are crawing again; it's time the deid should part the quick, Marjorie, I must be gane." It is noteworthy that in B and C the cocks crow before Margaret takes her walk with the ghost, whereas in A, the concluding stanzas of which have a modern ring, the cocks crow after the walk. In Herd's text (B) the "corruption of 'middle-earth,'" says Professor Ker, "into 'midd-larf,' . . . . has spoilt one of the most beautiful things in ballad poetry, the ghostly regret for the living world."[1] Herd's copy reads:

> *O cocks are crowing a merry midd-larf,*
> *A wat the wilde foule boded day;*

This should read: "Cocks are crowing on merry middle-earth."

In *The Wife of Usher's Well* (79) the warning signal (A) is given by the red cock and the gray. In C the reading is:

> *"The white cock he has crowed once,*
> *The second has, so has the red."*

The colorless "second" may correspond to the black cock of the Norse ballads. B 4 has the following: "O the young cock crew i the merry Linkem,[2] an the wild fowl chirpd for day." Though their color is not specified, the cocks crow in American variants of *The Wife of Usher's Well*.[3] It is

[1] On the History of the Ballads—1100–1500," *Proceedings of the British Academy*, IV, 7.

[2] Cf. "Merry midd-larf" (77 B) and see Glossary, Child, V, 354.

[3] *JAFL*, XXX, 306; McGill, *op. cit.*, p. 5.

not clear why the black cock should have been dropped from the English ballads and why in the foregoing ballad (79 A) the "gray," as Köhler points out,[1] should have taken its place. Is it because the black cock has been for so long associated with the devil?[2] In Scandinavian myth the black cock is heard in Niflheim, the "land of gloom."

Cockcrow puts a period to ghost walking in Mrs. Leather's text of *The Unquiet Grave:* "The cock does crow and we must part, I must return to my grave."[3] In *Young Benjie* (86 A 16), another supernatural ballad, cockcrow is concomitant with the speaking of a maiden's corpse or, rather, with the "thrawing" of the corpse, which thereupon speaks: "The cocks began to craw, and at the dead hour o the night, the corpse began to thraw." Cockcrow is potent in Greek superstition, according to which the Callicantzari vanish away at the crowing of the third cock. This third cock is black and the sound of its voice has greater power to frighten away evil spirits than has the voice of the white or the red cock.[4] In the Outer Hebrides "the red cock of autumn" would admit a goblin to the house, but not so the "black cock of the spring March."[5] In a sort of magic incantation the black and the red cock are found together in Peele's *Old Wives' Tale.*[6] The color triad of cocks recalls the black, the brown, and the white steeds of balladry, but it is the white horse and not the black or the brown that proves the most serviceable.[7]

In departing from the walks of the living the dead man of balladry is not, as a rule, ghostlike; that is, he does not, save in two or three suspicious texts, vanish as ghosts and spirits are often said to vanish—in a flash of fire or in a mist or cloud.[8] The matter-of-fact manner of his return to

---

[1] *Loc. cit.*

[2] See Henderson, *op. cit.*, p. 147 and n.

[3] *Op. cit.*, p. 203.

[4] J. C. Lawson, *Modern Greek Folk-Lore*, p. 195.

[5] *Folk-Lore*, X, 269.   [7] See *supra*, p. 188.

[6] See *JAFL*, XXXII, 457.   [8] See Brand, *op. cit.*, III, 70.

the upper world is characteristic of his departure there-from. The dead Sweet William (77 C), for example, makes his way prosaically enough to the churchyard, where he lies down in his grave, which has opened up to receive him:

> She followed him high, she followed him low,
>   Till she came to yon church-yard;
> O there the grave did open up,
>   And young William he lay down.

Back to their wormy bed the three sons in *The Wife of Usher's Well* (79 A) are hurried by the crowing of the cock, but they answer the summons in a natural and unsensa-tional manner. In lines "profoundly affecting" we find a leave-taking not at all theatrical or spooklike:

> "Fare ye weel, my mother dear!
>   Fareweel to barn and byre!
> And fare ye weel, the bonny lass
>   That kindles my mother's fire!"[1]

The revenant in Buchan's copy of *Proud Lady Margaret* (47 B 32) does not take his departure in true ballad fash-ion. The epithet "gloomy" is by itself enough to justify our suspicion of the following lines:

> "Wi that he vanishd frae her sight,
>   Wi the twinkling o an eye;
> Naething mair the lady saw
>   But the gloomy clouds and sky."

We have already called attention to the like false manner of the closing stanzas of Ramsay's copy of *Sweet William's Ghost* (77 A 15 f.). Here the ghost is said to vanish in "a cloud of mist."[2] But it is the affecting scene at the dead man's grave—a scene depicted in the foregoing text, as well as in other copies (B, D, F)—that gives us again the genuine ballad treatment of the revenant motif. All the

[1] See Child, II, 238.

[2] See *supra*, p. 228.

[252]

"live-lang winter night" the maiden has followed the "dead corp" and having, we may suppose, as in C, reached the grave, asks to be allowed to lie down with her lover:

> *"Is there any room at your head, Willy?*
> *Or any room at your feet?*
> *Or any room at your side, Willy,*
> *Wherein that I may creep?"*

> *"There's no room at my head, Margret,*
> *There's no room at my feet;*
> *There's no room at my side, Margret,*
> *My coffin's made so meet"* [A].

So, too, the vain lady in *Proud Lady Margaret* (47 A, B, C) would share a dead man's grave. The dead man in our best ballads is, let us repeat, a corporeal revenant and lives on in bodily form in the grave,[1] all of which precludes the idea that he dissolves into or is swallowed up in a magic mist.

MOTIVES FOR THE WALKING OF THE DEAD MAN

Before we inquire into those motives which actuate the nocturnal walking of the dead, let us examine whatever evidence the ballads yield of attempts to bar the ghost.[2] As regards this latter point, we must admit that the evidence is slight and even doubtful. In the first place, is there anything in our balladry to indicate a fear of the dead man? On the whole, there is not, as we may infer from those incidents treated in the foregoing pages where the dead and the living are seen to consort in such manner as to indicate anything but that our revenant is thought to be a demonic or malevolent being. Certainly, the "honour's gate," which the bereaved maiden in *Clerk Saunders* (69 E 21) would set up to facilitate the coming and going of her dead lover, reveals no fear of the ghost:

[1] See *supra*, pp. 229 ff.

[2] On barring the ghost see Frazer, *Psyche's Task* (2d ed.), pp. 111–53; Crooke, *op. cit.*, II, 55 ff.

"Go make to me a high, high tower,
Be sure you make it stout and strong,
And on the top put an honour's gate,
That my love's ghost may go out and in."

In our survey of blood-soul ideas we saw that a maiden (214) drinks the blood of her slain lover,[1] and under modes of enchantment we shall see that a maiden fears not to kiss the dead (77, 78).[2]

It seems not improbable, however, that in *The Cruel Mother* we find an instance of barring the ghost—this by fettering the limbs of the dead. Binding or tying the hands of the dead in order to prevent the ghost from walking is a common practice among many peoples, and it is interesting to note in connection with the babe ghosts of our ballad that the spirits of infants which die under three years are thought by the Manipuris to be extremely malicious.[3] In a Motherwell copy of *The Cruel Mother* (20 C), as well as in other texts, the murderess ties the babes, slays them, and buries them:

She took frae 'bout her ribbon-belt,
And there she bound them hand and foot.

She has taen out her wee pen-knife,
And there she ended baith their life.

Motherwell's other version (H) reads: "She took the ribbons off her head, she tied the little babes hand and feet"; the Pepys copy: "She took her filliting off her head, and there she ty'd them hand and leg";[4] an American variant: "She pulled down her yellow hair, and she bound it around their little feet and hands";[5] another American text: "She drew her garter from her leg and tied them up both hand and foot."[6] In H no mention is made of the mother's slay-

---

[1] See *supra*, pp. 73 f.   [4] Child, II, 500.

[2] See *infra*, p. 289.   [5] Campbell and Sharp, p. 29.

[3] *Folk-Lore*, XXIII, 463.   [6] Cox, *Folk-Songs of the South*, p. 30.

ing the babes before burying them, and from this, apparently, Child infers an instance of burial alive.[1] That this is to be understood is doubtful, for in C, E, O, and in the Campbell and Sharp text cited above, the mother not only ties them but slays them as well before she buries them. According to J, she strangles the babes with the ribbon from her head. But that she murders them in this fashion is not borne out by any other text. Again, in texts F and I we read that she "tied the baby hand and feet" or "bound their bodyes fast and sair."

It must be admitted, as we have already indicated, that the foregoing incident may or may not be taken as an instance of barring the ghost. The ballad narrative itself rather discredits the former view, for the babes do come back. The incident is interesting and suggestive, however, when read in the light of the widespread custom of fettering the dead in order to prevent their return. The ancient Hindus fettered the feet of their dead that they might not come back to the walks of men.[2] In Lincolnshire you must be sure to tie the feet, otherwise the dead may return.[3] In Jutland "the great toes [of the corpse] were tied together so that the legs could not be separated."[4] The thumbs and great toes of the corpse are fastened with iron rings in Northern India, and most Hindus tie the corpse to the bier.[5] In Afghanistan "the big toes of the dead person are tied with a strip of white muslin."[6]

In one copy of *Sweet William's Ghost* (77 D) Margret returns the dead man's troth by stroking him three times on the breast with a silver key. In the tradition of India, for example, keys and knives serve as a protection against devils and ghosts.[7] But the use of the key in our ballad

[1] *Op. cit.*, I, 218.

[2] Frazer, *op. cit.*, p. 137.

[3] *County Folk-Lore*, V, 240.

[4] *Folk-Lore*, XVIII, 366.

[5] Crooke, *op. cit.*, I, 270.

[6] *Folk-Lore*, XXX, 278.   [7] Frazer, *The Golden Bough*, III, 234 ff.

can hardly be taken as an instance of laying the ghost. The dying boy in *The Twa Brothers* (49 F, H) gives directions for his grave and says that a green turf laid on his breast will cause him to sleep soundly. In Silesia a sod of fresh turf before the door is proof against witches.[1] Dancing on the grave is designed in certain burial and mourning practices to prevent the ghost from walking.[2] Does some such purpose as this motivate the threat of the maiden in *The Brown Girl* (295) to dance on her lover's grave?

> *"I'll dance above your green, green grave*
> *Where you do lie beneath"* [B 16].

Whether or not we are safe in saying that our ballads reflect certain of those practices designed to bar the ghost, there is no question but that the dead of folksong do walk.[3] And it is not without reason that they come back to the haunts of men. Indeed, the motives for his return place our dead man among the dramatis personae of folk poetry. The ballad revenant is never brought in for mere purposes of background or atmosphere. Ballad atmosphere, if we may use the term with reference to folksong, is, in fact, never got up. Our dead man plays a legitimate rôle and revisits the "glimpses of the moon" for reasons germane to the story.[4]

Excessive grief on the part of the living causes the dead to return in *The Unquiet Grave* (78 A, B, D, E, F), *The Twa Brothers* (49 C), and, according to certain American variants, in *The Wife of Usher's Well*. This incident, as it occurs in balladry, has been considered in connection with the corporeity of the revenant.[5] We must be content here with a passage from *The Unquiet Grave* (78 A):

[1] *Ibid.*, II, 54.

[2] Oesterley, *The Sacred Dance*, p. 30.

[3] On various motives for the return of the dead see Pineau, *Les vieux chants scandinaves*, pp. 122–44; Hartland, *Perseus*, I, 182–224; Brand, *op. cit.*, III, 67 f.; Child, V, 59.

[4] Cf. Ehrke, *op. cit.*   [5] See *supra*, pp. 230 ff.

The twelvemonth and a day being up,
The dead began to speak:
"Oh who sits weeping on my grave,
And will not let me sleep?"

The foregoing incident reflects a belief which occurs in German, Scandinavian, and Indian tradition, as well as in that of the ancient Persians, the Greeks, and the Romans.[1]

The belief that the dead for this or that reason may come back to carry off the living is illustrated in *The Elfin Knight* (2), and belongs, it seems, to the original text of *The Unquiet Grave*.[2] According to one copy of *The Elfin Knight* (2),[3] a maiden escapes being carried off to the grave or the land of shadows by outwitting her dead lover, who sets her impossible tasks:

"Now thou hast answered me well," he said,
"Or thou must have gone away with the dead."

The riddle motif as illustrated in this and other ballads is considered in detail under the Otherworld spell.[4] In *Sweet William's Ghost* (77) the heroine would, of her own accord, apparently, accompany the dead to the grave. So, too, in *Proud Lady Margaret* (47) the vain lady would "go to clay" with her dead brother. In neither ballad, however, will the dead admit the living to the grave. Herd's copy of *Sweet William's Ghost* (77 B 10) gives, nevertheless, clear evidence of the belief that the dead may come back for the living:

"I thank you, Margret, I thank you, Margret,
And I thank you hartilie;
Gine ever the dead come for the quick,
Be sure, Margret, I'll come again for thee."

In the tale of which *The Suffolk Miracle* (272) is the representative in English song, the lover, brought back by the excessive grief of his sweetheart, carries her to the church-

---

[1] See Child, II, 234 ff.   [3] Child, IV, 440.
[2] See *infra*, pp. 306 f.   [4] See *infra*, pp. 301 ff.

yard and tries to drag her into the grave with him.[1] This important incident is absent from the British ballad, though the revenant does give the maiden a wild ride on her father's horse.

The notion that the dead may return to punish the living is reflected in at least one text of *James Harris* (243). The revenant, called a "spirit" in Pepys' copy (A), returns for the vows which his sweetheart, now married, had formerly made him—this in several copies (D, E, F)— and having carried her away in his ship, throws her "in the main" (D), drowns "baith ship and crew" (C), or sinks "the ship in a flash of fire, to the bottom of the sea" (E 18). The returned lover expressly says in Buchan's text (C 20) that he has brought the woman away to punish her for breaking her vows:

> "*I brought you away to punish you*
> *For the breaking your vows to me.*"

For his infidelity to the mermaid the hero of *Clerk Colvill* (42) pays the penalty of death. As regards the character of the preternatural being in *James Harris*, Child remarks:

In A the *revenant* is characterized as a spirit; in B, which is even tamer than A, he is called the mariner, and is drowned with the woman; in C he expressly says to the woman, I brought you away to punish you for breaking your vows to me. This explicitness may be prosaic, but it is regrettable that the conception was not maintained. To explain the . . . . ship-master, E–G, with a sort of vulgar rationalism, turn him into the devil, and as he is still represented in E, F (G being defective at the beginning) as returning to seek the fulfilment of old vows, he there figures as a "daemon lover." D (probably by the fortunate accident of being a fragment) leaves us to put our own construction upon the weird seaman; and, though it retains the homely ship-carpenter, is on the whole the most satisfactory of all the versions.[2]

A further motive for the return of the dead is illustrated in *Sweet William's Ghost* (77). Here the dead man comes back to regain his unfulfilled troth-plight. Herd's copy (B 5) reads:

[1] See Child, V, 60 ff.   [2] *Ibid.*, IV, 362.

"Cocks are crowing a merry mid-larf,
I wat the wild fule boded day;
Gie me my faith and trouthe again,
And let me fare me on my way."

The maiden questions him as to "what comes of women
. . . . that dy's in strong traveling," and then, upon re-
ceiving his answer, strokes her troth upon a long wand:

Up she has tain a bright long wand,
And she has straked her trouth thereon;
She has given [it] him out at the shot-window,
Wi many a sad sigh and heavy groan.

In A she stretches out her white hand, "to do her best;" in C "takes
up" her white hand, and strikes him on the breast; in E takes her white
hand and smooths it on his breast—all of which are possibly corruptions
of the ceremony performed in B. In D she takes a silver key and strikes
him three times on the breast.[1]

The dead man often asks for or returns plighted faith, as in
our ballad and in the *Child of Bristowe*.[2] According to
Scott's advertisement to *The Pirate*, a lady formally resumes her troth plight by touching the hand of her lover's
corpse. "Without going through this ceremony," Scott
says, "she could not, according to the superstition of the
country, have escaped a visit from the ghost of her departed lover, in the event of her bestowing upon any living
suitor the faith which she had plighted to the dead." Kinloch was informed by Scott that he had received this story
from an old woman in Shetland.[3] With respect to the ceremony portrayed in our ballad, Gummere remarks: "As for
the wand upon which Margaret 'strokes' her troth, it seems
not unlikely that we are dealing with a confused survival
of the common method by which savages and even European peasants get rid of a disease by rubbing the affected
part upon a stick, a tree, or what not."[4] The wand in
Sweet William's Ghost reappears in *The Brown Girl* (295).

[1] *Ibid.*, II, 227.   [2] Hazlitt, *Early Popular Poetry*, I, 120, 124, 128.

[3] See Child, II, 227 n.

[4] *Old English Ballads*, p. 349; cf. Tylor, *Primitive Culture*, II, 148 f.

[259]

A maiden strokes (B) a "white wand" on her dying lover's breast and says, "My faith and troth I give back to thee, so may thy soul have rest." In text A this passage occurs in a corrupted form. The wand in both the foregoing ballads recalls that in *Hind Horn* (17 A, B). Horn gives his mistress a silver wand with "seven living lavrocks sitting thereon." This wand, we may suppose, is a sort of love token. May the incident in *Sweet William's Ghost* (77) be regarded as a ceremonial return of troth plight by means of giving back a love token? This supposition is not, of course, inconsistent with the foregoing interpretation offered by Gummere. Certainly some kind of magic is at work here, and one is reminded of the peculiar incident in *The Lass of Roch Royal* (76 A, B, C, D, etc.). Love Gregory and his mistress, by way of effecting a love covenant, exchange their smocks:

> *"Have you not mind, Love Gregory,*
> *Since we sat at the wine,*
> *"We changed the smocks off our two backs,*
> *And ay the worst fell mine"* [A].[1]

In *The Clerk's Twa Sons o Owsenford* (72 C 35 ff.) two lovers, about to be hanged, request a return of their "faith and troth." A lady in *Prince Robert* (87 A 16, B 12, C 15) asks for the ring on her dead husband's hand.

To seek revenge and to punish, or at least admonish, the living are further motives for the return of the dead. In *The Cruel Mother* (20), two Danish versions of which approach "surprisingly near to Scottish tradition," a woman who has slain her newborn babes in order that she may appear a leal maiden is confronted by the murdered children and told what her future punishment is to be. In all but five of the Child versions of the ballad the returned babes are seen "playing at the ba"; so in a Motherwell text (C):

> *As she was walking by her father's castle wa,*
> *She saw twa pretty babes playing at the ba.*

[1] On exchange of costume between men and women see Frazer, *The Golden Bough*, VI, 260 f.

In the concluding stanzas, as in the Danish versions, the ghosts foretell the punishment in store for the mother—transformation into various shapes, bird, fish, and so on.[1]

Already considered in detail under ideas of the soul,[2] the incident of the singing bone in *The Twa Sisters* (10) need not detain us long. Through a harp, viol, or fiddle made entirely of her body or furnished from some part or parts thereof, a drowned maiden reveals the identity of her slayer. Vengeance is clearly the motive for the playing, speaking, or singing of the miraculous instrument—this in six texts (D, F, K, O, P, V). The mid-seventeenth-century broadside (A) reads:

> *Then bespake the treble string,*
> *"O yonder is my father the king."*

> *Then bespake the second string,*
> *"O yonder sitts my mother the queen."*

> *And then bespake the strings all three,*
> *"O yonder is my sister that drowned mee."*

The motive of revenge is not present in the foregoing text (A) nor in other texts aside from those listed above, nor is it found in Norse variants.[3] But in D, F, K the singing instrument demands that the murderess be hanged; in O, that she be drowned; in P and V, that she be burnt.

Again, as in *Young Hunting* (68), the soul of a slain man may return in the form of a bird to denounce the slayer.[4] Young Hunting has been murdered by his mistress, whom he has jilted. A bonny bird speaks out (A 7):

> *Out an spake the bonny bird,*
> *That flew abon her head:*
> *"Lady, keep well thy green clothing*
> *Fra that good lord's blood."*

[1] See *supra*, pp. 33 ff.

[2] See *supra*, pp. 68 ff.

[3] See Child, I, 122.   [4] See ideas of the soul (*supra*, p. 35).

In two versions (J 24, K 32) the bird directly testifies concerning the crime. In A, C, H, J, K it tells the seekers how to find the body by means of burning candles.[1]

The fine ballad of *Young Benjie* (86) depicts an old ceremony whereby a dead maiden is caused to speak and reveal the name of her murderer. There is no intervening metamorphosis here as in the case of the dead man in *Young Hunting*. With doors ajar, two brothers watch beside their dead sister until cockcrow at midnight, at which time the corpse thraws and begins to speak (A):

> "*O wha has done the wrang, sister,*
> *Or dared the deadly sin?*
> *Wha was sae stout, and feared nae dout,*
> *As thraw ye oer the linn?*"

> "*Young Benjie was the first ae man*
> *I laid my love upon;*
> *He was sae stout and proud-hearted,*
> *He threw me oer the linn.*"

In all texts of this song the corpse asks that the brothers punish the false lover by picking out his "twa grey eyes," a penalty which reminds us of that which the fairy queen would have inflicted upon Tam Lin (39).[2] Scott observes:

In this ballad the reader will find traces of a singular superstition, not yet altogether discredited in the wilder parts of Scotland. The lykewake, or watching a dead body, in itself a melancholy office, is rendered, in the idea of the assistants, more dismally awful, by the mysterious horrors of superstition. In the interval betwixt death and interment, the disembodied spirit is supposed to hover around its mortal habitation, and, if invoked by certain rites, retains the power of communicating, through its organs, the cause of its dissolution. . . . . One of the most potent ceremonies in the charm, for causing the dead body to speak, is setting the door ajar, or half open. On this account, the peasants of Scotland sedulously avoid leaving the door ajar while a corpse lies in the house. The door must either be left wide open, or quite shut; but the first is always preferred, on account of the exercise of hospitality usual on such occasions.[3]

[1] See *supra*, pp. 47, 83 f.

[2] See *infra*, p. 391.   [3] *Minstrelsy*, III, 10.

It should be noted that neither in Buchan's copy (B) of our ballad nor in the original of Scott's version (A) is anything said of the door's being ajar,[1] but in all versions the important incident of the talking corpse is present.

The evil doings of the living may cause the dead to walk. In *Proud Lady Margaret* (47), a ballad which has possible connections with popular tales, a dead man comes back to humble the haughty heart of his sister, whose cruelty has "gard" many a suitor die. The revenant proves himself in all copies of the ballad a match in riddlecraft for the heartless lady, and thereby wins a right to her love.[2] He then pronounces—this only in Scott's copy (A 15)— a curse upon the fertility of her land; in other texts warns her of the punishment which will overtake her because of her pride; reveals or admits his identity in all versions; announces the object of his visit (A); and in every copy, save A, says expressly that her pride has denied him peace in the grave, a motive which appears in corrupted form in certain American texts of *The Wife of Usher's Well* (79).[3] Scott's version of *Proud Lady Margaret* (47 A) gives the motive for the dead man's return:

> *"I am your brother Willie," he said,*
>   *"I trow ye ken na me;*
> *I came to humble your haughty heart,*
>   *Has gard sae mony die."*

D 11 reads:

> *"But I canna get peace into my grave,*
>   *A' for the pride o thee."*

In A 15 the dead brother makes the following dire prediction:

> *"And round about a' thae castles*
>   *You may baith plow and saw,*
> *But on the fifteenth day of May*
>   *The meadows will not maw."*

[1] See Child, IV, 478; V, 476: "The Dead."

[2] On riddlecraft see *infra*, pp. 301 ff.   [3] Campbell and Sharp, pp. 74 f.

This has double weight in coming from the dead, and recalls the deathbed testaments of other ballads (11, 12, 13).[1] In texts B, C, D, and E the revenant admonishes Lady Margaret to leave off the vanity of gold ornaments, and in B 31 warns her thus: "But if ye do not your ways refrain, in Pirie's chair ye'll sit";[2] C 18: "Or when you come where I have been you will repent it sore"; D 12: "If ye come the roads that I hae come sair warned will ye be"; E 11: "Ere ye see the sights that I hae seen sair altered ye maun be." The dead maiden in *Young Benjie* (86 A) is likewise concerned for the redemption of her slayer, and requests that a "green gravat" be tied round Benjie's neck to lead him "out and in," and that every "seven year's end" he be taken to the "linn," this to "scug his deadly sin." There is, however, no redemption for the murderess in *The Cruel Mother* (20). The dead babes announce that she must enter hell step by step (C)—steps which, though not given in this text, suggest the series of metamorphoses in other copies (I, J, K).[3] In the case of *Proud Lady Margaret* and likewise in that of *Young Benjie*, we are reminded of the close relationship which throughout balladry exists between brother and sister. In *The Cruel Brother* (11), as well as in other ballads (7, 8, 39 G, 65, 69, 71, 233), we find that fraternal authority is not to be slighted in the matter of a maiden's betrothal or amours, and in certain songs (14, 16, 50, 51, 52) brother-sister incest makes tragedy. The traditional "seven brethren" are found everywhere (7 B–F; 25 A; 48, stanza 21; 69 A, B, C, etc.; etc.).

The belief that a vengeful dead man may tear the living to pieces is recorded in *Willie's Fatal Visit*, in the Baring-Gould text of *The Unquiet Grave*, and in those tales of which *The Suffolk Miracle* is a ballad analogue. On his return from a night visit to his sweetheart,[4] the lover in

---

[1] See *infra*, p. 352. [2] See "Pirie's chair" (*infra*, p. 419).

[3] See *supra*, pp. 33 ff.

[4] See C. R. Baskervill, "English Songs on the Night Visit," *PMLA*, XXXVI, 565–614.

Willie's Fatal Visit (255), as a penalty for having said no prayer for his safety, is "riven" "frae gair to gair" by a female ghost, which is at once "great and grievous" and wan, weary, and smiling. Stanzas pronounced by Child as too good for the setting give us the ghost's accusation and its punishment of Willie.[1] The last of these stanzas may be quoted:

> Then she has taen him Sweet Willie,
> Riven him frae gair to gair,
> And on ilka seat o Mary's kirk
> O Willie she hang a share;
> Even abeen his love Meggie's dice,
> Hang's head and yellow hair.

The vindictiveness of our female ghost seems not sufficiently motivated, and one is inclined to supply a motive such as that in *Clerk Colvill* (42), where a sea-witch or mermaid, because of her earthly lover's infidelity, brings about his death.

Fear that his sweetheart may prove untrue prompts the dead man's threat in *The Unquiet Grave*—this only in the Baring-Gould versions:

> "Now if you were not true in word,
> As now I know you be,
> I'd tear you as the withered leaves
> Are torn from off the tree."[2]

The reason for a like ferociousness on the part of the dead man, in those continental tales of which *The Suffolk Miracle* (272) is a defective analogue, is not always clear.[3]

"The ballad of the dead mother's return to help her children," says Professor Ker, in his study of the Danish ballads, "is known to most of the Romance languages in the region described." But after comparing the plot of *Svend Dyring*, a Norse song in which this motive appears, with the plot as found in versions of Southern Europe, Ker notes further that "in Scotland there is apparently nothing

[1] See Child, IV, 415. [2] *Ibid.*, pp. 474 f. [3] See *ibid.*, V, 60 ff.

corresponding, beyond what is told by Jamieson in *Northern Antiquities*."[1] Concerning the presence of the story in Scotland, Jamieson says: "On the translation from the Danish being read to a very ancient gentleman in Dumfriesshire, he said the story of the mother coming back to her children was quite familiar to him in his youth, as an occurrence of his own immediate neighbourhood, with all the circumstances of name and place."[2] In Scottish balladry there is no lack of occasion, certainly, to justify the dead mother's return, for the traditionally cruel stepmother is active enough in the rôle of witch or enchantress.[3] And there is a suggestion in *Lady Isabel* (261)—unfortunately a poor ballad—of the motive which Professor Ker does not find in British folksong. The stepmother here, wicked enough for all purposes, accuses her stepdaughter of being leman to her father, and asks her to "drink the wine." Lady Isabel goes first, however, to Marykirk and into "Mary's quire" to consult her dead mother, whom she finds sitting in a "gowden chair." Advised by her mother to drink the "dowie drink" prepared by the stepdame, she returns home, wills—in true ballad fashion—her broaches and rings to her "Maries," drinks the poison, and dies, not before announcing, however, that her stepmother's bed shall be "in the lowest hell," her own "in the heavens high."

We may now give a moment's attention to the Danish ballad *Svend Dyring*. Ker says:

> Generally the southern versions have rather a different plot from the well known one of Jamieson's *Svend Dyring*. There the mother in heaven is grieved by her children's crying, and comes to the Lord to ask leave to return to middle-earth. In France, and generally in the South, the children go to the graveyard to find their mother; on the way they meet with Jesus Christ, who asks them where they are going, and calls their mother back to take care of them.[4]

Having lost his wife, Svend Dyring marries a "grim and harsh ill-favour'd dame," who kicks off his children, gives

[1] "On the Danish Ballads," *Scottish Historical Review*, I, 367.

[2] *Northern Antiquities*, p. 318.

[3] See *supra*, pp. 206 ff.   [4] *Loc. cit.*

them neither bread nor beer, makes them sleep on straw, and takes away their fire and light. But the dead mother hears the crying of her seven children, gets permission at God's high throne to succor them, rends her way through the earth and stones of her grave, and finally reaches her husband's courtyard gate:

> She reach'd her husband's courtyard gate,
> And there her eldest daughter sate.
>
> "O daughter mine, why so in tears?
> How fare my other little dears?"
>
> "No mother at all art thou of mine,
> Thou'rt not like her, though fair and fine;
>
> "My mother's cheeks were white and red,
> But thine are pale, and like the dead."
>
> "And how should I be fine or fair,
> When death has bleach'd the cheeks I bear?
>
> "Or how should I be white and red,
> So long, my child, as I've been dead?"
>
> She found her children's sleeping place,
> And wet with tears each little face.
>
> She nurs'd them all with mother's care,
> She comb'd and dress'd their silky hair.
>
> The infant babe she took on lap,
> And offer'd him the welcome pap.[1]

Thereupon she sends her eldest daughter to fetch Svend Dyring out of bed. She chides her negligent husband and warns him that it will be ill for him if ever his neglect of his children should occasion another visit from their dead mother. Nor is her warning without effect:

[1] Prior, I, 369.

Whenever hound was heard to whine,
They gave the children bread and wine.

Whenever hound was heard to bark,
They thought the dead walk'd in the dark.

Whenever hound was heard to howl,
They thought they saw a corpse's cowl.

In popular fictions a common motive for the return of the dead is to announce the death of the visitant.[1] Fair Margaret, jilted by Sweet William in the ballad which bears the names of these two lovers, goes forth "of her bower" never to come back, but that night her spirit appears "at William's feet" to tell of her death (74 A):

When day was gone, and night was come,
And all men fast asleep,
Then came the spirit of Fair Margaret,
And stood at William's feet.

"God give you joy, you two true lovers,
In bride-bed fast asleep;
Loe I am going to my green grass grave,
And am in my winding-sheet."

This incident occurs also in texts B and C, as well as in certain American variants,[2] and is found, too, in *Lord Thomas and Fair Annet* (73 E 32, F 28, I 32).

In Saxo's traditions and in Northern poetry the dead appear in visions, for the purpose, usually, of predicting the death of the person visited.[3] This motive is present in one version of *Lord Lovel* (75 I 1 ff.), and there is something of it in *The Cruel Mother* (20) and *Proud Lady Margaret* (47). *Lord Lovel* reads:

[1] See Child, V, 59.

[2] *JAFL*, XIX, 281; XXIII, 381; XXVIII, 154; Campbell and Sharp, pp. 62 ff.; McGill, *op. cit.*, p. 71; Wyman and Brockway, *Lonesome Tunes*, p. 99; Mackenzie, *Quest of the Ballad*, p. 125; Cox, *Folk-Songs of the South*, pp. 65 ff.

[3] Elton-Powell, *Saxo*, p. 42; Vigfusson-Powell, *op. cit.*, II, 330.

There came a ghost to Helen's bower,
Wi monny a sigh and groan:
"O make yourself ready, at Wednesday at een,
Fair Helen, you must be gone."

In *Proud Lady Margaret* the dead man predicts, as do the babes in *The Cruel Mother*, the punishments which the living must undergo as a consequence of wrongdoing.

We may conclude our discussion of the return of the dead with reference to *Sir Hugh* (155). In this ballad, the story of which is widely known in legend and song, Sir Hugh's mother makes an appointment to meet her murdered son's "dead corpse." In Jamieson's text (A) the appointment is not only made but kept. The dead Sir Hugh speaks to his mother from the draw-well, into which the Jew's daughter has thrown him:

"Gae hame, gae hame, my mither dear,
Prepare my winding sheet,
And at the back o merry Lincoln
The morn I will you meet."

Lady Maisry does as directed and then meets the "dead corpse." In other texts the appointment is made but nothing is said as to its being kept.[1]

---

[1] The motif of the grateful dead does not occur in the British traditional ballads, but it forms one thread of the plot in the verse narrative *The Factor's Garland*. See an oral version of this piece in *Texas and Southwestern Lore*, No. VI, pp. 56 ff. On the grateful dead man see Max Hippe, Herrig's *Archiv*, LXXXI, 141–83; G. H. Gerould, *The Grateful Dead*.

PART III

THE OTHERWORLD SPELL

INTRODUCTORY

❧

UNDER the chapter headings "Modes of Enchantment" and "Modes of Disenchantment" this section is devoted (1) to a discussion of those spells
or charms whereby mortals are brought within the jurisdiction of Otherworld powers, and (2) to a treatment of
those counterspells by means of which mortals evade, or
escape from, such jurisdiction. Relating as it does to necro-
mancy, witch beliefs, fairy-lore, and magic of various sorts,
the evidence herewith submitted is exceedingly significant
as proof of the basically pagan character of the ballads.
Indeed, the following pages present a world of pre- or non-
Christian thought, an array of beliefs and superstitions, as
well as practices, which in many cases may be said to go
far backward in time and not infrequently to reflect a way
of life unquestionably ancient or at least not to be explained
in the light of modern culture. Characteristic of the culture of early, backward, and primitive peoples the world
over are the types of taboo which find depiction in the
ballads—the eating and drinking taboo, the speaking taboo, name avoidance, and so on. Characteristic, moreover,
of early thought are the ballad examples of shapeshifting—
already discussed under ideas of the soul[1]—and the recovery, through magical procedure, of an original form. In its
portrayal of such operations, folksong illustrates the efficacy of fire, iron, milk, and water, as well as the power of
runes, riddlecraft, the magic wand, the magic circle, and
magic herbs, and furnishes instances, too, of the enchanted
apple tree, the tabooed or sacred grove, fairy wells, and
fairy hillocks, which, in one way or another, are associated
with the elfin spell. Finally, such ancient superstitions as

[1] See *supra*, pp. 44 ff.

the demon- or fairy-lover, the changeling, the mortal nurse in elfland, and the supernatural lapse of time in the fairy realm are all embodied in our popular poetry.

In the following chapters, however, as elsewhere in this volume, we encounter certain elements of ballad lore that may be described as Christian in character or that are tinged, at least, with Christian thought. Among such elements we find, in the present connection, the sign of the cross, the Holy Name, the Bible, baptism, and holy water—all these serving as charms against the spell of fairies and demons. In its portrayal of these counterspells balladry recognizes the line of demarcation that separated Christendom and heathendom.

Chapter IX
MODES OF ENCHANTMENT

❖

IN BRITISH balladry mortals are brought within the
jurisdiction of fairies, ghosts, and witches by the following methods: enchantment through eating, drinking, or speaking in the Otherworld; through physical contact with preternatural beings; through fairy gifts; through
elfin music, runic charms,[1] riddlecraft, and the fairy dart
or elf shot.[2] Folksong has something to say, moreover, of
the place of enchantment—beneath an apple tree, at the
fairy well, on the elfin hill, and in the magic or sacred wood.
The ballads exemplify, too, certain motives that lead the
fairies to capture earthly folk, motives illustrated chiefly
in the incidents of the mortal lover, the earthly nurse, and
the payment of the "teind to hell."

EATING, DRINKING, AND SPEAKING TABOOS

Taboos that have to do with eating, drinking, and
speaking in the abode of unearthly folk, as well as those
respecting personal contact with Otherworld creatures
and the acceptance of gifts from them, are common to the
traditions of peoples far and near.[3] The belief of early
Teutonic peoples in this matter of refraining from food and
drink in the Otherworld, as well as from other manner of

---

[1] The runic spell may, however, be claimed for English balladry only by
reference to Norse analogues of certain of our songs.

[2] In his dissertation *Zauber und Aberglaube* (Halle, 1907) Georg Rüdiger
offers a brief treatment of magic in the English ballads.

[3] See Schambach-Müller, *Niedersächsische Sagen und Märchen*, pp. 373–424;
Child, *Ballads*, I, 322 and n.; II, 505; Lang, *A Collection of Ballads*, p. 232;
Hartland, *Science of Fairy Tales*, pp. 43 ff.; MacCulloch, *Childhood of Fiction*,
p. 178 and n.

commerce with the preternatural beings therein, is strikingly exemplified in Saxo's account of King Gormo's visit to the enchanted realm of Guthmund. His sinister designs cloaked by a genial and hospitable mien, Guthmund tries in every way to induce his earthly visitants to partake of the good cheer of his realm. He offers them the delicious fruits of his garden and tempts them with the beautiful women of his household. But already instructed by Thorkill, their guide to Guthmund's land, Gormo and his men, save four, maintain their self-control and refuse to yield to the pleasures of the place. These four, "to whom lust was more than their salvation," succumb to the charms of the women and lose all recollection of their former life.[1] For the traditional poetry of England and Scotland *Thomas Rymer* (37), *Tam Lin* (39), and Jamieson's story of Child Rowland, part ballad, part tale,[2] furnish important parallels to the incidents in Gormo's Otherworld voyage. Like evidence, too, is supplied by Norse balladry.

True Thomas of our ballad must not touch the fruit of the Otherworld subterranean garden, for upon it fall all the "plagues that are in hell" (37 A):

> *O they rade on, and further on,*
> *Until they came to a garden green:*
> *"Light down, light down, ye ladie free,*
> *Some of that fruit let me pull to thee."*

> *"O no, O no, True Thomas," she says,*
> *"That fruit maun not be touched by thee,*
> *For a' the plagues that are in hell*
> *Light on the fruit of this countrie."*

The same prohibition occurs in B 7, I; in the related romance;[3] and in two other texts given by Child,[4] as well as in stanzas of Hutton's *Tam Lin* (39 M) that belong to

[1] See Elton-Powell, *Saxo*, pp. 344 ff.

[2] On the ballad elements in Jamieson's tale see Child, V, 201 and n.

[3] See *ibid.*, I, 328. [4] *Ibid.*, IV, 454 f.

Thomas Rymer.[1] The reading in C 17 of this latter piece retains the garden of paradise but is entirely perverted in that it makes the fairy offer Thomas for his wages an apple which will give him the "tongue that can never lie." Ogier the Dane, Thomas' analogue in romance, does, unlike Thomas, eat the apple of the Otherworld orchard, and thereby, we may well suppose, lays himself under the fairy spell. But according to texts A 10 and B 9 of the ballad, the fairy has provided for Thomas' safety by bringing along some honest bread and wine:

> *"But I have a loaf here in my lap,*
> *Likewise a bottle of claret wine,*
> *And now ere we go farther on,*
> *We'll rest a while, and ye may dine"* [A 10].

Matters are strangely mixed in our ballad. Thomas has already yielded himself to the elfin spell by having, earlier in the story (C 6), embraced the fairy,[2] a point to be considered shortly.

Matters are less entangled in the tale of Child Rowland, who, according to Jamieson's Scottish version of the story, is advised by the warlock Merlin that he "should neither eat nor drink of what was offered him in that country, whatever his hunger or thirst might be; for if he tasted or touched in Elfland, he must remain in the power of the Elves, and never see middle-eard again."[3] Tam Lin in the ballad of that name (39) probably had not abstained from fairy viands.[4] But his enchantment can be explained on other grounds, as we shall see later. To find parallels to our eating formula we need not go to romance, saga, or classic myth, but can find remarkable equivalents in savage traditions, such as that of the woman who visited her

[1] *Ibid.*, p. 458.

[2] The incident of embracing the fairy is absent from texts A and B but is present in the romance.

[3] *Northern Antiquities*, p. 399.

[4] Cf. Lang, "Fairy," *Encyclopaedia Britannica*, X, 134.

dead brother in Panoi, the Melanesian Otherworld, and
was there cautioned to eat nothing;[1] or that of Ahak-tah
who, according to a Sioux Indian legend, enters the realm
of the dead, but fortunately partakes of no food there;[2]
or yet again that of the New Zealand woman who, in her
visit to the land of spirits, is ordered by her father to refrain from eating.[3]

Norse balladry, in certain Otherworld pieces, preserves
the foregoing belief. Sir Bosmer, seduced by an "elfquean," quaffs a Lethean draught, prepared at the fairy's
command, and, like the four Danes in Saxo's story of King
Gormo's adventure in giantland who yield to the women
of Guthmund's household, he loses all knowledge of the
earthly world:

> *"Bring hither the goblet of red-deer horn,*
> *And cast in it grains of elfin corn."*

> *The maid came in at the chamber door,*
> *A goblet of horn in her hand she bore.*

> *"Now pledge me, Sir Bosmer, a friendship's cup."*
> *"If such is thy pleasure, I drink it up."*

> *He swallow'd the juice of the elfin grain;*
> *The world was lost to his wilder'd brain.*

> *His father and mother he clean forgot,*
> *His sisters and brothers remember'd not.*[4]

Bosmer's indiscretion recalls, of course, that of Proserpine
in eating the seven grains of a pomegranate which grew in
the Elysian fields, and that, too, of Ulysses' companions
in drinking from Circe's cup and eating the lotus. In Faro-

---

[1] Codrington, *The Melanesians*, p. 277.

[2] Eastman, *Dacotah*, p. 177; see Tylor, *Primitive Culture*, II, 52 n.

[3] Shortland, *Traditions of New Zealanders*, pp. 150 ff.

[4] Prior, *Ancient Danish Ballads*, III, 320.

ese versions of *Elveskud* the mortal knight meets his death by partaking of an elfin drink with an atter-corn, a poison grain, floating in it.[1] But this, apparently, is not the forgetful draught to which Bosmer owes his enchantment. Such a drink, however, is given the woman in the Danish *Jomfruen og Dværgekongen* as well as in Swedish and Norwegian variants of this piece.[2] A Norwegian version, Child's translation, reads:

> *Forth came her daughter, as jimp as a wand,*
> *She dances a dance, with silver can in hand.*

> *"O where wast thou bred, and where wast thou born?*
> *And where were thy maiden-garments shorn?"*

> *"In Norway was I bred, in Norway was I born,*
> *And in Norway were my maiden-garments shorn."*

> *The ae first drink from the silver can she drank,*
> *What stock she was come of she clean forgat.*[3]

The hero of the Danish song *Elvehöj* tricks the fairies by letting the wine flow on his breast:

> *I rais'd to my lips the silver cup,*
> *The wine on my breast let flow;*
> *The Elf-queans merrily clapp'd their hands,*
> *They thought they had won me so.*[4]

In the savage Otherworld tales referred to above, as well as in Saxo's story of Gormo's adventure and in the ballads *Thomas Rymer* and *Elveskud*, the mortal visitant to the land of the dead, to giantland, or to fairyland owes his salvation to the advice or orders of a ghost relative, to a well-informed guide, or to a well-disposed fairy, who, in the case of *Elveskud*, according to the variant we have quoted, is the visitor's own sister, herself a captive to the fairies.

[1] See Child, I, 375 and n. [3] *Ibid.*, p. 363 n.
[2] *Ibid.*, pp. 363 f. [4] Prior, III, 246.

The helpful ghosts of the savage stories and the kindly fairies of the ballads instance, of course, the significant mingling or paralleling of ghost and fairy beliefs, or perhaps, we should say, the identicalness of such beliefs. As for our eating formula, it is noteworthy that in Brittany if one should partake of food offered him by the dead he will be unable to go back to the land of living men. The enchantment is identical with that effected by the eating of fairy viands.[1]

It is barely possible that we find a curious reversal of this prohibition in the ghost ballad *The Wife of Usher's Well* (79). The revenant sons will not eat the food which their mother prepares for them. This incident appears neither in the Scott (A) text nor in the Kinloch (B) version. It is found, however, in Burne's Shropshire copy, but is best preserved in the Backus North Carolina text and in other American copies. The Backus version reads:

> *The table was fixed and the cloth was spread,*
> *And on it put bread and wine:*
> *"Come sit you down, my three little babes,*
> *And eat and drink of mine."*
>
> *"We will neither eat your bread, dear mother,*
> *Nor we'll neither drink your wine;*
> *For to our Saviour we must return*
> *To-night or in the morning soon."[2]*

According to the Burne text, the mother makes up a supper "as small, as small, as a yew-tree leaf, but never one bit they could eat."[3] In neither of these texts is the refusal to eat motivated by a lack of time, for afterward the sons go to bed and sleep until cockcrow or almost dawn. In two of the Campbell and Sharp variants, however, the babes

---

[1] See Le Braz, *La Légende de la Mort,* pp. 46, 47, and *passim* for this and other striking incidents that illustrate the similarity between fairies and the dead.

[2] Child, V, 294.

[3] *Ibid.,* III, 514.

will neither eat nor sleep, because the "Saviour dear" stands ready to take them.[1]

Analogous to the fairy-food taboo is the rule which prohibits speech with Otherworld folk. Thorkill, in Saxo's narrative, warns the Danes to be silent in Guthmund's realm; only those versed in the manners of the country should exchange words with its inhabitants. Thorkill's advice, however, seems to proceed from a fear that the Danes will offend the giants by uncivil words rather than from the belief that speaking per se is dangerous.[2] But Falstaff, as well as the fairy in *Thomas Rymer*, knows the rule when he says: "They are fairies; he that speaks to them shall die."[3] This superstition is somewhat allied to the belief in the power of the name, a type of magic which we have discussed under "Ideas of the Soul."[4] True Thomas of the ballad (37) has been duly warned by the queen to hold his tongue while in elfland no matter what he may hear or see, otherwise he will never get back to his own country:

> "*But Thomas, ye maun hold your tongue,*
> *Whatever you may hear or see,*
> *For gin ae word you should chance to speak,*
> *You will neer get back to your ain countrie*" [A 15].

According to the Campbell text (B), as well as one of Scott's copies[5] and also a stanza of *Tam Lin* (39 M 10) which belongs to *Thomas Rymer*, Thomas is urged to speak to no one but the queen, this by way of discretion in both the related romance (stanza 44) and in the Campbell text:

[1] *English Folk Songs from the Southern Appalachians*, pp. 73 f. See also text C (*ibid.*, p. 75). Cf. McGill, *Folk Songs of the Kentucky Mountains*, p. 5; *JAFL*, XXIII, 429; XXX, 305 ff. Cf. also Leather, *Folk-Lore of Herefordshire*, p. 199.

[2] See Elton-Powell, *op. cit.*, p. 346.

[3] *Merry Wives of Windsor*, V, 5.

[4] See *supra*, pp. 84 ff.

[5] Child, IV, 454.

> *It's when she cam into the hall—*
> *I wat a weel bred man was he—*
> *They've asked him question[s], one and all,*
> *But he answered none but that fair ladie* [B 12].

Or, according to another Scott text: "Now when ye come to our court, Thomas, see that a weel-learnd man ye be; for they will ask ye, one and all, but ye maun answer nane but me."[1] Just as Thorkill excuses the silence of the Danes in Guthmund's land, so the fairy in the romance of *Thomas of Erceldoune* is prepared to explain Thomas' silence by saying (stanza 45) that she took his "speche" beyond the "see"; in one of Scott's texts of the ballad, on the score that she got his "aith at the Eildon tree."[2] To conclude this matter of the speaking taboo, are the ghost babes in *The Cruel Mother* (20 L) aware of some form of prohibition which binds preternatural beings in telling of their Otherworld experiences? Describing the punishment which the false mother must undergo, the dead children say:

> *"Seven lang years ye'll ring the bell,*
> *And see sic sights as ye darna tell."*

But this may be just such a threat as that in *Proud Lady Margaret* (47 E 8) where the dead man thus admonishes or warns the vain woman: "Ere ye see the sights that I hae seen, sair altered ye maun be."[3]

PHYSICAL CONTACT WITH OTHERWORLD BEINGS

Superstitions relating to the fatal effect of personal contact with preternatural beings[4] are excellently illustrated for ghostlore in *The Unquiet Grave, Sweet William's Ghost,* and *The Twa Brothers;* for fairy tradition in *Thomas Rymer* and *Tam Lin.* Child remarks:

---

[1] *Ibid.,* p. 455.   [2] *Ibid.*

[3] Cf. B 26, C 18, D 12. Cf. the words of the ghost in *Hamlet* (I, v): "But that I am forbid to tell the secrets of my prison-house, I could a tale unfold, ..."

[4] On disenchantment through physical contact see *infra,* pp. 335 ff.

In this matter there is pretty much one rule for all "unco" folk, be they fairies, dwarfs, water-sprites, devils, or departed spirits, and, in a limited way, for witches, too. Thomas, having kissed the elf-queen's lips, must go with her. When the dead Willy comes to ask back his faith and troth of Margaret, and she says he must first kiss her, cheek and chin, he replies, "If I should kiss your red, red lips, your days would not be long."[1]

One recalls the men of Gormo's train, who, though warned by Thorkill to keep their hands off the servants and the cups of the people, cannot resist—four of them, that is— the blandishments of the Otherworld women. According to an exquisite Italian song, a lover visits hell, meets and kisses his mistress, and is told by her that he cannot hope ever to escape from her abode:

> "*Ora, mio caro ben, baciami in bocca,*
> *Baciami tanto ch'io contenta sia.*
> *È tanto saporita la tua bocca*
> *Di grazia saporisci anco la mia.*
> *Ora, mio caro ben, che m'hai baciato,*
> *Di qui non isperar d'andarne via.*"[2]

The important incident of how Thomas was enchanted by the elf queen, namely, by kissing or embracing her, is carefully detailed in the romance of *Thomas of Erceldoune*, but in the ballad versions of the story, save in Scott's copy, there is nothing of it. Wherever possible we cannot do better than to give Professor Child's analyses of certain ballad situations, and so here:

As C 5 stands, she challenges Thomas to kiss her, warning him at the same time, unnaturally, and of course in consequence of a corrupt reading, of the danger; which Thomas defies, C 6. These two stanzas in C represent the passage in the romance, 17–21, in which Thomas embraces the fairy queen, and are wanting in A, B, though not to be spared. It is contact with the fairy that gives her the power to carry her paramour off; for carry him off she does, and he is in great fright at having to go.[3]

[1] *Op. cit.*, I, 322.

[2] Tommaséo, I, 26; see trans. Busk, *Folk-Songs of Italy*, p. 89.

[3] *Op. cit.*, I, 320.

The two stanzas referred to by Child as C 5, 6, are in Scott's version of the ballad:

> *"Harp and carp, Thomas," she said,*
> *Harp and carp along wi me,*
> *And if ye dare to kiss my lips,*
> *Sure of your bodie I will be."*

> *"Betide me weal, betide me woe,*
> *That weird shall never daunton me;"*
> *Syne he has kissed her rosy lips,*
> *All underneath the Eildon Tree.*

> *"Now, ye maun go wi me," she said,*
> *"True Thomas, ye maun go wi me,*
> *And ye maun serve me seven years,*
> *Thro weal or woe, as may chance to be."*[1]

In the romance is described the melancholy transformation of the queen brought about by Thomas' embrace (stanzas 18 ff.), but this passage is not in keeping with the story of Ogier, which probably represents the original tale.[2]

The manner of Thomas' seduction by the elf queen is in part paralleled by the experience of the hero in *Tam Lin*, a ballad which, through the chief incident in the tale, the retransformation of Tam Lin, has connections with pre-Homeric Greek popular traditions.[3] According to Buchan's copy (G) of this piece, as well as one of Scott's versions, Tam falls asleep under an apple tree—a point to be noticed shortly—is there touched by the fairy queen, and must henceforth go in her company. It must be said, too, that he owes his misfortune partly, at least, to his being "ill sained" by his stepmother:

[1] Cf. text, *ibid.*, IV, 455, stanzas 6 ff.

[2] See *ibid.*, I, 320 and n.

[3] See *ibid.*, p. 336.

"When I was young, o three years old,
Muckle was made o me;
My step-mother put on my claithes,
An ill, ill sained she me.

"Ae fatal morning I went out,
Dreading nae injury,
And thinking lang, fell soun asleep,
Beneath an apple tree.

"Then by it came the Elfin Queen,
And laid her hand on me;
And from that time since ever I mind,
I've been in her companie" [39 G].

It is interesting to note, though this is a matter for later discussion, that Tam's disenchantment can be effected only in case his sweetheart holds him fast.[1] Moreover, whereas in *Thomas Rymer* and the ghost ballads, kissing Otherworld beings places one in their power, in *Kemp Owyne* (34) the situation is reversed. The transformed maiden is freed from the witch spell by the kemp's three kisses—this illustrating an incident common to saga, romance, ballad, and tale.[2]

Of a piece, no doubt, with foregoing beliefs respecting the fatal effect of contact with fairies is the incident related in *Clerk Colvill* (42), a ballad, the English texts of which are "deplorably imperfect," but which, were they given in full, would present a history similar to that of the Knight of Staufenberg, and which are matched by innumerable parallels in continental balladry, especially Scandinavian.[3] In two of the English texts (A 9, B 7) the tragic consequences of Clerk Colvill's unfaithfulness to the water nymph seem to be hastened by her prescription that he bind a "gare" of her "sark" about his aching head. What the "merfay" of the English ballad does to bring on the

[1] See *infra*, p. 338.
[2] See *infra*, pp. 335 ff.   [3] See Child, I, 372 ff.

[285]

headache is not clear, but reasons enough for the hero's sickness are brought out in foreign analogues—blows dealt him in Danish versions, poison elf drink administered in Faroese texts, elf-knife wounds in other Scandinavian versions.[1] There is no question, however, but that the gare of the fairy's sark when bound about the lover's head is by itself quite enough to effect the mermaid's wicked designs. Witness her exultation when Clerk Colvill carries out her instructions:

"But out ye tak your little pen-knife,
And frae my sark ye shear a gare;
Row that about your lovely head,
And the pain ye'll never feel nae mair."

Out he has taen his little pen-knife,
And frae her sark he's shorn a gare,
Rowed that about his lovely head,
But the pain increased mair and mair.

"Ohon, alas!" says Clark Colven,
"An aye sae sair's I mean my head!"
And merrily laughd the mermaiden,
"It will ay be war till ye be dead" [42 A].

Or, as in B 8: " 'And sairer, sairer ever will,' the maiden crys, 'till you be dead.' " Contact with the garment of an Otherworld being, such as a fairy or ghost, is, of course, on a par with kissing or embracing a preternatural creature. An instance for ghostlore is found in *The Suffolk Miracle* (272), which we shall consider presently.

Let us make somewhat of a digression at this point in order to illustrate for balladry the malicious activities of mermaids. A mermaid is partly responsible, at least, for the undoing of Sir Patrick Spens and his sailors (58),[2] and another water witch must take the entire blame for the

[1] *Ibid.*, pp. 375 ff.

[2] All texts except D and L–R, which are fragmentary.

fate of the ship and its crew in *The Mermaid* (289). Norse balladry preserves the tradition, as in *Sir Luno and the Mermaid:*

> *As steer'd Sir Luno across the sea,*
> *There met him a Mermaid, and wroth was she.*

> *"Hark thee, Sir Luno, and wend thee back,*
> *Or high on a rock thy ship I'll wrack."*[1]

But the mermaid's magic is counteracted by the power of runes, which the hero knows how to write. The shipwrecking propensities of the sea witch are found again in the Danish song *The Queen and the Mermaid:*

> *"The Mermaid I give not up to thee,"*
> *She trips on the floor so gay,*
> *"Seven ships of mine she has drown'd at sea,*
> *And would not my will obey."*[2]

The mermaid, like other fairies or witches described in balladry and elsewhere, assumes an entirely human form at will. So the "havfru" or mermaiden of the foregoing Danish song, since she is represented in the refrain as dancing on the floor, must, for the time being, have been in possession of a human shape.[3] It is clear, too, that the "merfay" in *Clerk Colvill* (42) has a human shape when on land, for when her false lover attempts to slay her, so the ballad reads (A 11), "she's become a fish again, and merrily sprang into the fleed"; or (B 9), "she was vanishd to a fish, and swam far off, a fair mermaid." But the mermaid has the power of transforming not only herself but others as well, this according to *Kemp Owyne* (34 B 15):

> *"O was it wolf into the wood,*
> *Or was it fish intill the sea,*
> *Or was it man, or wile woman,*
> *My true love, that misshapit thee?"*

[1] Prior, III, 257.
[2] *Ibid.*, II, 133.   [3] Cf. *ibid.*, p. 130.

To return to the superstition that it is dangerous to touch preternatural folk, *The Suffolk Miracle*, as we have already observed, illustrates possibly the same species of magic which we found to be exemplified in *Clerk Colvill* (42) when the mermaid's garment, or a "gare" of it, seals the lover's fate. The former piece, which preserves in a blurred manner the old idea of the procession of the dead, tells of a maiden who binds her handkerchief about the aching head of her dead lover, and afterward dies. But Professor Child can see no sense in the dead lover's head-ache.[1] Moreover, as the story goes, the maiden's death seems to be motivated by terror and grief, but it is probable that this is an instance of rationalization, and that originally the maiden, by virtue of a kind of sympathetic magic, owes her death to the fact that the ghost has gained possession of her handkerchief:

> But as they did this great haste make,
> He did complain his head did ake;
> Her handkerchief she then took out,
> And tyed the same his head about [272, stanza 14].

In the Cornwall tale which establishes the relationship between *The Suffolk Miracle* and its beautiful continental analogues, the maiden loses a piece of her garment to her dead lover and dies before morning.[2] It is true that in the ballad, as well as in the tale, the subsequent finding of the "handkerchief" in the grave of the dead lover, or of the piece of garment on his grave, seems intended to corroborate the girl's account of her experience, but even at this we may still suspect an underlying magic motif. For one to leave an article of his clothing, or any of his effects, for that matter, in the possession of the dead is commonly held to be very dangerous.[3] Certainly, in a Polish tale recorded by Grudziński and analogous to our ballad, magic

[1] *Op. cit.*, V, 59.

[2] *Ibid.*, p. 59 and n.

[3] For a number of examples see Hartland, *Perseus*, II, 89 ff.

is clearly present. Here the dead man is recalled from the grave by means of a spell wrought with a piece of his clothing.[1] To observe the superstition immediately to be presented for other ghost ballads, it is noteworthy that in American variants of *The Suffolk Miracle* the maiden kisses the ghost in addition to binding up his head.[2]

True Thomas' embrace of the elf queen, with his consequent enforced sojourn in the Otherworld, belongs to the same tradition as the fatal effect of kissing the dead. In *The Unquiet Grave* (78 A 5) the dead lover, a decidedly corporeal revenant,[3] thus warns his sweetheart, whose grief has brought him out of the grave:

> *"You crave one kiss of my clay-cold lips;*
> *But my breath smells earthy strong;*
> *If you have one kiss of my clay-cold lips,*
> *Your time will not be long."*

This commonplace is found in all the Child versions of our song, as well as in other variants both British and American.[4] It occurs also in *Sweet William's Ghost* (77 A, B, C, E), in *The Twa Brothers* (49 B), and likewise in American variants of this latter ballad.[5] It has been suggested that it is this fear of touching the dead which causes Margaret in *Sweet William's Ghost* (77) to return her lover's troth by means (B 9) of a "bright long wand" or (D 13) "a silver key."[6] But we must bear in mind—to defer to the ballad narrative or plot—that Margaret, inconsistently with this explanation, follows her lover and craves admission to his grave.

[1] *Lenore in Polen*, pp. 13 ff.; see Child, V, 60 f.

[2] Campbell and Sharp, pp. 130, 132.

[3] See *supra*, pp. 231 f.

[4] Sharp and Marson, *Folk Songs from Somerset* (1st ser.), p. 14; Leather, *op. cit.*, pp. 202 f.; *Journal of the Folk-Song Society*, I, 119, 192; II, 6 ff.; Sharp, *One Hundred English Folksongs*, pp. 56 f.

[5] Campbell and Sharp, pp. 35, 36.

[6] Stempel, *A Book of Ballads*, p. 232.

Illustrative of the same order of primitive thought as the foregoing superstitions relating to personal contact with Otherworld creatures, is the belief that it is dangerous to accept gifts from unearthly folk. Tam Lin's sweetheart proves herself a clever lass when, in addition to effecting her lover's retransformation, she refuses for him the "fee" offered by the elf queen:

> *"O stay, Tomlin," cried Elphin Queen,*
> *"Till I pay you your fee;"*
> *"His father has lands and rents enough,*
> *He wants no fee from thee"* [39 D 33].

G 50 has virtually the same reading. Sir Olave, the representative in Scandinavian balladry of our Clerk Colvill (42),[1] is proof against all the wonderful gifts with which the elf maid tempts him, but the maiden smites him to death for refusing her love:

> *"O keep to yourself your gold so red,*
> *For I must home to the maid I wed."*
>
> *She struck the knight on his cheek a stroke*
> *That splash'd the blood on his scarlet cloak.*[2]

Unlike Magnus in the Danish song *Herr Magnus og Bjærgtrolden*,[3] as well as in the Swedish analogue of this piece, *Hertig Magnus och Elfvorna*,[4] who comes off scot-free after having rejected the splendid gifts of an ugly hill troll, the hero in *Allison Gross* (35) suffers, for a similar offense, transformation into an "ugly worm." The witch offers the youth a "mantle o red scarlet, wi gouden flowrs an fringes fine"; a "sark o the saftest silk, well wrought wi pearles about the ban"; and, finally, "a cup of the good red gold, well set wi jewls sae fair to see." But our young man cries:

[1] See Child, I, 374 ff.

[2] Prior, II, 302.

[3] Trans. Prior, III, 344; see also Child, I, 314.

[4] Trans. Keightley, *Fairy Mythology*, p. 154.

"Awa, awa, ye ugly witch,
Had far awa, and lat me be;
For I woudna ance kiss your ugly mouth
For a' the gifts that ye coud gi."

True Thomas' seducer is a beauteous lady, and one feels that he must have doubly insured his Otherworld servitude by accepting the nine bells which the fairy holds in her hand (37 B 2) and which Thomas fancies have been promised him:

The horse she rode on was dapple gray,
And in her hand she held bells nine;
I thought I heard this fair lady say
These fair siller bells they should a' be mine.

In one of Scott's copies: "He thought he heard that lady say, 'They gowden bells sall a' be thine.' "[1] The bells here, however, as in A 2, C 2, hang at the horse's mane. Whether or not ornamental bells are to be regarded as distinctive of fairies,[2] it is obvious that in the above-quoted texts they serve to illustrate the fairy gift and imply the danger of accepting such gifts. Nor is it wholly absurd that the fairy queen in B 2 holds the bells in her hand. About the "middle" of the Elysianized hero in *Tam Lin* (39 G 2) there are nine "siller bells." According to the Brown (A 16) and the Scott (C 20) copies of *Thomas Rymer* (37), Thomas gets an elfin costume and is not seen on earth for seven years. Properly to be mentioned here, but already considered earlier in this work, are the golden slippers and the gilded boat which in *James Harris* (243) the demon-lover promises his mistress, and so, too, those Elysiums of golden mountains and castles painted by preternatural lovers who would lure earthly women to the fairy realm.[3]

THE ELF-SHOT MAN

Mortals may be charmed or even slain by the elf arrow or fairy dart. In the words of Allan Ramsay, elf shot

[1] Child, IV, 455. [2] See *ibid.*, I, 320 n. [3] See *supra*, pp. 143 ff.

means "bewitched, shot by fairies."[1] In his *Ode on the Popular Superstitions of the Highlands* Collins records the ancient superstition prevalent in the British Islands and in Scandinavia that the fairies destroy cattle by shooting them with their elf stones or flints:

> *There ev'ry herd by sad experience knows*
> *How, wing'd with fate, their elf-shot arrows fly,*
> *When the sick ewe her summer food foregoes,*
> *Or stretch'd on earth the heart-smit heifers lie.*

In *King Orfeo* (19) and notably in the Norse *Elveskud*, a parallel to *Clerk Colvill* (42), the elves put their weapons to a more loftily vengeful use, that, namely, of bewitching or slaying mortals. According to *King Orfeo*, which tells in little the story of the medieval romance of *Sir Orfeo*, Lady Isabel is charmed away to fairyland by being pierced with a fairy dart:

> *"For da king o Ferrie we his daert,*
> *Has pierced your lady to da hert."*

Even more tragic is the fate of Sir Oluf, the Norse representative of our Clerk Colvill. Sir Oluf is "ill handled and elf-shot, (*elleskudt*), because he would not be in the *elve-dance* with the *ellefolk*."[2] Child's excellent synoptical analysis of the Norse variants of the ballad of the elf-shot man may be given here:

Upon Oluf's now seeking to make his escape through the elves' flame, ring, dance, etc., Norwegian A, B, C, E, G, I, H, K, the elf-woman strikes at him with a gold band, her wand, hand, a branch or twig; gives him a blow on the cheek, between the shoulders, over his white neck; stabs him in the heart, gives him knife-strokes five, nine; sickness follows the stroke, or blood: Danish A, B, F, N, O, R, V, Z, Æ, Ø, Swedish D, G, Norwegian A–E, H, I, Icelandic. The knife-stabs are delayed till the elves have put him on his horse in Danish D, G, X; as he sprang to his horse the knives rang after him, H.[3]

---

[1] See Brand, *Popular Antiquities*, II, 491. On elf arrows see also Kirk, *Secret Commonwealth* (ed. Lang), pp. 19 f.; Keightley, *Fairy Mythology*, p. 352; Henderson, *Northern Counties*, pp. 185 ff.; Gummere, *Germanic Origins*, pp. 373 ff.

[2] Jamieson, *Popular Ballads*, I, 224. [3] *Op. cit.*, I, 377.

In analyzing Italian parallels of this ballad Child recalls the elf knives in Norse versions: "Shutting our eyes to other Romance versions, or, we may say, opening them to Scandinavian ones, we might see in these stabs the wounds made by the elf-knives in Danish D, G, H, N, O, R, X, Swedish G, Norwegian H, I."[1] In *Lady Isabel and the Elf-Knight* (4 A 12) the heroine charms her elf seducer to sleep and then stabs him with his "ain dag-durk." Nor must we overlook the "eldryge sword" of *Sir Cawline* (61) with which the earthly knight does such execution. The hillman in certain Norse analogues of *Hind Etin* (42) beats his earthly mistress with an elf rod.[2] Unfortunately, the ballads offer no parallel to that interesting ghost-shooter described by Codrington in his study of the Melanesians.[3]

FAIRY MUSIC

Of those charms which lure mortals to elfland, magic music is perhaps the most common and the most effective, that is, at any rate, according to folksong. Our ballads instance the power of the elfin strain to seduce human beings to the Otherworld, its power as a soporific spell, and its power over inanimate nature. To cite a case outside balladry, Bran, among the most celebrated of Otherworld itinerants, is overcome by the sweet music of the silver branch,[4] a branch, the melody of which is heard also by Cormac in his fairy adventure.[5] We have already called attention to the love of fairies for music and the dance,[6] a predilection which, interestingly enough, is characteristic of witches,[7] and, for that matter, characteristic of spirits, as well, for the Celts ascribe non-human music to

[1] *Ibid.*, 382 n.; cf. *Don Joan y Don Ramon* (*ibid.*, p. 385).

[2] See *ibid.*, p. 364.

[3] *Op. cit.*, pp. 205 f.

[4] See Meyer-Nutt, *Bran*, I, 2.

[5] *Ibid.*, p. 190.

[6] See *supra*, pp. 191 ff.

[7] See Murray, *Witch-Cult in Western Europe*, p. 137.

"fairy" or "spirit" agency.[1] Music, of course, like other fairy spells, may be employed in countercharming, as we shall see under "Modes of Disenchantment."[2]

In three of our best ballads of the supernatural, *The Elfin Knight* (2), *Lady Isabel and the Elf-Knight* (4), and *Hind Etin* (41), elfin love for mortal maiden is furthered by the notes of the fairy horn. Thus in *The Elfin Knight* (2 A):

> *The elphin knight sits on yon hill,*
> > *Ba, ba, ba, lilli ba*
> *He blaws his horn both lowd and shril.*
> > *The wind hath blown my plaid awa*

> *He blowes it east, he blowes it west,*
> *He blowes it where he lyketh best.*

> *"I wish that horn were in my kist,*
> *Yea, and the knight in my armes two."*

> *She had no sooner these words said,*
> *When that the knight came to her bed.*

The magic music is found also in texts B, C, D, and E,[3] likewise in I, but in this text the elf is replaced by an "auld, auld man," the devil, in other words—a natural-enough substitution.[4] In still another copy, where the blowing of the wind is substituted for the blowing of the elfin horn, the supernatural lover is a ghost.[5] The fairy horn is not found in those American texts I have examined, but we have it again in two good versions from Gavin Greig.[6] In both copies the horn is called a trumpet, and in one version

---

[1] Wentz, *Fairy-Faith*, p. 475 n.

[2] See *infra*, pp. 332 ff.

[3] Cf. text, Child, V, 206.

[4] See *ibid.*, I, 14.

[5] *Ibid.*, IV, 439.

[6] *Folk-Song of the North-East*, art. C. Cf. text, Greig, *Last Leaves*, p. 1.

there are "three trumpeters." The "Laird o' Elfin" himself is the trumpeter in the other text:

> *The Laird o' Elfin stands on yon hill,*
> *Ba, ba, ba, leelie, ba;*
> *And he blaws his trumpet lood and shrill,*
> *And the wind blaws aye my plaid awa.*

One is at a loss to account for the "three trumpeters":

> *"There stands three trumpeters on yon hill,*
> *Blow, blow, blow, winds blow;*
> *Blows their trumpet both loud and shrill,*
> *And the wind blows my plaid awa.*

In *Lady Isabel and the Elf-Knight* we again find the incident of a lass who is entranced by notes from an elfin horn and wishes that the fairy musician might he hers. In this case, however, the maiden goes away with her supernatural visitant, and, after discovering his diabolical designs on her life, turns the tables by slaying him—in text A by stabbing him, in other copies by drowning him, if such a fate may be said to be possible for an Otherworld being. If, as Miss Gilchrist points out, our supernatural wooer is a lineal descendant "of the malevolent waterspirit ('havmand') of Scandinavian ballads,"[1] we may account for his taking the maiden to "Wearie's Well" (B), to a "rock by the side of the sea" (C), and so on. But whatever his original character, he is, in our song, an elf-knight who knows the power of fairy strains:

> *Fair lady Isabel sits in her bower sewing,*
> *Aye as the gowans grow gay*
> *There she heard an elf-knight blawing his horn.*
> *The first morning in May*

> *"If I had yon horn that I hear blawing,*
> *And yon elf-knight to sleep in my bosom."*

[1] *Journal of the Folk-Song Society*, IV, 123.

This maiden had scarcely these words spoken,
Till in at her window the elf-knight has luppen.

"It's a very strange matter, fair maiden," said he,
"I canna blaw my horn but ye call on me" [4 A].

In B 2 the knight has a harp instead of a horn and with his playing sleep-binds all but the king's daughter. But we shall consider music as a soporific charm farther on. In Dutch and German parallels to our ballad the elfin horn is represented by an alluring song. "The elf-horn of English A," says Child, "is again represented by the seductive song of the Dutch ballad and of German G-R and Z."[1] To continue, and to read Child's note along with his text: "Though the lady is not lured away in the Scandinavian ballads by irresistible music . . . . the murderer has a horn in Swedish C, D, as also in the Dutch Halewyn and the German A, B, C, E, and the horn may be of magical power, but it is not distinctly described as such."[2] In certain continental versions of our song the maiden is lured away, not by music, but by the prospect of being taken to an Elysium or wonderland.[3] Foreign analogues of *Hind Etin* (41), as noticed by Child, do not employ the incident of magic music, but in Buchan's Scottish version the maiden is enticed to the elf wood, Elmond's wood, by an enchanted note:

She heard a note in Elmond's wood,
And wishd she there had been [A].

The "note" in A is in B mistaken for "nuts": "She spied some nuts growin in the wud, and wishd that she was there." According to C, the maiden is abducted under cover of a magic mist. But we find the fairy music again in a variant from Greig. The maiden hears a note in "Elwin's [Elfin's] wood," where dwells the etin, a "young hind chiel."[4]

[1] *Op. cit.*, I, 49; see also *ibid.*, p. 485; IV, 441. [2] *Ibid.*, I, 49 and n.
[3] See *supra*, pp. 143 f. [4] *Folk-Song of the North-East*, art. CLVII.

The knight in the Danish song *Hr. Tönne af Alsö* is overcome by the music of the dwarf maiden, who on her harp plays a runic strain:

> *She play'd a rune on golden harp,*
> *And, when she touch'd the string,*
> *The wild bird sitting on the bough*
> *His song forgot to sing.*

> *The wild bird sitting on the bough*
> *His song forgot to sing;*
> *The hart that in the green-wood skipp'd*
> *With joy forgot to spring.*

> *Charm'd with her runes the meadow bloom'd,*
> *And greener grew the wood;*
> *In vain Sir Tonné spurr'd his steed,*
> *Move he no longer cou'd.*

This spell, wrought by the elf's runic lay, is preserved in a Swedish version of the foregoing ballad Englished by Keightley.[1] The power of music over nature, whether the musician be an inspired mortal or an elf, we shall again have occasion to illustrate in connection with modes of unspelling.[2]

The soporific effect of enchanted music is no less strikingly instanced in balladry. The Otherworld knight in *Lady Isabel and the Elf-Knight* (4 B) initiates his nefarious wooing by the sleep-binding strains of his harp. He plays everybody to sleep save the king's daughter:

> *He's taen a harp into his hand,*
> *He's harped them all asleep,*
> *Except it was the king's daughter,*
> *Who one wink couldna get.*

Glenkindie likewise employs his harp (67 B 5, C 2) by playing a sleep spell to which all but his lady-love succumb.

[1] *Op. cit.*, pp. 97 f.   [2] See *infra*, pp. 332 ff.

[297]

But the enchanted music (B 14) is turned against Glenkindie himself when his man Gib, with designs on the lady
in question, harps his master asleep.[1] A "silly blind harper"
in the rather ineffective piece *The Lochmaben Harper* (192
A 9 f., B 5, C 7, D 7, E 8) accomplishes the theft of King
Henry's horse by first harping the court into forgetfulness
of the "stable-door." The incident of soporific music is of
frequent occurrence in popular literature, in Norse balladry, for example, in Highland story, or in Irish legend.[2]

THE RUNIC SPELL

Music is potent both as a charm and a countercharm,
and such reciprocity in magical procedure is characteristic
of other devices of enchantment. The power of the written
word or the magic rune, for instance, may be used not only
by the elves against mortals, but may be employed by
mortals against the powers of darkness. Ballad characters
are not unversed in "gramarye," and the heroine in *Lady
Isabel and the Elf-Knight* (4 A 11), to anticipate the study
of breaking the fairy spell, escapes from the Otherworld
knight by putting him to sleep with a "sma charm."[3] This
charm takes the place of the rune which produces magic
sleep in certain corresponding Norse ballads.[4] In one of the
Child variants (D 6), however, as well as in a Gavin Greig
text, it is the knight who employs the charm against the
maiden and so causes her to go with him:

> *From below his arm he pulled a charm,*
> *And stuck it in her sleeve,*
> *And he has made her go with him,*
> *Without her parents' leave.*

[1] Cf. No. 63 K (Child, V, 220), the first two stanzas of which belong to No.
67. For soporific music see also Nos. 62 E 14, F 24, J 46; 42 C 7.

[2] See Child, II, 137, 511 f.; V, 293. See also Wentz, *op. cit.*, p. 298; Meyer-
Nutt, *op. cit.*, I, 198; T. P. Cross, "Celtic Origin of the Lay of Yonec," *Revue
celtique*, XXXI, 452, n. 2.

[3] See *infra*, p. 348.

[4] See Child, I, 28, 48.

The reading in Greig's text is almost identical.[1] It is possible that in the original form of the ballad the elf enchants the maiden by some sort of runic spell, only to have his charm turned against him by his intended victim.[2] Such is the case in the Danish ballad *The Retorted Rune*, though, apparently, the lover here is not a supernatural being:

> *He took the runes, that royal prince,*
> *And so he threw them down,*
> *That just beneath her cloak they leap'd,*
> *Under her scarlet gown.*

> *Nine nights she sat and nine long days*
> *Out on the rocky fell,*
> *And then back on the Prince again*
> *She drove the runic spell.*[3]

In still other Danish ballads, *The Maid and the Dwarf-King*, analogue of *Hind Etin* (41), *Sir Peter and Mettelille*, *Sir Tideman*, and *Sir Buris and Christine*, a lover, elf or mortal, causes a maiden to follow him by the exercise of rune charms. According to the first of these, a princess, who would go to evensong, is compelled to repair to the elf hill through runic enchantment wrought by a dwarf.[4] Upon Mettelille Sir Peter places his irresistible spell; that is, throws "that fatal Rune" "beneath th' unwary maiden's cloak," so that she must follow him over the ocean.[5] Sir Tideman writes a "pair of potent runes," and tossing them toward the land bids them float ashore to Blidelil, thereby making good his boast to bring this fair maid aboard his ship.[6] In *Sir Buris and Christine*, which tells a cruel story

---

[1] *Folk-Song of the North-East*, art. CVI.

[2] In our English ballad and in certain German and Dutch analogues, the maiden is lured away by enchanting music, though not so in Norse variants; see *supra*, p. 296.

[3] Prior, III, 47.

[4] Grundtvig, No. 37.

[5] Prior, II, 349.   [6] *Ibid.*, III, 308.

widely spread over Northern Europe, a knight, at the instigation of his queen sister, succeeds in his wicked love by the aid of a runic spell:

> *Those fatal Runes he duly spread,*
> *Where the fair maid Christine must tread.*

> *And all o'erwhelm'd with shame and woe*
> *That night to Buris she must go.*[1]

According to the Swedish song *Sömn-runorna*[2] and the Danish ballad *Sövnerunerne*,[3] which tell a story somewhat similar to that in *The Broomfield Hill* (43), a song of witchcraft, a maiden preserves her chastity by means of runes written on sheets or featherbeds. A like incident occurs in the romance of Dolopathos, in a tale in the *Gesta romanorum*,[4] and in the romance *Sir Bevis of Hamptoun*,[5] as well as in other tales, in balladry, and in saga.[6] Our English ballad, *The Broomfield Hill* (43), tells how a maiden, under instructions from a witch woman, retains her honor by using sleep charms. She puts her lover to sleep by means of a combination of herbal and circle magic:

> *"But when ye gang to Broomfield Hills,*
> *Walk nine times round and round;*
> *Down below a bonny burn bank,*
> *Ye'll find your love sleeping sound.*

> *"Ye'll pu the bloom frae aff the broom,*
> *Strew't at his head and feet,*
> *And aye the thicker that ye do strew,*
> *The sounder he will sleep"* [C].

[1] *Ibid.*, II, 99.

[2] Arwidsson, II, 249.

[3] Grundtvig, II, 337.

[4] See Child's analyses (*op. cit.*, I, 391 ff.).

[5] Cited (*ibid.*, II, 506).

[6] See *ibid.*, I, 391 ff., 508; II, 506; III, 506; IV, 459.

Under "Modes of Disenchantment" we shall give further consideration to the broom as a magic plant.[1] The incident of the maiden's walking round and round the hill, a sort of circumambulatory charm, does not recur in other of Child's texts, but it is found in several versions recorded in the *Journal of the Folk-Song Society*.[2] These copies seem, however, to have lost the magical significance of the maiden's walking three, six, nine times round her lover. In Scott's text of the ballad (A 5) the sleeping knight has a "silver belt about his head," but Child thinks the belt meaningless and that it can hardly have anything to do with the lover's sleeping.[3] However, one recalls the belt and ring in *Kemp Owyne* (34 A) through which the hero acquires invulnerability. It is possible that the belt in *The Broomfield Hill* is intended as some kind of spiritual fetter.[4]

RIDDLECRAFT

There are still other ways by which ballad folk may fall within the jurisdiction of the Otherworld. Preternatural beings—ghosts, elves, and fiends—resort to riddlecraft in an effort to get mortals under their power. Through our riddle songs, *Riddles Wisely Expounded* (1), *The Fause Knight upon the Road* (3), and *The Unquiet Grave* (78), British traditional song has affinities with the remote past and with the ballads and tales of many peoples—this by virtue of the various situations in which riddlecraft figures.[5] In one type of riddle flyting, illustrated by certain texts of *Riddles Wisely Expounded* (1), an Otherworld personage can carry off his opponent if he can worst her in a question-and-answer contest, a sort of catechetical combat. In an important fifteenth-century text of the foregoing ballad, under the title *Inter diabolus et virgo*, the parties are the

[1] See *infra*, pp. 354 f.
[2] IV, 110 ff.
[3] *Op. cit.*, I, 391.
[4] See Frazer, *The Golden Bough*, III, 313 ff.
[5] See Child's introductions to Nos. 1, 2, 3, 45, 46, 47.

fiend and a maid, as in Motherwell's texts (C, D) and in Miss Mason's Northumberland copy (E).[1] In texts A and B the wooer is simply a knight, and Child at first supposed that the supernatural motif was a departure from the original story,[2] but upon his discovery of the above-mentioned fifteenth-century version he revised his opinion and concluded that the fiend rather than the mortal knight was the original character.[3] In *Inter diabolus et virgo*,[4] as well as in the Mason text (E), the fiend threatens rather than promises the maid that she shall be his in case of her failure to answer his questions. In the former text this threat is made after the putting of the questions:

> *"But þou now answery me,*
> *Thu schalt for soþe my leman be."*[5]

The questions vary in number according to different versions. In the foregoing text there are seven pairs of questions, all of which the maid answers successfully and thereby silences the "fovle fende."

The answers of the clever lass in one of Motherwell's copies cause the fiend to fly away in a blazing flame. This text we may quote, beginning with the diabolical wooer's announcement of his compact with the maid:

> *"Gin ye will answer me questions ten,*
> *The morn ye sall be made my ain.*

> *"O what is heigher nor the tree?*
> *And what is deeper nor the sea?*

> *"Or what is heavier nor the lead?*
> *And what is better nor the breid?*

---

[1] Child, V, 205.   [2] *Ibid.*, I, 3.

[3] *Ibid.*, V, 283: "The parties are the fiend and a maid, as in C, D, which are hereby evinced to be earlier than A, B."

[4] *Ibid.*, pp. 283 f.

[5] Cf. E, 5–7; and the promise, A 11, B 5, C 8. Cf. *The Elfin Knight* (2 I 3) where the "auld man" thus threatens the maiden: "I will ask ye questions three; resolve them, or ye'll gang wi me."

"O what is whiter nor the milk?
Or what is safter nor the silk?

"Or what is sharper nor a thorn?
Or what is louder nor a horn?

"Or what is greener nor the grass?
Or what is waur nor a woman was?"

"O heaven is higher nor the tree,
And hell is deeper nor the sea.

"O sin is heavier nor the lead,
The blessing's better nor the bread.

"The snaw is whiter nor the milk,
And the down is safter nor the silk.

"Hunger is sharper nor a thorn,
And shame is louder nor a horn.

"The pies are greener nor the grass,
And Clootie's waur nor a woman was."

As sune as she the fiend did name,
He flew awa in a blazing flame [C].

No other Child version gives this conclusion, but it is
found in Alfred Williams' interesting variant from the
Upper Thames:

Then he clapped his wings, and aloud did cry
And a flame of fire he flew away.[1]

D concludes by merely naming the fiend: "And the Devil's
worse than eer woman was"; B, by the knight's promising
to marry the lass; E, as well as the fifteenth-century text,
by the maiden's asserting her supremacy over the fiend.

[1] *Folk-Songs of the Upper Thames*, p. 37.

E, in which the fiend addresses his questions to all three sisters, reads: "Thus you have our answers nine, and we never shall be thine";[1] the Rawlinson copy:

> "*Now, thu fende, styl thu be;*
> *Nelle ich speke no more with the!*"

The device of naming the fiend is, of course, enough to send him packing, regardless of the maiden's success in solving his riddles, but in C the naming is clearly a part of the riddling. A German ballad which resembles *The Cruel Mother* (20) tells how Satan carries off to hell a woman who denies the evidence of her illicit love. Upon the bride's wishing that the devil may come for her if she has been unchaste, Satan appears, but there is nothing of riddlecraft in the story.[2]

In his Introduction to *The Elfin Knight* (2) Child observes that riddlecraft is practiced by divers preternatural beings, and draws for illustrations upon the mythology and lore of Scandinavia, Russia, Germany, Servia, Greece, and India.[3] But he thinks that the elf in the foregoing song is an intruder, for, to give his exact words, "An elf setting tasks, or even giving riddles, is unknown, I believe, in Northern tradition, and in no form of this story, except the English, is a preternatural personage of any kind the hero."[4] In connection with Child's observation it should be noted, however, that although riddling is not confined in our ballads to unearthly folk altogether, as witness *Captain Wedderburn's Courtship* (46) and *King John and the Bishop* (45), yet it is true that in nearly all our riddle songs one of the actors is a supernatural being—a fiend, a ghost, or an elf. We have already seen that Child grants priority to certain texts of *Riddles Wisely Expounded* (1) in which the riddle-monger is the devil—the devil being, therefore, the original of the mortal knight in texts A and B.[5] The devil as a riddle-monger is found not infrequently in popular

---

[1] Child, V, 205.   [2] See *ibid.*, I, 219 f., for the occurrence of this ballad.

[3] *Ibid.*, pp. 13 f.; cf. Kittredge, *Gawain and the Green Knight*, pp. 277, 280.

[4] *Ibid.*, I, 13.   [5] See *supra*, p. 302.

tales.[1] According to Child's own observation, the devil supplants the elf in certain texts of *The Elfin Knight*.[2] The elf in this particular song is probably the original character, although Child thinks that those opening stanzas which designate the hero as an elf belong more properly to *Lady Isabel and the Elf-Knight* (4).[3] In still another copy of *The Elfin Knight*, as we shall see presently, the elf is replaced by a ghost.

At any rate, whether in our ballad we are dealing with ghost, devil, or elf, we find here another form of riddlecraft, according to which, instead of question and answer, as in *Riddles Wisely Expounded*, there is a matching by one character of impossible tasks proposed by the other. This type of riddling occurs also in *The Fause Knight upon the Road* (3) and *The Unquiet Grave* (78). According to *The Elfin Knight* (2), to take a Baring-Gould text which "used to be sung as a sort of game in farm-houses," a maid escapes being carried off to the Otherworld by outwitting her dead lover. The impossible tasks set by him are met on her part by a proposal of tasks equally difficult. The ghost in this version, so Baring-Gould thinks, is the original of the elf in the other copies.[4] It will be enough to give the tasks set by the revenant:

"Thou must buy me, my lady, a cambrick shirt,
And stitch it without any needle-work.

"And thou must wash it in yonder well,
Where never a drop of water in fell.

"And thou must hang it upon a white thorn
That never has blossomed since Adam was born.

"And when that these tasks are finished and done
I'll take thee and marry thee under the sun."[5]

[1] See Child, I, 14.

[2] *Ibid.*

[3] *Ibid.*, I, 13.

[4] *Songs of the West*, p. 15 of the notes.

[5] Child, IV, 439 f.

Cleverly answered by the wise maiden, the ghost says:

"Now thou hast answered me well," he said,
"Or thou must have gone away with the dead."

In tales of this sort the acquittal of the person upon whom a task is imposed hinges upon that person's setting his opponent a task equally difficult that must be performed first.[1] So it is in the foregoing ballad, and again in *The Unquiet Grave* (78), a song of wide circulation, and which, in addition to the practice of riddlecraft, illustrates the belief, common to Persia and the Highlands of Scotland, that immoderate grief on the part of the living disturbs the rest of the dead.[2] Our ballad tells of a battle of wits between a maiden and her dead lover. The idea "on which [the piece] is based," in the words of Baring-Gould, "is that if a woman has plighted her oath to a man, she is still bound to him, after he is dead, and that he can claim her to follow him into the world of spirits, unless she can redeem herself by solving riddles he sets her."[3] This riddle motif is present in three of the Child versions of the ballad in question—E,[4] F,[5] and Hb[6]—and is found in one of Cecil Sharp's American variants.[7] According to the Baring-Gould copy, the ghost sets the following tasks, after having told the maiden that one kiss of his lips will be fatal:

"Go fetch me a light from dungeon deep,
Wring water from a stone,
And likewise milk from a maiden's breast
That never maid hath none [read *"babe had"*].[8]

In his notes on the foregoing text Baring-Gould gives the maiden's reply, which acquits her,[9] but Child does not

[1] Cf. *ibid.*, I, 8. [4] *Op. cit.*, III, 512.

[2] See *supra*, pp. 256 f. [5] *Ibid.*, p. 513.

[3] *Op. cit.*, p. 3 of the notes; see also *ibid.*, p. 15. [6] *Ibid.*, IV, 475.

[7] *One Hundred English Folksongs*, p. 56. Also in text, Williams, *op. cit.*, p. 76.

[8] Child, IV, 475. [9] *Op. cit.*, p. 15 of the notes.

OWAIN-

NINIAN- 80 BC Agricola

The Caliphs of Bagdad?

include this. A Cornwall variant of our ballad does not preserve the riddle incident, but, according to Robert Hunt, there ensued after the last stanza "a stormy kind of duet between the maiden and her lover's ghost, who tries to persuade the maid to accompany him to the world of shadows."[1] It must be that motives are mixed in our ballad or that the logic of ghostdom is other than that of mortals, else how explain the attempt of the dead lover to outriddle the maid and so carry her away to spiritland when he has already warned her that one kiss of his dead lips will be fatal?

The Fause Knight upon the Road (3), an old ballad with a striking parallel in a curious Swedish piece, furnishes still another example of riddlecraft. Matched by a witchlike old crone in the Swedish song,[2] the false knight here, none other than the devil himself, tries to nonplus a wee boy by asking him questions and making evil wishes. Needless to say, the youthful replicant is capable of clever rejoinders and has the last word, a matter of paramount importance in these verbal conflicts with Otherworld folk.[3] Child observes that our ballad is known only through Motherwell, but it is interesting that copies have been recovered in America by Phillips Barry, H. M. Belden,[4] and Cecil Sharp.[5] The false knight is called the "fol fol Fly" in Barry's Maine text, a probable corruption, as Barry points out, of "foul, foul Fiend." This text, Barry further observes, retains "a form of the theme more primitive than that of Motherwell's version."[6] An instance of flyting appears in *Harpkin*, a piece on the order of the foregoing ballad and given in Chambers' *Popular Rhymes of Scotland*.[7]

[1] *Popular Romances of the West of England* (3d ed., 1881), p. 27.

[2] See trans., Child, I, 21.

[3] On flytings see *ibid.*, pp. 21 n., 485; II, 496, 509; III, 496; IV, 440.

[4] *JAFL*, XXX, 286; XXIV, 344.

[5] *Folk Songs from the Southern Appalachians*, pp. 1 f.

[6] *JAFL*, XXIV, 344.

[7] P. 66; see Child, I, 21.

In a sort of scolding combat the hero of the poem outdoes a personage called Fin, an appellation of diabolical ancestry.

We may not dismiss the subject of riddlecraft without in the first place giving the opinion of Baring-Gould as to the evolution or genesis of the wooer in *The Elfin Knight* and allied pieces, and in the second place devoting a moment to those ballad incidents in which riddles are associated with wooing or marriage. With respect to the character of the wooer in such ballads as *The Elfin Knight* (2), Baring-Gould says:

> Apparently at some remote period a maiden who was pledged to a man was held to belong to him after he was dead, and to be obliged to follow her lover into the world of spirits, unless she could evade the obligation by some clever contrivance. When this idea fell away, either an elf was substituted or a man of low birth, or else the whole story was dropped; or, again, it was so altered that a knight was put in the place of the ghost, and it became the privilege of the shrewd girl who could answer the riddles to be taken as his wife.[1]

Concerning the "auld man," who in a Motherwell copy of *The Elfin Knight* (2 I) has displaced the elf of other versions and who is identical with the fiend of the Motherwell texts of *Riddles Wisely Expounded* (1 C, D),[2] Child says that this example of the substitution of the devil for the knight, unco or familiar, is natural enough for either of two reasons —"because the devil is the regular successor to any heathen sprite, or as the embodiment of craft and duplicity" he is introduced to "give us the pleasure of seeing him outwitted."[3] With however great certitude we may venture to define the original nature of the hero of these pieces who in shifting guise becomes ghost, elf, fiend, or mere mortal, it is noteworthy, as indicated in the preceding

[1] *Op. cit.*, p. 15.

[2] See also texts, Child, V, 205, 283 f.

[3] *Ibid.*, I, 14. On the devil as a riddle-monger see *ibid.*, pp. 14, 484. For Child's complete references to riddlecraft, flytings, etc., see his Index of Matters and Literature, *ibid.*, V, 469 ff., the following topics: "Devil gives riddles," "Dead lover sets tasks," "Flytings," "Foiling," "Nonplussing," "Riddlecraft," "Riddles," "Scolding," "Tasks," "Wit-combats."

pages, that in all our riddle ballads, except two (45, 46), a preternatural being of some kind is made to play a rôle (1, 2, 47, 78). And it would not be too great a hazard, perhaps, to venture a guess that one of these exceptions, *Captain Wedderburn's Courtship* (46), has supernatural affiliations by virtue of some as yet undiscovered text in which the maid or the hero is an Otherworld personage.

Lack of space forbids anything beyond a brief consideration of the association, in these ballads, of riddlecraft with wooing and marriage, a motive known to popular lore from remote times, and which finds its counterpart even in actual life. All three classes of riddle tales described by Child are represented in the traditional poetry of England and Scotland.[1] According to the first class, which apparently has nothing of the betrothal motive, and of which *King John and the Bishop* (45) is our sole specimen, the idea is that unless one party can guess another's riddles or give riddles of equal difficulty he must forfeit his life or some other heavy wager.[2]

The second and third classes of riddle stories have to do with courtship. In the third class, represented by certain texts of *Riddles Wisely Expounded* (1 A, B) and *The Elfin Knight* (2), a clever lass, by ingeniously answering her suitor's questions or matching the tasks he sets her, wins herself a husband or even a crown. German tradition has many ballads on the order of the two foregoing pieces,[3] and there is a well-known Gaelic ballad in which Fionn would marry no lady whom he could pose.[4] We should point out here, however, that our folksong represents a fourth type of riddling ballad, in which, as in the older versions of *Riddles Wisely Expounded* (1 C, D) and in certain texts of *The Unquiet Grave* (78), a mortal escapes being carried to the Otherworld by outriddling an elf, de-

[1] *Op. cit.*, I, 1 f.

[2] *Ibid.*, p. 1.

[3] *Ibid.*, p. 1 f.

[4] Campbell, *Popular Tales of the West Highlands*, III, 36.

mon, or ghost.[1] In his classification of riddle songs Child ignored the foregoing type because he had supposed the supernatural hero in texts C and D of *Riddles Wisely Expounded* (1) to be an intruder. This applies also to *The Elfin Knight* (2).[2] Without reference to the character of these riddle songs, we may note, in passing, that one of the tasks proposed by the Otherworld lover in *The Elfin Knight*, the task, namely, which requires the maiden to make her lover a shirt,[3] reflects a custom from actual life.[4] This incident is also illustrated elsewhere in British and Scandinavian balladry,[5] and is retained in American variants of *The Elfin Knight*.[6]

But let us touch briefly upon the second class of riddle stories, specimens of which are found in *Captain Wedderburn's Courtship* (46)[7] and *Proud Lady Margaret* (47). Here the situation is reversed. It is the suitor who must guess the riddles and rest the success of his courtship upon his ability to outwit the lady. The ingenious lover is not so popular a character as the shrewd lass, but he appears not infrequently in the tales of various peoples.[8] The proud lady in the second of the foregoing songs (47 A, B, C, D) has been accustomed to put riddles to her wooers, the penalty for their inability to answer being that they must die. This is expressly stated in A 6:

["*But ye maun read my riddle*," *she said*,
"*And answer my questions three*;
And but ye read them right," *she said*,
"*Gae stretch ye out and die*."]

[1] See *supra*, pp. 304 ff.

[2] See *supra*, pp. 302, 305.

[3] Texts A, B, C, D, F, G, H, I; also texts, Child, II, 495 f.; IV, 439 f.; V, 206; 284; and E.

[4] See Child, V, 284.   [5] *Ibid.*

[6] E.g.: *JAFL*, VII, 228 ff.; XIII, 121 f.; XVIII, 49 f., 212 ff.; XXVI, 174 f.; XXX, 285.

[7] See American texts: *ibid.*, XXIII, 377 f.; XXIV, 335 f.

[8] See Child, I, 416.

But the cruel lady of our ballad meets her master in the ghost of her dead brother, who, in the guise of a wooer, returns from the grave to reprove his sister. After he has answered her questions she says:

> *"Mony's the questions I've askd at thee,*
> *And ye've answerd them a';*
> *Ye are mine, and I am thine,*
> *Amo the sheets sae sma"* [B 18].

In like manner she admits her defeat in A 11, C 12. Among savages, riddles are employed in religious ceremonies relating to death or harvest.[1] But we should not, perhaps, infer that our vain lady is a practitioner of harvest magic when she says:

> *"And round about a' thae castles*
> *You may baith plow and saw,*
> *And on the fifteenth day of May*
> *The meadows they will maw"* [A 13].

Tales and ballads that contain this important incident of riddlecraft appear to reflect actual custom, for even among Russian peasants of today riddles play a part in marriage.[2]

THE APPLE TREE

In our traditional poetry there is no exact counterpart of the enchanting silver apple branch which initiates the fairy adventures of Bran and of Cormac,[3] nor is there any record of those venomous apples of Celtic tradition, but the apple tree figures in the enchantments in *Tam Lin*, *Thomas Rymer*, and *Sir Orfeo*—in these last two pieces, however, by reference to the kindred romances. The lore of the apple appears to be more extensive than that of any other fruit. We find it in the myths of all ages and countries.[4] And our balladry, as we have indicated, makes

[1] Kelso, "Riddle," *Encyclopaedia of Religion and Ethics*, X, 770.

[2] See Child, I, 418.

[3] See Meyer-Nutt, *op. cit.*, I, 3 ff., 189 f.

[4] Friend, *Flowers and Flower Lore*, p. 199.

[311]

somewhat of a contribution to these widespread traditions of the apple. According to the Swedish ballad *Agneta och Bergamannen* and the Danish song *Jomfruen og Dværge-kongen*, analogues of *Hind Etin* (41), a hillman or dwarf king throws gold apples into the lap of his earthly mistress, and thereby, so it seems, causes her to return with him to dwarfland.[1] The Danish piece reads:

> *The Dwarf on her lap gold apples threw,*
> [*That home to the cavern his lady drew.*]
>
> *Fair Hermeline up from the table sprang,*
> *The apples of gold they clash'd and rang.*
>
> *As Hermeline came to the mountain cave,*
> *The Dwarf on her ear a buffet gave.*[2]

In the Danish ballad *Swennendal* a golden ball thrown into the bower of a lady seems to have some magic power of attraction.[3] Golden apples of a magic or venomous character are often found in Celtic tradition,[4] as, for example, in certain incidents of the returning head.[5] We may recall here the apple or apples with which the Jew's daughter in *Sir Hugh* (155 A, B, C, D, etc.) lures her victim into her power, a noteworthy point if our ballad, as Charlotte Burne suggests, tells "the old, old story of the fatal love of the Siren in her garb of green, ..."[6] May we make anything of the heroine's saying in *Lord Thomas and Fair Annet* (73 I 24) that she got her surpassing beauty in her "father's garden, aneath an apple tree"? From some interestingly unknown source Fair Annet—jilted because of her poverty—is provided with rich clothes and an imposing retinue.

[1] See Child, I, 364.

[2] Prior, III, 340. Prior supplies the second line of the first stanza.

[3] See trans., Prior, II, 332; see also note, *ibid.*, III, 341 f.

[4] See Meyer-Nutt, *op. cit.*, I, 150, 169, 190, and *passim*.

[5] For examples see Kittredge, *Gawain*, pp. 153 f., 222, 275.

[6] *Shropshire Folk-Lore*, p. 532.

The apple tree, as we have already observed, plays a part in the enchantment of Tam Lin, according to two texts of the ballad of this name (39 G, K). Tam was asleep beneath an apple tree when he fell into the hands of the elf queen:

> *"I went out to my father's garden,*
>   *Fell asleep at yon aple tree:*
> *The queen of Elphan [she] came by,*
>   *And laid on her hands on me"* [K 14].[1]

G 26, 27: "And thinking lang, fell soun asleep, beneath an apple tree. Then by it came the Elfin Queen, and laid her hand on me." That Tam Lin was captured by the elf-queen while sleeping beneath an apple tree is in all likelihood a Celtic feature.[2] In the romance of Sir Orfeo, sleeping under an ympe tree exposes the queen to the enchantments of the fairy king, and it is probable that the ympe tree is an apple tree.[3] "Thomas of Erceldoune is lying under a semely (derne, cumly) tree, when he sees the fairy queen. The derivation of that poem from Ogier le Danois shows that this must have been an apple-tree."[4] The association of trees with enchantment is a common feature in old traditions.[5] We have already pointed out that transformed mortals, as in *Kemp Owyne* (34 A 6), are associated in one way or another with trees.[6] In Greece it is thought dangerous in summer and at noon to lie under certain trees, particularly the plane, the poplar, the fig, the nut, and St. John's bread, for one will in this way lay himself open to capture by the fairies.[7] "The elder and the linden are favorites of the elves in Denmark."[8]

---

[1] Child, IV, 456.

[2] Cf. Kittredge, "Sir Orfeo," *American Journal of Philology*, VII, 190.

[3] See *ibid*. and Child, I, 340.   [4] Child, I, 340.

[5] Kittredge (*American Journal of Philology*, p. 190 and n.) gives a number of instances. See also Friend, *op. cit.*, *passim*.

[6] See *supra*, pp. 124 f.

[7] See Schmidt, *Volksleben der Neugriechen*, p. 119; cf. Child, I, 340.

[8] Child, I, 340; see also *ibid.*, II, 505; III, 505; IV, 455 f.; V, 290.

THE MAGIC WOOD OR SACRED GROVE

Trespass upon fairy localities makes one liable to capture by Otherworld beings, a belief which finds illustration in *Tam Lin* (39 A–L) and *Hind Etin* (41 A, B). Janet's act of plucking a flower or breaking a branch in the enchanted wood summons Tam Lin, an elfin knight, and is the cause, apparently, of her falling into his power:

> *She had na pu'd a double rose,*
> *A rose but only twa,*
> *Till up then started young Tam Lin,*
> *Says, "Lady, thou's pu nae mae.*
>
> *"Why pu's thou the rose, Janet,*
> *And why breaks thou the wand?*
> *Or why comes thou to Carterhaugh*
> *Withoutten my command"* [39 A]?

A text in the *Journal of the Irish Folk-Song Society*[1] reads:

> *"What makes you pull those branches?*
> *What makes you pull those boughs?*
> *What makes you walk through these green fields*
> *Without the leave of me?"*

We have here something of an analogy to the theme of the forbidden chamber stories, prohibitions suggestive of primitive taboos, that, for instance, relating to the medicine man's fetish hut, which must not be approached or entered under penalty of death.[2] According to Grimm, Tam Lin finds a possible parallel in the dwarf Laurin, who does not allow trespassing in his rose garden.[3] As a parallel to the prohibition of breaking the bough in the grove of Diana at Aricia, Andrew Lang cites Tam Lin and his tabooed wood.[4]

In *Hind Etin* (41 A, B) a mortal maiden, trespassing

---

[1] I, 47 f.

[2] Cf. MacCulloch, *op. cit.*, pp. 315 f.

[3] *Deutsche Mythologie*, III, 130.

[4] "Breaking the Bough in the Grove of Diana," *Folk-Lore*, XVIII, 89–91.

upon the sacred grove, pulls "nuts" instead of roses. The "nuts," however, Child thinks less plausible than the "rose" in *Tam Lin*.[1] Earlier in this study we have given Gummere's interpretation of the *Hind Etin* incident, an interpretation which may well justify the reading "nuts."[2] This reading, it is important to note, is found in a Gavin Greig text of our ballad. Hearing a fairy horn, the maiden goes to Elwin's wood and begins gathering nuts. A "young hind chiel" appears and says:

> *"Oh, why pu' ye the nut, the nut,*
> *Or why break ye the tree?*
> *For I'm the guardian o' the wood,*
> *And ye maun let it be."*[3]

As a commonplace this passage or incident occurs also in *Babylon* (14 A, B, D, E), where a maiden—a maiden and her sisters—goes out to pluck flowers (A, B), a leaf (D), roses (E), and thereby summons an outlaw. It is found, too, in *The King's Dochter Lady Jean* (52 A–D). We find it again in *Jellon Grame* (90 C 24 ff.), though here the trespasser is a boy. In none of these three pieces, however, unless it be in the last, is the guardian of the wood a preternatural being.[4] The same incident appears in a Wendish analogue of *Lady Isabel and the Elf-Knight* (4).[5]

It is possible that our sacred-grove taboo finds an explanation in a remarkable Danish ballad *Trolden og Bondens Hustru*.[6] According to this piece, a farmer settles in a wood in a "Western isle," and there fells the oak, the birch, the beech, and the poplar. But the elves take offense at the encroachments of the foreigner:

[1] *Op. cit.*, I, 360 n.

[2] See *supra*, p. 123.

[3] *Folk-Song of the North-East*, art. CLVII. Cf. text, Greig, *Last Leaves*, p. 29.

[4] On the Silver Wood in *Jellon Grame* see *supra*, pp. 157 f.

[5] See Child, I, 41.

[6] Grundtvig, No. 52.

'Twas in a wood on a Western isle,
A farmer chose his ground;
He thought to spend the winter there,
And brought his hawk and hound.

He brought with him both hound and cock,
For long he meant to stay,
And much the deer, that roam'd the wood,
Had cause to rue the day.

He fell'd the oak, he fell'd the birch,
Nor beech nor poplar spared,
And much was griev'd the sullen Elf,
At what the stranger dared.

He hew'd him balks, he hew'd him beams,
With eager toil and haste;
"Who," ask'd the Elves in the mountain cave,
"Who's come our wood to waste?"[1]

The foregoing ballad is interesting in view of the ethnological theory as to the origin of fairies. Into the incident of the contest between the elves and the farmer one may read a reminiscence of the early struggles between aboriginal inhabitants of the Northern countries and the Scandinavian peoples.[2] In his assemblage of evidence to show that the fairy belief arose from the folk-memory of a prehistoric race, David MacRitchie cites the Danish ballad as well as our own Shetland song *King Orfeo* (19).[3]

Whether or not we may argue for balladry the ancient and widespread tradition of well worship, it is noteworthy that wells, springs, or rivers are associated in our folksong with fairy capture. When he came "in by Lady Well,"a magic or Otherworld sleep fell upon Tam Lin and made him an easy victim for the Queen of Faery:

[1] Trans. Prior, III, 165 f.; cf. other texts (*ibid.*, pp. 171 ff.).

[2] Cf. Prior, III, 164.

[3] *The Testimony of Tradition*, pp. 104 ff.

"If Charteris ha be thy father's,
I was ance as gude mysell;
But as I came in by Lady Kirk,
And in by Lady Well,

"Deep and drowsy was the sleep
On my poor body fell;
By came the Queen of Faery,
Made me with her to dwell" [39 E].

Or J 8: "When riding through yon forest-wood, and by
yon grass-green well, a sudden sleep me overtook, and off
my steed I fell." The wee wee man (38 A, B, D, E, F)is
spied "between a water and a wa," and Clerk Colvill's
tragic love for the mermaid (42) takes him (A 4) to the
"wall o Stream," (B 4) to the "wells of Slane," (C) to
"Clyde's water." It is to Wearie's Well that the Otherworld knight (4 B) leads the clever lass and there tries to
drown her as he has drowned seven other royal maidens.
The diabolical being in this piece is possibly a water
sprite.[1] The korrigan in *Le Seigneur Nann et la Fée* combs
her hair beside a woodland spring.[2] Nor should we fail to
mention the wife of Usher's Well and the ghost sons (79),
and also "Our Lady's draw-well," which is "fifty fathom
deep" and out of which the murdered Sir Hugh talks to
his mother (155 A). In other texts of this latter song we
have simply "Jew's draw-well," "draw-well," or "well."[3]
It is at "the well" (39 A, B, L) that Janet meets her elfin-
lover, who exacts forfeits of maidens who wear gold on
their hair:

O I forbid you, maidens a',
That wear gowd on your hair,
To come or gae by Carterhaugh,
For young Tam Lin is there.

[1] See *supra*, p. 138.

[2] See trans., Keightley, p. 434.

[3] For ballad wells see also Nos. 11 B 18; 58 B 14; 68 D 3, F 4; 231 C 6; and
Child, IV, 93, 105; V, 501: "Wells."

There's nane that gaes by Carterhaugh
But they leave him a wad,
Either their rings, or green mantles,
Or else their maidenhead [A].[1]

Arrived at Carterhaugh, Janet finds the elf at the well:

When she came to Carterhaugh
Tam Lin was at the well,
And there she fand his steed standing,
But away was himsel.

With reference to the second line of the first of the fore-going stanzas, we may quote Prior to the effect that "the crown of gold was an ornament which only maiden ladies were entitled to wear, and the loss of it prevented their being received in society."[2] Those who trespass on Hynde Henry's wood (90 C 25 ff.) must likewise pay a fine.

Carterhaugh provides at once a fairy region for the story of *Tam Lin* and an interesting example of localization.[3] Scott says:

Carterhaugh is a plain, at the conflux of the Ettrick and Yarrow, in Selkirkshire, about a mile above Selkirk, and two miles below Newark Castle; . . . . The peasants point out, upon the plain, those electrical rings, which vulgar credulity supposes to be traces of the Fairy revels.[4]

The place of Janet's fairy adventure is called "Carter-haugh" in texts A, B, H, I, Ib, and L; "Kertonha" in C; "Charteris ha," E; "Carden's Ha," J;[5] "Chaster's wood," "Chester wood," "Charter woods," D, Dc, F, G. It is "Crickmagh," according to a text in the *Journal of the Irish Folk-Song Society.*[6] Carterhaugh appears also in Scott's copy of *The Wee Wee Man* (38 C); in G: "Between Midmar and bonny Craigha." In the ballad of *Thomas*

---

[1] Cf. B, G, H, I.

[2] *Op. cit.*, III, 147.

[3] On localizing of ballad stories see Child, V, 487: "Localizing . . . ."

[4] *Minstrelsy* (ed. Henderson), II, 377.

[5] "Katherine's Hall," J, Child, III, 504.   [6] I, 47 f.

Rymer (37 B, C), as well as in the related romance, the scene of the hero's meeting with the elf queen is Huntly Banks and the Eildon Tree.[1] Murray says:

Eildon Tree, referred to in the Romance, and connected traditionally with Thomas's prophecies, stood on the declivity of the eastern of the three Eildon Hills, looking across the Tweed to Leader Water, Bemerside, Earlstoun, and other places connected with Thomas. Its site is believed to be indicated by the *Eildon Stone*, "a rugged boulder of whinstone" standing on the edge of the road from Melrose to St. Boswell's, about a mile south-east from the former town, and on the ridge of a spur of the hill.[2]

Other localities of fairy enchantment are mentioned by name in the ballads and have already been referred to here and there in the foregoing pages; for example, "Wormie's Wood" (34 B 18); "the wood o Tore" (18 B); "Elmond's wood" (41 A); "Craigy's sea," "Eastmuir craigs" (34 A, B); "Bunion Bay" (4 D 8) or "Binyan Bay" in a Greig text.[3] Sir Cawline (61, stanzas 14 ff.) meets the eldrige king on Eldrige Hill where "growes a thorne," a probable allusion to the thorn as a magic tree.

As for still other elfin localities, there are the fairy-haunted hills of balladry, the dwarf caverns, and the undersea realms, but these we have considered earlier in our study, chiefly in connection with the situation of the Otherworld.[4] We must bring to a close our discussion of modes of enchantment. Scott observes that the power of fairies was extended not only to unchristened babes[5] but to "full-grown persons, especially such as, in an unlucky hour, were devoted to the devil by the execration of parents and of masters; or those who were found asleep under a rock, or on a green hill, belonging to the Fairies, after sunset, or, finally, to those who unwarily joined their orgies."[6] We

[1] Cf. text, Child, IV, 455.

[2] *Thomas of Erceldoune, Early English Text Society*, LXI, l.

[3] *Folk-Song of the North-East*, art. CVI.

[4] See *supra*, pp. 127 ff.

[5] On christening and fairies see *infra*, pp. 373 f.

[6] *Op. cit.*, II, 366.

have already seen how Tam Lin (39 G, K) was captured by the elfin queen as he lay asleep beneath an apple tree.[1] And we have illustrated, too, the danger of having any sort of commerce with preternatural beings, such as embracing them or partaking of their food, or, again, joining in their dances. The apple-tree incident occurs only in texts G and K of *Tam Lin*. But in other copies, as he is returning from the hunt, he falls asleep on or near a green hill and is there caught by the queen of fairies:

> "*And ance it fell upon a day,*
> *A cauld day and a snell,*
> *When we were frae the hunting come,*
> *That frae my horse I fell;*
> *The Queen o Fairies she caught me,*
> *In yon green hill to dwell*" [39 A 23]

In D 13, 14, and I 29, 30, Tam falls asleep while he is hunting. In J 8, 9, he is out riding, falls asleep, and is captured.[2] According to B 22, he falls from his horse. In E 7, also, he is taken while asleep. In I 30 the sleep seems to be brought on by a "sharp wind and a snell" from the "north." According to D 13, his misfortune overtook him as he "rode east and west yon hill."

But let us illustrate another of the conditions mentioned by Scott as making one susceptible to the Otherworld spell, the circumstance, namely, of being devoted to the powers of evil by the "execration of parents and of masters." Buchan's copy of *Tam Lin* (39 G 25) leads us to think that the hero's undoing was the result of his stepmother's having "ill-sained" or ill-blessed him: "My stepmother put on my claithes, an ill, ill sained she me." The sign of the cross is, of course, proof against fairies, and we may well suppose that the stepdame maliciously exposed Tam to the elfin powers.[3]

[1] See *supra*, p. 313.

[2] Child, III, 504.

[3] On the sign of the cross see *infra*, pp. 367 ff.

THE TROLL MIST

The fairy or troll mist, by aid of which Hind Etin (41 C 3) carries off his mortal bride, may serve to bring to a close our examples of the Otherworld spell and the various means whereby elfin beings seduce their earthly victims:

> *Yet she preferred before them all*
> *Him, young Hastings the Groom;*
> *He's coosten a mist before them all,*
> *And away this lady has taen.*

A 15 has something of the magical mist: "I catchd her on a misty night, whan summer was in prime." The fairy hall (38 G 7) vanishes in a mist: "Out gat the lights, on cam the mist, ladies nor mannie mair coud see." The revenant in one copy of *Sweet William's Ghost* (77 A 15) vanishes in a "cloud of mist"; but this has a modern ring. It is not characteristic of the ballad ghost so to vanish. A magic cloud or mist figures in Saxo's story of Regner and Swanwhite. "Swanhwid . . . . cast off the cloud of mist which overshadowed her, ..."[1] This feature comes probably from Irish tradition, which, in its tales, furnishes many examples of the "druidical mist."[2] Finally, and to conclude our listing of charms, we may refer to the "glamer" which Johny Faa and his men cast over Earl Cassillis' lady in *The Gypsy Laddie* (200 A–F, Gb). In a Greig variant of this song "They cast their camprols o'er her O."[3]

MOTIVES FOR THE CAPTURE OF MORTALS

The methods whereby mortals are brought within the jurisdiction of preternatural powers are numerous and picturesque,[4] and the ballads record many of them. But

[1] Elton-Powell, *op. cit.*, p. 53.

[2] Cf. Bugge, *Home of the Eddic Poems*, p. 351; see also Meyer-Nutt, *op. cit.*, I, 180, 190; II, 171 ff.

[3] Greig, *Last Leaves of Traditional Ballads*, p. 126. On "camprol" (spell) see *ibid.*, p. 265.

[4] See Hartland, *Science of Fairy Tales*, chaps. iii, iv, v; Scott, *op. cit.*, II, 300 ff.; Wentz, *op. cit.*, *passim*.

let us now turn for a moment to those motives which gov-
ern fairies, demons, witches, and ghosts in their abduction
or enchantment of earthly folk. The love of elf for mortal
is enough in most cases. This motive colors completely or
in part the designs of the elves, trolls, and fiends in the
following pieces: *Riddles Wisely Expounded* (1), *The Elfin
Knight* (2), *Lady Isabel and the Elf-Knight* (4), *Hind Etin*
(41), *The Unquiet Grave* (78),[1] *Thomas Rymer* (37), and
Tam Lin (39). In these last two pieces there are other
elements which will be treated shortly. Love, wooing, and
marriage are present, or actuate the story, in *Clerk Colvill*
(42) and *The Great Silkie of Sule Skerry* (113), as well as in
Child Waters (63), *The Fair Flower of Northumberland* (9),
The Knight and Shepherd's Daughter (110), and *The Lass of
Roch Royal* (76). The evidence of fairy machinery is, however, slight and doubtful in these last-named pieces.
Fairies often find their lovers among mortal folk, but he
who would enjoy their charms must generally submit to
some sort of restriction or taboo, the violation of which
brings sorrow or even death to him. So Clerk Colvill (42)
dies because he has proved untrue to his mermaid mistress.
Likewise his Norwegian analogue is offered the alternative
of dying or marrying an elf maid:

> *Whether wilt thou go off sick, "under isle,"*
> *Or wilt thou marry an elf-maid?*

> *Whether wilt thou go off sick, under hill,*
> *Or wilt thou marry an elf-wife?*[2]

The rejected love of a witch is the theme of *Allison Gross*
(35).

The song of *The Wee Wee Man* (38) is apparently concerned with Otherworld adventure in and for itself. The
diabolical riddle-monger in *The Fause Knight upon the Road*
(3) seems to be governed by pure maliciousness in his attempt to outwit the clever boy. The jealousy and venge-

[1] On the riddle motif in this song see *supra*, pp. 306 ff.

[2] Trans. Child, I, 377.

fulness of a witch stepdame are at work in *Kemp Owyne*
(34) and *The Laily Worm* (36), and account for enchantments no less monstrous in *The Marriage of Sir Gawain*
(31) and *King Henry* (32). By its title alone *The Queen of
Elfan's Nourice* (40) reveals the nature of the superstition
which it embodies, a superstition which merits brief discussion farther on. *King Orfeo* (19) gives in traditional
song the medieval romance of Sir Orfeo. The motives for
the return of the dead have been considered earlier in this
study.[1]

The necessity of paying a tribute to hell actuates the
fairies in stealing mortal men, according to *Tam Lin* (39)
and *Thomas Rymer* (37). As a consequence of having at
stated intervals to pay this tax, tithe, or teind to hell, the
fairies, so it was formerly believed in Scotland, were accustomed to abduct earthly folk, whom they offered up as
a tribute to the fiend, a fine which must otherwise have
been met by sacrificing a member of their own order.[2]
After quoting certain passages from *Tam Lin* we may give
Professor Child's synoptical analysis of the incident in
question as it occurs in the several texts of this piece and
in *Thomas Rymer*. Eerie is the tale which Tam relates to
his sweetheart:

> "*And pleasant is the fairy land,*
> *But, an eerie tale to tell,*
> *Ay at the end of seven years*
> *We pay a tiend to hell;*
> *I am sae fair and fu o flesh,*
> *I'm feard it be mysel*" [39 A 24].

A stanza from Campbell's version (H 15) should also be
given as showing that the fairies, for lack of a human
victim, had to satisfy the tax by drawing upon their own
ranks:

[1] See *supra*, pp. 253 ff.

[2] See W. Henderson, *op. cit.*, p. 225; Gregor, *Folk-Lore of the North-East of
Scotland*, p. 60; Hartland, *Science of Fairy Tales*, p. 102 n.; Child, I, 339; V, 215.

> *Up bespack the Queen of Fairies,*
> *And she spak wi a loud yell:*
> *"Aye at every seven year's end*
> *We pay the kane to hell,*
> *And the koors they hae gane round about,*
> *And I fear it will be mysel."*

Professor Child's synopsis may now be given:

At stated periods, which the ballads make to be seven years, the fiend of hell is entitled to take his teind, tithe, or kane from the people of fairy-land: [39] A 24, B 23, C 5, D 15, G 28, H 15.[1] The fiend prefers those that are fair and fu o flesh, according to A, G;[2] ane o flesh and blood, D. H makes the queen fear for herself; "the koors they hae gane round about, and I fear it will be mysel." H is not discordant with popular tradition elsewhere, which attributes to fairies the practice of abstracting young children to serve as substitutes for themselves in this tribute: Scott's Minstrelsy, II, 220, 1802. D 15 says "the last here goes to hell," which would certainly not be equitable,[3] and C "we're a' dung down to hell," where "all" must be meant only of the naturalized members of the community. Poor Alison Pearson, who lost her life in 1586 for believing these things, testified that the tribute was annual. Mr. William Sympson, who had been taken away by the fairies, "bidd her sign herself that she be not taken away, for the teind of them are tane to hell everie year": Scott, as above, p. 208.[4]

This tribute or sacrifice to the devil[5] is also found in both the ballad and the romance of Thomas Rymer. Like the fairy in *Allison Gross* (35) and the household-familiar, Billie Blin, in *Willie's Lady* (6), who show themselves kindly disposed toward earthly folk by undoing witch charms, the fairy queen, in the case of True Thomas, shows herself equally friendly by hurrying Thomas back to the upper

---

[1] To which should be added J 9 (Child, III, 504), K 15 (*ibid.*, IV, 456), M 16 (*ibid.*, p. 458).

[2] Cf. K 15: "I'm so full of flesh and blood."

[3] Cf. J (Child, III, 504 f.): "The cleverest man . . . . to Pluto must go this year."

[4] *Op. cit.*, I, 338 f.

[5] See Murray, *Witch-Cult in Western Europe*, pp. 156–59, 246; Lady Wilde, *Ancient Legends*, I, 70; F. N. Robinson, "Human Sacrifice among the Irish Celts," *Kittredge Anniversary Papers*, pp. 185–97; MacCulloch, *op. cit.*, pp. 399 ff., 424 ff., and *passim*.

world the day before the fiend comes for his tribute. According to Tam Lin (39 A, D, G, K) the fiend prefers one who is fat and healthy or who is of "flesh and blood"; and so Thomas is in peculiar danger because, according to the romance, he is a "mekill mane and hende":

> "To morne of helle þe foulle fende
> Amange this folke will feche his fee;
> And þou art mekill mane and hende;
> I trowe full wele he wolde chese the" [stanza 57].

Or, according to one of Scott's texts of the ballad:

> "Ilka seven years, Thomas,
> We pay our teindings unto hell,
> And ye're sae leesome and sae strang
> That I fear, Thomas, it will be yeresell."[1]

In view of the changeling superstition it is noteworthy that Tam Lin, according to a text in the *Journal of the Irish Folk-Song Society*,[2] was stolen when he was a young baby. This version is given under the title *Lord Robinson's Only Child*:

> "My name is young Lord Robinson,
> Did you ever hear tell of me?
> I was stolen by the Queen of Fairies
> When I was a young babie."

So, too, in Buchan's text (G 25) Tam was stolen when he was young, "o three years old." According to I 29, he "was a boy just turnd of nine"; or A 23, B 22, he was out hunting with his grandfather when he was captured. The dwarf wife in the Danish song *Hr. Tönne af Alsö* says that she was taken by the dwarfs to wean:

> For I was born of Christian folk,
> Tho' dwarfs took me to wean."[3]

[1] Child, IV, 455, stanza 18.
[2] I, 47 f.
[3] Prior, III, 13.

Or, to give lines from a Swedish version:

And I was born of Christian kind,
And to the hill stolen in."[1]

Among the ballads mentioned above as depicting the various motives that impel Otherworld beings to enchant or steal mortal folk, that of *The Queen of Elfan's Nourice* (40) is especially important. The superstition of the fairy birth and the human midwife and nurse is so widespread in Northern traditions, German, Scottish, and Scandinavian, that we need hardly pause here for examples outside our ballad.[2] Gervase of Tilbury himself saw a woman who had been abducted to serve as a nurse in the household of a water sprite,[3] and Cromek details a similar experience— known to tradition—of a young woman of Nithsdale, who was visited by a fairy mother and asked to give the fairy infant "a suck."[4]

The Child collection contains only one copy of *The Queen of Elfan's Nourice* (40), but another version, unknown to Child, and in certain respects superior to the one given by him, has been recovered from Scotland by Mr. Claude H. Eldred.[5] In order to set forth the tradition of the mortal nurse somewhat in full, it will be well to quote from both versions. The Eldred variant pictures the coming of the little elf man[6] or troll, who requests the services of the mortal mother:

I heard a bonnie cow low, cow low, cow low,
I heard a bonnie cow low,
  Over the lea,

---

[1] Keightley, p. 100.

[2] For the occurrence of this tradition see references given by Child, I, 358 f.; II, 505 f.; III, 505 f.; IV, 459; V, 215, 290. See also Hartland, *Science of Fairy Tales*, chaps. iii, iv.

[3] Liebrecht, *Gervasius*, p. 38.

[4] *Remains of Nithsdale and Galloway Song*, p. 302.

[5] See *JAFL*, XX (1907), 155.

[6] On the size of fairies, see *supra*, pp. 168 ff.

An' it was an elf call, elf call, elf call,
An' it was an elf call,
  Calling unto me.

An' the little elf man, elf man, elf man,
An' the little elf man
  Said unto me:

"Come, nurse an elf child, elf child, elf child,
Come an' nurse an elf child,
  Down 'neath the sea."

The Skene copy in Child's collection does not make it clear that the lowing of the "bonnie cow" down in "yon glen" is an elf call. The next stanza of the Eldred copy shows the nurse moaning in elfland for her own bonnie lad, as in Skene's version, but the latter text gives the dialogue as taking place between the queen of Elfan and the human nurse. The elf king, who appears in the sixth stanza of the Eldred text, is not found at all in the Skene variant. The former version (stanzas 6, 9) reads:

"What do you moan for, moan for, moan for,
What do you moan for?"
  Elf-king said to me;

"'T is for my bonnie lad, bonnie lad, bonnie lad,
'T is for my bonnie lad
  That I never more shall see."

The earthly mother, according to Skene's text, has been carried away four days after bearing a son, but the Queen of Elfan promises that she may return home if she will care for the fairy bairn until it is able to use its legs:

"I moan na for my meat,
  Nor yet for my fee,
But I mourn for Christen land,
  It's there I fain would be."

"O nurse my bairn, nourice," she says,
"Till he stan at your knee,
An ye's win hame to Christen land,
Whar fain it's ye wad be.

"O keep my bairn, nourice,
Till he gang by the hauld,
An ye's win hame to your young son
Ye left in four nights auld."

The nurse's mourning for "Christen land" is evidential of that sharp line which Christianity was fond of drawing between itself and the "devils" of heathendom. We shall see more of this in our next chapter.

THE LAPSE OF TIME IN THE OTHERWORLD

According to the romance of *Thomas of Erceldoune*, True Thomas spends three years or more in the company of Otherworld folk, but, subject to the usual illusion respecting the time spent by mortals in paradisaic realms or fairyland,[1] he fancies the three years to be no more than three days (stanza 55). This, as Child observes, is "an almost moderate illusion compared with the experience of other mortals under analogous circumstances."[2] "Ogier le Danois hardly exceeded the proportion of the ordinary hyperbole of lovers: two hundred years seemed but twenty. The British king Herla lived with the king of the dwarfs more than two hundred years, and thought the time but three days: . . . ."[3] In the ballad of *Thomas Rymer* (37 A 16, B 5, C 20),[4] as well as in the Cambridge manuscript of the related romance, Thomas spends seven years in fairyland. This is in keeping with ballad tradition generally, which employs the number 7 with great fre-

---

[1] See Hartland, *Science of Fairy Tales*, chaps. vii, viii, ix.

[2] *Op. cit.*, I, 321.

[3] *Ibid.*, p. 321 n.; see also *ibid.*, V, 290.

[4] Also two texts, Child, IV, 454 f.

quency to describe periods of service, absence, penance, and so on:[1]

> *And till seven years were past and gone*
> *True Thomas on earth was never seen* [37 A 16].

But there is no indication in the ballad of a supernatural lapse of time. Tam Lin (39 M 17) begs Janet not to fail him: "And if ye miss me then, Janet, I'm lost for yearis seven." According to Buchan's copy of this ballad (G 10), Janet tarries "seven days" in the enchanted wood, where was "neither sun nor meen."

Numerous texts of *Tam Lin* (39 A–D, G–K, M), as well as one copy of *Thomas Rymer* (37),[2] tell us that at seven-year intervals the fairies "pay a tiend to hell." Hind Etin, an elfin-lover (41 A 9), keeps his earthly mistress in El-mond's wood for "six lang years and one"; for ten years (C 9). In the Fergusson variant of *The Great Silkie of Sule Skerry* (113),[3] a text unknown to Child and better than the version he gives, the seal husband directs his earthly wife to nurse his wee son for seven years, at the end of which time he will return and "pay the norish fee":

> *"Thoo will nurse my little wee son*
> *For seven long years upo' thy knee,*
> *An' at the end o' seven long years*
> *I'll come back an' pay the norish fee."*

The Spanish ballad *La infanta encantada*, which recounts a tale similar to that in *The Baffled Knight* (112), tells of a princess who has been held under the fairy spell for seven years.[4] Lady Margaret's dead lover (77 F 1) returns after "seven years were come and gane," as does also the demon-lover in *James Harris* (243 A 18, D 1, E 1, F 1).[5] To collate

[1] See Child, V, 490: "Numbers, favorite."

[2] *Ibid.*, IV, 455, stanza 18.

[3] Included by Sidgwick, *Popular Ballads of the Olden Time* (2d ser.), pp. 235–37.

[4] See Child, II, 480; Keightley, pp. 459 f.

[5] Cf. No. 48, stanza 2.

two old pieces, *The Cruel Mother* (20) and *The Maid and the Palmer* (21), which instance the belief in transmigration, a wicked mother must perform a series of seven-year penances by becoming a bird, a fish, a church bell, a stone, or a porter in hell. According to a Berwickshire tradition about the expiatory metamorphosis in Lamb's *Laidley Worm*, the transformed queen is confined in a cavern "whose 'invisible' door only opens every seven years, on Christmas eve."[1] Though not so popular as 3, the number 7 occurs with great frequency in the British ballads—a noteworthy point in view of the fact that it is said not to be a favorite number in England.[2] As regards certain ballad incidents it is probably of mystical significance. In folksong it is employed not only with reference to time but often with respect to people—seven sons, daughters, brothers, sisters, knights, butchers, uncles, maids—and is used miscellaneously: seven shirts, larks, flowers, diamonds, ships, hares, rats, rings, mills, letters, "seven-headed fiend," and so on.

[1] See Child, I, 311.

[2] See Cox, *Introduction to Folk-Lore*, pp. 22 f.

Chapter X

MODES OF DISENCHANTMENT

❖

BY WHAT means are earthly folk protected from witch magic, fairy charms, and the power of the dead, and how, once they have been carried off by elves and goblins, are mortals redeemed from fairyland, the grave, or the Otherworld in general? Here, as virtually everywhere in their depiction of Otherworld ideas, the ballads instance a confusion or merging of fairy and ghost superstitions. Any attempt to distinguish exactly between these conceptions seems unnecessary and, on the whole, inadvisable, if one is to keep in mind the point of view of folklore, which so often, and in this case particularly, recognizes a basic identification of beliefs which on the surface may appear to be far apart. By way of proof of this we may at this point cite merely such evidence as that given in our preceding chapter under the food taboo. There we found that a Polynesian story of the land of the dead contains an eating taboo identical with that in the fairy ballad of *Thomas Rymer* and with that in Saxo's account of King Gormo's visit to the realm of Guthmund.[1] Or, again, as further proof, we may refer to the notable confusion in certain riddle ballads of elf, demon, and ghost.[2]

The various ballad incidents of breaking the Otherworld spell belong, chiefly, however, to fairy-lore.[3] Among the means of effecting disenchantment or guarding against

---

[1] See *supra*, pp. 277 f.

[2] See *supra*, pp. 301 ff.

[3] On methods of disenchantment or escape from elfland see, for example, Hartland, *Science of Fairy Tales*, pp. 222–54; *Perseus*, I, 182–228; Kittredge, *Gawain and the Green Knight*, pp. 47 ff., 79 ff., 115 ff., 151 ff., 200 ff., 205 f., 236 ff., and *passim*.

the elfin spell are magic music, kissing, or physical contact in general, blood-drinking, the magic wand, verbal charms, circular magic, herbal magic, lustrative rites, the sign of the cross, holy water, the Holy Name, and other Christian charms or countercharms. A point to be stressed at the outset is that the methods of unspelling are not infrequently the same as those employed in spelling.

ORPHEAN MUSIC

The power of magical music works both ways: on the one hand, to seduce earthly maidens to the arms of elfin lovers, as in *Lady Isabel and the Elf-Knight;* on the other hand, to evoke the dead from the grave or to rescue a mortal from fairyland, as in *The Twa Brothers* and *King Orfeo*, respectively. These latter songs are mentioned by Professor Child in his observations on the wonders wrought by music in Norse balladry as well as in the traditional poetry of England and other nations:

> The marvellous power of the harp in B 2, C 1 [*Glasgerion* (67)] is precisely paralleled in the Scandinavian "Harpans Kraft," . . . . In these [the several texts of the Norse song] the fish is harped out of the water, the young from folk and from fee, the bairn from its mother's womb, the water from the brook, the hind from the wood, the horns from the hart's head, the bark from the tree, the dead out of the mould, etc., etc. These effects are of the same nature as those produced by the harp of Orpheus, and it is to be observed that in the ballad of "Harpans Kraft" the harper is a bridegroom seeking (successfully) to recover his bride, who has been carried down to the depths of the water by a merman. We have had something like these effects in "The Twa Brothers," No. 49, B 10, I, 439, where Lady Margaret harps the small birds off the briers and her true love out of the grave.[1]

This last-named piece reads:

> *She put the small pipes to her mouth,*
> *And she harped both far and near,*
> *Till she harped the small birds off the briers,*
> *And her true love out of the grave.*

[1] *Ballads*, II, 137.

In another text (C 18), weeping effects like marvels, but this stanza may be corrected by reference to the foregoing passage in B. According to an American variant, "She charmed the birds all out of their nests, and charmed young John all out of his grave."[1] Certain stanzas of *Charles Graeme* which belong to *The Unquiet Grave* (78) picture a maiden as sitting and harping on her true-love's grave. But the bereaved lass also weeps "saut tears."[2] Either harping or weeping is, in balladry, sufficient to cause a ghost to "peep," but it is altogether likely that the harping incident as it occurs in this piece is borrowed from *The Twa Brothers* or from some other source. In other texts of *The Unquiet Grave* it is merely the weeping of the maiden that brings the lover from his grave.[3]

The Shetland ballad of *King Orfeo* tells in traditional song the story of the medieval romance of Orpheus, in which elfland supplants Hades and the king of fairies takes the place of Pluto.[4] But the redemptive power of music has not waned. Our King Orfeo has sought out his queen in fairyland and rescues her with his playing:

> *And first he played da notes o noy,*
> *An dan he played da notes o joy.*

> *An dan he played da göd gabber reel,*
> *Dat meicht ha made a sick hert hale.*

> *"Noo tell to us what ye will hae:*
> *What sall we gie you for your play?"*

[1] Campbell and Sharp, *English Folk Songs from the Southern Appalachians*, p. 36.

[2] Child, IV, 475.

[3] See *supra*, pp. 256 f.

[4] See Child, I, 216; Kittredge, "Sir Orfeo," *American Journal of Philology*, VII, 188. On fairyland and the classical hell, see also Scott, *Minstrelsy* (ed. Henderson), II, 328 f.; Kirk, *Secret Commonwealth* (ed. Lang), pp. xxiii ff.; Wentz, *Fairy-Faith*, pp. 336 f.

"What I will hae I will you tell,
An dat's me Lady Isabel."

"Yees tak your lady, an yees gaeng hame,
An yees be king ower a' your ain."

According to Professor Sophus Bugge, the Norse ballad *Harpans Kraft*, like our *King Orfeo*, is derived from the romance of Sir Orfeo.[1] Foredoomed, like her two sisters, Sir Peter's bride falls from Ringfalla Bridge into the stream below and is there held captive by an ugly Neck until she, along with her sisters, is released by the harping of Sir Peter. Keightley's translation of the Swedish version reads:

The first stroke on his gold harp he gave
The foul ugly Neck sat and laughed on the wave.

The second time the gold harp he swept,
The foul ugly Neck on the wave sat and wept.

The third stroke on the gold harp rang,
Little Kerstin reached up her snow-white arm.

He played the bark from off the high trees;
He played Little Kerstin back on his knees.

And the Neck he out of the waves came there,
And a proud maiden on each arm he bare.[2]

The related Danish ballad gives much the same reading.[3]

Harping the dead from the grave, as in *The Twa Brothers* (49 B), recalls the incident of the harp, viol, or fiddle made from the drowned girl's body in *The Twa Sisters* (10), an instrument which, when played upon, reveals the identity of the girl's slayer.[4] The power of the witch over nature is illustrated in *The Laily Worm* (36,

[1] *Arkiv för nordisk Filologi*, VII (1891), 97 ff.

[2] *Fairy Mythology*, p. 150.

[3] Prior, *Ancient Danish Ballads*, II, 284.   [4] See *supra*, pp. 68 ff.

stanza 14), where a sorceress, by blowing her magic horn, calls up the fish from the sea. There is also a witch horn in *Allison Gross* (35). Other horns or bugles which possess more or less of magic power are found in *Sir Lionel* (18 C), *Little Musgrave* (81), *King Arthur and King Cornwall* (30, stanzas 71 ff.)—these in addition to the magic or elfin horn in *The Elfin Knight* (2) and *Lady Isabel and the Elf-Knight* (4).[1] But we digress from our discussion of modes of unspelling. That the elfin horn or harp may, in the hands of mortal men, exert power over unearthly folk is apparently shown in certain Scandinavian analogues of *Hind Etin* (41). Among the gifts which a maiden receives from her Otherworld lover in exchange for her honor is a harp; in a Norwegian text, a horn. At the request of her mother the heroine plays upon the elf instrument and thereby, it seems, summons the elf, who upbraids her for betraying him.[2]

PHYSICAL CONTACT

Just as music is employed in ballad story both as a charm and a countercharm, so personal contact, as in kissing or embracing, may produce enchantment or disenchantment.[3] Enchantment through physical contact is exemplified in the ballad and the romance of Thomas Rymer. Disenchantment through the same process is illustrated in certain of our transformation and fairy songs: *Kemp Owyne, Allison Gross, The Laily Worm, King Henry, The Marriage of Sir Gawain*, and *Tam Lin*.

Unspelling or restoration to human form is effected by kissing in *Kemp Owyne* (34), a ballad the hero of which is borrowed from one of Ritson's romances, but which, as regards the incident of the magic kiss, finds its general folklore connections through Scandinavian balladry, Ice-

---

[1] For references to ballad incidents of magic music see Child, V, 482, 483, 489: "Harp, power of"; "Horn"; "Music, harp, pipe." See also Kittredge, "Sir Orfeo," *American Journal of Philology*, pp. 187 f.

[2] See Child, I, 363.

[3] On disenchantment through physical contact see Kittredge, *Gawain and the Green Knight*, pp. 205 f., 216 f.

landic saga-lore, numerous German tales of *Schlangenjung-frauen*, certain forms of "Beauty and the Beast," as well as through romance[1] and through savage tradition.[2] According to Buchan's copy of *Kemp Owyne* (34 A), Dove Isabel is transformed by a traditionally wicked step-mother into a "savage beast," so that her breath grew strong, her hair grew long and twisted thrice about the tree. Her enchantment is to last until she is "borrowed" by Kemp Owyne with kisses three. "In many tales of the sort," says Child, "a single kiss suffices to undo the spell and reverse the transformation; in others, as in the ballad, three are required."[3] Having heard news of the dragon, Kemp Owyne, the king's son, arrives, and, made invulnerable in the event of each kiss by a talisman—a "royal belt," a "royal ring," and a "royal brand"—succeeds in unspelling Dove Isabel. It is noteworthy that the gifts come from Dove Isabel herself, and an interesting phase of the whole procedure is that along with each stage of the disenchantment the monster's hair is unwound from about the tree. The story of the unspelling proceeds by incremental repetition, and so it will be enough to give the third stage of the retransformation:

> *"Here is a royal brand," she said,*
> *"That I have found in the green sea;*
> *And while your body it is on,*
> *Drawn shall your blood never be;*
> *But if you touch me, tail or fin,*
> *I swear my brand your death shall be."*
>
> *He stepped in, gave her a kiss,*
> *The royal brand he brought him wi;*
> *Her breath was sweet, her hair grew short,*
> *And twisted nane about the tree,*
> *And smilingly she came about,*
> *As fair a woman as fair could be* [A].

[1] See Child, I, 306 ff.; II, 502; III, 504; V, 290.   [2] See *ibid.*, V, 215.
[3] *Ibid.*, I, 307; see also Scott, *op. cit.*, III, 290 ff., 299.

According to B, the beast is "the fieryest beast that ever was seen," but the talismanic gifts are absent. These re-occur, however, in the Sharpe version, which closely resembles A.[1] Child observes:

The triplication of the kiss has led in A to a triplication of the talisman against wounds. The popular genius was inventive enough to vary the properties of the several gifts, and we may believe that belt, ring, and sword had originally each its peculiar quality. The peril of touching fin or tail in A seems to correspond to that in the saga of hesitating when the sword is thrown up.[2]

Disenchantment, wrought by kissing, occurs in the Danish ballad *Trolden og Bondens Hustru*. An elf, foul and ugly, will refrain from destroying a farmer's household only on condition that the housewife embrace and kiss him. The elf becomes a knight upon his deliverer's kissing him the third time, this contrary to Child's observation that in such matters a single kiss suffices:

> *Him must she take in arms, and kiss,*
> *And keen she felt the pain;*
> *For ill and strangely he was shaped,*
> *As eye shall see again.*

> *The housewife's heart was like to break,*
> *"O give me, God, thine aid":*
> *The third time she must kiss his mouth,*
> *A knight that Elf was made.*[3]

By the same means a like evil spell is broken in the Danish songs *Jomfruen i Ormeham* and *Jomfruen i Linden*. In both these pieces, however, a single kiss is sufficient. According to the former ballad, a maid becomes a snake on the stroke of every midnight hour, but the evil enchantment is broken when Sir Jenus kisses the little snake:

[1] Child, V, 213 f.; see also Lamb's *Laidley Worm* (*ibid.*, I, 311 ff.; II, 502 f.) and the Grow copy (*ibid.*, II, 503 ff.).

[2] *Op. cit.*, I, 307.

[3] Prior, III, 174; cf. other texts, pp. 165 ff., 175 ff.

Sir Jenus over the saddle bent,
The bright little snake he kiss'd,
And straight there was smiling a lovely maid,
Where even a snake had hiss'd. [1]

A spell no less cruel yields to a brother's kiss in *Jomfruen i Linden:*

He found the linden, kiss'd her wood,
And there at once a maiden stood. [2]

In this matter of personal contact, whether it be kissing or blood-drinking, a type of disenchantment presently to be illustrated, one recognizes merely another example of sympathetic magic, as in the power of the name, in signing with one's own blood a pact with the devil, or as in the identification of a person with his clothes, parts of his body, and so on. Tam Lin's escape from fairyland is made possible only if his sweetheart holds him fast in spite of the fearful shapes he assumes, a precautionary measure found in a Cretan fairy tale from Chourmouzis;[3] in the story of the forced marriage of Thetis with Peleus, according to Apollodorus; and paralleled in the Odyssean tale of Menelaus and Proteus, as well as in the classic myth of Hercules and Nereus.[4] With respect to each of his successive transformations, Tam Lin enjoins Janet as follows:

"They'll turn me in your arms, lady,
Into an esk and adder;
But hold me fast, and fear me not,
I am your bairn's father" [39 A].

The same directions are found in texts B–K inclusive. In connection with this incident we again encounter the striking similarity between fairy and ghost beliefs when we find

[1] Prior, III, 137.

[2] *Ibid.*, p. 142.

[3] See Schmidt, *Das Volksleben der Neugriechen*, pp. 115–17.

[4] See Child's analyses of these tales with reference to the ballad incident (*op. cit.*, I, 337, 338 n.).

in a North Berwick story, given by Scott, that a dead woman in process of recovery from the Otherworld must be, according to her own directions, detained or held fast no matter what shapes she may assume.[1]

Before taking up the other processes and conditions of disenchantment set forth in *Tam Lin* we must give brief attention to the retransformation incidents in *King Henry* (32) and the related ballad *The Marriage of Sir Gawain* (31). According to these pieces, a hideously shaped woman is restored to her proper shape when she succeeds in obtaining absolute sovereignty over a man's will. In both ballads, upon being bedded, she turns out to be a beautiful lady. *King Henry*, as Scott observes, is paralleled by an episode in Hrólfr Kraki's saga,[2] which in turn finds a near counterpart in the Gaelic tale *Nighean Righ fo Thuinn, The Daughter of King Under-Waves*.[3] The incidents as related in *The Marriage of Sir Gawain* are found with a slight variation in a romance in Madden's *Syr Gawayne*,[4] and both Gower and Chaucer have the tale, with an important variation, in *Confessio Amantis* and *The Wife of Bath*.[5] The story of Grímr in Icelandic saga likewise parallels our ballad,[6] stories resembling which were doubtless widely current during the Middle Ages. The Scandinavian ballad *Lindormen* yields a kindred incident. A maid, being entreated, lies with a linden worm and discovers a king's son by her side the next morning[7]—a widespread story found again, for example, in the German *Ode und de Slang*[8] or in a tale of the Monferrato in De Gubernatis.[9] The incident of the bespelled person's having one shape by night, another

---

[1] *Op. cit.*, II, 371. [2] *Ibid.*, III, 339 f.

[3] Campbell, *Popular Tales of the West Highlands*, III, 421 ff.

[4] See Child, I, 289 ff. [5] See *ibid.*, pp. 291 f.

[6] See *ibid.*, pp. 292 f. On the resemblances of No. 110 to tales of the Gawain class see *ibid.*, II, 458.

[7] For various Norse texts see *ibid.*, I, 298.

[8] Müllenhoff, *Sagen, Märchen und Lieder*, p. 383.

[9] *Zoölogical Mythology*, II, 418.

by day, a common feature in popular fictions,[1] is present in *The Marriage of Sir Gawain*. And doubtless, according to certain lost stanzas, the monstrous lady in *King Henry* is subject to the same law.[2] The trait is found in the poor ballad of *The Earl of Mar's Daughter* (270), as well as in the related and more effective Danish *Ridderen i Fugleham*. In one of Grundtvig's texts of this latter piece it is noteworthy that in the process of his shapeshifting the bird-lover takes the maiden by the hand:

> *"You've plighted your word, and now be true,*
> *Give hither your hand, my claw take you."*

> *The lady she gave the bird her hand,*
> *And free from feathers she saw him stand.*[3]

To illustrate the manner of unspelling as depicted in stories on the order of *King Henry* and *The Marriage of Sir Gawain* it will suffice to quote the final stanzas of the former ballad:

> *"Tak aff your claiths, now, King Henry,*
> *An lye down by my side!"*
> *"O God forbid," says King Henry,*
> *"That ever the like betide;*
> *That ever the fiend that wons in hell*
> *Shoud streak down by my side."*

> *Whan night was gane, and day was come,*
> *An the sun shone throw the ha,*
> *The fairest lady that ever was seen*
> *Lay atween him an the wa.*

> *"O well is me!" says King Henry,*
> *"How lang 'll this last wi me?"*
> *Then out it spake that fair lady,*
> *"Even till the day you dee.*

---

[1] See numerous references, Child, I, 290 and n., 291; IV, 454; V, 39 f., 289.

[2] On the derivation of the hideous woman in English romances see *ibid.*, II, 502; IV, 454; V, 289.

[3] Prior, III, 209. For analyses of other Norse versions see Child, V, 39.

"For I've met wi mony a gentle knight
That's gien me sic a fill,
But never before wi a courteous knight
That ga me a' my will."

In Scott's copy the lady says that she has been "witched to a ghastly shape" all by her "stepdame's skill."[1] The nearness of the lore of romance and balladry to primitive tradition is seen at once when we find in a Kaffir tale an incident analogous to that in *King Henry*. According to this tale, a girl weds a crocodile, originally a handsome man who was bewitched by the enemies of his father's house. The evil enchantment is broken, however, when the bride licks her crocodile-husband's face.[2]

Under the head of unspelling through personal contact may be included disenchantment by means of drinking human blood. If, as Grundtvig suggests, the magic blood of Saint Paul in *Leesome Brand* (15 A), along with the incident of the white hind in the same ballad, points to a lost Scottish ballad on the order of the Danish song *Jomfruen i Hindeham*,[3] then our folksong has a claim upon the notion, present in still other Norse ballads, that unspelling may be effected by blood-drinking. According to *Jomfruen i Hindeham*, a maiden is freed from the animal shape wrought by her stepmother only when she drinks her brother's blood.[4] The Norse ballad *Nattergalen* tells how a youth, transformed by his stepmother into a wolf, dissolves the enchantment by tearing out the heart and drinking the blood of the sorceress—this according to a tale told by a nightingale, the youth's sister, who is under the spell of the same enchantress:

"In wolfish guise for seven long years
He roam'd the murky wood;
For bound he was in runic spell,
Till he should drink her blood.

[1] Child, I, 300.   [2] Theal, *Kaffir Folk-Lore*, p. 37.   [3] See Child, I, 178.

[4] Grundtvig, No. 58. Drinking blood likewise dissolves enchantment in Grundtvig, Nos. 55 and 56.

"One day, as through the Rose-tree grove
All gaily dress'd she came,
He slily watch'd her, lay in wait,
And caught that hateful dame.

"He griped her fast with wolfish claw,
And then with deadly bite
Tore out her heart and drank her blood,
And so stood up a knight."[1]

To lift the curse from the bird maiden it suffices to draw her blood. This is accomplished by the knight to whom she has told her story. Before the knight makes the incision for blood, the maiden, as does Tam Lin (39), passes through a series of animal shapes:

To lion and to bear she turn'd,
And many monsters more;
Or as an ugly lindworm laugh'd
And seem'd athirst for gore.

He cut her with his little knife,
And drew a stream of blood,
And there at once before his eyes
A blooming maiden stood.

Drawing the blood of a transformed being brings to an end a snake metamorphosis in a story from Annam,[2] and likewise a turtle metamorphosis in a tale from Brittany.[3] A legend of Auvergne tells how a wicked baron wanders as a *loup-garou* until a woodcutter, a Christian man, wounds him and draws his blood, thereby restoring him to his human shape.[4] Disenchantment by decapitation does not occur in British balladry, but in his study of this type of

[1] *Ibid.*, No. 57; trans. Prior, III, 118.

[2] Landes, *Contes et Légendes Annamites*, pp. 12 f.

[3] Sébillot, *Contes populaires de la Haute-Bretagne*, I, 13 f.

[4] Antoinette Bon, *Revue des Traditions populaires*, V, 217 f.

unspelling Professor Kittredge gives an example from the Norwegian ballad *Asmund Fregdegævar*.[1]

THE MAGIC WAND

The ceremony of stroking with the hand or with a wand effects disenchantment[2] in *Allison Gross* (35) and *The Laily Worm* (36), and is employed as a protective charm in *Lady Isabel and the Elf-Knight* (4). The incident in *Allison Gross* of the fairy queen's undoing a witch spell, by means of which a young man has been reduced to the shape of an "ugly worm," is, according to Child's knowledge, not paralleled in English or Northern tradition.[3] Child must have overlooked, however, the case in *Willie's Lady* (6) where the well-known ballad familiar, Belly Blind, speaks "aye in good time" and suggests ways and means of reversing the spells of the witch mother-in-law. Moreover, the elf queen's kindness to the hero of *Thomas Rymer* (37) brings to mind the humanitarian instincts of the fairy in *Allison Gross*. The Greek nereids, who, in these matters, are akin to Northern elves, have a queen who is friendly toward mortals and who even repairs the mischief wrought by subordinate sprites.[4] But let us give the lines from *Allison Gross* (35) which illustrate disenchantment by stroking with the hand:

> *She took me up in her milk-white han,*
> *An she's stroakd me three times oer her knee;*
> *She chang'd me again to my ain proper shape,*
> *An I nae mair maun toddle about the tree.*

The number 3 is employed frequently in magic, ritual, and folklore, and is by far the most popular number in British balladry.

Breaking a witch spell by three strokes of a magic wand

[1] "Disenchantment by Decapitation," *JAFL*, XVIII, 2 n.

[2] On magic wands see MacCulloch, *Childhood of Fiction*, pp. 205 ff.

[3] *Op. cit.*, I, 314.

[4] See Schmidt, *op. cit.*, pp. 100 f., 107, 123.

occurs in *The Laily Worm* (36), which, like *The Marriage of Sir Gawain* (31) and the Norse *Nattergalen*, sings of a double transformation, the metamorphosis of brother and sister. There is, however, in *The Laily Worm* no good fairy as in *Allison Gross* to undo the evil enchantment, and the wicked stepmother must dissolve her own spells. The manner of the sister's restoration is not given, but the brother is restored by the stroking of a "siller wan":

> She has tane a siller wan,
> An gien him strokes three,
> And he has started up the bravest knight
> That ever your eyes did see.

By the use of a "sma charm," probably the rune charm of related Norse ballads, and by some sort of stroking magic the clever lass in *Lady Isabel and the Elf-Knight* (4 A 11) gets the demon within her power and lulls him fast asleep:

> She stroakd him sae fast, the nearer he did creep,
> Wi a sma charm she lulld him fast asleep.

As we have already pointed out under "Modes of Enchantment," the foregoing ceremony is probably a case of retorting upon the elfin knight his own magic, for in version D 6, as well as in a Gavin Greig variant of our ballad, the sprite seduces the girl by means of a "charm" which he sticks "in her sleeve."[1]

Given detailed discussion in our chapter on the return of the dead, the incident in *Sweet William's Ghost* (77) of Margret's stroking her troth upon a "bright long wand" and handing it to her dead lover "out at the shot-window" need only be mentioned here.[2] In *Young Beichan* (53 M 19) and in *The Knight and Shepherd's Daughter* (110 E 22) a wand is stroked about as a protective ceremony—in the first piece before venturing upon a sea voyage, in the second to insure the safe and rapid passage of a stream. This latter piece, with Billy Blin in three texts (D, F, G) and a magic wand in E, retains vestiges of fairy machinery.

---

[1] See *supra*, pp. 298 f.   [2] See *supra*, pp. 258 ff., 289.

Moreover, parts of the ballad are rather closely analogous to tales on the order of *The Marriage of Sir Gawain*.[1] But let us give the incident of the wand, an instrument which, like the pointing sticks or bones of savage peoples, enables one to control even the elements:[2]

> *She's taken the wand was in her hand*
> *And struck it on the faem,*
> *And before he got the middle-stream*
> *The ladye was on dry land.*

According to *King Arthur and King Cornwall* (30, stanza 67), three strokes with a gold wand inspire a refractory steed to spring forth "as sparke doth out of gleede." Harris' *Sir Colin* (61b, stanza 11), which Child regards as a *rifacimento* of Percy's *Sir Cawline*, has a "lang, lang wand" which confers invulnerability.

NAME MAGIC AND VERBAL CHARMS

At the expense of repeating certain matters already discussed in our chapter on "Ideas of the Soul," we may here give brief consideration to the magic of the personal name. The power of the name seems to play a part in the hero's recovery from elfland in the song of *Tam Lin* (39). According to a Motherwell version of this ballad (E 20), it is imperative that Lady Margaret, in addition to keeping a firm grip on her lover during the course of his retransformation, continually cry out his name:

> *They next shaped him into her arms*
> *Like the laidliest worm of Ind;*
> *But she held him fast, let him not go,*
> *And cried aye "Young Tamlin."*

That Lady Margaret should retain control over her elfin lover by calling his name is not surprising to one familiar with superstitions about the name, with the idea, for

[1] Cf. Child, II, 458.

[2] See MacCulloch, *op. cit.*, pp. 205 ff. The purpose of the "cane" (possibly a wand) in Nos. 39 J 16, 76 G 3, 97 B 20, is not clear.

example, current among primitive peoples, that the name of the dead is often taboo, for to name the departed is to invoke their return.[1] In another Motherwell text (D 9) the elfin lover explains that his Otherworld name is Tomlin, a significant explanation when coupled with the incident in E 20 of Lady Margaret's crying his name. Additional light is thrown upon the episode by the Danish ballad *Rosmer*, which closely parallels Jamieson's tale of Child Rowland.[2] The giant Rosmer, at the request of Swanelille, his earthly mistress, has borne back to the land of sun and moon Swanelille's youngest brother, and asks in return for his services no other boon than that this brother refrain in the upper world from mentioning his sister's name:

> *"And now I've borne thee to thy home,*
> *The land of sun and moon;*
> *I beg thee name not Swanelille,*
> *And ask no other boon."*[3]

It appears that by naming his sister the brother could re-call her to the land of mortals. Something of this power of the name seems evident in Buchan's copy of *Tam Lin* (G 9) when the elf vanishes upon his earthly love's turning about to "spier her true-love's name." Already noted earlier in our study are further instances of name magic[4] —the exorcism effected in *Riddles Wisely Expounded* (1 C 18 f.) by a maiden's giving her demon suitor his prop-er name of "Clootie," and, to mention no others, the dead-naming incident which may be restored in full to *Earl Brand* (7) and *Erlinton* (8) by reference to Norse balladry.

Among those verbal charms, written or spoken, where-by mortals turn aside magic which is directed against them or, once enthralled, release themselves from the fairy spell, may be mentioned especially runic charms and those incan-

---

[1] See Clodd, *Magic in Names*, pp. 123 ff.; Frazer, *The Golden Bough*, III, 349 ff.

[2] *Northern Antiquities*, p. 398.

[3] Prior, III, 56.

[4] See *supra*, pp. 84 ff.

tations which we may venture to see in the flower burdens of our ballads. Runes, which were so potent in early days —when etched, for example, upon the warrior's sword blade, or written to effect magic in divers other ways[1]— make their power felt throughout Norse balladry both in spelling[2] and unspelling. As countercharms they play an important rôle in the Norse songs *Peter Gudmanson and the Dwarfs*,[3] *How Sir Hylleland Wins his Bride*, and *Sir Luno and the Mermaid*. They are employed for like purposes in Norse analogues of *Lady Isabel and the Elf-Knight*. By writing a rune, Sir Luno, the hero of the Danish ballad, counteracts the magic wiles of the sea witch who is on the point of wrecking his ship:

> *Said then the steersman, "Has none the skill*
> *With Runes the Mermaid's wrath to still?"*
>
> *Up spake Sir Luno, that worthy knight,*
> *"The Runes myself I have learnt to write."*
>
> *On staff so slender he wrote the Rune,*
> *And bound the struggling Mermaid down.*
>
> *He wrote the Rune on a twig so small,*
> *Yet bound her fast on a stone withal.*[4]

The malice of a loathsome witch is rendered innocuous by the potent runes which Sir Hylleland writes and lays under the threshold floor:

> *Sir Hylleland laid the potent runes*
> *Just under the threshold floor;*
> *So soon as the witch had trodden thereon,*
> *She threaten'd their lives no more.*[5]

[1] See L. F. A. Wimmer, *Die Runenschrift* (German trans. by Holthausen), p. 57 and *passim*; for a specific instance see Vigfusson-Powell, *Corpus poeticum boreale*, I, 114.

[2] See *supra*, pp. 298 ff.

[3] See trans., Prior, III, 200.

[4] *Ibid.*, p. 258.   [5] *Ibid.*, p. 227.

In Scandinavian analogues of *Lady Isabel and the Elf-Knight* (4) the demon-lover's sleep is induced by the power of runes, to match which we find in the Scottish ballad (A 11) a soporific "sma charm":

> *She stroakd him sae fast, the nearer he did creep,*
> *Wi a sma charm she lulld him fast asleep.*

Among the several devices, again, which the woman employs in order to get the murderer into her power, the original would seem to be her inducing him to lay his head in her lap, which gives her the opportunity (by the use of charms or runes, in English A, Danish G, Norwegian F, H, and one form of B) to put him into a deep sleep.[1]

According to the Swedish ballad *Sömn-runorna* and the Danish *Sövnerunerne*, which tell a story somewhat similar to *The Broomfield Hill* (43), a maiden puts a man to sleep by the aid of rune charms and so preserves her chastity.[2] An inscription written in "grammarye" in the foreheads of King Estmere and his brother (60, stanza 41) proclaims these two "the boldest men that are in all Christentye,"[3] but there is nothing to indicate that this inscription, like the magic herb in the same story, makes our heroes invulnerable. A possible instance of verbal magic is to be found in both *The Elfin Knight* (2 A 3, B 4, C 3, E 3) and *Lady Isabel and the Elf-Knight* (4 A 3 f.) when the shrewd lass summons her fairy-lover by simply wishing that he were in her arms. The former piece (A 3 f.) reads:

> *"I wish that horn were in my kist,*
> *Yea, and the knight in my armes two."*

> *She had no sooner these words said,*
> *When that the knight came to her bed.*

In another version of this piece[4] the lover comes in the guise of a dead man:

[1] Child, I, 48.

[2] See *ibid.*, p. 391. For other examples of rune slumber and sleepthorns in romance, ballad, and tale see *ibid.*, pp. 391 f.; II, 506; III, 506; IV, 459.

[3] Cf. the inscription on the hand or the breastbone of Gil Brenton's heir: No. 5 A 74, B 60, C 85, D 54, E 30.

[4] Child, IV, 439.

The maiden she sighed; "I would," said she,
"That again my lover might be with me!"

Before ever a word the maid she spake,
But she for fear did shiver and shake.

There stood at her side her lover dead;
"Take me by the hand, sweet love," he said.

In addition to runic spells and the power of the name, what else do the ballads offer of verbal magic, of those incantations known to folklore generally, those spoken charms or formulas of such frequent occurrence in *Märchen* and in primitive ritual? Miss Lucy Broadwood's significant observations on the flower burdens of riddle songs like *The Elfin Knight* and *Riddles Wisely Expounded*[1] will serve at once to dispose of whatever else the ballads hold of pagan verbal charms and introduce for brief discussion the subject of talismanic flowers, herbs, and trees. The plant refrain in *The Elfin Knight* (2 G) is a very probable survival of an incantation used against the demon-suitor:

"Can you make me a cambrick shirt,
Parsley, sage, rosemary and thyme
Without any seam or needle work?
And you shall be a true lover of mine."

The burden varies with different texts and becomes in one copy (L), "Sing green bush, holly and ivy." In other copies the reading is that found in G,[2] a reading which in H is corrupted to "Every rose grows merry wi thyme"; in M to "Every rose springs merry in't' time"; in F to "Sober and grave grows merry in time."[3] A text in *Folk Songs from Somerset* has "Sing Ivy leaf, Sweet William and Thyme."[4] *Riddles Wisely Expounded* (1 B) reads: "Jennifer gentle and

[1] *Journal of the Folk-Song Society*, III, 12.

[2] Child, II, 495, 496; V, 284.

[3] See also *ibid.*, V, 284.

[4] Sharp and Marson (3d ser.), p. 27.

rosemaree"; (A) "Lay the bent to the bonny broom"; (E) "Lay the bank with the bonny broom"; (C) "Sing the Cather banks, the bonnie brume."

Says Miss Broadwood:

> On studying this type of riddle-ballads one cannot fail to be struck by the extraordinary frequency with which "plant-burdens" occur in them.[1] Both abroad and in the British Isles one meets still with so many instances of plants being used as charms against demons, that I venture to suggest that these "plant-burdens," otherwise so nonsensical, are the survival of an incantation[2] used against the demon-suitor. That *he* should have disappeared from many versions of the riddle-story (where the dialogue only survives), is most natural, seeing that to *mention* an evil spirit's name is to *summon* him, in the opinion of the superstitious of all countries. Every one of the plants mentioned in the burdens above quoted is, as a matter of fact, known to folk-lorists and students of the mythology of plants, as "magical." That is to say, from the earliest times they have been used both as spells by magicians, and as counter-spells against the evil powers who employ them. . . . . It is perhaps hardly necessary to remind our readers that, from earliest times, the herbs or symbols efficacious against the evil eye, and spirits, are also invariably used on the graves of the dead, or during the laying of the dead to rest.[3]

Miss Broadwood's observations on the magical properties of the plants represented in the burdens of *The Elfin Knight* (2) and *Riddles Wisely Expounded* (1) may be summarized as follows:[4] parsley, used by the ancient Greeks at funerals, and on graves, and employed magically in Germany, the British Isles, and in Europe generally; sage, a magic plant in England, and proof against the evil eye in Spain, Portugal, etc.; rosemary, called "Alicrum" or "Elfin Plant" in Spain and Portugal, is worn there against

---

[1] For Child's remarks on burdens see his *Ballads*, I, 7 n., 484; II, 204 n.

[2] Miss Broadwood has this note (*op. cit.*, III, 14): "In one form of this riddle-song we get burdens which seem to be a corruption of a Latin exorcism (see 'My true love lives far from me' in Halliwell's *Nursery Rhymes*). 'He sent me a goose, without a bone; Perrie, Merrie, Dixie, Domine; He sent me a cherry, without a stone, Petrum, Partrum, Paradise, Temporie, Perrie, Merrie,' etc."

[3] *Ibid.*, pp. 12–14.

[4] Miss Broadwood's analysis of the plantlore in question is based upon Friend's *Flowers and Flower Lore*, a work compiled from all the most important European books on the subject.

the evil eye, burnt against witches in Devonshire, and everywhere associated with funerals and death; thyme, a chief ingredient in a recipe (*ca.* 1600) for an eye-salve for beholding without danger the most potent fairy or spirit, and associated with death and the grave in England; juniper, sacred to the Virgin in Italy and France, and especially potent against evil spirits; the gentle (thorn or bush), the name used all over Ireland for the large hawthorns which are regarded as holy and sacred to the "gentry"—"gentle people" or fairies who inhabit them; holly and ivy used magically from the earliest heathen times, holly being particularly abhorred by witches in England and other countries of Europe; broom, most potent against witches and spirits, and per contra, often used by witches in their spells; the bent or rush, protective against the evil eye, and, as Miss Broadwood points out, doubly powerful when combined with the broom, as in the refrain (1 A), "Lay the bent to the bonny broom." We may dismiss the subject of the incantation refrain by quoting a note from Scott, which goes no little way toward proving Miss Broadwood's point that our plant burdens are incantations directed against evil spirits:

> The herb vervain, revered by the Druids, was also reckoned a powerful charm by the common people; and the author recollects a popular rhyme, supposed to be addressed to a young woman by the devil, who attempted to seduce her in the shape of a handsome young man:—
>
> > *"Gin ye wish to be leman mine,*
> > *Lay off the St. John's wort and the vervine."*[1]
>
> By his repugnance to these sacred plants, his mistress discovered the cloven foot.[2]

Finally, as for incantations in our balladry—without reference, however, to disenchantment—there is the charm (the formula not given) muttered by the witch in *Allison Gross* (35) as she transforms the young man who has

---

[1] Both St. John's wort and vervain are widely known as magical plants (Friend, *op. cit.*, pp. 37, 73, 107, and *passim*).

[2] Scott, *op. cit.*, IV, 275; cf. Broadwood, *op. cit.*, III, 15.

scorned her love. Tom Potts (109 A 75, B 82) stops the
bleeding of his wound "with some kind of words." Moreover, we may, in passing, refer to the ballad oath and
curse[1] and specifically to those deathbed testaments in
Lord Randal (12), *Edward* (13), and *The Cruel Brother* (11).
In these testaments[2] our dying heroes and heroines will
undying hatred in such eloquent bequests as the "gallows"
or the "curse of hell." It is not improbable that the ill
wishes conveyed in these legacies indicate popular ascription of supernatural power to the words of the dying.[3]

HERBAL MAGIC

The lore of ballad plants and flowers, illustrated in part
by the foregoing observations on the magical refrain,
would of itself make a study of no mean proportions, but
lack of space limits the present survey to only the principal
examples of herbs, flowers, and trees as they are employed
in countermagic. Traditions relating to the apple tree and
the Otherworld spell, evidences of the sacred character of
the birch, indications of ancient tree cults, and the idea
that the soul may at death pass into a tree or flower, have
all been considered earlier in this work.[4] Several trees and
plants to which our folksong ascribes magical qualities remain to be discussed—the rowan or mountain ash, the
woodbine, the broom, and the thorn.

Employed as a countercharm, the rowan is found in
Lamb's *Laidley Worm*, a poem closely related to *Kemp
Owyne* (34); in *Hustru og Mands Moder*, the Danish ana-
logue of *Willie's Lady* (6); and in certain texts of *Willie o*

---

[1] See *supra*, p. 92; *infra*, pp. 362, 378 f.

[2] See Perrow, "*The Last Will and Testament in Literature*," *Transactions of
the Wisconsin Academy of Arts and Sciences*, Vol. XVII; H. Tardel, "Die Testa-
ments-idee als dichterisches Formmotiv," *Nd. Zs. f. Volkskunde*, IV (1926),
72–84; V (1927), 43–51, 102–15.

[3] Cf. Prior, II, 369; cf. also the following (*Fafnismol*): "Sigurth concealed
his name because it was believed in olden times that the word of a dying man
might have great power if he cursed his foe by his name."

[4] See *supra*, pp. 38 ff., 122 ff., 155 ff., 311 ff.

Douglas Dale. A mystic and sacred tree, known throughout Europe as a preservative against magic, especially so in England, Scotland, Germany, and Sweden, and representative in Europe of the Indian palasa and mimosa, similarly obnoxious to practitioners of the black art,[1] the rowan tree needs no introduction to students of folklore.

> *"Roan-tree and red thread,*
> *Haud the witches a' in dread."*

So runs the old rhyme; and the witch hags of the evil queen in Lamb's *Laidley Worm,* a tale of magic black and white, are powerless against the Child of Wynd's ship, for its masts are of rowan-tree wood:

> *The hags came back, finding their charms*
> *Most powerfully withstood;*
> *For warlocks, witches, cannot work*
> *Where there is rowan-tree wood.*[2]

The witch charms of the cruel mother-in-law in the Danish *Hustru og Mands Moder,*[3] analogue of *Willie's Lady* (6), are potent over sun, moon, and earth, and are employed in the ballad to arrest childbirth, but they have no power over the spot where stands the young wife's chest of red rowan. So, all that is needed to break the black spell is to move the heroine's bed to the place the chest had occupied. Thereupon Ellen gives birth to a pair of children. The rowan chest retains its power against the witch in a Danish tale into which the ballad has been resolved: "If I have not succeeded in bewitching the woman," says the witch, "she must have found the place where the damned rowan chest stood."[4]

---

[1] See Friend, *op. cit.,* pp. 195, 272 f., 284 f., 353–56, and *passim*; W. Henderson, *Northern Counties,* pp. 201, 224–26, 293 f.; George Henderson, *Survivals in Belief among the Celts,* p. 180; Scott, *op. cit.,* IV, 274, 395; Frazer, *The Golden Bough,* II, 53 f.; IX, 267; X, 154, 327 n.; XI, 184 n., 185.

[2] See Child, II, 503; also texts (*ibid.,* I, 312; II, 504).

[3] Grundtvig, No. 84.

[4] See Child, I, 82 ff., for an analysis of this tale and of the various Norse variants of *Willie's Lady.*

According to *Willie o Douglas Dale* (101 A 20), which relates the important and not uncommon ballad incident of birth in the forest, a woman, about to enter upon her travail, asks her lover to get her a "bunch of red roddins," the berries of the rowan tree or mountain ash.[1] Her request is grounded, no doubt, in the superstition that protective measures must, at childbirth, be taken against the spirits of darkness and that the rowan is particularly efficacious against such spirits:

> He's pu'd her a bunch o yon red roddins,
> That grew beside yon thorn,
> But an a drink o water clear,
> Intill his hunting-horn.

On a similar occasion the heroine in *Willie and Earl Richard's Daughter* (102 B 11) asks for "a few of yon junipers." In folk-medicine rowan berries play an important rôle.[2] Version B 23 of our ballad describes the "bush o roddins" as growing on "yonder thorn." That the drink of water in this text is said to come from "Marywell" may bear out the idea that the woman was seeking protective charms. The rowan or mountain ash as a magical tree may be dismissed with reference to Glasgerion's (67 A 18) "full great othe, by oake and ashe and thorne," though the ash here may not be the rowan.

The broom as a countercharm against evil powers has already been considered in connection with the plant burdens of *Riddles Wisely Expounded* (1). *The Broomfield Hill* (43) furnishes further evidence that this plant may be employed in magical procedure. A maiden keeps an appointment with her lover—so runs the ballad story—and at the same time succeeds in retaining her honor—this by causing him to fall asleep beneath the soporific power of broom blossoms, a bit of strategy suggested by an old witch woman. In the related Swedish song *Sömn-runorna*

[1] For descriptions of the rowan tree and its berries see Friend, *op. cit.*, pp. 284, 346.

[2] See Black, *Folk-Medicine*, p. 39.

and the Danish *Sövnerunerne* a like result is brought about by the power of runes.[1] The Scottish ballad (43 C) reads:

> *"But when ye gang to Broomfield Hills,*
> *Walk nine times round and round;*
> *Down below a bonny burn bank,*
> *Ye'll find your love sleeping sound.*
>
> *Ye'll pu the bloom frae aff the broom,*
> *Strew't at his head and feet,*
> *And aye the thicker that ye do strew,*
> *The sounder he will sleep."*

According to A and B, the broom (roses, D) is strewn merely to show that the maiden has kept tryst, but version C gives unquestionably the correct reading. In Icelandic tales a sleep-thorn, probably "a thorn inscribed with runes," is used to induce supernatural slumber. "The thorn is stuck into the clothes or into the head . . . ., and the sleep lasts till the thorn is taken out."[2] If we may go by the ballad of *Tam Lin* (39 A 40, B 38, I 52) fairies are not averse to the broom, for it is "out of a bush o broom" that the "Queen o Fairies" bewails the loss of her earthly knight.

The woodbine is known as a magic plant employed frequently in the service of mortals. It avails, for example, to keep witches from the cows on May Day or to confer health upon sickly children.[3] It plays a contrary rôle, however, in *Willie's Lady* (6). Among other devices it is there used by the witch mother-in-law to hold the young wife spellbound in an attempt to arrest childbirth. The undoing of the wicked spell under the direction of the beneficent household-familiar, Belly Blind, consists partly in removing the bush of woodbine which hangs between the bower of the mother-in-law and that of the bride. Our ballad

---

[1] See *supra*, p. 300.

[2] See Child, I, 392 f. Cf. the small charm which the elfin knight sticks into the sleeve of the maiden in Greig's version of No. 4; see *supra*, pp. 298 f.

[3] See Frazer, *The Golden Bough*, II, 53; IX, 267; XI, 184.

may be taken to illustrate modes of enchantment as well as of disenchantment, and so the various modes of dissolving the witch spell may be given here.

Upon the advice of the Belly Blind, there is fashioned a child of wax[1] wherewith to deceive the mother-in-law, who, thinking the image to be the newborn son whose birth she had so long obstructed, is betrayed into revealing her various charms and the means of breaking them. But behind this incident of the wax child there is probably more than the ballad relates. The means employed in our song to undo the witch enchantment is simulation and resembles other instances of simulatory magic, such as those designed to bring about conception—rocking an empty cradle, or placing a doll therein.[2] As for the episode of the malicious arrest of childbirth by magical devices, there are numerous parallels in addition to those furnished by the Norse analogues of our ballad.[3] Classic mythology, for example, relates two cases in the familiar stories of Latona and Alcmene. Sicilian tales have the incident, as have also a Roumanian and a Wallachian story, as well as a story in Heywood's *Hierarchy of the Blessed Angels*.[4] Nor is such a procedure vouched for only by fiction; it is believed to be actually possible among the Swabians[5] and in Arran.[6]

But to return to our ballad. Acting upon his knowledge of the charms as enumerated by his witch mother, Willie, in the following manner, lifts the evil spell from his household and gets himself a "bonny young son":

> O Willie has loosed the nine witch knots
> That was amo that ladie's locks.

[1] The Danish parallels of *Willie's Lady* fall into two classes chiefly by reason of their employing or not employing the trick of wax children (see Child, I, 82).

[2] See Hartland, *Perseus*, III, 176–79; cf. Scott, *op. cit.*, III, 214.

[3] See Child's synoptical analyses of the Norse songs (*op. cit.*, I, 82–84; also *ibid.*, II, 498; III, 497; V, 207, 285).

[4] See *ibid.*, I, 84 f.

[5] Lammert, *Volksmedizin in Bayern*, p. 165.

[6] *Folk-Lore Record*, II, 117.

And Willie's taen out the kaims o care
That hang amo that ladie's hair.

And Willie's taen down the bush o woodbine
That hang atween her bower and thine.

And Willie has killed the master kid
That ran beneath that ladie's bed.

And Willie has loosed her left-foot shee,
And letten his ladie lighter be.

And now he's gotten a bonny young son,
And mickle grace be him upon.

The magical power of the woodbine has already been considered. As for the "master kid" we may well suppose that we have represented here the traditional compact of witch with devil. The left shoe figures not infrequently in witchcraft and medicinal magic.[1] Child says:

> With respect to the knots . . . . , it is to be observed that the tying of knots (as also the fastening of locks), either during the marriage ceremony or at the approach of parturition was, and is still, believed to be effectual for preventing conception or childbirth.[2]

A text of our ballad recorded by the late Gavin Greig[3] throws additional light upon the procedure of the witch. According to this version the sorceress, deceived, as in Child's text, by an image "o the clay" with a "face o wax," divulges her wicked charms. Not only has she bound the lady's arms but has locked her bedstock—devices, neither of which appears in the Child version:

> *"Wae worth the han's that brak the ban's*
> *That I had on his lady's arms,*

[1] See Black, *op. cit.*, p. 190.

[2] *Op. cit.*, I, 85.

[3] *Last Leaves of Traditional Ballads and Ballad Airs*, pp. 4 f., 249.

"Wae worth the key that opened the lock
That I had on his lady's bed-stock;

"Wae worth the knife that killed the ted
That I'd aneath his lady's bed!"

It is to be noted that for the "master kid" of Child's text the Greig version has a "ted" or fox.

With respect to the foregoing song we may suppose that the man's mother, in perfecting her enchantments, went through the usual procedure—procuring locks of her victim's hair, her left-foot shoe, and so on. Among savage peoples and even races more advanced it is a common precaution to guard the hair, the clothes, and other personal belongings with great care for fear that they will fall into the hands of an enemy who might work therewith his evil spells.[1] The unspelling of the enchanted bride in the Danish *Hustru og Mands Moder* consists in laying the prospective mother on that spot which the enchantress has not bewitched. Tricked by the artifice of the wax children, the sorceress betrays herself:

"What? did I not then with key and ring
Reverse and spell-bind every thing?

"I surely the room with spells possess'd,
Save under Thorelille's bridal chest."

Full quickly they made the chest give place,
And laid her down on the vacant space.

She scarcely a moment was seated there,
Before she two healthy children bare.[2]

According to the belief of peoples widely distributed over the globe, the peasants of Germany and Scotland, for example, and the natives of Sumatra, childbirth may be

[1] See Hartland, *Perseus*, II, 64–74, 86–92, and *passim*.
[2] Prior, II, 368.

[358]

facilitated by unlocking doors and chests, opening windows, and uncorking bottles—practices which exemplify homeopathic magic.[1] It is to defeat the beneficent ends of such magic that the witch of the Danish ballad employs her key. The "ring," like the key, is employed to "fetter" the bride and so prevent her delivery, serving, of course, the same purpose as the "witch-knots" in the Scottish ballad.[2] Circular magic will be treated farther on in our study. It is with a "silver key" that the maiden in *Sweet William's Ghost* (77 D 13) strokes her troth and thereby returns to her lover his vows.

Magic facilitation of childbirth brings to mind the strange incident of shooting the arrow in *Leesome Brand* (15 B) and the closely related *Sheath and Knife* (16). In the former piece the heroine, about to enter upon her travail, requests her lover to shoot his bow when she gives a cry:

> *"When ye hear me give a cry,*
> *"Ye'll shoot your bow and let me lye."*

Earlier in this work we have given Child's interpretation of the similar incident in *Sheath and Knife;* namely, that when the arrow leaves the bow the soul of the woman shoots from the body.[3] But is it not possible that in both songs the shooting of the arrow is meant to simulate childbirth and thereby facilitate delivery? That the songs end tragically need not tell against this explanation—an explanation offered here, of course, merely as a suggestion. Whatever the exact significance of the incident, it is interesting to observe that in the island of Saghalien when a woman is in labor the husband—among other things that he does—"withdraws the cartridges from his gun, and the arrows from his crossbow." On a like occasion, in some

---

[1] See Frazer, *The Golden Bough*, III, 296.

[2] On magic knots see Cox, *Introduction to Folk-Lore*, pp. 22 f.; Black, *op. cit.*, pp. 79, 120, 185 f.; Frazer, *The Golden Bough*, III, 293 ff.; "Knots," *Encyclopaedia of Religion and Ethics*, VII, 747-51.

[3] See *supra*, pp. 53 f.

parts of Java, swords are unsheathed and spears drawn out of their cases.[1] The Galelareese say that shooting with a bow and arrow under a fruit tree will cause the tree to cast its fruit "even as the arrows fall to the ground."[2] The Berwickshire tradition about the wicked queen in *The Laidley Worm*—a poem related to *Kemp Owyne* (34)—has it that the hero in disenchanting the queen must unsheathe and resheathe his sword thrice.[3] According to the foregoing poem—both in the Lamb and the Grow version—the hero is required to bend his bow in the process of breaking the heroine's enchantment. In effecting the final stage of the retransformation—this only in the Grow copy—the hero unbends his bow.[4] We may make reference here to the naked sword as an emblem of chastity in *Lord Ingram and Chiel Wyet* (66 B 15, E 30):

> Then he's taen out a trusty brand,
>   Laid it between them tway;
> Says, Lye ye there, ye ill woman,
>   A maid for me till day.[5]

To continue our survey of herbal magic is to carry our study somewhat outside its proper confines into a consideration of folk-medicine. It may not be amiss, however, to give a passing glance at certain incidents in *Tam Lin* and *Mary Hamilton*, according to which a maiden seeks out medicinal or magical herbs for the purpose of abortion. It is especially noteworthy that the belief in the efficacy of churchyard plants[6] is illustrated in a copy each of the foregoing songs. In a Motherwell text of *Tam Lin* (39 F 5) the heroine's mother knows of the medicinal properties of such herbs and thus advises her daughter:

[1] Frazer, *The Golden Bough*, III, 297, 298.

[2] *Ibid.*, I, 143.

[3] See Child, I, 311.

[4] See *ibid.*, p. 313; II, 504 f.

[5] For the occurrence of this incident outside our ballads see *ibid.*, II, 127 and n., 511; III, 509; V, 292.

[6] See Black, *op. cit.*, pp. 95 f.

Up starts Lady Margaret's mother,
An angry woman was she:
"There grows ane herb in yon kirk-yard
That will scathe the babe away."

In texts A 20, B 19, I 25 a rose is plucked to "scathe" the babe away. In F 8 rose, tree, and herb are all mentioned. In D 10 and G 18 the herb is a "flower" with "pimples gray" or "the pile o the gravil green." According to Donaldson, the "gravil" is a plant, "graymill or gromwell," anciently used in the cure of gravel and also in producing abortion, but Child questions this.[1] In *Lord Thomas and Fair Annet* (73 C 18 f.) we have, perhaps, a variety of cherry employed as a cosmetic: It was in her father's garden, "below an olive tree" that the heroine got the "water-cherry" which "washes" her so white. "And whair gat ye that rose-water?" asks the nut-brown bride in another version. "Into my mither's wame," replies Annet. It is "roseberry-water" (e 13 f.), or it is "water" from "a well in my father's land, a place you'll never see (f 14).

Mary Hamilton (173), an ancient ballad, tells a story of child murder. The lover himself, no other than a king, goes to the "Abbey-tree" to find the means of relief for his mistress:

The king is to the Abbey gane,
To pu the Abbey-tree,
To scale the babe frae Marie's heart,
But the thing it wadna be [I 6].

In C 3 the maiden it is who goes to "pull the leaf aff the tree." The tree is the "sycamore," according to X 3; the "deceivin tree," N 3; the "savin," D 4. "Deceivin" and "Abbey" appear to be corruptions of "savin."[2] The savin is a juniper, has medicinal properties, and is used as an abortifacient. But we must forego the interesting study of folk-medicine in balladry and make mere mention of such

[1] *Op. cit.*, V, 341.

[2] Cf. *ibid.*, III, 380 n.

incidents as the "gallow tree" cure of leprosy[1] in *Sir Aldingar* (59 A 49, 53),[2] and resuscitation by means of "three draps o' Saint Paul's ain blude" in *Leesome Brand* (15 A 44-47), a conspicuous example of hagiolatry in folk-medicine.[3]

Before leaving herbal magic we should point out that the belief in the magic power of certain trees or plants survives in a number of ballad oaths. We have already mentioned the oath by "oake and ashe and thorne" in *Glasgerion* (67 A 18). The thorn is again sworn by—this in moments of great crisis—in *Young Hunting* (68 K 26) and in *Fair Janet* (64 G 11). The latter song reads: "And Willie swore a great, great oath, and he swore by the thorn." In other versions of *Young Hunting* (A 16, D 21, G 7) there is swearing by the "corn," the "grass-green growing corn," or the "grass sae greene" and the "corn." "I wish I was at yonder thorn," says the dying bride in *The Cruel Brother* (11 L 18), "I wad curse the day that ere I was born." Swearing "vpon this holy grass" occurs in a Robin Hood piece (147, stanza 21). Vestiges of nature worship are found in still other pagan oaths, such as oaths by the sun, the moon, the stars, and the earth. There is swearing, too, by the body or by parts of the body.[4]

THE MAGIC CIRCLE

Of great efficacy in magical procedure, in enchantment, disenchantment, and protective ceremonies, the magic

---

[1] Leprosy, says Scott (*op. cit.*, III, 74), was "formerly very common in Scotland."

[2] On the gallows and the hangman's rope in medicine see Aubrey, *Remaines*, pp. 118, 198, 241; Black, *op. cit.*, p. 100; *Folk-Lore Record*, III, 137, 142; V, 177; *Folk-Lore*, VII, 268, 272.

[3] On saints in folk-medicine see Black, *op. cit.*, pp. 75–94.

[4] Oaths by sun, moon, stars, and the "mold": Nos. 35, stanza 8; 44, stanza 4; 68 A 17, D 21; 110 E 10, 12; 156 F 6; 200 B 9, 17. By "salt and bread": No. 99, stanza 3 (Child, V, 234). By body or parts of the body: Nos. 64 E 12 and text, Child, IV, 465, stanzas 21, 22; 104 B 2, 3; 140 A 17; by the truth of the right hand, as in No. 100 A 11, is a ballad commonplace; so also by "faith" or "truth" of "my body": Nos. 140 A 17, B 7, 15; 145 A 24; 149, stanza 33; 161 A 16; 186, stanza 7; 176, stanza 6; 190, stanza 31.

circle is well known to folklore.[1] In several of our ballads, as also in Jamieson's tale of Child Rowland, it is employed in counterspelling. May not something of ritualistic intent in the way of circle magic account for the ballad formula of turning "right and round about" when swearing, as in *The Knight and Shepherd's Daughter* (110 E 11), *Allison Gross* (35, stanza 8), or in *Young Hunting* (68 A 16, 17)?

> *She has turnd her right and round about,*
> *She sware now by the corn,*
> *"I saw na thy son, Young Hunting,*
> *Sen yesterday at morn."*

> *She has turnd her right and round about,*
> *She swear now by the moon,*
> *"I saw na thy son, Young Hunting,*
> *Sen yesterday at noon."*

This commonplace of turning right and round about is found, however, not only with swearing. It occurs on other occasions, as in connection with grief (39 G 9; 49 E 18; 65 H 12; 81 L 35; 99 A 14; 100 G 10; 194 C 7; 213, stanza 7; 217 L 18; 229 B 3; 243 F 3; 257 A 26).

But let us take up our more obvious examples of circle magic. In order to gain admittance to the fairy hill wherein his sister is held captive, Child Rowland, according to Jamieson's story,[2] must walk round the hill three times *widershins*, backward, that is, or contrary to the apparent motion of the sun, and, upon each completion of the circuit, cry, "Open door! Open door!" The third time the door opens. This procedure may, of course, be made to serve the purposes of black as well as of white magic. *Marstig's Daughter*, a Norse song, tells a story of a merman who braves Christendom in order to win an earthly bride, just

---

[1] See articles "Circumambulation" and "Magical Circle," *Encyclopaedia of Religion and Ethics;* also Brand, *Observations on Popular Antiquities*, III, 58; W. Henderson, *op. cit.*, p. 62; Black, *op. cit.*, pp. 172 ff.

[2] *Northern Antiquities*, p. 400.

as Child Rowland assails the stronghold of goblindom in order to recover his sister.

> *He's tied his steed to the kirk-stile,*
> *Syne wrang-gaites round the kirk gaed he;*
> *When the Mer-Man entered the kirk-door,*
> *Awa the sma' images turned their e'e.*[1]

The expression "wrang-gaites" says Jamieson, "may signify either *backward*, or what the Scots call *widdershins*, in a direction contrary to the apparent motion of the sun; a kind of motion of mighty efficacy in all incantations."[2] Circle magic plays a part in an incident reported by Scott as having occurred at the town of North Berwick. According to the story, which parallels rather closely the main episode in *Tam Lin* (39), a certain dead woman could be redeemed from fairyland if her rescuer could grasp her animated corpse before it had thrice encircled the church.[3]

Lord Gregory in *The Lass of Roch Royal* (76) is apparently held captive under a witch spell or fairy enchantment. His sweetheart (F 7 f.) attempts to free him by sailing round and round the tower in which he is imprisoned:

> *And when she saw the stately tower,*
> *Shynand sae cleere and bricht,*
> *Whilk proud defies the jawing wave,*
> *Built on a rock a hicht,*

> *Sche sailed it round, and sailed it sound,*
> *And loud, loud cried she,*
> *"Now break, now break, ye fairy charms,*
> *And let the prisoner free."*

In Pitcairn's copy (C 10) Gregory denounces his dame as a "witch mother,"[4] but Child sees no call for magic or witch-

---

[1] Jamieson, *Popular Ballads and Songs*, I, 210.

[2] *Ibid.*, p. 213. See also W. Henderson, *op. cit.*, p. 61 n.; *Encyclopaedia of Religion and Ethics*, III, 658.

[3] *Op. cit.*, II, 371.

[4] On the witch mother in this song see *supra*, pp. 211 f.

craft in the case.[1] Nevertheless, as evidence in other than the foregoing copies seems to suggest, magic may well be present in this song. For one thing, in nearly all texts (B, C, D, E, F)[2] the heroine sails over the sea to find her lover. In one version she finds him on an island, a possible reference to an oversea Elysium.[3] Moreover, the idea of sailing round the castle to break the fairy spell is borne out by two versions (A, B) besides Herd's (F), and the reading in one of Scott's texts[4] is virtually identical with that of the Herd copy.

Among the devices to which Lady Margaret has recourse in redeeming Tam Lin (39 D 25) from fairyland is that of casting a compass round with holy water:

> *She rid down to Miles Cross,*
> *Between twelve hours and one,*
> *Took holy water in her hand,*
> *And cast a compass round.*

This incident appears in only one other text (G 44), and it may be that the holy water is a relic of the water or milk bath in other versions.[5] Still, the efficacy of holy water against Otherworld powers is well-enough known,[6] and the protective ceremonial here involves, no doubt, the exercise of a double countercharm more or less Christianized. The idea seems to be that the lovers by staying within the sacred circle are protected against the spell of the fairies. Bearing in mind that it is at Miles Cross—possibly a crossroads—that Tam's sweetheart casts her compass of holy water and recaptures her lover from the elves, it is interesting to note the following belief from Indian tradition. In

[1] *Op. cit.*, II, 214 and n.

[2] And texts (*ibid.*, III, 510; IV, 471).

[3] *Ibid.*, III, 510, stanza 5.

[4] *Ibid.*, IV, 472.

[5] Cf. *ibid.*, I, 338 n. The compass of holy water occurs also in a Greig text, *Traditional Ballads*, p. 28.

[6] Tylor, *Primitive Culture*, II, 188, 439 ff.; Cox, *op. cit.*, p. 8; Brand, *op. cit.*, II, 255; Black, *op. cit.*, pp. 73, 88, 89, 92, 102, 103.

India one may secure control of a spirit by making at a crossroads a circle carefully guarded with iron and water and sitting inside it and mumbling spells.[1]

The Broomfield Hill (43) gives further evidence of the magic circle, but the story here is one of enchantment rather than disenchantment. Preliminary to the ritual of strewing soporific broom flowers about her lover, the heroine, bent upon preserving her honor, and acting under instructions from an old witch woman, walks the hill nine times round (C 12). This incident occurs in no other Child text, but it is found in several versions recorded in the *Journal of the Folk-Song Society*.[2] According to the first of these versions, the maiden walks three times "round the crown of his head," "twice around the soles of his feet," and three times kisses his cherry cheeks. In the second version it is "three times" throughout, but in a variant of this stanza of the second version we find "nine times" round the crown of his head, etc.; in the third copy, "three" again; in the fourth, "three," "six," and "nine." In this last copy she rides. There is something of all this in Child's E 4. In Scott's version of the ballad (A 5) the sleeping knight has a "silver belt about his head," but Child thinks the belt meaningless and that it can hardly have anything to do with the lover's sleeping.[3] The belt may, however, serve as some sort of spiritual fetter.[4] One recalls the belt and ring in *Kemp Owyne* (34 A)[5] which confer invulnerability upon the wearer. This same piece seems further to illustrate the magic circle. The enchanted maiden's hair, wound three times about "the tree," is un-

---

[1] *Folk-Lore*, XXXIV, 281 f.

[2] IV, 110 ff. It occurs also in Gavin Greig, *Traditional Ballads*, p. 31: "nine times" round his head, "nine times" round his feet.

[3] *Op. cit.*, I, 391. In the Greig text (*Last Leaves*, p. 31) we read: "Wi his silvery bells an' the gay old oak, an' the broomstick lay under his head." Cf. the "silvery bells" with the "silver belt" of Child's A 5. The "gay old oak" of Greig's text is probably a corruption of "gay goss-hawk."

[4] See Frazer, *The Golden Bough*, III, 313 ff.

[5] And the text (Child, V, 213 f.).

wound once for each of the three countercharms employed by the hero. In the Danish ballad *Orm Ungersvend og Bermer-Rise*, a ballad possibly affiliated with our *King Estmere* (60),[1] a friendly mermaid tells Childe Orm that he can unspell his bewitched sword by swinging it three times round his head and then sticking it in the ground:

> *He swung it three times round his head,*
> *And stabb'd it in the mould,*
> *Heav'd then one blow, and at his feet*
> *Both Gerd and Arland roll'd.*[2]

Finally, for circumambulatory or circle magic we may cite the Danish ballad *Agnete og Havmanden*, an analogue of *Hind Etin* (41). As a means, apparently, of gaining entrance to the mountain cave of the dwarf king, Agnes circles the mountain three times:

> *Thrice went fair Agnes the mountain round,*
> *And enter'd the cave beneath the ground.*[3]

Her reason for circling the mountain is made clearer in a Swedish variant of the song:

> *So she goeth around the hill compassing,*
> *Time with me goes slow.—*
> *So there openeth a door, and thereat goes she in,*
> *But that grief is heavy I know.*[4]

THE SIGN OF THE CROSS

The sign of the cross is widely employed in defensive magic and countermagic.[5] Like the name of Jesus or our sacrament of baptism, it may, as it occurs in British balladry, be regarded as belonging, on the whole, to those

---

[1] This according to Bugge; see Child, II, 49 f.

[2] Prior, I, 138.   [3] *Ibid.*, III, 336.   [4] Keightley, p. 104.

[5] See Cox, *op. cit.*, pp. 7, 10, 268; W. Henderson, *op. cit.*, pp. 257 f.; Burne, *Shropshire Folk-Lore*, pp. 167, 185, 273; Black, *op. cit.*, pp. 85 ff., 128; "Charms and Amulets," *Encyclopaedia of Religion and Ethics*, III, 426; "Cross," *ibid.*, IV, 328.

charms which, whatever their basis in more primitive ritual, came to be peculiarly Christian. Magic of the cruciform variety is found, of course, in non-Christian practice. The cross is employed by the Amerindians, for example, in rain-making ceremonies.[1] Crossing as a protective charm is in evidence in several of our ballads, but British folksong furnishes no such example as that in the Danish piece *Trolden og Bondens Hustru*. Calling for help upon "Jesus, Mary's son," the farmer makes a cross in every nook of his house and thereby sends packing every ugly elf save one who had no fear "for sign of cross":

> *In every nook he made a cross,*
> *But most about his room,*
> *And off flew many a frighten'd Elf,*
> *Back to his forest gloom.*[2]

According to another text of this ballad, the sign of the cross is made following cockcrow, which alone should have sufficed to drive off the invading elves.[3] The ceremony of crossing is in this instance probably an addition of Christian times. Chaucer, in his *Miller's Tale*, records the popular notion that crossing is a powerful charm against elves:

> *"Awake, and thenk on Cristes passioun;*
> *I crouche thee from elves and fro wightes!"*

As already pointed out under "Modes of Enchantment," it is because of his having been "ill-sained" or ill-crossed by his stepmother that Tam Lin (39 G 25) is made the more susceptible to the fairy spell. In *Archie o Cawfield* (188 A 37) we read: "For the man had needs to be well saint that comes thro the hands o Dicky Ha." As a preliminary to the business of redeeming Tam Lin from the fairies, Lady Margaret (39 G 48) "loots her low, and sains hersell." The place at which Tam's redemption occurs is Miles Cross or Corse (A 26, B 24, D 25, G 32, I 34, K 16),[4]

---

[1] See "Cross," *op. cit.*, IV, 330.   [2] Prior, III, 167.

[3] *Ibid.*, III, 177; cf. *ibid.*, pp. 310 f.

[4] And texts (Child, III, 505; V, 215).

Rides Cross, Miles Moss (D 16, 17, Da 17, Db 16, 25),
Blackning Cross (H 8), Blackstock (E 8), Chester Bridge
(F 9), Carden's Ha, Carden's stream (J 12). The locality
indicated here may be at a crossroads or at a cross or wayside crucifix. "Miles Moss" (D 16) is clearly a corruption
of "Miles Cross," unless, that is, it has reference to a moss
or swamp. In the latter case it may be read with "Chester
Bridge" (F 7) and "Carden's stream" (J 12), and hence
may imply some sort of water barrier against the fairies.
This, however, is to conjecture. If a crossroads is meant
(A 26, B 24, etc.), then we have an instance of the widespread belief that divinities and fairies, or witches, ghosts,
and demonic beings generally—*bhuts* in India, the *jinn* of
Mohammedan tradition, vampires in Russia—frequent or
haunt crossways on the occasion, say, of their festivals or
for the practice against mortals of their evil charms.[1]
Witches are occasionally thought to lose their power at a
crossroads, a belief which may be related to Christian
magic in that a crossroads has the form of the cross and
may, therefore, as possibly in the case of Tam's rescue,
serve as a prophylactic charm. If we are dealing here, however, with a wayside crucifix—and this is perhaps the most
plausible supposition—then it is apparent that Tam's
choice of a spot for his rescue is made with a view to bringing into play against the elves one of the most efficacious of
Christian charms:

> "*Just at the mirk and midnight hour*
> *The fairy folk will ride,*
> *And they that wad their true-love win,*
> *At Miles Cross they maun bide*" [A 26].

The "Scottish cross" in *The Fair Flower of Northumberland*
(9 B 5, E 7) may give some magical significance to the
story. The tale is that of an eloping maiden betrayed by
a false lord from Scotland. The knight shows his true
colors when, with the maiden, he arrives at a Scottish
cross:

---

[1] See "Cross-Roads," *Encyclopaedia of Religion and Ethics*, IV, 331.

> *O when they came to the Scottish cross,*
> *A may's love whiles is easy won*
> *"Ye brazen-faced whore, light off o my horse,*
> *And go get you back to Northumberland"* [B 5].

Commenting on this episode as paralleled by an incident
in a Polish ballad of the class of *Lady Isabel and the Elf-
Knight* (4), a song of magic and countermagic, Child remarks: "By a curious accident, it is at a wayside crucifix
that the man begins his change of demeanor in Polish CC
2 . . . . , as in B 5, E 7, of this ballad, it is at a Scottish
cross."[1]

The power of the cross finds recognition in the oath by
the "Rood" or the cross, an oath which occurs in *Old
Robin of Portingale* (80, stanza 8), *Robin Hood and the
Tanner* (126, stanza 26), and *Sir Andrew Barton* (167 A 3),
as well as in several other pieces (137, stanza 16; 142 A 2;
156 E 6, 7; 157 A 12). Johny Faa, in *The Gypsy Laddie*
(200 C 7), swears by the top of his spear or (A 5) by the
"hilt" of his sword. Johny's oath may well be an example
of swearing by the cross or rood.[2] That the oath in *The
Gypsy Laddie* is a Christian ceremony seems borne out by
a similar oath in *Gude Wallace* (157 B 11): "The captain
sware by the root of his sword." Child remarks that "root
of his sword" arises "simply from ignorance of the meaning
of the rood, by which the captain swears in A 12; rood of
his sword is hardly to be thought of."[3] One recalls, however, Horatio's oath by the sword[4] and the assertion of
some commentators on *Hamlet* that here is a Christian
rite, a rite which seems to have sprung from the Crusades
with their mixture of military and religious fanaticism.[5]

[1] *Op. cit.*, I, 113 n.

[2] Examples of swearing by sword given by George Henderson in his *Survivals in Belief among the Celts*, pp. 77 f., indicate that this practice is pre- or non-
Christian.

[3] *Op. cit.*, III, 275.

[4] *Hamlet*, I, v.

[5] See Dyer, *Folk-Lore of Shakespeare*, p. 509.

To conclude our evidence of the sign of the cross we have the incident in that heroic piece *The Battle of Otterburn* (161 A 44) where Percy's men are commanded each one to "marke hym to the Trenite," to commit himself to the fight by making the sign of the cross. Upon setting out for the Holy Land, Old Robin of Portingale (80, stanza 32) burns a cross in his right shoulder, but this incident may mean nothing more than an expression of Christian faith. Robin "burns the cross in with a hot iron, as was done sometimes by the unusually devout or superstitious, or for a pious fraud."[1] The custom is reflected in romance and tale, as in the romances of Isumbras and of King Richard,[2] and was so common in actual practice[3] as to be forbidden by the canon law—this according to certain editions of the *Sarum Missal*.[4]

LUSTRATIVE RITES

The widely prevalent notion, common to Protestant and Catholic communities alike all over Europe, that baptism is a protective charm against the powers of darkness, is not absent from the lore of the ballads. Baptism is, of course, a pagan as well as a Christian rite,[5] but it is Christian thought which in *Little Musgrave* (81 B 13) pronounces the unbaptized babe a "heathen child." The sudden remorse which overtakes Lord Barnard after his victims lie dead about him is doubly significant with respect to the death of the unchristened infant:

> "*Soe haue I done a heathen child,*
> *Which ffull sore greiueth mee.*"

In Norway within recent times it appears that an unbaptized child, as well as a woman between childbirth and

---

[1] Child, II, 240.

[2] See *ibid.*, p. 513; III, 514.

[3] See *ibid.*, II, 240; IV, 476; V, 225.   [4] *Ibid.*, IV, 476.

[5] See "Water," *Encyclopaedia of Religion and Ethics*, XII, 706; Cox, *op. cit.*, pp. 203, 231; Tylor, *op. cit.*, II, 440 ff.; MacCulloch, *op. cit.*, p. 76 and nn.; "Baptism," *Encyclopaedia of Religion and Ethics*, II, 367–75.

churching, was designated as heathen. The same is true in Icelandic usage for a boy or girl before confirmation—this, however, from confusion of baptism and confirmation.[1]

British balladry gives evidence of the sanctity of milk and its use in baptismal and purificatory ritual.[2] "And wash my son in the morning milk," commands Gil Brenton (5 B 61, F 57, G 33, C 82), voicing a commonplace which occurs in a number of other songs (20 C 8; 63 B 35, C 35; 101 A 25; 104 A 8, B 14). It is very probable that Gil Brenton's direction concerning his newborn son has to do with some sort of lustrative rite meant to purify the child against evil spirits. The Cromek version (C 82) seems to bear this out:

> "O wash him purely i the milk,
> And lay him saftly in the silk."

In his contribution to the article "Milk" in the *Encyclopaedia of Religion and Ethics*[3] Gomme sees in our incident, as it occurs in Jamieson's *Burd Ellen*, an allusion to the use of milk in funeral rites. But he bases his observation on those concluding stanzas which are of Jamieson's own invention and which are omitted by Child from Jamieson's text. In all the Child versions, the ballad, *Child Waters* (63), has a happy ending. There is perhaps an allusion to milk lustration as a burial rite in the children's game of "Green Gravel," from the general movements of which Lady Gomme infers derivation from a funeral ceremony. The most constant formulas in the game rhymes contain the words, "Wash them in milk and clothe them in silk."[4]

In Tam Lin (39) immersion in milk plays an important part in the restoration of an enchanted mortal to his original shape.[5] And milk baptism is unquestionably referred

---

[1] Child, II, 243; see also *ibid.*, p. 513.

[2] See "Milk," *Encyclopaedia of Religion and Ethics*, VIII, 633 ff.

[3] VIII, 634.

[4] *Traditional Games of England, Scotland, and Ireland*, I, 171 ff.

[5] See *infra*, pp. 388 ff.

to in the ecclesiastical ballad of *The Cherry Tree Carol* (54 C 12). Among other luxuries that the Christ Child must forego is that of baptism with milk or wine:

> *"He neither shall be christened*
> *in milk nor in wine,*
> *But in pure spring-well water,*
> *fresh sprung from Bethine."*

Texts B 13, D 9 read: "white wine nor red"; a Greig variant: "Wi brandy nor wine."[1] Milk in primitive baptism is discussed by J. E. Harrison in her *Prolegomena to the Study of Greek Religion*,[2] and, keeping our ballad in mind, it is curious to find that the rite of "milk baptism" was in ancient Ireland reserved for the sons of wealth. We may quote Benedict of Peterborough (A.D. 1172): "Mos enim prius erat per diversa loca Hiberniae, quod statim cum puer nasceretur, pater ipsius vel quilibet alius eum ter mergeret in aqua. Et si divitis filius esset, ter mergeret in lacte."[3] There may be something of the old belief in the magic properties of milk in our ballad *King Arthur and King Cornwall* (30, stanzas 69 ff.) where a horn cannot be sounded until there is poured into it a certain powder "blent" with "warme sweet milke."

The belief that unchristened children are at the mercy of the powers of darkness explains in part, no doubt, the solicitude of the son in *Hind Etin* (41 A 48)—a tale of a troll's marriage to a mortal bride. The youth longs to see himself and brothers christened:

> *"I wish we were in the good church,*
> *For to get christendoun."*

The mother in this same ballad (A 50, C 9), wife against her will to an etin, desires for like reasons, one must suppose, the purificatory rites of churching:

---

[1] *Folk-Song of the North-East*, art. CLX.

[2] Pp. 596 f.

[3] As quoted in Warren, *Liturgy and Ritual of the Celtic Church*, p. 67.

> *"For ten lang years now I hae lived*
> *Within this cave of stane,*
> *And never was at gude church-door,*
> *Nor got no gude churching"* [C 9].[1]

And so (C 14) she leaves the elfin wood and with her children goes to the kirk "where the gude priest them christened, and gave her gude kirking." In the ballad of *Child Waters* (63 A 38, B 36, C 34, D 30, E 26, G 22, J 48, K 34), a piece with some vestiges of fairy-lore, the much-abused mistress is promised both marriage and "kirking" after having borne her cruel lover a "bonny son." That the rite of baptism was regarded as a protective ceremony is clearly shown in a Swedish variant of our *Hind Etin* (41). Through the rite of christening—it is to be noted that the parent herself performs the rite—a mother would insure her daughter's future immunity from supernatural lovers:

> *"Nay," said the mother, "now thou art mine,"*
> *And christened her with water and with wine.*[2]

Hind Etin of the British variant is by reference to foreign parallels strictly a supernatural character—a dwarf king, elf king, hill king, or even a merman—and we are not surprised to find (41 B 19) that he had "neer got christendame."

All these matters reflect the ancient attitude of the Church toward fairies, trolls, and other preternatural creatures of pagan tradition. It is unfortunate that our versions of the *Hind Etin* story do not bring out, as do foreign variants, certain important traits—those taboos, for example, with which the hillman would hedge his mistress about on the occasion of her visit to her Christian home, or, again, the visit of the troll to the church. In his analyses of the Norse versions of *Jomfruen og Dværgekongen* and the related *Agnete og Havmanden* Child includes these significant details. His synopsis of the former piece reads:

---

[1] On the churching of women see Brand, *op. cit.*, II, 75 f.; Gregor, *Folk-Lore of North-East Scotland*, p. 6; W. Henderson, *op. cit.*, p. 16.

[2] Trans. Child, I, 366.

After her eight or nine years with the hill-man the woman longs to go home, Danish E, F, I, Swedish A, F, I, Norwegian D; to go to church, Danish L, M, N, P, T, Norwegian F; for she had heard Denmark's bells, church bells, Danish L–P, T, Swedish G, Norwegian D, F. She had heard these bells as she watched the cradle, Danish T, P, Swedish G; sat by the cradle and sang, T 4; compare English C 7. She asks the hill-man's permission, and it is granted on certain terms: she is not to talk of him and her life in the hill, Danish E, I, Swedish A, F, I, is to come back, Danish F, must not stay longer than an hour or two, Norwegian D; she is not to wear her gold, her best clothes, not to let out her hair, not to go into her mother's pew at the church, not to bow when the priest pronounces the holy name, or make an offering, or go home after service, etc., Danish I, L–P, T, Norwegian F. All these last conditions she violates, nor does she in the least heed the injunction not to speak of the hill-man. The consequence is that he summarily presents himself,[1] whether at the church or the paternal mansion, and orders her back to the hill, sometimes striking her on the ear or cheek so that blood runs, or beating her with a rod,[2] Danish E, I, L, M, S, T, Swedish A, B, C, H, I, Norwegian F.[3]

The sharp cleavage between the Church and the devils of heathendom is equally well illustrated in *Agnete og Havmanden*, particularly in the incident of the merman's entering the church:

As she is sitting and singing by the cradle one day, she hears the bells of England, Danish A, C, D, E, H, I, K, Swedish D [church bells, bells, F, G], Norwegian A, C. She asks if she may go to church, go home, and receives permission on the same terms as in the other ballad. . . . . When the merman comes into the church all the images turn their backs, Danish A, D, K, Swedish D, F, G, Norwegian A, C; and, in some cases, for Agnes, too.[4]

According to various texts of the German song *Die schöne Agniese* from which the Norse forms of *Agnete og Havmanden* were derived,[5] when Agnes

enters the church everything in it bows, A, B, F. . . . . As she goes out of the church, there stands the merman, A, B, E, F. Her parents take her home in D, G, H. They seat her at the table, and while she is

---

[1] The speaking taboo is, of course, an instance of name magic.

[2] See *supra*, pp. 292 f.

[3] *Op. cit.*, I, 363 f.

[4] *Ibid.*, pp. 364 f.   [5] See Grundtvig, IV, 812.

eating, a gold apple falls into her lap (cf. "The Maid and the Dwarf-King," Danish E, Swedish G), which she begs her mother to throw into the fire; the merman appears, and asks if she wishes him burnt, G, H.[1]

The churchly status of Tam Lin, enchanted mortal, is not always clear. In certain texts (39 A, B) of the song in which he figures he makes no reply to his earthly sweetheart's insistent questioning as to whether he had ever stood in holy chapel or got "christendom" or "christendom did see":

> "O tell me, tell me, Tam Lin," she says,
> "For's sake that died on tree,
> If eer ye was in holy chapel,
> Or christendom did see" [A 21]?

In two versions (D 12, G 24), however, he says that he has "been at good church-door, and aff her yetts within." And in still two other texts (H 9, I 38) he says that the fairies especially honor him because he is a "christened knight." But in A 29, B 27, D 20, G 35 he is thus honored simply because he is an "earthly knight." The honor consists in the fairies' letting him ride on a "milk-white steed" "ay nearest the town." It is altogether probable that Tam Lin had never been duly christened or that, as he remarks in G 25, he had been "ill-sained" by his stepmother, and so became an easy victim to the fairy spell.

But we must conclude our survey of ballad allusions to christening. We may pass over most of these allusions with mere reference to the ballad texts (6 A 32; 102 B 27; 103 A 13; 107 A 85; 73 G 21, H 33), and pause a moment over the name christening "at the crystal stream" in *Jellon Grame* (90 C 17):

> He's washen him at the crystal stream,
> And rowd him in a weed,
> And namd him after a bold robber
> Who was calld Robin Hood.

[1] Child, I, 365.

It is noteworthy that the birth and naming take place in the "gude greenwood." Hind Horn (17 G 2, H 2), we may recall, was born in "gude greenwud." There is an allusion to christening in *Willie's Lady* (6 A 32), and *The Kitchie-Boy* (252 C 36) makes mention of a "christening-feast."

OTHER CHRISTIAN COUNTERCHARMS

From the dawn of the Christian Era the name of Jesus has been regarded as all-powerful against evil spirits of every description. "In My Name shall they cast out demons . . . . they shall take up serpents . . . . they shall lay hands on the sick and they shall recover." Such, according to the Gospel of Mark, were the parting words of Jesus. The ballad of *Sir Cawline* (61) sings of a fight between an earthly champion—a man of Christendom—and an elfin king. Because he has not "minged" or named Christ (stanzas 21, 25) the Eldrige king can naught avail against the knight who has lived by Christ's law:

> *Ffor because thou minged not Christ before,*
> *Thee lesse me dreadeth thee.*

So, too, Charles Nevill in *The Earl of Westmoreland* (177) is strong in the might of the Lord and takes off the head of the "heathen soldan." "Thou spekest soe litle of Gods might," cries Nevill, with his child's voice (stanza 71), "much more lesse I doe care for thee." By speaking the name of Jesus, the revenant in the Danish ballad *Aage og Else*, analogue of *Sweet William's Ghost* (77), proves itself a "spirit of health":

> *Up spake the Lady Elsey,*
> *And tears were on her cheek;*
> *"Come, if the name of Jesus*
> *Thou still dost dare to speak."*

> *"Rise then, dear Lady Elsey,*
> *And open me the door,*
> *For name I can Lord Jesus,*
> *As I could do before."*[1]

[1] Prior, III, 77.

[377]

Lack of space forbids our dwelling on the Christian oath. The oath by the rood has already been considered.[1] Some other common oath formulas are "by him that was crownd with thorn (9 C 4); by *that* birth Marye bore" (48, stanza 15); by Our Lady herself (89 A 17, 32; 116, stanza 60; 305 B 17; 123 B 8; 147, stanza 7; 161 A 42; 177, stanza 29); by the Trinity (9 A 10; 30, stanzas 6, 33, 37; 31, stanza 56; 109 A 29, B 32; 117, stanzas 180, 359; 121, stanzas 38, 57; 161 A 44); by "God that dyed on a tre" (117, stanza 101; 39 B 20); by "St. Andrewes bones" (159, stanza 38); or by various other saints (8 C 24; 21 A 7; 45 A 25, 29; 116 stanzas 102, 155; 117, stanzas 91, 315, 390). The swaggering Robin Hood ballads fairly ring with oaths mainly Christian. The salutation "Weel may ye save," in which "weel" is a euphemism for God (37 B 3; 157 B 3; 217 C 13, G 4, 21; 305 B 9), or "Christ you saue and see," and imprecations like "Nowe Christ*es* cors on his crowne" (59 A 15; 63 A 2; 111, stanza 16; 112 A 10; 117, stanza 177; 140 A 13; 162 A 20) still retain something of their original force. Enough of oaths, however, pagan or Christian. Nor have we time to pause over those effective imprecations in *The Wife of Usher's Well* (79 A), *Fair Annie* (62 A, B, C, E, G, I, J), *The Maid Freed from the Gallows* (95 I), and *Proud Lady Margaret* (47 A), as well as in other songs (73 H 7; 88 C 6; 90 A 22; 114 D 3; 164, stanza 9; 120 A 8; 216 A, B, C; 257 A 16). The ballad of *The Twa Magicians* (44, stanzas 4, 6) gives preference to the Christian oath "by the mass" over the good pagan oath "by the mold." "An ill death may you die" is a common wish formula in balladry, a wish, by the way, which strikes home on every hand. The devil, under the euphemistic title "shame," lends weight to imprecations in two ballads (62 A 15; 185, stanzas 11, 44, 52, 58). The evil wish "fause fa thee" occurs in *Captain Car* (178 F 5). Maternal curse gives a title as well as a tragic turn to the ballad of *The Mother's Malison* (216). The deathbed testaments in *The Cruel Brother* (11), *Lord Randal* (12), and *Edward* (13) may be regarded as

---

[1] See *supra*, pp. 370 f.

curses—in those of their bequests, that is, whereby misfortune is willed to the enemies of the testator.

Another important example of Christian countermagic is found in *King Arthur and King Cornwall* (30). The fire-breathing fiend, Burlow Beanie, though proof against sword, knife, and ax, succumbs to a "surer weapon," "one litle booke," found by the sea, a book which our Lord had written with his hands and sealed with his blood. "It was probably a book of Evangiles," observes Child, and ". . . . in a manner takes the place of the relics in the French tale," the romance of Charlemagne's Journey to Jerusalem.[1] This "litle booke" seems, however, to be not a book of Evangiles but an example of the letters from heaven which are used as charms against witchcraft, and which are found from Massachusetts to the Malabar Coast. Mr. Alfred Ela says:

> In general, the letter is written by Christ Himself, in letters of gold, or with His blood. It is carried to earth by the archangel Michael, or falls from Heaven, at Rome on the tomb of St. Peter, at Jerusalem, at Bethlehem, or in other celebrated places.[2]

Our ballad reads:

> *But now is the knight left without any weapons,*
> *And alacke! it was the more pitty;*
> *But a surer weapon then he had one,*
> *Had neuer lord in Christentye;*
> *And all was but one litle booke,*
> *He found it by the side of the sea.*
>
> *He found it at the sea-side,*
> *Wrucked upp in a floode;*
> *Our Lord had written it with his hands,*
> *And sealed it with his bloode.*

And with this "surer weapon" the Green Knight "coniures" the "fowle feend" in such manner as to transform him into a serviceable demon (stanzas 55 ff.).

[1] *Op. cit.*, I, 280.

[2] *Folk-Lore*, XXVIII, 318 ff.

In addition to those ceremonies and charms already discussed, such as baptism and the sign of the cross, our ballads yield few other examples of what may be called Christianized or perhaps distinctly Christian rites and counterspells. To the incidents already listed may be added the following. In *Tam Lin* (39 J 15)[1] Tam's sweetheart must, among other things which she does, take the Bible in her right hand, with God to be her guide.[2] According to tales which more or less parallel *The Suffolk Miracle* (272), a maiden resorts to various Christian charms in order to escape from her dead lover. Child's analysis reads: The dead man who is disposed to help the lover capture the maiden is

prevented from helping because the maid has laid her cross, scapular, on his coffin, 4, 17; (two dead, because she has laid her rosary on the feet of one, her prayer-book on the feet of the other, 32;) the maid throws at him beads from her rosary, which check his movements until the string is exhausted; the maid puts up three effectual prayers, 35; Ave sounds, 48. . . . . The cock crows, and the dead fall powerless, return to their places, turn to pitch, vanish, ... and the maid is saved.[3]

The ballad of *The Jew's Daughter* (155) reflects the custom of burying belongings with the dead. Sir Hugh asks that there be buried with him or placed at his head and feet a Bible, a Testament, a catechise-book (E 20, F 14, N 16, H 7, I 5, M 6, S 7, T 7). Sir Hugh's request is no doubt motivated in his concern for the safety of his soul. Swearing on the Bible or on a book occurs in several ballads (64 F 26; 138, stanza 13; 271 A 73); swearing by the "holy grass" (147, stanza 21); by "my silver miter" (145 B 26). A Turkish oath "by Acaron" or Alcoran is found in one ballad (129, stanza 32). It seems that the transformed maiden in *The Laily Worm* (36) has the power of resuming her original shape on Saturday. The same rule may apply to the metamorphosed man in *Allison Gross* (35, stanza

[1] Child, III, 505.

[2] On the Bible as a protective charm, see Cox, *op. cit.*, pp. 14, 231; Hartland, *Science of Fairy Tales*, p. 95.

[3] *Op. cit.*, V, 61 f.

10).[1] One wonders what is the significance of the etin's building his earthly mistress (41 A 7) a bower near by a "hallow seat," a saint's place.

A passing allusion is perhaps due any miracles of Christian hagiolatry found in balladry. But the saints, though often sworn by and invoked, enter scarcely at all into the ballad story. *Brown Robyn's Confession* (57) instances virtually our sole miracle of the Virgin, though there is a hint of this class of legends in *Sir Hugh* (155) and perhaps in *A Gest of Robyne Hode* (117), if we take seriously the outlaw's view of his loan.[2] The common saintly miracle of restoration to life is illustrated in Buchan's copy of *Leesome Brand* (15 A), when "wi three draps o' Saint Paul's ain blude" the hero brings back his lady and his son. The interposition of Providence is again seen in Percy's *Child Waters* (63 A 16) in the event of Our Ladye's bearing up Ellen's "chinne" as she swims the "water." As Steenstrup observes for Danish balladry, however, the ecclesiastical element gets small leave to appear in British traditional poetry:

> Concerning all others the rule holds good that however many remarkable and marvelous things happen, miracles never find a place. It is not by prayers and petitions to God and to the saints that metamorphosed knights and maidens get their own shape back again, nor is it by making the sign of the cross nor by reading the Scriptures that evil is bested. The intervention of the Virgin Mary or of holy men is unnecessary; that which heals or reshapes, that which draws the frigid lover to longing is mysterious remedies, the various instruments of superstition, the token and the mystic word.[3]

TAM LIN'S ESCAPE FROM FAIRYLAND

No other single ballad illustrates better than does the traditional song of *Tam Lin* the essentially heathen character of our folksong. And bearing in mind the foregoing observations of Steenstrup, in which he points out how

---

[1] See *ibid.*, I, 315.   [2] *Ibid.*, II, 13.

[3] For Steenstrup's observations in full, see the general Introduction to this work (*supra*, p. 11).

foreign and intrusive are the Christian elements which appear in Scandinavian balladry, we may proceed to a consideration of the pagan and primitive magic incorporated in this remarkable song of *Tam Lin*, a ballad purely traditional and found among no people save the Scottish. Through the chief feature in the story, however, the retransformation of Tam Lin, it is allied with ancient Greek tradition.[1]

The important magical ceremony of immersion in water or milk as a means of effecting restoration to an original shape is depicted in *Tam Lin*. This rite will be discussed immediately following an examination of those preliminary stages of Tam's retransformation and with respect to which the incident of immersion is or should be the culminating stage. In justice to the ballad story and for the sake of clearness it will be well at the outset to give the situation somewhat in full, chiefly as it occurs in Johnson's version of the ballad (A). According to the Johnson copy, as well as others, Tam Lin has instructed Janet to attempt his rescue on Hallowe'en[2] at Miles Cross,[3] and has also told her how she may recognize him in the fairy train. Next follow explicit directions as to Janet's procedure in winning her lover from the elves. A significant point in the entire business is that Tam Lin can do nothing in his own behalf. Thus to begin with and to follow for a moment the Glenriddell text, Janet must with great expedition pull her lover down from his fairy steed, an incident lacking in the Johnson version:

> *"Then hie thee to the milk-white steed,*
> *And pu me quickly down,*
> *Cast thy green kirtle owr me,*
> *And keep me frae the rain"* [B 29].

Tam is likewise pulled from his horse or falls from it in texts C 7; D 21, 28; E 15 f.; F 14; G 37; H 10; I 49; J 17;[4]

---

[1] Child, I, 336. Cf. the transformations in the Danish song *Nattergalen, supra*, p. 342.

[2] See *infra*, p. 396.   [3] See *supra*, pp. 368 f.   [4] Child, III, 505.

K 19. We may now return to Johnson's text, which presents the steps of the disenchantment more nearly in their right order:

> "*They'll turn me in your arms, lady,*
> *Into an esk and adder;*
> *But hold me fast, and fear me not,*
> *I am your bairn's father.*
>
> "*They'll turn me to a bear sae grim,*
> *And then a lion bold;*
> *But hold me fast, and fear me not,*
> *As ye shall love your child.*
>
> "*Again they'll turn me in your arms*
> *To a red het gaud of airn;*
> *But hold me fast, and fear me not,*
> *I'll do to you nae harm.*
>
> "*And last they'll turn me in your arms*
> *Into the burning gleed;*
> *Then throw me into well water,*
> *O throw me in wi speed.*
>
> "*And then I'll be your ain true-love,*
> *I'll turn a naked knight;*
> *Then cover me wi your green mantle,*
> *And cover me out o sight*" [A].

With regard to the foregoing magical procedure the following points are especially noteworthy: (1) the necessity of Janet's holding her lover fast throughout his shapeshifting —a matter already discussed in connection with physical contact and disenchantment; (2) the series of animal transformations; (3) the mutations into a red-hot bar of iron and into a burning coal; and (4) the act of immersion in well water.

These matters may wait a moment, however, upon a recognition here of Child's observations on the important connections which *Tam Lin* has with Greek tradition, ancient and modern. Although this fine ballad, as Child remarks, is not, "as might have been expected, found in possession of any people but the Scottish,"[1] yet it has affiliations, "through the principal feature in the story, the retransformation of Tam Lin, with Greek popular tradition older than Homer."[2] A Cretan fairy tale, recovered by Chourmouzis[3] from tradition, furnishes a surprising parallel to the principal motive of the Scottish song, and includes all the important circumstances of Thetis' forced marriage with Peleus, as given by Apollodorus.[4] The tenacity of tradition as evidenced by the striking relationship between the Greek stories is pointed out by Professor Child:

> The Cretan tale does not differ from the one repeated by Apollodorus from earlier writers a couple of thousand years ago more than two versions of a story gathered from oral tradition in these days are apt to do. Whether it has come down to our time from mouth to mouth through twenty-five centuries or more, or whether, having died out of the popular memory, it was reintroduced through literature, is a question that cannot be decided with certainty; but there will be nothing unlikely in the former supposition to those who bear in mind the tenacity of tradition among people who have never known books.[5]

We may now take up our survey of the retransformation incidents in *Tam Lin*, in connection with which we shall consider the parallel circumstances of the foregoing tales along with other related matter from kindred tradition. Among the important incidents in the unspelling of Tam is that of his shapeshifting. Assuming just now for purposes of analysis that the right order in the series of transformations prevails throughout the various texts of the ballad, what are the several animal shapes through which Tam passes on the way to the recovery of his original form? According to Johnson's text, which does keep

---

[1] There is a text, however, in the *Journal of the Irish Folk-Song Society*, I, 47.

[2] *Op. cit.*, I, 336.

[3] See Bernhard Schmidt, *op. cit.*, pp. 115–17.

[4] See Child, I, 337.   [5] *Ibid.*, pp. 337 f.

the right order, the metamorphoses range throughout the following shapes. We may include also Tam's metamorphosis into a red-hot bar of iron and into the burning gleed or fire: (A) esk, adder, bear, lion, red het gaud of airn; according to Glenriddell's text (B): adder, snake, greyhound, red hot gad o iron; according to Herd's copy (C): esk, adder, toad, eel, dove, swan. In other texts there are certain variations with respect to the animal forms, but the snake form is constant for all versions except two, and the red-hot iron, or fire of some description, occurs in every copy save one. The order and character of the transformations in texts other than A, B, and C are as follows: (D) savage wild, adder or snake, iron in strong fire; (E) adder or snake, wood black dog to bite, red-het gaud o airn, laidliest worm of Ind; (F) eagle, ass (probable corruption of "esk" or "ask" in other texts), flash of fire, naked man; (G) wolf, fire burning bold, iron cauld, adder, snake, deer sae wild, silken string, naked man; (H) ask, adder, snake, warld's make; (I) adder, snake, ask, red-hot gad o airn, toad, eel, dove, swan, mother-naked man; (J) adder, eel, hot as any coal, adder, snake; (JJ)[1] adder, snake, two red gads of airn, all things vile, naked knight; (K) fire burning bold, iron cold, fire burning wild, father of child. A text in the *Journal of the Irish Folk-Song Society* has the following: a worm so long, a fiery snake, a bird so wild.[2]

Chourmouzis' analogous fairy tale relates how a nereid becomes in the grasp of her lover a dog, a snake, a camel, and fire before she resumes her proper shape:

A young peasant of the village Sgourokepháli, ... used to be taken by the nereids into their grotto for the sake of his music. He fell in love with one of them, and, not knowing how to help himself, had recourse to an old woman of his village. She gave him this advice: that just before cock-crow he should seize his beloved by the hair, and hold on, unterrified, till the cock crew, whatever forms she should assume. The peasant gave good heed, and the next time he was taken into the cave fell to playing, as usual, and the nereids to dancing. But as cock-crow

[1] *Ibid.*, III, 505.

[2] I, 47. Cf. the excellent text in Greig, *Traditional Ballads*, p. 28: "Fire that burneth bold," "iron cold," "hound that runneth wild," "nakit man."

drew nigh, he put down his instrument, sprang upon the object of his passion, and grasped her by her locks. She instantly changed shape; became a dog, a snake, a camel, fire. But he kept his courage and held on, and presently the cock crew, and the nereids vanished all but one. His love returned to her proper beauty, and went with him to his home.[1]

The related story of Thetis and Peleus gives the shapes as fire, water, and a wild beast.[2] Shapeshifting of a like order is found in the stories of Menelaus and Proteus, Hercules and Nereus, and in tales of the White Ladies, which, according to Mannhardt,[3] bear a relation to these Greek traditions.[4] Andrew Lang in *A Collection of Ballads* adds a Senegambian ballad, *Penda Baloa*.[5]

The foregoing animal and bird transformations reflect, of course, a widespread and primitive philosophy, familiar to every student of folk-belief and treated in the present work under "Ideas of the Soul."[6] But the "primitive" rationale of Tam Lin's turning into a "red het gaud of airn" in escaping from the elves is somewhat puzzling in view of the well-known effect of iron upon fairies, demons, and spirits generally. According to the tale of Thetis and Peleus, Thetis, wishing to make her son immortal, buries him in fire by night in order to burn out his human elements. In becoming once more a mortal, however, Tam passes through a fire metamorphosis. Still it is to be noted that this fire shape is wrought by the fairies in an effort, so we must suppose, to stay off Tam's resumption of his human form. Looked at in this way, the incident is doubtless analogous to the episode of Thetis and her son. Of course one must refuse to concede a point to the exigencies of the narrative and dismiss our ballad episode with the explanation that red-hot iron, more than any other shape

[1] Child's analysis (*op. cit.*, I, 337).

[2] See *ibid.*, pp. 337 f.

[3] *Wald- und Feldkulte*, II, 60–64.

[4] See Child's analyses of the Greek traditions (*op. cit.*, I, 337, 338 n.).

[5] P. 231, citing Bérenger-Féraud, *Contes populaires de la Sénégambie*.

[6] See *supra*, pp. 44 ff.

that her lover might assume, would cause Janet to release her hold of him. It is true that the order of the metamorphoses in texts A, B, D, E may be taken to bear out this interpretation, the iron coming as it does toward the last. It is probable that the fairies, in turning their captive into (A) a burning gleed or (B) a red-hot bar of iron, were merely exerting a magic force, a sort of fire spell, which was commonly employed against themselves or other supernatural beings by mortals. Thus,

In Asia Minor, "if a person is believed to be possessed by an evil spirit, one form of treatment is to heat an iron-chain red-hot, form it into a ring and pass the afflicted person through the opening, on the theory that the evil spirit cannot pass the hot chain, and so is torn from his victim and left behind."[1]

In Lancashire a witch may be driven away by putting a hot iron into the churn, an operation consistent enough with customary magical procedure against the fairy and the witch world.[2]

As we have already indicated, the laws of magic may be made to serve both mortal and fairy, and probably there is present in the foregoing mutation into hot iron, as in the following change into the burning gleed (A), nothing more than a reversal of a magical operation. Parallels to Tam Lin's fire metamorphosis, as noted above, are found in the kindred Greek traditions of Thetis and Peleus, Hercules and Nereus, and in the Cretan analogue of the former of these.[3] According to the several variants of the ballad, our hero is turned into a "burning gleed," a "flash of fire," a "fire burning bold," or a "fire burning wild." As a lustrative force fire is no less efficacious than water and is regarded the world over as a charm against evil or demoniacal influences. We may mention the practice common to Germans, Danes, the Irish, and other peoples, of burning a light in the chamber of an unbaptized babe; or the custom of throwing a live coal after a mother

[1] Frazer, *The Golden Bough*, XI, 186.

[2] W. Henderson, *op. cit.*, p. 183.   [3] See Child, I, 336 ff.

as she goes to be churched, or a burning coal after a troll wife or witch; or, again, the practice of carrying a firebrand after dark to ward off evil powers.[1] These examples, of course, view the matter from the standpoint of mortals rather than from that of fairies, and are not exact parallels to the fire metamorphoses of Tam Lin. In the Danish ballad *Sir Magnus and the Elf-Maid* a fairy maiden when cut to fine bits turns to a blazing flame:

> *The maiden turn'd to a blazing fire,*
> *And rose in angry flake,*
> *And made the mightiest forest trees*
> *To tremble all and quake.*[2]

Immersion in water or milk as a ceremony for effecting transformation from a non-human to a human shape, or vice versa, is a familiar trait in many popular tales as well as in romance. It occurs, for example, in Ulrich's romance of Lanzelet, in a Greek tale, *Goldgerte*, in an Albanian story, *Taubenliebe*, and in an ancient version of the story of Melusina.[3] Other instances are abundantly supplied by Child and Professor Kittredge,[4] and Andrew Lang finds precedents for our incident in "*Old Deccan Days*, in a Hottentot tale by Bleek, and *Les Deux Frères*, the Egyptian story."[5] In but three of the Child copies of *Tam Lin* (39 A 34, B 34, I 43) does immersion in water or milk play a part in the retransformation process, and in only one of these texts (A) does the rite occur at the proper place in the series of changes through which the elf passes. The holy water in D 17 and G 32 is probably a relic of the water bath.[6]

[1] For these and other examples of prophylactic fire see Tylor, *op. cit.*, II, 194 ff., 281, 429 ff.; Hartland, *Science of Fairy Tales*, pp. 96 f.

[2] Prior, III, 345.

[3] See Child's analyses of these tales (*op. cit.*, I, 338, 339 and n.).

[4] *Ibid.*, II, 505; III, 505; V, 39 f.; also Kittredge, "Disenchantment by Decapitation," *JAFL*, XVIII, 4.

[5] *Op. cit.*, p. 231.

[6] Child, I, 338 n.

According to various texts, the end of the shapeshifting is a naked man (F, G, J), a naked knight (A, JJ),[1] a mother-naked man (B, I), a perfect man (C), her earthly mate (D), "warld's make" or mate (H). If we bear in mind the magic law of Tam's world, this conclusion, it is clear, should be preceded by the incident of throwing the elf into "well water" (A), or of dipping him first in a "stand o milk" and then in a "stand o water," as in Glenriddell's text. This variant, however, confuses the natural order of the metamorphoses:

> "They'll turn me in your arms, lady,
> A mother-naked man;
> Cast your green kirtle owr me,
> To keep me frae the rain.

> "First dip me in a stand o milk,
> And then a stand o water;
> Haud me fast, let me na gae,
> I'll be your bairnie's father" [B].

Both milk and water are employed in only one other text (I 43), but here also, as in B, they are used out of their proper order in the retransformation process. Child says:

In Scott's version, I, transformations are added at random from C, *after* the dipping in milk and in water, which seems indeed to have been regarded by the reciters only as a measure for cooling red-hot iron or the burning gleed, and not as the act essential for restoration to human nature.[2]

Child's observations on the right order in the series of Tam's mutations may be given here:

The end of the mutations, in F 11, G 43, is a naked man, and a mother-naked man in B 33, under the presumed right arrangement; meaning by right arrangement, however, not the original arrangement, but the most consistent one for the actual form of the tradition. Judging by analogy, the naked man should issue from the bath of milk or of water; into which he should have gone in one of his non-human shapes, a dove, swan, or snake (for which, too, a "stand" of milk or of water is

[1] *Ibid.*, III, 505. [2] *Ibid.*, I, 338 n.

a more practicable bath than for a man). The fragment C adds some slight probability to this supposition. The last change there is into "a dove but and a swan"; then Tam Lin bids the maiden to let go, for he'll "be a perfect man": this, nevertheless, he could not well become without some further ceremony. A is the only version which has preserved an essentially correct process: Tam Lin, when a burning gleed, is to be thrown into well-water, from which he will step forth a naked knight.[1]

According to our ballad, Carterhaugh is a fairy domain or at least a place where the fairies are seen by mortals. It is noteworthy that tradition once preserved, possibly still preserves, the story of Tam Lin's milk and water bath at this spot.

> The peasants point out, upon the plain, those electrical rings, which vulgar credulity supposes to be traces of the Fairy revels. Here, they say, were placed the stands of milk, and of water, in which *Tamlane* was dipped, in order to effect the disenchantment; and upon these spots, according to their mode of expressing themselves, the grass will never grow.[2]

In connection with baptism as a countercharm we pointed out the efficacy of milk in defensive magic. By way of stressing the fact of the wide currency of folk-superstitions we may refer to Professor N. N. Puckett's work on the beliefs of the southern Negro in which we find that the Negro believes that sweet milk may be used to drive off ghosts.[3]

As a final act in redeeming Tam Lin from fairyland, Janet (A 35, B 37, F 16, I 51) must cover him with her green kirtle or mantle. In B she does this to keep her lover "frae the rain"; in A to "cover" him "out o sight," that is, it appears, to hide him from elfin eyes. In F and I this procedure seems to be a necessary part of the entire process of Tam's redemption:

> *They turned him into a flash of fire,*
> *And then into a naked man;*
> *But she wrapped her mantle him about,*
> *And then she had him won* [F 16].

[1] *Ibid.*, p. 338.   [2] Scott, *op. cit.*, II, 377.
[3] *Folk Beliefs of the Southern Negro*, p. 142.

In A, B, and I the mantle or kirtle is said to be green, a very popular color in balladry so far as woman's dress is concerned. But it is a color, too, which is peculiar to fairies and witches and is therefore regarded as unlucky. In our Tam Lin incident Janet's green mantle has possibly a countermagical significance. Moreover, the fact that Tam is again clothed in human garments may go far to insure his complete immunity to the fairy spell.

Tam Lin's escape from elfdom concludes dramatically enough when the fairy queen (A 42, B 40 f., D 34, E 21, H 14) cries that had she known her earthly knight's purpose she would have taken out his "twa gray een" and put in "twa een o tree," and in addition would have deprived him of his "heart o flesh" and replaced it with a "heart o stane" or of "tree." A common stipulation between elf and mortal was that the mortal, in case he broke faith, should sacrifice his heart and eyes.[1] The Glenriddell copy of our ballad (B 40 f.) reads:

> *"Had I kend, Thomas," she says,*
> *"A lady wad hae borrowd thee,*
> *I wad hae taen out thy twa grey een,*
> *Put in twa een o tree.*
>
> *"Had I but kend, Thomas," she says,*
> *"Before I came frae hame,*
> *I had taen out that heart o flesh,*
> *Put in a heart o stane."*

"I'd take out your false, false heart, and put in one of clay," is the reading in a variant recorded in the *Journal of the Irish Folk-Song Society*.[2]

That the heart has been and still is thought to be the seat of life, the embodiment of the soul, and that eating a man's heart will enable one to acquire the qualities of the man are widespread beliefs and find partial reflection in the foregoing passage.[3] Child observes:

[1] See Child, I, 339; Gummere, *Germanic Origins*, p. 380.   [2] I, 47 f.

[3] See "Heart," *Encyclopaedia of Religion and Ethics*, VI, 556 ff.

The taking out of the eyes would probably be to deprive Tam of the faculty of recognizing fairy folk thereafter. Mortals whose eyes have been touched with fairies' salve can see them when they are to others invisible, and such persons, upon distinguishing and saluting fairies, have often had not simply this power but their ordinary eyesight taken away. . . . . Grimm has given instances of witches, Slavic, German, Norse and Italian, taking out the heart of man (which they are wont to devour), and replacing it in some instances with straw, wood, or something of the kind; nor do the Roman witches appear to have been behind later ones in this dealing.[1]

The belief that the witch was given to devouring the heart of her victim points no doubt to cannibalistic practice. We have already seen in our survey of soul ideas that balladry records the custom of blood-drinking and of eating the heart, a custom which, however, it should be said, can only be inferred from certain of our examples of transformation magic.[2] But let us at this point—at the expense of digressing from our study of disenchantment—give other ballad incidents that seem to reflect more directly the practice of cannibalism.[3] Our folksongs are replete with barbarous practices, such as various forms of mutilation employed chiefly in matters of blood vengeance but likewise in the exercise of public justice.[4] Nor are traces of cannibalism and human sacrifice entirely absent from British balladry. Our popular poetry can boast of a cannibalistic feast in the incident of the "thirtie . . . . heades" of his enemies, which Andrew Barton (167)[5] sent home "to eate with breade":

> *"Once I met with the Portingaills,*
> *Yea, I met with them, ye, I indeed;*
> *I salted thirtie of ther heades,*
> *And sent them home to eate with breade."*

[1] *Op. cit.*, I, 339. See also *ibid.*, II, 505; III, 505; V, 290; and *Journal of the Folk-Song Society*, III, 14 ff.

[2] See *supra*, pp. 73 ff.

[3] On cannibal rites in the British Islands see Gomme, *Ethnology in Folklore*, p. 192.

[4] See my study, *Death and Burial Lore*, pp. 8 ff.

[5] Child, IV, 505, stanza 42.

Something there is in this of gasconade, to be sure. And, as Child observes, it may be "a ferocious addition of the ballad."[1] But one must hasten to say, as in the matter of blood-drinking, it is an addition that reflects, however indirectly, an actual practice. That it is the ballad and not history which fastens this barbarity upon Andrew and his friends at home[2] does not alter the case. It is even possible that history fails to give the true account; but the veracity of the historical record aside, there is no question that our song reflects a custom to which Andrew's prototypes were given before or even after his day. It is altogether probable that the ballads hold as close to folkways as do popular tales, of which, with respect to cannibalistic incidents, J. A. MacCulloch says: "Some of the incidents of folk-tale cannibalism are copied exactly and with a curious minuteness, from actual practice."[3] "The folk-tales [of India]," observes Crooke, "also disclose ample evidence of cannibalism."[4]

History sometimes paints the darker picture, or goes hand in hand with tradition. Scott says in his notes on *Lord Soulis:*

> The tradition regarding the death of Lord Soulis, however singular, is not without a parallel in the real history of Scotland. The same extraordinary mode of cookery was actually practised (*horresco referens*) upon the body of a sheriff of the Mearns. This person, whose name was Melville of Glenbervie, bore his faculties so harshly, that he became detested by the barons of the country. Reiterated complaints of his conduct having been made to James I. (or, as others say, to the Duke of Albany), the monarch answered, in a moment of unguarded impatience, "Sorrow gin the sheriff were sodden, and supped in broo!" The complainers retired, perfectly satisfied. Shortly after, the Lairds of Arbuthnot, Mather, Laureston, and Pittaraw, decoyed Melville to the top of the hill of Garvock, above Lawrencekirk, under pretence of a grand hunting party. Upon this place (still called the *Sheriff's Pot*), the barons had prepared a fire and a boiling cauldron, into which they plunged the unlucky sheriff. After he was *sodden* (as the King termed

[1] *Ibid.*, p. 502.

[2] See *ibid.*

[3] *Op. cit.*, p. 305 n.   [4] *Folk-Lore of Northern India*, II, 168.

it) for a sufficient time, the savages, that they might literally observe the royal mandate, concluded the scene of abomination by actually partaking of the hell-broth.[1]

If the terrible blood-smelling giants of folktale, and the witches and fairies who cut out the hearts and eyes of their captives, are to be regarded as traditional representatives of actual cannibals, then British folksong, through the ballad of *Tam Lin* and the part ballad, part tale, of Child Rowland, may lay claim to a share in preserving the customs of man-eating folk. The story of Child Rowland, fragmentary in ballad form but rounded out in detail by Jamieson's country tailor,[2] includes the incident of the man-eating ogre, known, with his dreadful formula, all over Europe:

> *"Fee, fie, fo, fum,*
> *I smell the blood of some earthly one."*

"A hostile race of giants," says Gomme, in connection with this incident and concerning the traditions of the Celtic Aryans, "having their sense of smell for human flesh peculiarly sharp, ate their captives and revelled in their blood."[3] And according to Mr. Campbell, the "Fee-fo-fum" of Cornwall is "Fiaw-fiaw-foaghrich" in Argyll, sounds which may not impossibly be corruptions of the language of real big-bodied savages now magnified into giants.[4]

One should proceed cautiously and armed with reservations when approaching the question as to whether human sacrifice is reflected in balladry. The vestiges of such sacrifice are seen in the practice of British Islanders who offer up animals for the cure of disease in both men and animals. The immolation of a black cock for the cure of epilepsy, and of a bull for the recovery of health, rites "frequently performed," is noted by Henderson in his *Northern Coun-*

[1] *Op. cit.*, IV, 242 f.

[2] *Northern Antiquities*, p. 398.

[3] *Op. cit.*, p. 157. [4] *Popular Tales of the West Highlands*, I, xcii.

ties,[1] and various sacrificial customs among the Irish are discussed by Professor Robinson in his study "Human Sacrifice among the Irish Celts."[2] In the black cock which crows in the Scandinavian *Niflheim*, the counterpart of which is found in English folksong,[3] we have a vestige of offerings to the powers of darkness. And, as already pointed out earlier in this study, one may urge a strong implication of the traces of human sacrifice in the fairy ballads of *Tam Lin* (39) and *Thomas Rymer* (37). According to both these pieces, stories of fairy capture, the elves at the end of every "seven years" must pay a "tiend" or tax to hell, the victim to be one of their own number unless they can find a substitute among earthly men. This tax or tithe, considered earlier in this study with reference to its occurrence in the various texts of the foregoing ballads, need only be touched upon here.[4] Tam Lin, an earthly knight who is captive to the fairy powers, says to his true-love;

> "*And pleasant is the fairy land,*
>   *But, an eerie tale to tell,*
> *Ay at the end of seven years*
>   *We pay a tiend to hell;*
> *I am sae fair and fu o flesh,*
>   *I'm feard it be mysel*" [39 A 24].

According to a Motherwell copy (D 15), the fiend, as in the foregoing text, prefers "ane o flesh and blood." In his criticism of Lady Wilde's conclusion that the same incident in *Thomas Rymer* points to human sacrifice, Mr. Hartland is of the opinion that the folklorist must await more complete evidence, evidence obtainable elsewhere than from a "literary work of the fifteenth century, and ballads derived therefrom."[5] But Mr. Hartland is seemingly unaware that this incident is present in the best texts of the purely tradi-

---

[1] Pp. 147 ff.

[2] *Kittredge Anniversary Papers*, pp. 185–97.

[3] See *supra*, pp. 248 ff.

[4] *Supra*, pp. 323 ff.   [5] *Science of Fairy Tales*, p. 102 n.

tional and "unliterary" ballad of *Tam Lin* and that the tradition is familiar in Scotland outside the ballads.[1] May one venture to see evidences of devil worship and sacrificial rites in the story told in a German analogue of our *Lady Isabel and the Elf-Knight*? A rich leper is advised by the devil that he may be rid of his disease by bathing in the blood of twelve pure maidens,[2] a prescription in keeping with the idea prevalent in the Middle Ages that the blood of children or of virgins was a specific for leprosy.

But we must return to the proper business of this chapter, a discussion of modes of disenchantment, a matter which we have well-nigh concluded, for little remains to be said as to the manner in which ballad actors evade, or escape from, the Otherworld spell. According to Scott, the feat of recovering a person abstracted by fairies was "reckoned an enterprise of equal difficulty and danger, [and] could only be accomplished on Hallowe'en, at the great annual procession of the Fairy court."[3] The various texts of *Tam Lin* (39) agree in appointing this as the time for Margaret to rescue her lover:

> "*The morn at even is Halloween;*
> *Our fairy court will ride,*
> *Throw England and Scotland both,*
> *Throw al the world wide;*
> *And if ye would me borrow,*
> *At Rides Cross ye may bide*" [D 16].

In yet another fairy ballad, *Allison Gross* (35, stanza 12), an earthly being is disenchanted on Hallowe'en, a matter not unworthy of note since the ballad calendar is on the whole unusually incomplete. The ballads make reference to the following special days: "Scere-thorsday" (23, stanza 1); Christmas (29, stanza 22; 31, stanza 3; 54 Ab 11; 149, stanza 8; 258, stanza 4); Yule or Yuletide (68 C 7; 72 A 16, B 6, C 18, D 13; 79 B 1; 91 B 27, D 9, F 13; 94, stanza

---

[1] See Child, I, 338 f.

[2] See *ibid.*, p. 47.   [3] *Op. cit.*, II, 369.

1; 236 A 6; 300, stanza 17); "New Yeers day" (31, stanza 12); "Newyeeres euen" (167 A 71); "Easter-day" (54 A 12, B 17); "Pasche" (68 B 9, C 7; 155 T 1; 289 A 2); "Lammas-tide" (68 C 16; 84 C 1; 161 A 1, B 1, C 1; 227, stanza 1; 262, stanza 1); "Martinmass" (79 A 5; 81 M 1; 91 B 27; 158 C 1; 178 A 1, D 1, E 1, F 1; 190, stanza 1; 240 C 2; 275 A 1; 290 A 1); "Whitsunday" (91 D 9), "Whitsontide" (119, stanza 3); "Candlemas" (91 F 13); "St. Andrew's day" (107 A 23); "Michaelmas" (124 A 9, 13); "St. George's day" (145 A 11, 12); "St. James his day" (168, stanzas 1, 2); "St. Nicholas' day" (179, stanza 13); "Saint Innocent's day" (302, stanza 6).

PART IV
THE CHRISTIAN OTHERWORLD

INTRODUCTORY

❧

CERTAIN conceptions of the Otherworld as portrayed in British balladry are more or less Christian in character. But we should repeat here, what we have already observed from time to time in the preceding chapters, that Christian thought in our popular poetry is on the whole alien and intrusive. Our best ballads are pagan at heart, fully as much so as the traditional songs of Scandinavia, and their religion is as heathen as that of the Helgi lays. The amalgamation of heathen beliefs with the ideas of a later or alien faith—the Christianizing process, in a word, so apparent in the religious thought of the Celts, for example, or of the Teutons—is illustrated here and there in our balladry, but throughout these simple little songs the world of paganism enjoys a hardy survival. This is not, of course, to say that the ballads antedate the introduction of Christianity into the British Islands. It is to say, however, that English folksong has caught up and carried along a great *corpus* of beliefs which do antedate and are independent of Christian thought.

The intrusion of Christian thought is easily detected and has invariably the effect of emasculating the ballad story. This is excellently illustrated in Miss Burne's Shropshire version of *The Wife of Usher's Well* (79 C). In order that the dead sons may return to their mother, it is necessary, according to this text, that Jesus breathe life into their bodies, an incident which is a clear case of an attempt at Christian rationalization of a purely pagan story:

> *Then he went and rose up her three sons,*
> *Their names, Joe, Peter, and John,*
> *And did immediately send them to far Scotland,*
> *That their mother may take some rest.*

The singer's orthodoxy might go unquestioned had he named the sons James, Peter, and John. Such Otherworld features as the mountains or hills of heaven and hell in *The Daemon Lover* (243) and in the ballad and romance of True Thomas, the arctic hell in the former piece, the Scandinavian water hell in the latter,[1] are seen at once to belong to pagan tradition. And this is true no less of the paradisaical birch in *The Wife of Usher's Well* (79 A) and of the beflowered heaven in *Sweet William's Ghost* (77).[2] Occasionally, the ballads themselves draw the line of demarcation—rather unsatisfactorily, it is true—between Christian and heathen conceptions, as in *Thomas Rymer*, where the Elf Queen's interesting cosmography divides the subterranean region into four otherworlds, this after she has already guided Thomas through the dark waters of what seems to be a fifth.[3] We encounter a distinction between the Church and heathendom in such ballads as *Sir Cawline* (61), *Tam Lin* (39), and *Hind Etin* (41), where the claims of a rather nominal Christendom are maintained against the jurisdiction of heathen sprites and magic.[4] Although its intrusion is readily enough detected, the later faith enters again, for example, when True Thomas mistakes the Queen of Faery for the Queen of Heaven.[5] The Lass of Roch Royal (76) would father her bairn on the "king o heaven," and Lady Masery, remembering, no doubt, the practice of the Israelites,[6] would father her babe on stock or stone (66 B 14) rather than accept Lord Ingram's chivalrous offer of paternity. But Young Beichan "wadna sae much as bow a knee" to "onie of their stocks" in "Grand Turkie" (53 H 2).[7]

After all, however, Christianity plays virtually no part in the ballad story if we except such ecclesiastical pieces

---

[1] See *supra*, pp. 128, 132 f.

[2] See *infra*, p. 409.

[3] See *supra*, pp. 116 ff., 128.

[4] See *supra*, pp. 368 ff., 377.

[5] See *supra*, p. 179.

[6] See *infra*, pp. 407 f.

[7] Cf. E 2, I 2. Cf. also No. 62 J 31: "Ye'll wed your brother on a stock, sae do ye on a stane." Cf. text in Greig, *Last Leaves*, p. 49, stanza 27.

as *Judas* (23), *St. Stephen and Herod* (22), *The Carnal and the Crane* (55), *Brown Robyn's Confession* (57), with its miracle of the Virgin, and *Sir Hugh* (155), perhaps, bearing in mind its Chaucerian analogue, *The Prioresses Tale.* We should not overlook the ecclesiastical calendar nor Christian charms against the powers of evil, matters which have been considered earlier in this work.[1] We have already noted, too, the fair sprinkling of Christian oaths throughout the ballads—"by him that was crowned with thorn," "by God and good St. John," "by the Trynyte," "bi hym that dyed on rode," or "by Goddës pyne."[2] To "scug his deadly sin" Old Robin shapes a cross in his right shoulder (80, stanza 32) and makes a pilgrimage to the "holy land," and the ballads picture yet other penances for sin (20; 21; 65 C 22; 66 A 30, E 42). We are reminded, moreover, of the devout oaths of Robin Hood and his merry men, the honor in which the Virgin was held by that ideal outlaw and the not infrequent aid she rendered him. We recall, too, Robin's war on the Church in behalf of a democratic Christianity, the masses he forced from the lips of bishop and abbot (143, stanza 23; 144 B 11; 145 B 40; 154, stanza 25) and particularly his request for his "houzle" at the hands of Little John. Red Roger has died in sin; Robin has time to confess (120 A 22 f.):

> *Says, Ly there, ly there, Red Roger,*
> *The doggs they must thee eate;*
> *"For I may haue my houzle," he said,*
> *"For I may both goe and speake.*

> *"Now giue me mood," Robin said to Litle Iohn,*
> *"Giue me mood with thy hand;*
> *I trust to God in heauen soe hye*
> *My houzle will me bestand."*

"Giue me mood" has something to do, no doubt, with the "houzle"[3] or communion, and Professor Child is inclined

[1] See *supra*, pp.367 ff., 371 ff., 377 ff., 396 f.   [2] See *supra*, p. 378.

[3] Cf. Nos. 59 A 46; 156; 165, stanza 13; 96 B 14.

to regard Robin's request as signifying *give me my God*, this in view of an equivalent phrase in the *Romaunt of the Rose*, "yeve me my savyour."[1] A domestic religious service is reflected in the frequent formula "When bells were rung, and mass was sung, and a' men bound to bed" (5 A 27, B 19, C 40; 62 A 21, C 23, E 13, F 20, I 31; 63 B 21, C 24; 66 A 20, C 26; 73 F 26, I 31; 89 B 4; 110 F 52, G 29, N 36; 155 A 10, C 17, D 10, E 13, Lb 9; 196 A 5, B 6; etc., etc.).[2]

[1] *Ballads*, V, 359; see also *ibid.*, III, 103 n.; V, 240, 297.

[2] Cf. Nos. 11 A 27; 81 A 1, C 1; 96 A 24, C 30, E 31, etc.; 44, stanza 6. There is a reference to "Adam" in No. 2 D 7, F 4, G 3, H 4, J 5. The allusion to "God" in No. 4 B 14 is merely one of many ways of emasculating a good ballad. The following miscellany of matters and allusions also occurs: Haman (59 B 32); Mary Magdalene (76, stanzas 12 f., Child, IV, 472); "flood o Noah" (46 Bd 10); possible reference to scourging of Jesus (61, stanza 29); "parish mass" (61, stanza 6); "the prime," first canonical hour (26, stanza 9); two souls fly up to heaven (92 A 11); miracle of the obedient tree (54); miracle of men and dogs rendered powerless to afflict Lazarus (56 A, B). In No. 196 C 9 we find mention of the "fiftieth psalm and three." The foregoing references are not, of course, meant to be exhaustive, but they are representative and illustrate the ballad's incidental treatment of Christianity.

Chapter XI

HEAVEN

IN ADDITION to obviously pagan conceptions of the Otherworld and aside from any amalgam of the older and the later faith, we encounter in balladry, as we have already observed, certain ideas which may fairly be classified as Christian, and which, derived from whatever source, are representative of medieval Christian notions about heaven, hell, and purgatory. In the ballad and the romance of True Thomas we find the traditional "narrow way" to heaven, a "road" pointed out by the Elf Queen:

> "*O see not ye yon narrow road,*
> *So thick beset wi thorns and briers?*
> *That is the path of righteousness,*
> *Tho after it but few enquires*" [37 A 12].

C 11 gives the same reading; B 11 reads: "It's dont ye see yon narrow way, that leadeth down by yon lillie lea?" This latter passage is virtually the same as those in Child's remaining variants.[1] According to the related romance, the road to heaven is a "faire waye" and lies over a "heghe mountayne."[2] The same road, as described in *The Queen of Elfan's Nourice* (40), is a "narrow road up by yon tree." The gates of paradise are mentioned in *The Wife of Usher's Well* (79 A 6) and in *Sweet William's Ghost* (77 D 12). In the former ballad, the dead sons are said to wear hats of "the birk" which grew at "the gates o Paradise."[3] Urging

---

[1] *Ballads*, IV, 454, 455, 458.

[2] See locality of the Otherworld, *supra*, p. 123.

[3] See *supra*, pp. 155 ff., 243.

Margret to return his faith and troth, Sweet William says that the "gates o heaven will be shut" and that he'll "be mist away." Just how the dead lover returns to heaven is a question, for in the foregoing text, as in other variants of this ballad, he simply goes back to his grave and lies down in it. The reference to heaven is not at all plausible unless, as we have already indicated in our chapter on the dead, we think of William as leading a sort of dual existence.[1]

The Christian heaven is of course high, "heyer than ys the tre," according to a fifteenth-century version of *Riddles Wisely Expounded* (1),[2] as well as other texts (C 14, D 6) of this piece, and according, moreover, to *Captain Wedderburn's Courtship* (46 A 13, B 17, C 9).[3] Still another copy of the former ballad has "higher than the clouds."[4] "O cursed mother, heaven's high," say the dead babes in *The Cruel Mother* (20 C 10), and in other copies (D, E, F, H) they testify in like manner to the highness of heaven. Into their statement as to the remoteness of heaven from one guilty of infanticide, the dead children let enter nothing of the ameliorating skepticism of a later day, nor can they, if they would, be intercessors at the throne of grace for their wicked mother (E 18 f.):

> "*But now we're both in [the] heavens hie,*
> *There is pardon for us, but none for thee.*"

> "*My pretty boys, beg pardon for me!*"
> "*There is pardon for us, but none for thee.*"

Robin Hood, in his last moments (120 A 23), trusts "to God in heauen soe hye" that his "houzle" will him "bestand." The "hie, hie heaven, just by our Saviour's knee" to which the dead William refers (77 D 11) implies some sort of ordering of the celestial realm according to degrees of highness, a popular recognition, no doubt, of the familiar

[1] See *supra*, p. 236.

[2] Child, V, 283.

[3] Also text (*ibid.*, p. 216).   [4] *Ibid.*, p. 205.

classifications of theology. But there is no need to multiply further ballad allusions to the highness of heaven.

Of greater moment is the celestial economy.[1] What of the sovereign powers of heaven, of the inhabitants of the Christian home of the blessed, who may arrive there and who may not, and what pleasures are to be found in that realm? The Virgin's familiar title, the Queen of Heaven, is, through True Thomas' error, conferred upon the Queen of Faery (37 A 3):

> "*All hail, thou mighty Queen of Heaven!*
> *For your peer on earth I never did see.*"

But "that name does not belong to me," says the Queen of Faery (A 4, C 4). "B 3," says Child, "has suffered a Protestant alteration which makes nonsense of the following stanza."[2] "Qwene of heuene ne am I noghte, ffor I tuke neuer so heghe degre," replies the Elf Queen in the romance (stanza 15),[3] rebuking her admirer for using "swylke wordes." Thomas may be pardoned, however, on the score that his antecedent in romance, Ogier le Danois, was guilty of the same sacrilege.[4] Young Beachen knows better (53 D 4), and so makes his moan, not to stock or stone, but to the Queen of Heaven. The name of the Virgin, as we have already observed, lends weight to many a ballad oath.[5] The King of Heaven plays a lesser rôle in balladry, but in the absence of her bairn's earthly father a ballad maiden (76 D 4) may take Christian consolation:

> *But the king o heaven maun father her bairn,*
> *Till Love Gregor come hame.*

Rather than avail herself of Lord Ingram's offer to stand father to her child, Lady Masery (66 B 14) would father

---

[1] Cf. the government of fairyland, *supra*, pp. 197 ff.

[2] *Op. cit.*, I, 320.

[3] See *ibid.*, p. 327.

[4] See *ibid.*, p. 319; III, 504. Cf. No. 76, *ibid.*, IV, 472.

[5] See *supra*, p. 378.

her babe on stock or stone.[1] Except the "lord of heauen" be her speed, fair Ellen (63 A 15) will never get safely through the water into which her cruel lover leads her. Invoking the aid of the Deity or swearing by the Deity, one encounters as often as supplications to the Virgin.[2] "Awaken, Dowglas, for hys love that syttes in trone," cries the Scottish knight (161 A 21) who would arouse Douglas against the proud Percy. And in another heroic piece (118, stanza 52) Little John will now be delivered "with Christs might in heauen." The most desirable seats in heaven are, it seems, those "down at the foot of our good Lord's knee" (77 B 7) or those (D 8) "just by our Saviour's knee." The bereaved mother in the Backus text of *The Wife of Usher's Well* (79, Child, V, 294) prays to "a king in the heavens above that wears a golden crown."

The angels of heaven get scant notice in the ballads. The ecclesiastical song *Dives and Lazarus* (56 A 10, B 11), traceable to the sixteenth century, pictures two angels as guides to heaven:

> *As it fell out upon a day,*
> *Poor Lazarus sickened and died;*
> *Then came two angels out of heaven*
> *His soul therein to guide.*

And for Lazarus there is "a place prepared in heaven, to sit on an angel's knee," a fate not so happy as that of those whose beds are (77 B 7) "down at the foot of our good Lord's knee," but preferable certainly to that of Dives (56 B 14) who must sit in hell "upon a serpent's knee." In the poor ballad of *Lady Isabel* (261, stanza 23) the reward of an abused stepdaughter is a bed "in the heavens high, amang the angels fine," a bed, by the way, to which the flight of her soul is instantaneous. By virtue of two ballad oaths, a place in heaven must also be granted the saints: "By all the sayntes that be in heaven," swears the king in *Adam Bell* (116, stanza 155), and this oath sounds again,

---

[1] Cf. Jer. 2:27; see Frazer, *The Golden Bough*, V, 107.

[2] See *supra*, pp. 377 f.

but from a mouth not royal, in *Robin Hood and the Butcher* (122 A 6).

But who of the ballad dead may enter the gates of the Christian paradise, and what are the joys of that realm? "But now we're in the heavens hie, and ye've the pains o hell to drie," announce the murdered babes to the cruel mother (20 D 11) and so bespeak an ethical division of the Otherworld, eloquently voiced again in our ballad of *Dives and Lazarus* (56). In another ballad, Lady Margaret, with her necromantic questioning (77 D 7 f.), inquires of her dead lover concerning the future state of unbaptized children:

> "*But your faith and troth ye'se never get,*
> *Till you tell me again;*
> *Till you tell me where the children go*
> *That die without a name.*"

> "*O they gang till the high, high heaven,*
> *Just by our Saviour's knee,*
> *An it's a' clad ower wi roses red,*
> *A lovelie sicht to see.*"

The ballads know nothing apparently of the *limbus infantium*,[1] but they have authority for their disposal of women who die in childbed. The state of such women is inquired into by Margret (77 B 6 f.), who, we must suppose, has her own case in mind:

> "*Thy faith and trouth thou shall na get,*
> *Nor our trew love shall never twin,*
> *Till ye tell me what comes of women*
> *Awat that dy's in strong traveling.*"

> "*Their beds are made in the heavens high,*
> *Down at the foot of our good Lord's knee,*
> *Well set about wi gilly-flowers,*
> *A wat sweet company for to see.*"

[1] On beliefs about the souls of unbaptized children see W. Henderson, *Northern Counties*, pp. 130 ff.

One recalls here the incident of the "white hinde" in *Lee-some Brand* (15 A), which depicts the death of a woman in childbirth. The white hind is probably to be explained as an animal form into which the soul of the mother passes, though the death in travail need, of course, have no bearing upon such a transmigration.[1] "According to the old Mexicans, the souls of women who died in labour went to a place of delight in the temple of the sun."[2] "In Corea the souls . . . . of women who expire in childbed, invariably take up their abode in trees."[3] Another text of *Sweet William's Ghost* (77 D 11) likewise describes the future state of women who die in childbed and illustrates a ceremony which was possibly thought to be performed in lieu of earthly rites of purification:

> "*O they gang till the hie, hie heaven,*
> *Just by our Saviour's knee,*
> *And every day at twal o clock*
> *They're dipped oer the head.*"[4]

The dying lover in *Bonny Bee Hom* (92 B 16) requests that his riches be dealt most liberally to "women in child-bed laid." Those women (stanza 17) "that neer had children born, in swoon they down fell there."

In speaking of celestial delights the Kinloch text of *Sweet William's Ghost* (77 E 12 f.) is content with the abstraction "pleasures of heaven," pleasures which the dead man confesses he knows not of. According to the Elf Queen in the romance of True Thomas, heaven is where "synfull sawles are passed" their "payne,"[5] and "it's weel's the man," she says in the ballad analogue (37 B 11), that walks in "yon narrow way." The bells and the psalms of heaven are mentioned in *Sweet William's Ghost*—this as a

---

[1] See *supra*, pp. 52 ff.

[2] Lean, *Collectanea*, II, 102, citing Pritchard, *History of Mankind*, V, 366.

[3] Frazer, *op. cit.*, II, 31; see also *ibid.*, VIII, 97 f.; Toy, *Introduction to the History of Religions*, p. 35.

[4] On the churching of women, see *supra*, pp. 373 f.

[5] See Child, I, 328, stanza 38.

sort of Christian palliative, perhaps, for the distinctly
pagan elements which enter into this song, even into
heaven iself:

> *"But gie me my faith and troth, Margrat,*
> *An let me pass on my way;*
> *For the bells o heaven will be rung,*
> *An I'll be mist away"* [77 D 4].

In the foregoing as well as in another text (B 8) the dead
man would return before the psalms of heaven are sung:

> *"The salms of Heaven will be sung,*
> *And ere now I'le be misst away."*

Our ballad exemplifies something of that interesting combination of Christian and pagan Otherworld ideas found in
the *Voyage of the Húi Corra*, where, among other things,
we encounter a psalm-singing old man, as well as "fair,
builded churches" and beautiful altars.[1] The dying bride
and bridegroom of the Norse ballad *The Compulsory Marriage* hear the bells of heaven and the beckoning song of
God's angels;[2] and for Queen Dagmar, in another Norse
song, the bells of heaven are chimed.[3]

In her discussion of the traditional carol *Over Yonder's
a Park*, Miss Gilchrist questions the folk-origin of the
refrain, in which occurs an allusion to the "bells in Paradise":

> *"Over yonder's a park which is newly begun,*
> <u>*All bells in Paradise I heard them a-ring,*</u>
> *Which is silver on the outside and gold within,*
> <u>*And I love sweet Jesus above all things."*</u>[4]

Interpreting the carol symbolically, Miss Gilchrist sees
traces therein of the dogma of transubstantiation, and sup-

[1] See Stokes' trans., *Revue celtique*, XIV, 49, 53, 59, etc.

[2] See Prior, III, 448 f.

[3] See *ibid.*, II, 140.

[4] *Journal of the Folk-Song Society*, IV, 62.

ports her view with references to the ringing of bells in connection with eucharistic rites. But Frank Sidgwick feels "uncertain how far one ought to press symbolism and discredit the picturesqueness and imagination of the folk mind," and goes on to say that "Miss Gilchrist's ingenious arguments about the 'bells of Paradise' must fall to the ground."[1] There is nothing in *Sweet William's Ghost* to tempt one into the mazes of symbolical interpretation, and Mr. Sidgwick's suggestion as to a folk-origin for the "bells of Paradise" in the carol may readily be applied to the "bells o heaven" of our ballad, a song to which, strangely enough, neither Miss Gilchrist nor Mr. Sidgwick makes reference.

[1] *Ibid.*

Chapter XII

HELL AND PURGATORY

❖

THE dualism of Christian thought as reflected in
the ballads finds expression in antithetical descriptions of the Otherworld—the highness of
heaven, the lowness of hell; the path to the realm of the
blest, the road to the regions of the damned; the pleasures
of the former place, the pains of the latter. To match the
thorn-beset "narrow road" to heaven, the Elf Queen shows
True Thomas (37 A 13) the lovely "braid braid road" to
hell:

> *"And see not ye that braid braid road,*
> *That lies across yon lillie leven?*
> *That is the path of wickedness,*
> *Tho some call it the road to heaven."*

Other texts of *Thomas Rymer*, as does the related romance,
anticipate the joys of paradise by picturing the road to
heaven as "faire" (R, stanza 38)[1] or as winding (B 11)
"down by yon lillie lea,"[2] and predict the hardships of the
lower world by describing the way to hell as leading (B 10)
"down by yon skerry fell" or as lying "out-owr yon frosty
fell."[3] This "frosty fell" recalls the "mountain of hell" "so
dreary wi frost and snow" within sight of which the demon-
lover (243 F 14) carries his earthly mistress, and which
represents some sort of arctic hell.[4]

The gates of "paradise" and of "heaven" in *The Wife*

[1] Child, *Ballads*, I, 328.

[2] Also texts (*ibid.*, IV, 454, 455, 458).

[3] *Ibid.*, p. 455, stanza 15; cf. text (*ibid.*, 458, stanza 8).

[4] See *supra*, pp. 132 f.

of Usher's Well (79 A 6) and in *Sweet William's Ghost* (77 D 12) are matched in *Thomas Rymer* (37 B 10) by the "gates o hell." In *The Cruel Mother* (20 K 7, I 15) and *The Maid and the Palmer* (21 B 2) we find the traditional hell porter. A high heaven[1] calls for a low or deep hell, as in *Riddles Wisely Expounded* (1 A 16, B 9, C 14)[2] and other pieces (20 C 11, 46 A 13), where the contrast is effective enough:

> "*O heaven is higher nor the tree,*
> *And hell is deeper nor the sea*" [1 C 14].

The phrase "pit o hell" occurs in one text of *Thomas Rymer* (37);[3] "lowest hell," in another.[4] This latter phrase implies degrees of punishment, a matter to be discussed shortly. "To get a drop" of his "heart-bluid," Johnie Cock's enemies (114 B 1) "would sink a' their souls to hell," or for the same purpose (A 3) they "wad ride the fords of hell." This brings to mind those Otherworld waters through which ride Thomas and the Fairy Queen (37), and in general such rivers of woe as the rivers Styx and Acheron.[5]

The ballad descriptions of hell—a punitive hell, with degrees and kinds of punishment—are quite fragmentary and cannot, of course, rival that elaborate portrayal in the Apocalypse of Peter nor those later *Visions*, precursors of Dante's *Comedy*. But there is something in British balladry of the retributive economy of the Catholic region of torment, with its careful adjustment of penalty to sin. Ritson's *Deadman's Song* goes, it is true, into a more minute portrayal of what each vice must expect below,[6] and Norse balladry, as we shall see presently, instances

---

[1] See *supra*, p. 406.

[2] And the fifteenth-century text (Child, V, 283, stanza 15).

[3] *Ibid.*, IV, 455*b*, stanza 15.

[4] *Ibid.*, p. 454*b*.

[5] See "The Otherworld Journey," *supra*, pp. 116 ff.

[6] *Ancient Songs*, p. 287.

similar depictions of the fate of the damned. The *Lay of the Sun* or *Sólar-Lióð*, which may "be paralleled by some fragments in North-English ballads, such as Clerk Saunders [*Sweet William's Ghost* (77)]," details through the mouth of a dead father six of the joys of heaven, and ten varieties of torment for different kinds of sin.[1]

With the exception of *Sweet William's Ghost* (77), *Proud Lady Margaret* (47), *The Cruel Mother* (20), and *The Maid and the Palmer* (21), our ballads fail to particularize respecting the Otherworld torments in store for the earthly malefactor and seldom go beyond such generalities as the "plagues," the "pains," or the "fires" of hell. But the fires of the ballad hell still burn with the old medieval fury and are satisfyingly corporeal. Done to death by his false "true-love," Lord Randal (12 A 10) leaves his murderess "hell and fire." And the stricken hero in *Edward* (13 A 12) probably has like fires in mind when, in a bequest no less eloquent, he wills his wicked mother "a fire o coals to burn her." On the point of plucking the fruit of the subterranean garden, True Thomas (37 A 9)[2] is saved from the plagues of hell by the warning of the Elf Queen, a fairy whose instincts are notably humanitarian:

> "O no, O no, True Thomas," she says,
> "That fruit maun not be touched by thee,
> For a' the plagues that are in hell
> Light on the fruit of this countrie."

According to the romance (stanza 35),[3] his "saule" will go to the "fyre of helle," there in "payne ay for to duelle." In both the romance and the ballad of *True Thomas* and also the ballad of *Tam Lin* (39), the fairies must at seven-year intervals sacrifice to hell one of their number unless they can capture an earthly being and offer him as the sacrificial victim.[4] While her innocent babes are in the

---

[1] Vigfusson-Powell, *Corpus poeticum boreale*, I, 203, 204 ff.

[2] Cf. B 8, C 17, and texts (Child, IV, 454 ff.), and on the Otherworld garden, see *supra*, pp. 153 ff.

[3] Child, I, 328. [4] See *supra*, pp. 323 ff.

"heavens hie," the cruel mother (20 D 11) will have "the pains o hell to drie." "The pleasures of heaven I wat not of," says the dead Sweet William (77 E 13), "but the pains of hell I dree."

We may now take up those ballads in which Otherworld tortures are granted more generous depiction. It is paganism, however, rather than Christianity, which prescribes in *The Cruel Mother* (20) certain expiatory metamorphoses —a sort of Pythagorean dispensation, and a type of punishment which, it is conjectured, originally followed the violation of the eating taboo in Saxo's *Voyage of Guthrum Haraldson to Giant-land*.[1] Already discussed under transmigration beliefs, these examples of metamorphosis as well as those in *The Maid and the Palmer* (21) need not detain us here.[2] In both the foregoing ballads, however, one of the punishments enumerated is that of serving as a porter in hell (20 I 15, K 7; 21 B 2). Thus in a Motherwell copy of *The Cruel Mother* (20 K 7):

> "*Seven years to ring a bell,*
> *And seven years porter in hell.*"

"To lead an ape in hell" is another penalty specified in *The Maid and the Palmer* (21 A 14),[3] "a burlesque variation," says Child, "of the portership."[4]

Sweet William's Ghost and *Proud Lady Margaret*, although disappointingly fragmentary as regards the matter in hand, portray more fully than do other ballads the pains of the nether world. That our folksong recognizes the familiar gradations of hell, such as the circles of Dante's inferno, is evidenced by the following expressions: "lowest hell" (37),[5] "low, low hell" (77 D 6), "lowest seat o hell" (47 B 31), and "a dismal place, prepared in hell" (56 A 13). But what of those penalties which are attached specifically

---

[1] See Elton-Powell, *Saxo*, p. lxxii.

[2] See *supra*, pp. 33 ff.

[3] See *infra*, pp. 426 f.

[4] *Op. cit.*, I, 230.   [5] *Ibid.*, IV, 454.

to particular sins? The dialogue between Margaret and her dead lover in *Sweet William's Ghost* brings out several such penalties, a dialogue which, observes York Powell, must originally have been the central part of the poem and which is "of the same kind as the old heathen necromantic questioning of which there are several examples among the Eddic Lays."[1] Until he has told her what becomes of women who "hang themsell for sin," Margaret will not return the dead William's faith and troth (77 D 5 f.):

> *"Yere faith and troth ye' se never get,*
> *Till ye tell me this ane;*
> *Till ye tell me where the women go*
> *That hang themsell for sin."*

> *"O they gang till the low, low hell,*
> *Just by the devil's knee;*
> *It's a' clad ower wi burnin pitch,*
> *A dreadfu sicht to see."*

Sweet William's Danish analogue, Sir Ogey in *Aage og Else*, speaks of a kind of barrow hell, a grave torment which results from his lady's weeping:

> *"So oft as thou art weeping,*
> *And grievest thee so sore,*
> *Is brimming full my coffin*
> *With blood and gore.*

> *"Above my head is growing*
> *The grass so sweet,*
> *But lothely snakes are twining*
> *About my feet."*[2]

These "lothely snakes" bring to mind the "channerin worm" in *The Wife of Usher's Well* (79 A 11). It is possible that *Sweet William's Ghost*, if we grant a borrowing from the Danish *Aage og Else*, has given Sir Ogey's grave

---

[1] Vigfusson-Powell, *op. cit.*, I, 506.

[2] Prior, *Ancient Danish Ballads*, III, 78.

torture a Christian coloring, and thus widened the bounds of the dead man's barrow to the larger confines of the Catholic hell.

The circle of hell "just by the devil's knee" (77 D 6) is antipodal to that place which (B 6 f.) is reserved for women who die "in strong traveling," that place, namely, "at the foot of our good Lord's knee."[1] It probably corresponds, moreover, to that uncomfortable position assigned in the nether regions to the rich Dives (56 B 14):

> *"Rise up, rise up, brother Diverus*
> *And come along with me;*
> *There is a place prepared in hell,*
> *For to sit upon a serpent's knee."*

The Sylvester text (A 13) of *Dives and Lazarus* reads: "A dismal place, prepared in hell, from which thou canst not flee."[2] In *Allison Gross* (35) and *The Laily Worm* (36) a maiden in the former piece, a machrel in the latter, combs "upon her knee" the head of an "ugly" or "laily" worm. Commenting upon this incident, Child says respecting the "serpent's knee" in *Dives and Lazarus:* "Dives, in one version of a well-known carol, has 'a place prepared in hell, to sit upon a *serpent's knee.*' The pious chanson in question is a very different thing from an old ballad, which, it is hoped, no one will think capable of fatuity."[3] "Serpent" should doubtless in this case be taken as a name for the devil. Lazarus, in the same ballad (56 A 11, B 12), has a place prepared in heaven "to sit on an angel's knee." True Thomas (37 A 11, C 10) lays his head on the Elf Queen's knee and is shown "fairlies three," that is, wonders three.[4]

To return for a moment to *Sweet William's Ghost* (77), we find that the dead lover in the Kinloch version (E 13) speaks of hanging as a punishment for "huring" and "adulterie":

[1] See *supra*, p. 409.

[2] Cf. text (*Journal of the Folk-Song Society*, I, 17).

[3] *Op. cit.*, I, 315 n.   [4] Cf. Nos. 4 A 10; 34 B 1; 39 F 2.

"The pleasures of heaven I wat not of,
But the pains of hell I dree;
There some are hie hangd for huring,
And some for adulterie."

According to Buchan's copy of *Proud Lady Margaret* (47
B 30 f.), "Pirie's chair," the "lowest seat o hell," is the
portion of those who are guilty of pride. The dead brother,
returned from the grave because of his sister's vanity, concludes his visit with these words:

"You're straight and tall, handsome withall,
But your pride owergoes your wit,
But if ye do not your ways refrain,
In Pirie's chair ye'll sit.

"In Pirie's chair you'll sit, I say,
The lowest seat o hell;
If ye do not amend your ways,
It's there that ye must dwell."

The proud man, we may recall, fares exceedingly ill in
Dante's inferno. The Child glossary offers two suggestions
as to the meaning of "Pirie's chair," both of which are
rather plausible:

For the derivation Sir W. D. Geddes suggests as possible le pire,
which would be in the way of the Scottish "ill chiel." Professor Cappen
writes: "Familiar name in doggerel lines recited by boys in their games.
One boy stood back against the wall, another bent towards him with
his head on the pit of the other's stomach; a third sat upon the back of
the second. The boy whose head was bent down had to guess how many
fingers the rider held up. The first asked the question in doggerel
rhyme in which Pirie, or Pirie's chair, or hell, was the doom threatened
for a wrong answer. I remember Pirie (pron. Peerie) distinctly in
connection with the doom. Pirie's chair probably indicates the uncomfortable position of the second boy . . . . whose head or neck was confined in some way and squeezed after a wrong answer."[1]

A German ballad, probably a variant of *The Cruel Mother*
(20), tells of a seat in hell prepared for a murderess: "Dein
Sessel," says the devil, "ist dir in der Hölle gebaut."[2] A

[1] *Op. cit.*, V, 365a.   [2] See *ibid.*, I, 219 f.

French tale tells of a lover who goes to hell where he
sees his dead mistress sitting on a fiery chair and devoured
by serpents night and day.[1]

In texts of *Proud Lady Margaret* (47) other than the
version quoted above, the ghost does not specify the kind
of fate which will befall Lady Margaret, but is content
with warnings like the following: "When you come where I
have been you will repent it sore" (C 18); "If ye come the
roads that I hae come, sair warned will ye be" (D 12);
"Ere ye see the sights that I hae seen, sair altered ye maun
be" (E 11). To his false mother Edward (13 B 7) be-
queaths the "curse of hell," a curse heavy enough if we
are to believe the cruel mother in another ballad (20 J 12).
Guilty of infanticide, the murderess in the latter piece is
willing to do penance by becoming a "bird," a "fish," or
an "eel," but prays to be kept from the terrors of hell:

> *"Welcome, welcome, eel i the pule,*
> *But oh for gudesake, keep me frae hell!"*

So in I 17 and in *The Maid and the Palmer* (21 B 3).
Riddles Wisely Expounded (1 C 15) testifies to the specific
gravity of sin: "O sin is heavier nor the lead." But to
return to the particular tortures of the damned, we may
quote the Norse ballad *Saint James and the Vision of Hell*,
in which a dead man says that he has been down to the
gates of hell. He then details the punishments of that
place, mentioning among other things a red-hot stool on
which the matricide must sit. This fiery stool recalls
"Pirie's chair" of *Proud Lady Margaret* (47 B 30 f.). The
Norse song reads:

> *"And down to the gates of hell I've gone,*
> *Where those must sit, who ill have done;*

> *"Seen her, who once her mother slew,*
> *On red-hot stool the murder rue;*

[1] F. M. Luzel, *Contes populaires de la Basse-Bretagne*, I, 44, 45; see Child,
I, 426.

"Seen him, by whom his father died,
  In hell on red-hot saddle ride;

"The hostess, she who mix'd her wine,
  In hell I've seen her sit and pine;

"The trader, he who falsely weigh'd,
  In hell I've seen his theft repaid;

"The bailiff too, with hat so high,
  In hell I've heard for taxes cry;

"And seen the spoilt unruly chit
  In hell on glowing iron sit.

"Over them hangs a cloak of lead,
  And melts, as burns the fire so red."[1]

As for the duration of hell, the ballads are not unaware of the popular computations—that, for example, according to which a decillion of years are but "as a second of time in the sufferance of the damned." This is not so eloquent as the despairing calculation of Dives in our ecclesiastical ballad *Dives and Lazarus* (56 A 15):

"Oh had I as many years to abide
  As there are blades of grass,
Then there would be an end, but now
  Hell's pains will ne'er be past."

"Blades of grass" is likewise the reading in one version of this carol in the *Journal of the Folk-Song Society;*[2] "stars in the sky," in another text.[3] The romance of *Thomas of Erceldoune* speaks of the unending hell whence souls come "neu<u>er</u> owte or domesdaye" but are there "in payne aye for to duelle."[4] The various animal forms or other shapes which the cruel mother (20) and the murderess in *The*

---

[1] Prior, II, 31 f.   [3] IV, 48.
[2] V, 17.   [4] See Child, I, 328.

Maid and the Palmer (21) must assume by way of penance are to endure for seven years each. And these seven-year metamorphoses prescribe the time which our two infanticides must spend in hell: "seven years a porter in hell" (20 I 15, K 7; 21 B 2), "seven years doon into hell" (20 J 10), "other 7 to lead an ape in hell" (21 A 14). But a text of *The Cruel Mother* from Nova Scotia knows better, and to top off the expiatory metamorphoses predicts an eternity in hell: "The rest of your time shall be in hell, and it's there you'll be fixed for eternity."[1]

The denizens of hell as popularly conceived or as pictured in medieval theology are not unknown to English and Scottish folksong. That the arch fiend of balladry, like Dante's Lucifer, occupies the nethermost sphere of the Underworld is evident in lines from *Sweet William's Ghost* (77 D 6):

> *"O they gang till the low, low hell,*
> *Just by the devil's knee."*

The hungry maw of hell's monarch is implied in the heroic words of Will Scadlock in the pseudo-chivalrous romance *Robin Hood and the Prince of Aragon* (129, stanza 45). Having brought the giant to his knee, Robin's follower cries:

> *"The devil cannot break his fast,*
> *Unless he have you all three."*

But the lord of hell is not always mentioned by his right name. He occasionally hides behind such euphemisms as "auld man" (2 I 2); "Wearie" (4 B); "Clootie" (1 C 18); "shame" (62 A 15; 185, stanza 11). "Most like a feend of hell" is the bewitched lady in *The Marriage of Sir Gawain* (31), and a similar figure delineates the frightfully deformed woman in *Sir Henry* (32); she seems to be the very "fiend that wons in hell."

In a Robin Hood ballad (122 A 29) the devil's dame is mentioned when the sheriff complains of the outlaw: "But

---

[1] Mackenzie, *Quest of the Ballad*, pp. 105 ff.

such favor as he shewed me I might haue of the devills dam." As for the lesser powers in hell we have the following from *Clerk Colvill* (42 C 11):

> *"I will lie here an die," he said,*
> *I will lie here an die;*
> *In spite o a' the deils in hell*
> *I will lie here an die."*

But "deils in hell" is a popular and opprobrious designation for Otherworld beings of whatever denomination—of sea fairies, as in the foregoing ballad; of elves generally, as when Child Rowland in Jamieson's story thus defies the king of the trolls: "Strike, then, Bogle of Hell, if thou darest."[1]

Somewhat in the fashion of Burns, *The Farmer's Curst Wife* (278 A 5 ff.) illustrates certain popular notions of Satan—his habit of carrying off mortals on his back, his domain with its "hell's door," its wall, and its imps. "A curst wife who was a terror to demons," remarks Child, "is a feature in a widely spread and highly humorous tale, Oriental and European."[2] Our ballad, in preserving this incident, offers something of that comedy which is so conspicuously absent from British folksong:

> *Now Satan has got the old wife on his back,*
> *And he lugged her along, like a pedlar's pack.*

> *He trudged away till they came to his hall-gate;*
> *Says he, Here, take in an old Sussex chap's mate.*

> *O then she did kick the young imps about;*
> *Says one to the other, Let's try turn her out.*

> *She spied thirteen imps all dancing in chains,*
> *She up with her pattens and beat out their brains.*

---

[1] *Northern Antiquities*, p. 398.

[2] *Op. cit.*, V, 107; see also *ibid.*, p. 305.

> *She knocked the old Satan against the wall:*
> *"Let's turn her out, or she'll murder us all."*

> *Now he's bundled her up on his back amain,*
> *And to her old husband he took her again.*

Another version of the same piece (B 5) speaks of "hell's door,"[1] and of "seven wee deils a sitting in a raw." Texts recovered since Child read: "two young devils in chains";[2] "three young devils a-hanging in chains";[3] "little devils were playing with chains."[4] Satan is called the "auld Deil" in version B of Child's collection. The young devils in a later text speak of Satan as their "father."[5] According to Child's B, the curst wife was "seven years gaun, and seven years comin"; according to a version since Child, "seven years going and nine coming back."[6] The number 7, as we have already noted earlier in this work, is in balladry used with great frequency with reference to periods of time.[7] In a copy of the foregoing ballad recorded in the *Journal of the Folk-Song Society*[8] the devil's prong performs its traditional function: "The devil he took her upon his prong, and into hell he put her headlong." According to another variant found in the same periodical, the old woman is bundled out "over the wall" and comes down "on the earth a most terrible fall."[9]

Serpents are seldom absent from medieval descriptions and paintings of hell, and we need not go elsewhere to find a precedent for or parallel to the serpents mentioned in the carol *Dives and Lazarus* (56 A 12, B 13). Monstrous pagan "worms" our balladry may boast of in certain trans-

---

[1] Cf. "hell's hall-door" (*Journal of the Irish Folk-Song Society*, XVIII, 27).

[2] *Journal of the Folk-Song Society*, II, 184.

[3] *Ibid.*, III, 132.

[4] *Journal of the Irish Folk-Song Society*, loc. cit.

[5] *Journal of the Folk-Song Society*, II, 184.

[6] *Journal of the Irish Folk-Song Society*, loc. cit.

[7] See *supra*, pp. 328 ff.   [8] II, 184.   [9] III, 132.

formation pieces,[1] but with these, of course, the foregoing carol has nothing to do. To offset the angels which in the Gospel narrative conduct Lazarus to Abraham's bosom, the ballad introduces two serpents, which guide Dives to hell:

> *As it fell out upon a day,*
>   *Rich Dives sickened and died;*
> *Then came two serpents out of hell,*
>   *His soul therein to guide.*

But this is not enough, and according to one version of our carol (B 14), the rich man must sit in hell "upon a serpent's knee." The serpent here, however, as we have already noted, is probably Satan himself.[2] It is possibly a popular recollection of that passage in Revelations where the adversary is spoken of as the "Old Serpent."[3]

The "three hell-hounds" of Motherwell's *Sweet William's Ghost* (77 C 13) are not so easy of explanation as are the serpents of Dives' hell:

> *"What three things are these, Sweet William," she says,*
>   *"That stands here at your feet?"*
> *It is three hell-hounds, Marjorie," he says,*
>   *"That's waiting my soul to keep."*

"These verses . . . . cannot be an accretion of modern date," says Child.[4] As for hell-hounds, one recalls Cerberus, the watch dog of Hades; Milton's "Hell-hounds" with their "wide Cerberean mouths";[5] or Shakespeare's "hell-hound that doth hunt us all to death."[6] The hounds of the ballad may be representative of that class of spirits known to Welsh tradition as *Cwn Annwn*, or "dogs of hell," which are at times thought to be the hell-hounds that pursue through the air the spirit of the evil man the moment it leaves the body.[7] Gwynn ab Nudd, king

---

[1] See *supra*, p. 62.

[2] See *supra*, p. 418.

[3] Chap. xx, 2; also chap. xii, 9.

[4] *Op. cit.*, II, 227.

[5] *Paradise Lost*, II, 655.

[6] *Richard III*, IV, iv, 48.

[7] Sikes, *British Goblins*, p. 234.

of the realm of the dead in Welsh mythology, hunts the souls of the dying with his fierce hell-hounds.[1] But the lore of the dog of the Underworld is too extensive for further illustration here.

Peter is not found in our ballads in his rôle of heavenly porter, but the porter of hell, a familiar figure in Catholic mythology, is mentioned in two of our songs, *The Cruel Mother* and *The Maid and the Palmer*. To be a porter in hell is among the several penalties to be suffered by the murderess in each of these songs; thus in the former piece (20 I 15):

> "*Seven years to be a church bell,*
> *Seven years a porter in hell.*"

According to a Motherwell variant of *The Cruel Mother* (20 K 7), the punishment antecedent to that of being hell porter is ringing a bell for seven years. May not the bell-ringing and the portership be taken together as reflecting the old belief that a porter standing at hell's gate announces by ringing a bell the entrance of each new culprit? Another version of the ballad (L 9) seems to bear this out:

> "*Seven lang years ye'll ring the bell,*
> *And see sic sights as ye darna tell.*"

Our ballad porter recalls the porter in *Macbeth*, a character derived from the porter of hell in the old Mysteries.

A penance found in *The Maid and the Palmer* (21 A 14), that of leading an ape in hell for seven years, is, says Child, "a burlesque variation of the portership":[2]

> "*Other seaven a clapper in a bell,*
> *Other 7 to lead an ape in hell.*"

The reference here is to the belief that women who die old maids lead apes in hell.[3] Shakespeare alludes to this

---

[1] Rhŷs, *Arthurian Legend*, p. 155.

[2] *Op. cit.*, I, 230.

[3] See Murray, "Ape," *New English Dictionary*.

incident.[1] The allusion in *The Taming of the Shrew* (II, i, 34) clearly parallels that in our ballad.[2] It occurs in connection with the custom of dancing barefoot on a wedding day. Katherine, speaking of Bianca, says: "I must dance bare-foot on her wedding day, and, for your love to her, lead apes in hell."[3]

According to a variant of *Dives and Lazarus* (56) in the *Journal of the Folk-Song Society*, hell is "full of mice":

> *"Oh, hell is dark, oh, hell is deep,*
> *Oh, hell is full of mice."*[4]

Other versions from the same source give "mist," "lies," or "lice."[5]

In *Adam Bell* (116, stanza 63) there is an allusion to the harrowing of hell:

> *"[N]owe we are in," sayd Adam Bell,*
> *"[T]herof we are full fayne;*
> *[But] Cryst knoweth that heroued hell,*
> *[H]ow we shall come oute agayne."*

Of purgatory, that middle state of the dead, the ballads have virtually nothing to say. The prospective sojourn of the cruel mother (20) in hell—"seven years a porter in hell," this following a series of transmigrations[6]—may, it is true, be taken to reflect indirectly the medieval conception of purgatorial expiation. The infanticide in *The Maid and the Palmer* (21 A 13 ff.) may by undergoing penances similar to those prescribed in *The Cruel Mother* satisfy the demands of divine justice:

> *"Penance I can giue thee none,*
> *But 7 yeere to be a stepping-stone.*

---

[1] See Thistleton-Dyer, *Folk-Lore of Shakespeare*, p. 332.

[2] Cf. *Much Ado about Nothing*, II, i, 40.

[3] For the opinions of a number of commentators on "leading apes in hell" see Dyer, *loc. cit.*

[4] IV, 48.

[5] IV, 48 n.   [6] See *supra*, pp. 33 ff.

> *"Other seaven a clapper in a bell,*
> *Other 7 to lead an ape in hell.*

> *"When thou hast thy penance done,*
> *Then thoust come a mayden home."*

By consulting foreign versions of *The Maid and the Palmer*
—specifically, Norse versions and a Finnish variant—we
discover the true characters of the maid and the mysterious
palmer. With respect to these foreign analogues, Child
says:

> The story of the woman of Samaria, John, iv, is in all these blended
> with mediaeval traditions concerning Mary Magdalen, who is assumed
> to be the same with the woman "which was a sinner," in Luke, vii, 37,
> and also with Mary, sister of Lazarus. This is the view of the larger
> part of the Latin ecclesiastical writers, while most of the Greeks dis-
> tinguish the three. It was reserved for ballads, as Grundtvig remarks,
> to confound the Magdalen with the Samaritan woman.[1]

The names Maria, or Magdalena, Jesus, or Christ, occur
in most of the Norse versions of our ballad.[2] The mother
in the Shropshire version of *Usher's Well* (79 C 12 f.) has
nine days to repent before entering heaven:

> *Nine days then was past and gone,*
> *And nine days then was spent,*
> *Sweet Jesus called her once again,*
> *And took her to heaven with him.*

There are allusions in *Thomas Rymer* (37) to heaven
and hell and to fairyland, but for an allusion to purgatory
we must turn to the related romance *Thomas of Erceldoune*,
the Thornton manuscript: The queen, having first pointed
out the way to hell and that to heaven, shows Thomas a
third "waye," which lies under yon "grene playne." This
is the "waye, wi*th* tene and traye" where sinful souls
suffer their "payne."[3]

[1] *Op. cit.*, I, 228.

[2] See *ibid.*, pp. 228 ff.

[3] See *ibid.*, p. 328, stanza 40.

BIBLIOGRAPHY

BIBLIOGRAPHY

Archaeological Review. 4 vols. London, 1888–90.

Archivio per lo studio delle tradizioni popolari (rivista trimestrale, diretta da G. Pitrè e S. Salomone-Marino). Palermo, 1882——.

ÁRNASON, JÓN. *Icelandic Legends* (trans. G. Powell and E. Magnússon). 2 vols. London, 1864–66.

ARON, ALBERT W. *Traces of Matriarchy in Germanic Hero-Lore*, "University of Wisconsin Studies in Language and Literature," No. 9. Madison, 1920.

AUBREY, JOHN. *Remaines of Gentilisme and Judaisme* (ed. and annotated by James Britten). London, 1881. (Folk-Lore Society.)

BALDWIN, C. S. *An Introduction to English Medieval Literature.* New York, 1914.

BARBEAU, MARIUS, AND SAPIR, EDWARD. *Folk Songs of French Canada.* New Haven, 1925.

BARING-GOULD, S., AND SHEPPARD, H. F. *Songs of the West* (5th ed. in 1 vol.). London, 1913.

BASKERVILL, CHARLES READ. "English Songs on the Night Visit," *Publications of the Modern Language Association,* Vol. XXXVI (1921).

BASTIAN, A. *Allerlei aus Volks- und Menschenkunde.* 2 vols. Berlin, 1888.

BELDEN, H. M. "The Relation of Balladry to Folk-Lore," *Journal of American Folk-Lore,* Vol. XXIV (1911).

BELLOWS, H. A. *The Poetic Edda.* New York, 1923.

BÉRENGER-FÉRAUD, L. J. B. *Contes populaires de la Sénégambie.* Paris, 1885.

BLACK, W. G. *Folk-Medicine.* London, 1883. (Folk-Lore Society.)

BOAS, FRANZ. "Tsimshian Mythology," *Bureau of American Ethnology* (31st rept.). Washington, 1909–10.

——. "Mythology and Folk-Tales of the North American Indians," *Anthropology in North America.* New York, 1915.

BÖCKEL, OTTO. *Psychologie der Volksdichtung.* Leipzig, 1906.

BÖHME, FRANZ M. *Altdeutsches Liederbuch.* Leipzig, 1877.

BRAND, JOHN. *Observations on Popular Antiquities* (new ed., with the additions of Sir Henry Ellis). 3 vols. London, 1900.

BRAZ, A. LE. *La Légende de la Mort en Basse-Bretagne* (avec une introduction de L. Marillier). Paris, 1893.

BROADWOOD, LUCY. *English Traditional Songs and Carols*. London, 1908.

BRYANT, FRANK EGBERT. *A History of English Balladry*. Boston, 1913.

BUGGE, SOPHUS. *Studien über die Entstehung der nordischen Götter- und Heldensagen* (trans. into German by Oscar Brenner). München, 1889.

———. *The Home of the Eddic Poems* (rev. ed.; trans. W. H. Schofield). London, 1899.

BURNE, CHARLOTTE SOPHIA. *Shropshire Folk-Lore* (from the collections of Georgina F. Jackson). London, 1883.

BURNHAM, JOSEPHINE M. "A Study of Thomas of Erceldoune," *Publications of the Modern Language Association*, Vol. XXIII (1908).

BUSK, R. H. *The Folk-Songs of Italy*. London, 1887.

CAMPBELL, J. F. *Popular Tales of the West Highlands* (new ed.). 4 vols. London, 1890–93.

CAMPBELL, J. G. *Superstitions of the Highlands and Islands of Scotland*. Glasgow, 1900.

———. *Witchcraft and Second Sight in the Highlands and Islands of Scotland*. Glasgow, 1902.

CAMPBELL, OLIVE D., AND SHARP, CECIL J. *English Folk Songs from the Southern Appalachians*. New York, 1917.

CHAMBERS, E. K. *The Mediaeval Stage*. 2 vols. Oxford, 1903.

CHILD, FRANCIS JAMES. *The English and Scottish Popular Ballads*. 5 vols., 10 parts. Boston, 1882–98.

CLODD, EDWARD. *Magic in Names*. London, 1920.

CODRINGTON, R. H. *The Melanesians: Studies in Their Anthropology and Folk-Lore*. Oxford, 1891.

COSQUIN, EMMANUEL. *Contes populaires de Lorraine*. 2 vols. Paris, 1887.

County Folk-Lore. 7 vols. London, 1895–1912. (Folk-Lore Society.)

COURTHOPE, W. J. *History of English Poetry*, Vol. I. New York, 1895.

COX, JOHN HARRINGTON. *Folk-Songs of the South*. Cambridge: Harvard University Press, 1925.

COX, MARIAN R. *An Introduction to Folk-Lore*. London, 1904.

———. *Cinderella*. London, 1893. (Folk-Lore Society.)

CROMEK, R. H. *Remains of Nithsdale and Galloway Song*. London, 1810.

CROOKE, WILLIAM. *The Popular Religion and Folk-Lore of Northern India* (new ed., revised and illustrated). 2 vols. London, 1896.

CROSS, TOM PEETE. "The Celtic Origin of the Lay of Yonec," *Revue celtique*, Vol. XXXI (1910).

DALYELL, J. G. *The Darker Superstitions of Scotland*. Glasgow, 1835.

D'ARBOIS, H. *Les Druides et les dieux celtiques à formes d'animaux*. Paris, 1906.

DASENT, GEORGE W. *Popular Tales from the Norse* (2d ed.). Edinburgh, 1859. (A translation of the collection of Asbjørnsen and Moe.)

DURKHEIM, ÉMILE. *The Elementary Forms of the Religious Life* (trans. J. W. Swain). London, 1915.

DYER, T. F. THISTLETON. *Folk Lore of Shakespeare*. London, 1883.

ECKSTORM, FANNIE H., AND SMITH, MARY W. *Minstrelsy of Maine*. Boston, 1927.

EHRKE, KONRAD. *Das Geistermotiv in den schottisch-englischen Volksballaden*. Marburg, 1914.

ELTON, OLIVER, AND POWELL, FREDERICK YORK. *Saxo Grammaticus*, London, 1894. (Folk-Lore Society.)

FEHR, BERNHARD. *Die formelhaften Elemente in den alten englischen Balladen*. Berlin, 1900.

Folklore Fellow Communications. 1910——.

Folk-Lore. London, 1890——. (Organ of the Folk-Lore Society.)

Folk-Lore Journal. 7 vols. London, 1883–89. (Organ of the Folk-Lore Society.)

Folk-Lore Record. 5 vols. London, 1878–82. (Organ of the Folk-Lore Society.)

FRAZER, JAMES G. *Folk-Lore in the Old Testament*. 3 vols. London, 1919.

——. *Psyche's Task* (2d ed.). London, 1913.

——. *The Belief in Immortality*. 3 vols. 1913–24.

——. *The Golden Bough*. 12 vols. London, 1907–15.

——. "The Language of Animals," *Archaeological Review*, Vol. I (1888).

FRIEND, HILDERIC. *Flowers and Flower Lore* (2d. ed. in 1 vol.). London, 1884.

GEROULD, GORDON H. "The Ballad of the Bitter Withy," *Publications of the Modern Language Association*. Vol. XXIII (1908).

——. *The Grateful Dead*. London, 1908. (Folk-Lore Society.)

GOMME, ALICE B. *The Traditional Games of England, Scotland, and Ireland*. 2 vols. London, 1894–98.

GOMME, GEORGE L. *Ethnology in Folklore*. London, 1892.

——. *Folklore as an Historical Science*. London, 1908.

GÖRBING, FRIEDRICH. *Die Elfen in den englischen und schottischen Balladen*. Halle, 1899.

GREGOR, WALTER. *The Folk-Lore of the North-East of Scotland*. London, 1881. (Folk-Lore Society.)

GREIG, GAVIN. *Folk-Song of the North-East* (articles contributed to the *Buchan Observer*), "*Buchan Observer* Works." Peterhead, 1909 and 1914. 2 series.

——. *Last Leaves of Traditional Ballads and Ballad Airs* (ed., with an introductory essay, collations, and notes, by Alexander Keith). University of Aberdeen, 1925.

GRIMM, JACOB. *Teutonic Mythology* (trans. J. S. Stallybrass). 4 vols. London, 1880–88.

———. *Kinder- und Haus-Märchen* (gesammelt durch die Brüder Grimm). 17te Auflage. Berlin, 1880.

GRUNDTVIG, SVEND. *Danmarks gamle Folkeviser* (completed by Axel Olrik), Vols. I–VIII. 1853–99.

GUBERNATIS, ANGELO DE. *La Mythologie des Plantes.* 2 vols. Paris, 1878, 1882.

———. *Zoölogical Mythology.* 2 vols. London, 1872.

GUMMERE, FRANCIS B. "Ballads," *Cambridge History of English Literature.* Vol. II (1908).

———. "Primitive Poetry and the Ballad," *Modern Philology,* Vol. I (1903–4).

———. "The Ballad," *A Library of the World's Best Literature,* Vol. III (1902).

———. "The Mother-in-Law," *Kittredge Anniversary Papers.* Boston, 1913.

———. "The Sister's Son," *An English Miscellany* (the Furnivall memorial volume). Oxford, 1901.

———. *Germanic Origins: A Study in Primitive Culture.* New York, 1892.

———. *Old English Ballads.* Boston, 1894.

———. *The Oldest English Epic.* New York, 1914.

———. *The Popular Ballad.* Boston, 1907.

HALLIDAY, W. R. *Folklore Studies Ancient and Modern.* London, 1924.

HART, WALTER M. "Professor Child and the Ballad," *Publications of the Modern Language Association,* Vol. XXI (1906).

———. *Ballad and Epic.* Boston, 1907.

———. *English Popular Ballads.* New York, 1916.

HARTLAND, E. S. *Primitive Paternity.* 2 vols. London, 1910.

———. *The Legend of Perseus.* 3 vols. London, 1894–96.

———. *The Science of Fairy Tales.* London, 1891.

HASTINGS, JAMES. *Encyclopaedia of Religion and Ethics.* Edinburgh, 1908–27.

HENDERSON, GEORGE. *Survivals in Belief among the Celts.* Glasgow, 1911.

HENDERSON, T. F. *Scottish Vernacular Literature.* London, 1898.

———. Ed. Sir Walter Scott's *Minstrelsy of the Scottish Border.* 4 vols. London, 1902.

———. *The Ballad in Literature.* London, 1912.

HENDERSON, WILLIAM. *Folk-Lore of the Northern Counties* (new ed.). London, 1879. (Folk-Lore Society.)

HILDEBRAND, KARL. *Die Lieder der älteren Edda.* Paderborn, 1876.

HOLINSHED, R. *Chronicles of England, Scotland and Ireland.* 6 vols. London, 1807–8.

HULL, ELEANOR. *The Cuchullin Saga.* London, 1898.

HUNT, ROBERT. *Popular Romances of the West of England* (1st ser.). London, 1865.

HYDE, DOUGLAS. *Beside the Fire: A Collection of Irish Gaelic Folk Stories.* London, 1890.

International Folk-Lore Congress, The, Papers and Transactions of (ed. Joseph Jacobs and Alfred Nutt). London, 1892.

JAEHDE, WALTER. *Religion, Schicksalsglaube, Vorahnungen, Träume, Geister und Rätsel in den englisch-schottischen Volksballaden.* Halle, 1905.

JAMIESON, ROBERT. *Illustrations of Northern Antiquities.* Edinburgh, 1814.

——. *Popular Ballads and Songs.* 2 vols. Edinburgh, 1806.

JEVONS, FRANK B. *An Introduction to the History of Religion* (7th ed.). London, 1918.

JEWETT, SOPHIE. *Folk-Ballads of Southern Europe* (trans. Sophie Jewett; Introduction and notes by Katharine L. Bates). New York, 1913.

Journal of American Folk-Lore, Boston, 1888——. (Organ of the American Folk-Lore Society.)

Journal of the Folk-Song Society. London, 1899——.

Journal of the Irish Folk-Song Society. London. 5 vols., 1904–7.

KEIGHTLEY, THOMAS. *The Fairy Mythology.* Bohn's Antiquarian Library. London, 1900.

KER, W. P. "On the Danish Ballads," *Scottish Historical Review,* Vol. I (1904); Vol. V (1908).

——. "On the History of the Ballads: 1100–1500," *Proceedings of the British Academy,* Vol. IV (1909). London.

——. *English Literature: Mediaeval.* Home University Library. New York and London, 1914.

——. *Epic and Romance.* London, 1897.

KIRK, ROBERT. *The Secret Commonwealth of Elves, Fauns, and Fairies* (ed. Andrew Lang), London, 1893.

KITTREDGE, G. L. "Disenchantment by Decapitation," *Journal of American Folk-Lore,* Vol. XVIII (1905).

——. "Sir Orfeo," *American Journal of Philology,* Vol. VII (1886).

——. *English and Scottish Popular Ballads* (ed. from the Child collection). Cambridge, 1904.

——. *Gawain and the Green Knight.* Cambridge: Harvard University Press, 1916.

KÖHLER, R. "Der weisse, der rothe und der schwarze Hahn," *Germania,* Vol. XI (1866).

LADY WILDE. *Ancient Legends, Mystic Charms, and Superstitions of Ireland.* 2 vols. London, 1887.

LAMMERT, G. *Volksmedizin in Bayern.* Würzburg, 1869.

LANDES, A. *Contes et Légendes Annamites.* Saigon, 1886.

LANG, ANDREW. "Ballads," *Encyclopaedia Britannica* (11th ed.).
———. "Fairy," *ibid*.
———. "The Ballads," Chambers' *Cyclopaedia of English Literature* (new ed.), Vol. I (1901). London.
———. *A Collection of Ballads*. London, 1907.
LARMINIE, WILLIAM. *West-Irish Folk-Tales and Romances* (collected and translated). London, 1893.
LAWSON, J. C. *Modern Greek Folklore and Ancient Greek Religion*. Cambridge, England, 1910.
LEACH, H. G. *Angevin Britain and Scandinavia*. Cambridge: Harvard University Press, 1921.
LEAN, V. S. *Collectanea*. 4 vols. Bristol, 1902–4.
LEATHER, ELLA MARY. *The Folk-Lore of Herefordshire*. London, 1912.
LUZEL, FRANÇOIS MARIE. *Contes populaires de la Basse-Bretagne*. Paris, 1887.
MACCULLOCH, J. A. *The Childhood of Fiction*. London, 1905.
———. *The Religion of the Ancient Celts*. Edinburgh, 1911.
MCGILL, JOSEPHINE. *Folk Songs of the Kentucky Mountains*. New York, 1917.
MACKENZIE, W. ROY. *The Quest of the Ballad*. Princeton, 1919.
MACRITCHIE, DAVID. *The Testimony of Tradition*. London, 1890.
MANNHARDT, WILHELM. *Wald- und Feldkulte*. 2 parts. Berlin, 1875–77.
MARETT, R. R. *The Threshold of Religion* (2d ed.). New York, 1914.
MAURY, L. F. A. *Les Fées du Moyen Age*. Paris, 1843.
MEYER, KUNO, AND NUTT, ALFRED. *The Voyage of Bran*. 2 vols. London, 1895, 1897.
MOSS, ROSALIND. *The Life after Death in Oceania and the Archipelago*. Foreword by R. R. Marett. Oxford University Press, 1925.
MÜLLENHOFF, KARL. *Sagen, Märchen und Lieder der Herzogthümer Schleswig-Holstein und Lauenburg*. Kiel, 1845.
MURRAY, JAMES A. H. *Thomas of Erceldoune*, "Early English Text Society," Vol. LXI. London, 1875.
MURRAY, MARGARET A. *The Witch-Cult in Western Europe*. Oxford, 1921.
NAPIER, JAMES. "Old Ballad Folk-Lore," *Folk-Lore Record*, Vol. II (1879).
NAUMANN, HANS. *Primitive Gemeinschaftskultur*. Jena, 1921.
OESTERLEY, W. O. *The Sacred Dance*. Cambridge, England, 1923.
OLRIK, AXEL. *Danske Folkeviser i Udvalg*. Copenhagen, 1899.
———. *The Heroic Legends of Denmark* (trans. L. M. Hollander). New York, 1919.
PATCH, HOWARD. "Some Elements in Mediaeval Descriptions of the Otherworld," *Publications of the Modern Language Association*, Vol. XXXIII (1918).
PHILPOT, J. H. *The Sacred Tree*. London, 1897.

PINEAU, LÉON. *Les Vieux Chants Populaires Scandinaves.* Paris, 1898.

PITCAIRN, ROBERT. *Criminal Trials in Scotland.* 3 vols. Edinburgh, 1833.

POUND, LOUISE. "Oral Literature," *Cambridge History of American Literature,* Vol. IV (1921).

———. "The Term 'Communal,'" *Publications of the Modern Language Association,* Vol. XXXIX (1924).

———. *American Ballads and Songs.* New York, 1922.

———. *Poetic Origins and the Ballad.* New York, 1921.

PRATO, STANISLAS. "Psyché," *Bulletin de Folklore,* Vol. I (1892).

PRATT, JOHN B. *Buchan* (4th ed.). Aberdeen, 1901.

PRIOR, R. C. ALEXANDER. *Ancient Danish Ballads.* 3 vols. London, 1860.

Publications of the Modern Language Association of America. 1884——.

PUCKETT, NEWELL N. *Folk Beliefs of the Southern Negro.* Chapel Hill, N. C., 1926.

Revue celtique. Paris, 1870——.

Revue des traditions populaires. Paris, 1886——. *Société des Traditions Populaires.*)

RHŶS, SIR JOHN. *Celtic Folk-Lore.* 2 vols. Oxford, 1901.

———. *The Arthurian Legend.* Oxford, 1891.

RICHARDSON, ETHEL P., AND SPAETH, SIGMUND. *American Mountain Songs.* New York, 1927.

ROBINSON, F. N. "Human Sacrifice among the Irish Celts," *Kittredge Anniversary Papers.* Boston, 1913.

RÜDIGER, GEORG. *Zauber und Aberglaube in den englisch-schottischen Volksballaden.* Halle, 1907.

Rymour Miscellanea. Edinburgh, 1906——.

SANDBURG, CARL. *The American Songbag.* New York, 1927.

SCARBOROUGH, DOROTHY. *On the Trail of Negro Folk-Songs.* Cambridge: Harvard University Press, 1925.

SCHAMBACH, GEORG, AND MÜLLER, WILHELM. *Niedersächsische Sagen und Märchen.* Göttingen, 1855.

SCHMIDT, BERNHARD. *Das Volksleben der Neugriechen und das hellenische Alterthum.* Leipzig, 1871.

———. *Griechische Märchen, Sagen und Volkslieder.* Leipzig, 1877.

SCHOFIELD, W. H. *Studies on the Libeaus Desconus,* "[Harvard] Studies and Notes in Philology and Literature." 1895.

SCOTT, SIR WALTER. *See* HENDERSON, T. F.

SÉBILLOT, PAUL. *Contes populaires de la Haute-Bretagne.* 3 series. Paris, 1880–82.

———. *Le Folk-Lore de France.* 4 vols. Paris, 1904——.

———. *Traditions et Superstitions de la Haute-Bretagne.* 2 vols. Paris, 1882.

SÉBILLOT, PAUL. *Le Paganisme Contemporain chez les Peuples Celto-Latins.* Paris, 1908.

SHARP, CECIL J., AND MARSON, CHARLES I. *Folk Songs from Somerset.* 5 series. London, 1904–9.

———, AND OTHERS. *Folk-Songs of England,* Books I–V. London, 1908–12.

———. *One Hundred English Folksongs.* New York, 1916.

———, AND CAMPBELL, OLIVE D. *English Folk Songs from the Southern Appalachians.* New York, 1917.

SHARPE, CHARLES K. *A Historical Account of the Belief in Witchcraft in Scotland.* London, 1884.

SHOEMAKER, HENRY W. *North Pennsylvania Minstrelsy* (2d ed., revised and enlarged). Altoona, Pa., 1923.

SHORTLAND, EDWARD. *Traditions and Superstitions of the New Zealanders* (2d ed.). London, 1856.

SIDGWICK, FRANK. *Popular Ballads of the Olden Time.* 4 series. London, 1903–12.

SIKES, WIRT. *British Goblins.* London, 1880.

SMITH, C. ALPHONSO. "Ballads Surviving in the United States" (reprinted from the *Musical Quarterly*). New York, 1916.

SMITH, G. GREGORY. *The Transition Period.* New York, 1900.

STEENSTRUP, JOHANNES C. H. R. *The Medieval Popular Ballad* (trans. E. G. Cox). Boston, 1914.

STEMPEL, G. H. *A Book of Ballads Old and New.* New York, 1917.

STOKES, WHITLEY. "Translation of the *Voyage of the Húi Corra,*" *Revue celtique,* Vol. XIV (1893).

STOLL, E. E. "The Objectivity of the Ghosts in Shakespere," *Publications of the Modern Language Association,* Vol. XXII (1907).

SWAINSON, CHARLES. *The Folk Lore and Provincial Names of British Birds.* London, 1886. (Folk-Lore Society.)

TACITUS. *Germania* (ed. Henry Furneaux). Oxford, 1894.

TAYLOR, TOM. *Ballads and Songs of Brittany.* London, 1865.

Texas and Southwestern Lore (ed. J. Frank Dobie, 1927), Vol. VI. Austin, Tex., 1927. (Texas Folk-Lore Society.)

THEAL, GEORGE M. *Kaffir Folk-Lore.* London, 1882.

TRUMBULL, H. C. *The Blood Covenant and Its Bearing on Scripture* (3d ed.). Philadelphia, 1898.

TYLOR, EDWARD B. *Primitive Culture* (4th ed.). 2 vols. London, 1903.

VIGFUSSON, G., AND POWELL, F. YORK. *Corpus poeticum boreale.* Oxford, 1883.

WAGNER, ALFRED. *Die sittlich-religiöse Lebensanschauung des englischen und schottischen Volkes nach den Volksballaden.* Halle, 1910.

WEBSTER, HUTTON. *Primitive Secret Societies.* New York, 1908.

WENTZ, W. Y. EVANS. *The Fairy-Faith in Celtic Countries.* Oxford, 1911.

BIBLIOGRAPHY

WILLIAMS, ALFRED. *Folk-Songs of the Upper Thames*. London, 1923.

WIMBERLY, LOWRY CHARLES. *Death and Burial Lore in the English and Scottish Popular Ballads*, "University of Nebraska Studies in Language, Literature, and Criticism," No. 8 (1927).

WIRTH, A. *Formelhafte und typische Elemente in der englisch-schottischen Volksballade*. Halle, 1897.

WUNDT, WILHELM. *Elements of Folk Psychology* (trans. E. L. Schaub; rev. ed.). London, 1921.

WYMAN, LORAINE, AND BROCKWAY, HOWARD. *Lonesome Tunes*. New York, 1916.

INDEX

Abortifacients, herbs as, 360 f.

Adder, transformation into, 61 f., 385

Adultery, Otherworld punishment for, 418 f. *See also* Chastity; Incontinence

After-life: belief in, 30 f.; the grave associated with, 99 ff.; various conceptions of the, 29 f. *See also* Otherworld; Soul, forms of the

Alcoran, swearing by, 380. *See* Oaths

Allison, a witch name, 212

Al Sirât, bridge to the Otherworld, 113

Angelica, Otherworld, 156

Angels: the dead examined by, on the journey to the Otherworld, 113; song of, 411; soul guided to heaven by, 408

Animal lovers, 54, 67; parentage, 67, 134

Animals: list of ballad, 66; power of magic music over, 332 ff.; power of witch over, 207; sacred, 120; soul in the form of, 52 ff.; tabooed, 67 n. 1; talking and helpful, 45, 66 f.

Animism, 35, 91 f., 230, 236. *See* Pre-animism

Apes led in hell, 426 f. *See* Hell

Apple: forbidden Otherworld fruit, 154; fairy gives mortal, for wages, 277

Apples: gold, enchantment by means of, 312; green, dreaming of, 241

Apple tree: enchantment associated with the, 311 ff.; lore of the, 311; Otherworld, 154; sleeping under, makes one liable to fairy capture, 313

Arctic hell, 132 f.

Arrow: shot from bow as soul leaves the body, 54; shot to locate grave, 53 f.; shot to simulate childbirth, 359. *See also* Bow

Arrows, elf, 195, 291 ff.

Ash tree, swearing by the, 123

Atter-corn, elfin, 279

Austerities, 35. *See also* Penances

Backbone, fiddle made of dead girl's, 70. *See also* Breastbone; Fiddle; Harp; Skull

Backwards, walking, as a magical procedure, 363 ff.

Baldwin, C. S., on ballads and romances, 14

Ball: fairies play, 194; game of, occurrence in balladry, 194 n. 2; ghosts play, 245 f.; magic gold, 312

Ballads: actual beliefs reflected in, 29, 38, 39 and n. 1; British and Danish, 11; ecclesiastical, 33 ff., 402 f.; Eddic poetry and, 15; folktales and, 3 f., 7, 9, 39 n. 1; humor in, 225; metaphor in, 16 ff.; romances and, 4 f., 12 ff., 202; shapeshifting, 37; theories as to the origin of, 20 f.; tragedy in, 225; vestigial supernatural features in certain, 124 n. 2, 147 f., 184, 211, 344 f.

Bands, childbirth obstructed by, 357. *See also* Keys; Knots; Left-foot shoe; Locks; Ring

Baptism: of child by mother, 374; fairy capture and, 319; protective ceremony, 371 ff.; with milk, 372 f.; with water, 373 f.; with wine, 373 f.;